Contents

viii

List of Contributors

Monty Armstrong Cerritos High School, Cerritos, California

Davina Baird Horizon Honors High School, Phoenix, Arizona

Jerry H. Bentley University of Hawaii, Honolulu, Hawaii

Jack Betterly Emma Willard School, Troy, New York. Member of the Board of World History Connected. Deceased March 7, 2008.

Maryann Brown University of Ballarat, Ballarat, Victoria, Australia

Michael S. Brown Massaponax High School, Fredericksburg, Virginia

Barbara Brun-Ozuna Paschal High School, Fort Worth, Texas

Steven L. Buenning William Fremd High School, Palatine, Illinois

Mike Burns Concordia International School, Shanghai, China

Dave Clarke Nathan Hale High School, West Allis, Wisconsin

Sharon Cohen Springbrook High School, Silver Spring, Maryland

Steve Corso John H. Glenn High School, New York's Elwood School District, New York

David Dorman Manhasset High School, Manhasset, New York

Ryba L. Epstein Rich East High School, Park Forest, Illinois

William Everdell Saint Ann's School, Brooklyn, New York

Morgan Falkner Rio Rico High School, Rio Rico, Arizona

Christopher Ferraro Spring Valley High School, Spring Valley, New York

Helen Grady Springside School, Philadelphia, Pennsylvania, retired

Dale Griepenstroh Chula Vista High School, Chula Vista, California

Nancy Jorczak Council Rock High School North, Newtown, Pennsylvania, retired

Tom Laichas Crossroads School, Santa Monica, California

Suzanne Litrel Bay Shore Senior High School, Long Island, New York

Janet Martin W.T. Woodson High School, Fairfax, Virginia

William H. McNeill University of Chicago, Chicago, Illinois

Thomas Mounkhall State University of New York, New Paltz, New York

Marita Nicholas Belmont High School, Belmont, Geelong, Victoria, Australia

Chris Peek Bellaire High School, Bellaire, Texas

Sigrid S. Reynolds George Washington High School, Cedar Rapids, Iowa

Mary Rossabi Ethical Culture Fieldston School, New York, New York, retired

Cristóbal T. Saldaña Harlingen High School, Harlingen, Texas

Peter N. Stearns George Mason University, Fairfax, Virginia

Bill Strickland East Grand Rapids High School, East Grand Rapids, Michigan

Angela Wainright Kinkaid School, Houston, Texas

Beth Williams DeKalb School of the Arts, Atlanta, Georgia

Introduction

HEIDI ROUPP

Experience matters. Because a global perspective of world history is a relatively new subject, teachers new to the field find themselves poorly prepared and lacking the advice of a world history mentor. The authors who have contributed chapters to *Teaching World History in the Twenty-first Century* are educators, recognized by colleagues and students as teaching masters. These chapters address the needs of teachers who are new to the field and professors who are preparing students for teaching careers in social studies.

Developing a successful world history class is not an easy task. Through trial and error, over the last decade, world history teachers have shaped a new course, one intended for students who are preparing for twenty-first–century citizenship in a globalized economy. The chapters these teachers have contributed describe their best ideas for teaching in ways that strengthen student learning.

World history is a collaborative effort. Because no one can claim to have become an authority in the teaching of world history, discussion, research, collaboration and review continue to be essential ingredients in course development. The authors have donated the royalties from *Teaching World History in the Twenty-first Century* to *World History Connected Inc.*, an academic journal devoted to the scholarship of teaching world history (www.worldhistoryconnected. org). Peter N. Stearns's chapter leads the way with a discussion of how the teaching course developed. David Dorman and William Everdell identify some of the many reasons why individual teachers have engaged in a lifelong pursuit of learning and teaching world history. Suzanne Litrel's "A Low-Tech Approach to Teaching World History (Or, Real Learning on the Cheap)" reminds us that nothing much happens in any subject without engaging students.

Teachers new to the field often wonder how they can teach the history of the whole world in nine short months. Follow the textbook? That may seem the easy solution.

However, textbooks do not teach world history; teachers do. Selecting a textbook before learning the fundamentals is rather like buying a car without knowing how to drive. Careful, systematic preparation is critical. Developing a conceptual framework for the course is the first task. William H. McNeill suggests that the term *civilization* is a less effective concept for organizing a world history course than thinking of human activity across the globe as an expanding web of human exchange through time. Tom Laichas proposes an organizational model for embedding current events within the historical context of the course. Michael S. Brown has individualized student learning through technology. His chapter describes changes in his teaching that may reflect radical changes in twenty-first–century education. Professors preparing students for careers in social studies will be interested in Thomas Mounkhall's chapter about the most common questions asked by pre-service teachers. More interesting are his answers. Morgan Falkner demonstrates how useful world history themes are in the selection of subject matter, an essential step if students are to develop a global perspective. Christopher Ferraro takes the conceptualization process one step further, illustrating how the selection and rejection of content in a world history course differs from the selection of content for European history. To develop a conceptual framework and become acquainted with world history themes and scholarship, teachers can read basic world histories from Thomas Mounkhall's list or Mike Burns's recommendations or Jerry H. Bentley's bibliography.

Authors in the next unit, Teaching Basics, are teachers who share their basic teaching strategies for building student success. Teaching students to memorize content without practicing history leaves students with perhaps half the benefits of a good history class. World history offers students the opportunity to develop critical thinking. The process for teaching students to think historically requires coaching. Learning to think historically is a process that begins with reading, discussion, research, and writing. Chapters by Davina Baird, Jack Betterly, Ryba L. Epstein, Dave Clarke, and Bill Strickland offer the teaching basics to weave into the fabric of the course. Long after students have forgotten Mansa Musa, they will still have the opportunity to think historically.

How does a teacher integrate teaching content with the coaching needed to help students think historically and complete the course in nine months? Mike Burns develops a step-by-step plan chock-full of teaching tips and practical advice. Chris Peek and Angela Wainright address the Achilles heel of world history teachers: time management. Monty Armstrong presents a checklist of good organizational practices, the "nuts and bolts" of world history. Steve Corso follows with lessons learned, insights in how to avoid problems. Sigrid S. Reynolds reassures new teachers that, by the second year, teaching world history becomes less of a challenge and much more fun.

Teaching is an art. Just as no two students are alike, no two classes are the same. Teaching requires as many different approaches and ideas as there are students and classes. Helen Grady leads the way into Teaching Skills with a plan for the first day, the day that sets the pace for the year. Janet Martin follows with ideas to get students' attention on those days when students arrive in the classroom thinking about the basketball game or the prom or getting to work on time. When attention begins to slip, Beth Williams offers ideas for kinesthetic learning. Nancy Jorczk reminds us of ways to integrate local change into a global history course. Barbara Brun-Ozuna focuses on how to teach world religions in world history. Steve L. Buenning directs our attention to the importance of teaching about leadership through time in a variety of world cultures; and Mary Rossabi invites teachers and students to learn more

about world art by studying processions. Using these suggestions as models, new teachers can develop a variety of lessons to keep students engaged.

Analyzing what learners say about their learning and understanding is a guide to what comes next: to review, reteach, enrich, or introduce new material. Chapters in the next section illustrate methods for analyzing student responses that reflect their learning and understanding. Maryann Brown and Marita Nicholas analyze the challenge of teaching across a cultural divide, Sharon Cohen considers student responses to gender studies, and Dale Griepenstroh describes a week's worth of coaching as his students learn to think historically. Each of these chapters demonstrates an approach for analyzing student progress. Systematic review and analysis of student responses lead to better teaching. Building on lessons learned from one year to the next improves teaching practices the next year and the year after that and the following year, too.

If the quest for a textbook reflects a lack of academic background, no textbook can solve that problem; nor can content items listed in this index, which relate to specific lessons and teaching strategies in the chapters. Teachers must learn world history in order to teach the subject well. Cristóbal T. Saldaña reminds us that the historiography of world history is essential to understanding and teaching the course. Jerry Bentley has provided an annotated bibliography for world history. Using the bibliography, teachers can develop a reading plan or establish a world history book club online to become acquainted with world history scholarship.

Teachers are the tour guides to human history around the world and through time. The devotion of teachers to their students, and their commitment to learning and to improving the tour, have made world history the success it has become. This difficult work enables students to leave class better prepared for twenty-first–century life. We owe world history teachers our gratitude.

PART I

TEACHING WORLD HISTORY

CHAPTER 1

Where Did World History Come From?
The Origins of a Vital Subdiscipline

PETER N. STEARNS

The rise of world history as a teaching field and, to a lesser extent, a research field is one of the major developments in the discipline over the past three decades. The expansion of the field very much responded to needs, and at the same time it did not follow the most conventional pattern. Unlike Western civilization courses in the early twentieth century, for example, world history was not birthed in one of the prestigious Ivies, nor did it spring primarily from research innovation. Indeed, the emergence of significant new scholarship in many ways followed from the prior efflorescence of world history teaching, though it has come to embellish and sustain the field in many ways. The question of origins is not particularly thorny, because the impelling factors are not obscure. But the distinctive evolution is nevertheless interesting, and it also helps explain some of the hesitations and controversies that have surrounded the teaching of world history and surround it still.

In a formal sense, of course, world history is by no means entirely new. Historians delight in showing that origins of phenomena go back farther than anyone expects, but it is important to have an accurate perspective. Patrick Manning, in his vigorous guide to world history, appropriately traces efforts to provide a world perspective—in terms of what was known of the world at the time—in historical efforts from Herodotus to Ibn Khaldun and into more modern times. Any full exploration of world history must take these important scholarly precedents seriously, particularly since they emanate from the historiographical traditions of several different societies.[1]

It is also true, however, that the rise of nationalism and the strong impulse to associate history with the national story, from the nineteenth century and into our own time, moved against these important antecedents, toward a narrowing of scope. Even historians who worked on societies other than their own tended to adopt the national framework so that they became (in the United States) a British, or a German, or a Chinese historian, with most graduate and upper-level undergraduate coursework defined accordingly. Larger ventures, like the important *Encyclopedia of World History* that was imported from Germany and moved forward under American editorship by the 1920s, divided most of the world into nations and also made it clear that the story of Western nations was far more important and known in far greater detail than that of the rest of the world.[2]

This was the setting in which, during the 1960s, some pioneering efforts to define a world history approach emerged more self-consciously than ever before. Leften Stavrianos at Northwestern University and William McNeill at the University of Chicago launched serious programs to promote world history as a teaching field and a subject of potentially wide interest to the general public. McNeill's *Rise of the West*, which did indeed gain substantial public attention, admittedly connected to conventional assumptions about special qualities of the Western role in modern times but did so in a clearly world history context and with an awareness of the existence of other major civilizational traditions of a stature worth comparison with the West. Stavrianos's efforts were more strictly confined to classroom materials, but both he and McNeill generated important textbooks in the field. Both also lectured widely, seeking to promote world history and providing guidance in making the field not only valid but also manageable; it was Stavrianos, for example, who urged budding world historians that their first lesson must be "Dare to omit."[3]

These foundational efforts connect directly to the rise of world history more recently, aided by the fact that McNeill, in particular, continued to provide important studies from a world history vantage point. It is fair to note, however, that neither scholar generated the kind of educational current, in the 1960s and 1970s that they hoped for. William

McNeill, as a history administrator, helped convert the History Department at the University of Chicago to a significantly global enterprise, with scholars in various Asian, African, and, to a lesser extent, Latin American fields. But as an educator, McNeill failed to persuade relevant groups at the University of Chicago to move world history into a clear curricular position, as against a cherished Western civilization course. While he offered a stand-alone course successfully, no larger role emerged. Despite powerful statements that unquestionably helped generate the later surge in the field, the 1960s were not yet a hospitable climate for a larger world history current.

More decisive developments took shape during the 1980s, which is when the contemporary trend took clear root. World history courses emerged at scattered four-year state colleges and at a few community colleges. A number of high school teachers at some private institutions and a few public high schools began moving in the same direction. A world cultures rubric, which was not entirely new, allowed the introduction of more world history materials, often alongside the Western canon.

In the early 1980s the College Entrance Examination Board assembled a group of historians (and this was done in other fields as well) to discuss what secondary school students should learn in order to be ready for college. The effort produced a 1983 pamphlet, *Academic Preparation for College: What Students Need to Know and Be Able to Do*—an institutional statement of good faith that, although not widely influential, proved to be unexpectedly revealing of changes brewing in the history discipline.[4] The history committee, consisting of a mix of university historians and secondary teachers, yielded a surprising verdict in favor of world history as one of the key areas essential to successful high school preparation. Several committee members had prepared for the meeting on the assumption that discussion would focus on standards for U.S. history (an inescapable staple, which was indeed addressed) but also on its well-established complement, the Western civilization or European history survey. After all, the College Board itself offered U.S. and Western options—though not world history—in its advanced placement (AP) program; indeed an older European history and world cultures achievement test had collapsed from disuse. But against these expectations, several persuasive high school teachers argued that the history compass had changed direction and that it was now a world approach that deserved pride of place. The resultant standards called for understanding of the international context for contemporary economics and diplomacy; grasp of the major societies and cultures in the world and their similarities and differences; and exposure to major developments in world history like the Renaissance or the spread of Islam. The statement was an early effort, to be sure: few contemporary compilations would suggest a pairing of Renaissance and Islam in terms of global significance. But the world focus was clear, and it even spilled over to the U.S. standards with a plea to relate developments in the United States to "trends elsewhere in the world" and to subject them to wider comparisons—a battle still being waged as world history scholars try to help their Americanist colleagues to think of the U.S. survey in more global terms.

Again, the College Board effort was symptomatic, not itself a major new impulse. And even the College Board would fail to follow up with any real changes in test development for over fifteen years, at which point work on the AP World History course at last began in the late 1990s. Hesitation was widespread, given the tug of conventional staples and the intellectual challenge involved in accepting a new entrant to the disciplinary arsenal.

Clearly, however, the factors pushing for world history were abundantly visible by the 1980s, as they had not been twenty years before, and they lay behind the persuasive advocacy of a growing number of individual history teachers. Factor number one involved changes in American student demography, along with increasing assertiveness by African-American voices. Significant numbers of students were urging that the non-U.S. history they consumed must reflect origins with which they could identify—which meant less Europe. Even when students did not make the claim, many teachers did, believing that more of their charges would learn history seriously if they had more means of recognizing their own identities through dealing with societies of origin and faced less pressure to assume that things Western constituted the only standard of importance. One reason that world history initiatives emerged so surprisingly from certain high schools and four-year colleges involved the rapid appearance of the new demography in these settings and the attendant early assumption that students' interest in history depended on a serious change in focus. But student pressures spilled into other venues as well: by the late 1980s Stanford students were protesting against a required, exclusively Western history survey, and while this protest did not initially produce a fully world history curricular response, it did generate some very imaginative comparative options, sometimes highlighting Africa and Latin America around such themes as urbanization. Similar student prods would occur, though later, even at such classic Western civ bastions as Columbia.

Obviously, an increasingly diverse student body could prompt educators to insist even more strongly than before on the need for Western history exposure, on grounds that resultant familiarity with Western values was an essential integrating device; this was indeed a strong impulse among conservatives concerned about the expansion of minorities (whether willing to admit to this concern openly or not). And a bow to student identity issues could lead to patchwork approaches, like a barely modified Western civ course that did however add a section on the Sudanic kings, to provide a touchstone for African-Americans. On balance, however, at least over time, the interest in responding to changes in student composition and political awareness contributed notably to the context in which world history courses began to expand.

The second main spur to world history sprang not from domestic, demographic changes but from shifts in the world outside. For it was also by the 1980s that many history faculty members, again at several educational levels, began to seek a curricular counterpart to the obvious fact that the United States was now operating in a global environment in which many societies began to rival or surpass Western Europe in their bearing on the national interest. As William McNeill once argued, the Western civ survey had arguably served the United States well in providing relevant public awareness and a background for politicians and policy-makers when the main challenge lay in responses to Europe—through the 1930s and 1940s. But now the demands on history were different simply because the global context was different, amid decolonization, cold war pressures in Asia and Africa, and the economic and cultural developments that would ultimately be called globalization. World history would help prepare students for this framework, just as Western civ courses had once done for a more Atlantic focus.

This second factor could blend nicely with the responses to student diversity in promoting new attention to Asia, Africa, and Latin America—that kind of world history that urged students to be aware of a number of major traditions that, though continually evolving, contributed to a diverse world. It could also promote efforts to instill not only an awareness of cultural differences (and similarities) but also capacities in comparative analysis. Properly construed, however, it also suggested the need, in world history teaching, to complement a civilizational approach with attention to the ways in which larger interregional and ultimately global systems and patterns of contact developed, an area at least as important to the linkage between history and contemporary perspective as the appreciation of international diversity.

There was one other twist on this second factor that probably influenced at least some of the new voices in the world history field: a concern about political balance. With the rise of President Ronald Reagan, the 1980s saw a rejuvenation of American conservatism and a measurable increase in nationalism. For some historians, already interested in a global approach, this development added urgency to their sense that students needed a broader international perspective and, more particularly, some critical capacity to examine pro-American or pro-Western claims. World history, however specifically defined, required a rebalancing in regard to the West, in contrast to the Western civ tradition that put Europe and its relationship to the United States

in the limelight. Political concerns, in a more nationalist environment, might additionally inject a bit of anti-Western spice to the mix. Some world historians wanted their courses to expose flaws in the Western tradition—for example, Western responsibilities for the Atlantic slave trade—and corresponding virtuousness in the less familiar traditions of other societies. This agenda was never fully spelled out and it was not essential to the world history program in a larger sense, but it did enter into and may have contributed to the fact that it was the 1980s that finally combined the factors that undergirded what quickly became a real movement for curricular change in the history discipline.

The 1980s context, finally, helps explain why the world history movement, as a movement and not just an interest on the part of individual history scholars, emerged first and to an extent rather distinctively in the United States. Key elements of the causation, in other words, were clearly American, relating to national foreign policy issues broadly construed and to the new student mix forged by changing patterns of immigration. A somewhat ironic tension between world history as an American initiative in history and partially different (and in many cases slower) impulses toward world history in other societies was one ongoing result.[5]

Certainly within the United States, the 1980s formed a crucial turning point between strong but individual efforts to carve a space for world history, as by McNeill and Stavrianos, and a larger, increasingly collective momentum. It was in 1982 that the World History Association formed, symbolizing the field's new level of visibility and greatly furthering additional developments. Compared to most other academic organizations in history, the association had an unusual mission statement that accurately reflected the effective origins of the world history movement overall. It formed as a result of interests by teachers and academics alike, "determined to address the needs and interests of what was then a newly emerging historical subdiscipline and teaching field." The association deliberately united schools and universities, teaching with research. Even as the field developed further and amid some admitted tensions over how much to emphasize research credentials, the union between secondary and postsecondary educators was maintained, with a primary emphasis on teaching concerns. The association was also active in providing forums for the "discussion of changing approaches to the study and teaching of world history at all levels" in the meetings of other disciplinary organizations, notably the American Historical Association. Finally, and again revealingly, the vast majority of the association's members continued to be based in the United States, though over time the organization did make efforts to contact world historians elsewhere; by 2008, professionals in thirty-five countries participated.[6]

By the mid-1980s then, for several good reasons reflecting both key changes in American interests both domestic and foreign and the imaginative responses of numerous individual teachers at various levels, world history was truly launched in American schools and colleges. New courses began springing up regularly, although almost entirely at the introductory survey level.

Innovation, however, clashed with well-established practices and routines. Many teachers remained either unaware of world history as an option or frightened by its novelty and expanse or dismayed at the cherished subjects that would have to be truncated or redefined to fit into a world history framework—or experienced various combinations of all three sources of hesitancy. While some historians in the 1980s used prominent professional journals to herald the end of the Western civ courses,[7] in fact the traditional teaching field remained alive and well, often defiantly resistant to world history inroads. Resistance to world history also emanated from other civilization specialists, perhaps particularly from East Asian study centers, worried that world history would cut into their enrollments as "non-Western caves" (where requirements were expanding in response to some of the same issues as those motivating world history itself) and convinced that world history generalizations would not do justice to the subtle details of their own fields.

Resistance and innovation combined, finally, to produce predictably hackneyed compromises by some of the institutions most involved in shaping the history enterprise. The College Board, for example, having listed world history as a preferred secondary school option, did not seriously take up the subject as an option for advanced placement courses until the mid-1990s, content to continue to emphasize the successful and rapidly growing APs in American and European history. The disparity between professed goals and practical implementation seemed to be barely noticed, in an organization understandably concerned about the actual costs and exertions of developing a new testing program or promoting a new field prematurely.

Responses by textbook publishers were equally revealing. The fledgling world history movement did call forth some response, at both collegiate and high school levels, but almost entirely in terms of adjusting (and renaming) some best-selling Western civilization texts rather than introducing really new entries. High school European histories were thus embellished, in their medieval sections, with a chapter on the Sudanic kings, although no larger context or connection was established. College-level European histories added a few more chapters about Asia, while resolutely preserving a preponderance of European materials and a European-based periodization scheme. Arguably genuinely global texts—aside from the still-available efforts by McNeill and Stavrianos—did not emerge from mainstream publishers until the early 1990s, and even then many were timidly presented, without the expensive, full-color, test-bank supplements productions that, for better or worse, constituted the standard of the textbook field.

Only in the later 1990s did world history texts win full publisher endorsement, in terms of a felt need to produce fully competitive, independent titles, and even then only at the college level and amid some continued availability of the warmed-over Western civ ventures.

State educational agencies, responsible for school curricula, were similarly hesitant. Between the 1980s and the early 1990s, many states began to set up social studies standards with references to world history. Occasionally, they consulted practicing historians and history teachers, though often they operated independently. Occasionally also, these efforts actually discouraged pure European history at the high school level—in Texas, for example. Even when relabeling, however, most state standards remained predominantly or at least disproportionately Western in practice. California painstakingly established a sequential program labeled world history, with courses at several grade levels beginning in middle school. The first portions of the sequence, to 1500 CE, demonstrated impressive balance among different parts of the world, with serious attention to Asia, Africa, and indigenous societies in the Americas. After 1500, however, the sequence turned to fascination with Western phenomena, dealing in loving detail with familiar staples such as the Renaissance, the Reformation, absolutism, and the Enlightenment, with little space for other regions of the world and a tone that could easily be taken to suggest that these regions were waiting around for fuller contact with the West. Only in the twentieth century did a somewhat more global treatment return. As states began to introduce not only curricula but also testing programs, preoccupation with European developments and patterns further constrained any larger move toward world history. The same constraints continued to affect textbook production for the secondary schools, with the detail needed to live up to state standards for European history seriously limiting any move toward a more global framework. In contrast to the college level, where the views of teaching faculty and textbook authors had freer play and where promptings toward more balanced coverage increased steadily, high school textbook production and characteristically in-house staff authorship were agonizingly sensitive to the need to adhere to every official stipulation, particularly in the large markets like Texas and New York.

At least one other significant limitation bedeviled the otherwise ascending field from the 1980s onward, to some extent even to the present day. Training facilities for world history teachers were sorely lacking. The history department at the University of Hawaii, which was unusually interested in East-West encounters and which had established a pioneering world history course as early as 1945, did introduce a PhD field in world history in 1986 (followed four years later by the establishment of the *Journal of World History*, another landmark development for the field as a whole). The move was not only early, but exceptional, however. Few other history departments made this kind of commitment to training, although by the 1990s a handful of programs did at least establish a potential PhD field in world history. The sense that world history was more a teaching than a research endeavor and the dearth of committed world historians at the university level significantly retarded PhD training. As a result, however, a growing number of colleges were establishing world history survey courses for which none of the faculty was explicitly trained to teach; world history continued to depend disproportionately on individual efforts at retooling or the sometimes grudging commitment on the part of non-U.S. specialists to swallow a dose of world history teaching every so often. The training issue affected the high school level as well. With many college departments offering only a freshman survey in world history (and some offering nothing at all, through a continued attachment to separate civilizations courses), many new high school teachers found themselves assigned to a world history course (even when this was only a partially reworked European venture) without having had any college exposure at all, thanks in part to a lack of trained faculty at this level in turn. All of these makeshifts compounded a general problem in history teaching at the precollege level, with many instructors lacking much subject-matter experience save what they gained in on-the-job training.

By the 1990s, in sum, world history was moving forward, with a growing cluster of devoted advocates and skilled practitioners, important aids to further training through the sessions sponsored by groups like the World History Association and, now, the *Journal of World History* (the two would link directly a decade later), and the first emergence of genuine world history textbooks for college courses. Compromises, like the partially redefined European courses that now tacked on a world label (which most "real" world historians rejected as merely "the West and the rest"), were inevitable in a time of transition. On the one hand, they signaled the power of the world history argument and the factors that lay behind it; on the other hand, by confusing key terminology and leading many students to believe that they had gained more global exposure than was in fact the case, they arguably retarded the process of real conversion. Amid undeniable change, the situation was mixed, and key elements of this mixture persist to the present day.

Then, in 1994, came a new setback, at least on the surface, and a loud one at that. Conservative educators, eager to see Western civilization as part of a set of core values that must be defended from change, had been expressing concern about the rise of world history for some time. A variety of motives entered in. Tendencies in the 1960s to reduce course requirements were part of that decade's legacy that many conservatives vowed to reverse, and reinstituting a Western civ obligation was a key part of this quest. The very forces of immigration and globalism that motivated world history's rise could seem to some viewers as com-pelling reasons to insist even more strongly on the need to make sure that students knew and cherished the Western experience. (As one commentator put it, inaccurately as well as illogically, students must focus on Western civilization because it alone was tolerant of other traditions.) In 1994, world history was placed squarely among the battlegrounds of the so-called culture wars. A movement had developed in the 1980s, with support from various governors, to develop national standards in key learning fields, history among them. In consequence, a large commission of university and school historians had met to formulate goals for this discipline, with both world and U.S. history as targets. The commission drew advice from a wide range of teachers and scholars and, in the autumn of 1994, issued its two reports. The commission's National Standards in world history were carefully done in many respects, providing a well-reasoned periodization, lists of individual topics within each major time period, examples of key questions and exercises, and a useful discussion (if overshadowed by the empirical detail) of the kinds of analytical habits world history should inculcate. But the Standards did tend to present civilizations outside the West in a uniformly positive light, while noting some of the drawbacks as well as the benefits of the Western experience and global impact. This discrepancy, but even more the sheer fact that it was the world and not the West alone that focused attention, drew conservative ire, right at the moment that a new election produced an assertive conservative majority in Congress while correspondingly intimidating normally independent liberal voices. The U.S. Senate roundly rejected both the U.S. and the world standards in a 99–1 vote, and while attention focused primarily on presumed sins of commission and omission on the U.S. side, the vote explicitly renounced at least this particular effort at world history for failing to provide "adequate respect" for the virtues of the Western tradition.[8]

This vote, unprecedented in the experience of history as a discipline in the United States, reflected some genuine, deep divisions in the American public over what to teach about the past and created real outrage among partisans of the Standards effort. However, the Senate vote had surprisingly little lasting effect. After all, the factors that promoted world history in the first place continued to gain ground, backed now by the growing cadre of historians and history teachers committed to the field and eager to promote its expansion. The impact was further muted because Congress had relatively little mandate to intervene in these matters, which were normally the provinces of states and local school districts. It was true that, given the vote, the national standards movement tended to dissipate in history, inhibiting the development of any federally sanctioned testing program at a time when other fields continued to be involved; and while many historians rejoiced in their freedom from the federal hand, the exclusion of history may have been a drawback in the discipline's status in the schools overall. The subsequent overemphasis on reading and mathematics, in the No Child Left Behind legislation of the early twenty-first century, still further reduced history's role particularly in grade school education, and this arguably affected exposure to world history as well. There were important issues here, for all history fields. But the adverse vote barely dented the continued gains (and limitations) of world history within the discipline itself, through the later 1990s and beyond.

Thus, on the strength of growing college survey courses, almost all the major textbook companies had developed at least one explicitly world history product by the end of the decade. Additionally, documents collections and thematic series (from presses like Westview and Routledge) began to emerge to supplement the standard textbook fare, another sign of world history's arrival. Thus: the American Historical Association increased its commitment to the promotion of annual convention sessions devoted to world history, even as the World History Association expanded its outreach independently. Thus: a growing number of states defined curricula and testing standards in what they called world history, even though the global component continued to be subordinate to the West in most resultant programs; only the almost uniform absence of professional historians from the state standards committees reflected the setback of the congressional vote, which so strongly suggested that history was too important to be left to historians. The world history momentum, in other words, continued much as before this skirmish of the culture wars, with continued gains but also continued compromises and constraints.

With time, furthermore, the echoes of the culture wars themselves receded. The terrorist attack on the United States in September 2001 produced a faint revival. Most historians, and most interested elements of the general public, took the attacks as a reason to invest more energy in world history, to gain perspective on contemporary divisions and tensions. But a conservative group explicitly argued that the attacks provided yet another reason to circle the educational wagons around Western civilization, without succumbing to the temptation to dilute the Western message through attention to other parts of the world or to larger global processes. This little flurry soon forgotten, trends resumed as before—and since the trends largely worked in favor of more attention to world history, they also permitted further innovation.

For there were some genuinely new components in the world history movement from the late 1990s onward. The most concrete forward step involved the establishment of an Advanced Placement World History program. A committee was established in the mid-1990s to justify the new program, which it did, and then to prepare the parameters of the course and program. Standards were available by 2001, with the first test administered in the spring of 2002 to 21,000 students, the largest group ever presenting for an initial AP exam. Massive growth occurred thereafter, again more rapid than in any previous AP program, with well over 100,000 test-takers within five years. The program was not without internal controversy. An initial committee effort to make the course more manageable by emphasizing a beginning date of 1000 CE, with an introductory Foundations segment establishing previous highlights such as the major religions, met with fierce resistance, particularly from the World History Association, insistent on doing more with world history origins. An ensuing compromise added a more historical approach to the Foundations segment, along with modest expansion but still a relatively summary approach, and an ensuing periodization beginning with 600 CE that allowed for more attention to the spread of the world's religions and the growth of interregional trade.

The AP program had a number of practical consequences, beyond reflecting the growing popularity of the world history field. Training for high school teachers, now thrown into an area of obvious student demand, had to be stepped up, with regular workshops and refresher courses at many sites; other groups, like the National Council for Social Studies, began to provide brief training sessions at annual meetings as well. Whether the response kept pace with teachers' needs might be open to question, but at least there were new channels of communication. Pressures on colleges to provide teachers-to-be with world history experience mounted as well, though with even less systematic effects. Textbook publishers, quickly receptive to a new market, began to put out special editions of relevant college texts, and their interest in the product in general intensified. The AP program also encouraged further discussions of world history pedagogy, for example about the kinds of analytical habits ("habits of mind") world history should promote and how they might best be instilled and tested, with immensely promising effects.

Two other consequences of the AP program, though desired by many participants, were less conclusive, probably needing more time to mature. Many AP proponents hoped that the program would affect high school world history teaching more generally, for example by scaling back the amount of time devoted to Western history (the AP program specified no more than 30 percent of attention to the West). And of course increased teacher training and familiarity might also conduce to the same result, when AP teachers did some conventional courses as well. State standards remained an inhibition, however, and results remained unclear. Advanced placement also potentially implied the desirability of developing more advanced collegiate world history courses, beyond the survey, for undergraduates who came in with AP experience. A number of curricular proposals did emerge, but many departments were content to point to conventional non-Western civilization courses, and in any event many high-scoring AP students took their success in credits rather than further placement in the field.

The AP program was not the only important innovation

in the latest phase of the world history movement, though it was the most concrete. It was clear from the late 1990s onward that a genuine world history scholarship was emerging, with a number of stimulating books as well as articles in the *Journal of World History* and beyond. Research contributions, for example on patterns of trade, travel and culture contact, had their greatest effect in altering conventional understandings of the postclassical (600–1450) and early modern periods, but there were impacts on other eras as well. The rise of scholarship produced some new frictions between researchers and teachers, now that the field could be defined in conventional prestige terms, but to date these have proved manageable.

Growing research of various sorts also began to produce genuine interpretive debates within the field, another sign of mounting maturity with important and salutary implications for teaching. A largely textbook approach to world history, after all, hardly produced major analytical tensions. The texts disagreed on specifics, and of course authors badly wanted to outcompete each other, but defining areas of contention was not a normal part of the textbook process, and in fact the major authorial groups agreed on key aspects of periodization and on the need to find ways to rebalance and reduce conventional Western coverage. Between the mid-1990s and the present, however, discussion focused on issues such as China's role in the world economy, the comparative reasons for ultimate Western rather than Chinese leadership in generating the first industrial revolution, and, more generally, the appropriate framework for discussing what the world economy is from the early modern period onward.[9] Still more fundamental were objections to the use of civilizations as an organizing principle in world history: concerns here combined efforts to reduce distinctions among different types of societies in favor of more evenhanded treatments and to use intersocietal contacts and cross-cutting global forces as organizing principles rather than a comparative focus on civilizations. On another front, a group of "new global" historians proudly proclaimed their distinction from world historians more generally on the basis of arguments about the radical novelty of global developments over the past half-century; their claims were disputed in turn by world historians who took a more evolutionary view and by a new group who pointed to a reinterpretation of the late nineteenth century in globalization terms.[10] Yet another cluster of historians emerged around a "big history" approach into which world history would fit in new ways, placing the human experience within the larger contours of terrestrial evolution and emphasizing larger stages (like the "agricultural phase" of the human journey) and interactions with the natural environment, placing the question of how far back to go in time into dramatically new dimensions.[11] These broad new approaches, of course, came on top of more specific controversies around issues such as an appropriate global (and not just Western or American) definition

of consumerism or the causes of the abolition movements in the nineteenth century seen in global terms. World history was coming alive intellectually, with the disputatious results common to the historical endeavor and (one hopes) productive in the long run of further analytical advance.

With maturation, world historians—scholars and teachers alike—began also to pay more attention to social history topics, such as the organization of inequality, labor systems, and gender systems, which most earlier versions of world history had downplayed in favor of greater interest in formal political and intellectual patterns. The results were still somewhat hesitant, the generalizations more tentative than those applied to political forms like empires, but the notion that world history must embrace ordinary people, and topics beyond politics and ideas, was advancing steadily.[12]

Finally, and here the AP movement claimed significant but not exclusive leadership, world historians participated increasingly in the larger disciplinary effort to emphasize the inculcation of habits of mind, and not simply or primarily factual memorization, as the organizing principle in both teaching and the long-term assessment of results. World history could join in general disciplinary goals of training in the handling of sources of evidence and in dealing with issues of interpretation; it could enter strongly into the core effort of understanding change, causation, and continuity, with emphasis, of course, on changes in large global frameworks and patterns of contact. World history added, however, a distinctive concern for comparative skills and for understanding relationships between the local and the global, thus adding to the discipline's conceptual arsenal and to its training goals. Discussions of how to move both the shared and the distinctive skills along, in a world history context, became an important part of pedagogical interactions in the subfield and also allowed world history to enter into the field of learning research.[13]

The markers of growing establishment and sophistication were significant as the field emerged from a status of claimant (1980s–mid-1990s) to that of relatively mature participant in the history endeavor. Older issues lingered: questions of appropriate and extensive training and of building beyond the survey course had not been resolved. While world history courses gained ground steadily—entering almost all the Ivy League institutions during the past decade—there were still abundant contests over whether world or European history should be the non-U.S. staple of choice. High school textbooks inched toward becoming more global, but they were constrained by Westcentric state standards (which were changing less rapidly) and publishers' sensitivity to the need never to be very daring. Links between American world historians and those in other countries, though accelerating, formed another ongoing challenge. Relationships between world history and American history formed an interesting tension that had not been so clearly established in prior decades. World historians had initially tended to leave Americanists to their own devices, on grounds that their field offered abundant occupation. But by the 1990s it was clear that the United States had to be given some attention as part of world history, which then raised the question of additional possible relationships within a larger curricular program. One response, in the past five years, has been a growing plea for "internationalizing" the U.S. survey course, which would among other things make it more compatible with the world history program.[14] But whether this movement would make any real headway against entrenched national interests was unclear, and the huge federal investment in teaching American history, with no compensatory attention to a world history counterpart, served as a reminder that powerful interests had yet to be converted from a disproportionately national agenda.

Hardly surprisingly, in a field that despite prior antecedents was effectively only a generation old and despite a robust trajectory, a host of basic issues remained.

About the Author

Peter N. Stearns is provost and professor of history at George Mason University. He chaired the committee that developed the AP World History course. He has taught a freshman world history course at least once a year since 1982 and regularly participates in training workshops for high school teachers. He has published widely in the field, both at the textbook level and through thematic studies in a world history framework. His most recent work in that vein is *Sexuality in World History* (2009) and the forthcoming *Globalization in World History* (2010).

Notes

1. Patrick Manning, *Navigating World History* (New York: Palgrave Macmillan, 2003).

2. William Langer, ed., *An Encyclopedia of World History, Ancient, Medieval and Modern, Chronologically Arranged* (New York: Houghton Mifflin, 1948).

3. William McNeill, *The Rise of the West: A History of the Human Community* (Chicago: University of Chicago Press, 1992); Leften Stavrianos, *A Global History: From Prehistory to the 21st Century,* 7th ed. (New York: Prentice Hall, 1998).

4. *Academic Preparation for College* (New York: College Entrance Examination Board, 1983).

5. At a 2006 conference in Germany, designed to spur the really hesitant European efforts in world history, accusations were made that world history was part of an American imperialist agenda. Given what American world historians think they are trying to do, the charge seemed ludicrous, but there was some relevant context given the extent to which world history did respond to specifically American issues. It is also fair to note that Europeans were surprisingly slow to move into world history, some important individual scholars aside, because of the strong pull of the nationalist traditions (in some cases exacerbated by reactions to new levels of immigration) now overlaid with efforts to use history to help establish a European identity—an arguably worthy goal that nevertheless raised tensions concerning a more global agenda.

6. www.thewha.org/history_mission.php.

7. Peter N. Stearns, *Western Civilization in World History* (New York: Routledge, 2003).

8. Gary Nash, Charlotte Crabtree, and Ross Dunn, *History on Trial: Culture Wars and the Teaching of the Past* (New York: Vintage Books, 2000).

9. Immanuel Wallerstein, *World-Systems Analysis: An Introduction* (Durham, NC: Duke University Press, 2004); Kenneth Pomeranz, *The Great Divergence* (Princeton, NJ: Princeton University Press, 2000).

10. Bruce Mazlish, *The New Global History* (New York: Routledge, 2006).

11. David Christian and William H. McNeill, *Maps of Time: An Introduction to Big History* (Berkeley: University of California Press, 2005).

12. Paul Adams, Eric Langer, Lily Hwa, and Peter N. Stearns, *Experiencing World History* (New York: New York University Press, 2000).

13. Peter N. Stearns, Peter Seixas, and Sam Wineburg, *Knowing, Teaching, and Learning History* (New York: New York University Press, 2000).

14. Thomas Bender, *A Nation Among Nations: America's Place in World History* (New York: Hill and Wang, 2006); Carl Guarneri, *America in the World: United States History in Global Context* (Boston: McGraw Hill, 2006); Carl Guarneri, *America Compared: American History in International Perspective,* 2 vols. (Boston: Houghton Mifflin, 2005).

CHAPTER 2

What Sixth Graders Can Teach You About World History

WILLIAM EVERDELL

I started teaching a course called World History (632–2000) at Saint Ann's School in Brooklyn in 2001, after—not before—I was recommended to serve on the first Advanced Placement World History Test Development Committee. The titles of my courses for the previous four years had been Ancient History (sixth grade), Nineteenth- and Twentieth-Century World History (ninth grade), Modern European Cultural History, 1350–1998, alternating with Economics 101 (eleventh and twelfth grades), Twentieth-Century Ideas, and Debate (both high school seminars). My books were on French Christian thought in the Enlightenment, modernism in the West from 1872 to 1913, and the republican political tradition from the prophet Samuel in the Bible to Senator Sam Ervin. When Larry Beaber, one of the two staffers for the Educational Testing Service World History development committee, called me up to say the committee was considering me, he said, "We're not sure you teach world history," to which I replied, "Actually, I think I've been teaching it for over thirty years." I meant it. For me, the whole point of teaching history has been to introduce young people to the disorienting but maturing and potentially exhilarating truth that they are not alone in the universe. That project makes world history the most important course in the curriculum, whether you teach it in one year or seven. In 1974 when Saint Ann's was still new, our history department set up a four-year chronological world history curriculum: ancient history in sixth grade, medieval history in seventh, early modern history in eighth, and nineteenth- and twentieth-century world history in ninth grade, followed by electives for juniors and seniors that cover smaller parts of the same ground more intensively. And I have tried to make every class period and assignment count toward that goal of reducing natural self-regard by passing on at least one unexpected comparison of their world with the larger one and at least one counterintuitive truth.

This is not so easy. Adolescents in particular are champion solipsists and can be hard to convince even of the existence of some of their own classmates. No less hard to convince are large numbers of my fellow Americans, who are now famous for confusing Sweden with Switzerland and—a graver fault—not learning any language but their own. Most of them embrace the individualism in our public philosophy, and some of the smartest of them go all the way to making a virtue of selfishness. Long after being brought up by attentive parents to be considerate of others, some find it painful to discover how many billions of people there are and already have been on our shared planet and how few of them know or ever have known about Terry Schiavo, Grandmaster Flash, D-Day, Babe Ruth, Billie Holiday, or Thomas Jefferson. Or, more importantly, how few of them are disposed to agree with American judgments about what makes governments legitimate or what constitutes a fair allocation of the planet's resources.

I have had, however, one quite large advantage—my school, which (despite its name) is independent of both church and state. Independent schools have a special value to the profession because teachers can experiment there. Compared to faculty at public or parochial schools, teachers at independent schools have more autonomy, partly because they are hired primarily on the ground that they have extraordinary knowledge of the subject they will teach, not that they have formally studied ways to teach it. What I have learned over the years about teaching world history is not really startling, and much of it can be made use of by teachers in other subjects.

Let me begin with patience: you must maintain it, even as your dome grays and fundamental student errors become endlessly repeated evergreen classics. My students are admitted to my school based on measurements of their intelligence—the speed with which they can learn—but that only makes lapses of a teacher's patience more destructive. Almost every time, a student's failure to grasp something is an indication of a hitherto unchallenged preconception in his or her head. You have to back up and explain. No, medieval

Europeans (and Arabs) did not think the world was flat rather than spherical, though the early Chinese, the Sumerians, and the authors of Genesis did. No, capital is not money; it's a good that produces commodities. No, the strongest political party in the U.S. South has been—historically—the Republican Party but the Democratic Party. No, neither the French revolutionaries of 1789–1791 nor the Founders of the United States of America set up a democracy, nor is *democratic* the right word to describe laws protecting the rights and privileges of minorities, which democratic majorities are always itching to restrict. No, the high schools of France, Germany, and the nonanglophone world in general do not have their own sports teams; nor is what the whole world calls "football" the same game as what American students call "football." No, although liberalism and socialism, under those names, began together around 1800 in the West, they began as bitter enemies and they are neither the same nor versions of each other—except in the United States. Yes, commercial advertising direct to consumers predates the invention of Coca-Cola and of television, but not the invention of the periodical newspaper. No, there are more than nine times as many Muslims in Indonesia as there are in Iraq, nearly twice as many Muslims in North America as there are Jews, and nearly ten times as many Africans were brought as slaves to Brazil than were brought to the southern colonies of eighteenth-century British America. Many of my students can take all such paradoxes in stride, except possibly when History dashes the hopes of my would-be urban sophisticates that religion can be deleted from human experience.

But even more important than encouraging inquiry by upending preconceptions, I have come to think, is to get the proportions of the world history course right. Like most world history teachers, I see three dimensions to the subject: chronological periods, cultural regions, and cultural facets or themes. The six periods are a given that I have never seen any reason to question: Foundations to 632 (roughly, what Europeanists call ancient history), 632–1150, 1150–1500 (medieval), 1500–1750 (early modern), and 1750–1914 and 1914–present (modern). The cultural regions are somewhat less fixed but must certainly include these eight: sub-Saharan Africa, the Middle East (West Asia and North Africa), Central Asia, South and Southeast Asia (India to Indonesia), East Asia (China, Japan and Korea), Europe, and the Americas. The themes are slightly more fixed at six or seven, with acronyms like PERSIA, PERSIA-T, or SPRITE (*p*olitical, *e*conomic, *r*eligious, *s*ocial and gender, *i*ntellectual, *a*rtistic, *t*echnological). Those three dimensions give a total of more than 330 slots to deal with, but although teachers should think beyond the usual two-dimensional review chart, they need not pull out something like a Wii controller and draw and label three-dimensional boxes in the air above the desks. For one thing, the task of keeping the three dimensions in balance is simplified by a few of the newer textbooks,

especially the ones that, like Bulliett's and Tignor's, limit the number of pages and the amount of material.[1] For another, the most important question in the course is not how change occurs in any one cultural region or even how changes in one culture compare with those in another. The most important question for the leaders of the world history discipline—and thus for the teachers and students—has always been how those cultures and cultural regions interact with each other and how their exchanges of everything from foods to philosophies change over time. This is a rather limited number of rather precise parameters, and together they make world history genuinely manageable.

It can be done (as I got in the habit of saying to student-teachers in my summer institute at Taft School in Connecticut) even if, like me, you cannot speak Chinese or Urdu or Farsi, have never been to India or Japan, and depend on anglophone writers for the history and anglophone editors and translators for most of the documents you will study with your classes. Just remember not to spend more time on North America than you spend on China or Japan. And start with alertness to and respect for the differences between history as seen by Westerners and history as seen by West Asians.

It is hard for some men to admit that although purely military history can be catnip, it is catnip almost exclusively for boys. So is the broad history of the "rise and fall" of civilizations, at least when it is explained militarily (which is only too easy to do) and not related to the feelings and hopes of the people who survive such events. I've learned that my best document for teaching World War I is the poetry of Siegfried Sassoon, Wilfred Owen, Guillaume Apollinaire, and Anna Akhmatova, and that tells me that the *P* of PERSIA must be presented more broadly, with *S*, *I*, and *A*. The *S*, or social history of ordinary people, is also catnip, but almost exclusively for girls, unless we take care to relate it to love, lust, birth, death, and ambition, show how it differs among cultures and how it has continued to change.

The history of technology, the *T* in PERSIA-T, can and should be taught because it both fascinates and explains. Students of world history should know not just that electricity comes out of a plug in the wall; they should know in some detail how it contrived to get there (beginning in New York in 1882) and why a society that has learned to depend on its being there can have a very hard time when the blackouts come, whether in New York or Baghdad. Students should know how to spin thread, too, not because hand-spinning looks to be in demand again, but because they need to know how a society that hand-spins its own thread thinks about the value of clothing, gender relations, class markers, economics, communal loyalties, architecture, and just about everything else. The same must be learned about societies whose fastest form of communication runs at about twenty miles per hour or at the speed of light and about societies whose fastest form of transportation is the sailboat or the rocket. Students should know how much the grand strategy of both the Axis and the "United Nations" in World War II depended on the oil supplies of Sumatra, Indonesia; Baku in the Russian Caucasus; Ploesti, Rumania; Texas; and Iraq. Furthermore, I do not think that students should be allowed to leave an American or any other high school without learning enough about computers to understand why e-mail transmitted by packet-switching is more robust and better able to survive disasters than telephone communication by a single circuit of twisted pairs of wires, enough about the chemistry of the nitrate radical to understand why the manufacture of fertilizer leads directly to the manufacture of high explosives, and enough about the manufacture of nuclear weapons to judge whether any given shipment of "aluminum tubes" is intended for the centrifuge separation of fissionable isotopes of uranium or for the assembly of bicycles.

Finally, let me offer what I think might be the best advice I have, advice that is simultaneously about teaching students to think historically and about our own pedagogy. Saint Ann's is heavily committed to the arts, among them theater, and I have again and again found that the best written documents for future citizens of a democratic society like that of the United States (no less than that of the ancient or than the modern city of Athens) are the theatrical ones, artifacts of dramatic conflict (αγον) including not only plays themselves, but speeches, debates, and trials—for example, *Shakuntala*, *Bhagavad-Gita*, the *Iliad*, the *Birds* of Aristophanes, the *Birds* of Fariduddin Attar, the trial records of Joan of Arc and of the Sufi mystic Abu al-Hallaj, James Madison's *Notes of Debates in the Constitutional Convention*, and *Year One of the Empire*, the play by Elinor Fuchs and Joyce Antler composed entirely of documents generated by the U.S. wars against Spain and the new Philippine Republic. What they all have in common is the opportunity to sympathize with real passion and commitment as found on more than one side. Students are usually put to sleep by history presented—as it is too often—as a fait accompli. For the most important historical conflicts they need to know which sides people took and why, and how to argue the issues for themselves. This consideration also explains how I lost my suspicion of film and video. Once the students have seen key scenes of *Gandhi* together with most of *The Battle of Algiers*, they will never again be dismissive of what I take to be the great political issues of the twentieth century—the self-determination of peoples and the limits of violence.

I assign my students roles in model debates, like those of the U.S. Founders in their highly dramatic debate on banning the slave trade. It happened in Philadelphia on August 21–22, 1787, and the script is found in Madison's *Notes* (www.yale.edu/lawweb/avalon/debates/822.htm). There is also the Senate debate on the U.S. use of waterboarding torture (the "water-cure") in the Philippines in 1901. More often, I let students debate what they want to debate by helping them find a debatable issue that will honestly divide the class, assigning it both as a written essay and as what we teachers call "class discussion." I do not begin with the formal apparatus of debate because I find that students are quick to realize the usefulness of the more fundamental of Robert's *Rules of Order* and will pick them up as we go along—especially if the chair of the debate has been elected by the class. Successful questions for debate, which are always not only historical but ethical, have ranged from "Resolved: Every people is justified in resorting to violence to form a state of its own" or "Resolved: There can and should be a market for everything" to "Resolved: Qin Shihhuangdi was bad for China," "There is no excuse for the British Empire," and "The First French Republic was right to close the churches."

It is beginning to look as if the great debates of the twenty-first century will be about energy and resources. I want to have been responsible for producing students who retain the hope that such issues can be best illuminated by debate and best settled by the votes of the largest number of those affected. If H.G. Wells was right about history being a race between education and catastrophe, we are in a profession as ideally adapted for our own century as Wells's profession was for both of his. There is still time to win.

About the Author

William Everdell (BA, Princeton, 1964; MA, Harvard, 1965; PhD, New York University, 1971) teaches World History to students from sixth grade to adult extension classes at Saint Ann's School in Brooklyn. He is the author of *The End of Kings: A History of Republics and Republicans* (1983, 2000) and *The First Moderns: Profiles in the Origins of 20th-Century Thought* (1998).

Note

1. Richard W. Bulliet, Pamela Kyle Crossley, Daniel R. Headrick, Steven W. Hirsch, Lyman L. Johnson, and David Northrup, *The Earth and Its Peoples: A Global History* (New York: Houghton Mifflin, 2nd edition, 2001). This edition is now, of course, out of print. I do not know whether subsequent editions are as compact, though their pages are, of course, renumbered and their price is higher, with the apparent goal of requiring the textbook buyer to commit to replacing an entire class's worth of books every three years or so. Robert Tignor Jeremy Adelman, Stephen Aron, Stephen Kokin, Suzanne Marchand, Gyan Prakash, Suzan . . . , *Worlds Together, Worlds Apart—A History of the Modern World From the Mongol Empire to the Present* (New York: W.W. Norton, 2002) has been replaced by Jeremy Adelman, Stephen Aron, Peter Brown, and Benjamin Elman, *Worlds Together, Worlds Apart: A History of the World from the Beginnings of Humankind to the Present*, (New York: W. W. Norton, 2nd ed., one volume, 2008), adding two earlier time periods but more than doubling the price.

CHAPTER 3

Why I Teach World History

DAVID DORMAN

As a high school student I took a social studies class called Area Studies. When studying about the Soviet Union and Eastern Europe, I learned a little about Russian history. I learned about the Mongols who came thundering out from the east. They burned, raped, looted, killed, and pillaged everything in sight. Some time later, when studying about China, another of the "areas" in the course, I again learned about the Mongols. This time they were thundering from the west. They burned, raped, looted, killed, and pillaged everything in sight. I was flabbergasted. Could the Russian Mongols and the Chinese Mongols be one and the same? How could they be everywhere? Or were they two different peoples? My teacher had no satisfactory answers for my questions. And certainly there was no coherent awareness of an interconnected ecumene that for over a thousand years had linked the trading and traveling networks of Africa, Europe, and Asia.

In college and all through my studies toward a doctorate, the pedagogy never changed, and at times it was worse. Memorable was the master's-level course in ancient history that was described in the catalog as a study of the world's earliest civilizations. On the first day of class, the professor announced that he was an Egyptologist and he intended to teach nothing but Egyptian history. Students were invited to drop the course if that was not acceptable. I took the course and learned more about how not to be a good teacher than I did about Egypt.

My first few years as a high school social studies teacher found me teaching American history and senior electives in modern Asian and modern world history. Much to my surprise, the students were asking me the same kinds of questions—about the interconnections and interactions of peoples across both time and place—that I had asked when I was in their shoes. As a result, early in my career, I began to shape units of instruction so as to include global connections. This history made more sense to students, and it was far more satisfying for me. The unsatisfied student of "area studies" had become a world history teacher.

Thus, I was a teacher of world history before there was a course by that name. *Global studies* was as close as any course title came to what I had come to understand as the way to teach human history to my students. More often than not, the evolving courses, state syllabi, and textbooks were little more than what was euphemistically referred to as "the West and the rest," not a coherent, interconnected narrative of world history. Then an interesting phenomenon began to occur in my school: new students began to appear from around the globe—Asia, Africa, Latin America, and the Islamic world. My classes became less homogeneous. My students' backgrounds, values, and points of view created a classroom dynamic that presented real challenges and real opportunities. At the same time, national and world events conspired to create an environment that encouraged the teaching of a coherent world historical narrative. For me this narrative had become the only way I could hope to prepare high school students for the changing world in which they would soon be taking their places as adults.

Here is an example of what I mean by a new classroom dynamic. Recently, while examining the rise of various belief systems, it became clear to my students that different peoples in different places throughout the world were approaching the same fundamental questions, but developing different myths, heroes, rituals, and belief systems with which to try to answer those questions. Lively discussions ensued as my classes analyzed excerpts drawn from the literature of the world's various belief systems. Our task was to compare and contrast various myths, rituals, and values and their effects upon the worldview of different societies. Sitting in my classes were students whose backgrounds reflected Buddhist, Hindu, Muslim, Jewish, and Christian (Catholic, Orthodox, and Protestant) thought and belief. The modern, twenty-first–century world has brought each of these cultural traditions into juxtaposition with the others. To introduce my class to the world's history and its cultural traditions in the manner by which they were taught to me would be tantamount to educational malpractice.

In a world that has become flattened and globalized, the

development of national standards in history, along with the appearance of an advanced placement (AP) World History course, could not be timelier. That AP World History is supported by teacher-training institutes helps to ensure that, increasingly, high school students will be presented with a historical narrative that fully develops the themes and concepts of an interconnected history of the world. It is axiomatic for world history teachers that the world was interconnected long before political, economic, and other observers and pundits began to say it was. Indeed, the events that shape the world do not occur in a vacuum—they have causes, often many causes, that may lie deep in the recesses of an interconnected world historical narrative. Teaching about the historical routes and processes by which diplomats, warriors, merchants, ideas, technology, and diseases traveled the world gives today's student a clearer understanding of today's world and the possibilities for its future.

Thus far, my discussion has focused on the cognitive aspects of a good world history course, and frankly, that is the easy part. What puts a superior course, such as AP World History, in a class of its own is the affective component. I refer to the skills of analysis, critical thinking, and writing that develop habits of mind that will benefit students in all their courses and throughout life. These skills are achieved through the close reading of a text. Much is made of textbook selection, but I believe that the text is secondary to the teacher's ability to focus students' attention on the necessary themes, concepts, and global interconnections. In fact, I think that teachers, when selecting a text, should look for one that is strong where they are not. Another consideration regarding the selection of a text is the level of preparation with which students arrive in the class at the start of the school year. If a course is offered as a senior elective, all the students have already had some instruction in the subject; in a ninth- or tenth-grade course, however, students may arrive with no background whatsoever. Some texts assume that the student has some background understanding of the subject, while others do not. All the texts are supposed to be college-level books, so the problem is not with the book itself or its author; the problem is that of the high school AP teacher or any social studies teacher who must choose the text that will best meet the needs of both instructor and students. In addition to the text, supplementary materials should be used to add to the text's narrative and further enliven and enrich daily lessons.

As for the officially sanctioned AP World History course, the themes[1] and concepts are all reasonable, and it should be the goal of every world history teacher to present lessons that revolve around them in a coherent way. The thinking skills that are called for are also essential.[2] Problematic is that the course, structured around six chronological periods that run from approximately 8000 BCE to the present, is to be taught in one school year. In other words, students and teachers are expected to survey the entire panorama of human history in roughly 180 days. Realistically, even less time is available. After all, there are scheduled school holidays and unscheduled, unavoidable missed classes.

Teachers also set aside time for review prior to the AP exam in May. This time scheme presents both teacher and student with a daunting challenge. The result is a sprint through world history that rarely allows students to stop for thought and reflection. The course ends up being a mile wide and an inch deep. This is no way to develop in students an appreciation—indeed a love—of history. As a result, some teachers have said that they either skip the entire Foundations unit (covering the first period—to 600 BCE) or race through it or in some other way give it short shrift. If it is part of the syllabus, it ought to be taught and students ought to give some thought to the material, both the content and the necessary comparative historical analysis that we say an AP history course is all about.

The solution to this dilemma is to organize and present the AP World History course over a two-year period. Because I have the good fortune to teach in New York State, where global history and geography are a two-year requirement, I am able to do precisely that. My students are ninth and tenth graders who come to the course with no real content background. Two years allows for periodic in-depth study of selected topics and high-interest activities. Students also undertake summer reading and writing assignments and extra classes devoted to the development of the skills necessary to write coherent, analytical essays. Teacher and students must still adhere to a carefully structured schedule, but it is doable. At the start of the first year, I tell my students and their parents that if the students and I do our jobs competently, by the end of the second year they will see current events as the unfolding of current history. Contemporary world events will make sense because they will be seen in the light of a global historical ecumene that did not begin with the Mongols, nor will it end with us.

About the Author

David Dorman attended Temple University, Queens College, and New York University and has earned baccalaureate, master's, and doctoral degrees. He is a Woodrow Wilson fellow in world history. He has been a teacher at Manhasset High School in Manhasset, New York, for forty-six years. He is the coordinator of pre-AP vertical instruction in social studies, has published several articles on teaching and on selected topics in Asian history, and has presented world history institutes throughout the United States.

Notes

1. Interactions between humans and the environment; development and interaction of cultures; state-building, expansion, and conflict; creation, expansion, and interaction of economic systems; development and transformation of social structures.
2. Historical argumentation, chronological reasoning, comparison and contextualization, historical interpretation and synthesis.

CHAPTER 4

A Low-Tech Approach to Teaching World History
(Or, Real Learning on the Cheap)

SUZANNE LITREL

"Um, Mrs. Litrel . . . what's that underneath the horse?" It was early October, and my tenth-grade advanced placement (AP) students were still overly polite and hesitant. This would never do. Not in a course with a curriculum as vast as world history, where the students really have to wade into material, wrestle with it, and emerge by early May, muddy and grinning. They needed to get down and dirty. There are no neat formulas or clear answers when it comes to—as national award-winning teacher Michele Forman once called it—"the study of our humanity." Life is not neat, and it is often unpredictable.

Most world history courses begin with the Neolithic Revolution and chronologically, at least, end in the twenty-first century. Ten thousand years' worth of ideas, turning points, philosophies, revolution, and upheaval seems more than a little daunting. But the study of millions of lives and the events that shaped them is manageable, however, with reach and reflection—and not without a little humor. For me, a real marker for success is when a student writes on the end-of-the-year survey, "I've never worked so hard and had so much fun in my life!"

In my first year of teaching high school social studies, a thirty-year veteran took me aside to whisper a few helpful hints. "First, scare the life out of them," he said. "Don't even try to be nice to them until January." I nodded uncertainly. Then he added some classroom management tips. "Then—when all else fails, give 'em blood, guts, and sex. That'll get their attention." That I understood. After all, what else sells in this country?

This advice, however, went against all that I had learned from student teaching the previous year. Joseph Nardi, my mentor and former New York City teacher, had always insisted on direct student participation in the learning process. He measured success by hands in the air, rather than by order in the classroom. I once saw him control a mutinous class of thirty-four ninth-graders by assigning the ringleader a leadership position in an impromptu debate. He also put *me* through the wringer by having me co-teach with him from day one—and so I learned to adapt to changing classroom conditions on the fly. It was a far more effective learning experience than writing neat lesson plans with all the correct standards attached. As a student teacher, I was expected to know content *and* adapt to changing circumstances in the classroom in order to facilitate maximum student involvement. That experience—heart pounding and gut wrenching—was the best lesson of my life, as this would-be academic found that she could not hide behind neat, carefully planned and detailed lesson plans. Life—classroom life—does not work that way.

If there is one thing I have learned, it is that to the extent that students own a learning experience, it is theirs—forever. Thus I had decided to shake up my super-reserved and anxious AP World History sophomores. They were very smart, that much was clear, but they were way too quiet for me. How could they learn the material without challenging it?

"You can't compete with iPods and cell phones," I had been told. "Kids these days really need to be stimulated—and technology is the only answer!" This was certainly not the answer for me. I have not had a properly working Proxima in . . . forever. The Internet connection is shaky at best. I do not have a SMART Board, whatever that is, and the most reliable piece of technology in my classroom is an overhead projector from the 1960s. But as my grandmother, a painter, once told me, "Good artists never blame their tools." Good artists also connect with their audience. This was the task set before me.

So in an attempt to reach my AP World History students, I reworked my pivotal questions; the response was lukewarm. We jigsawed some fascinating (to me, anyway) Indian Ocean documents; the students were still only mildly interested. So, six weeks into the school year, I decided to take another approach. In an attempt to get a handle on the autocratic nature of Muscovite rule, I put a particularly gory woodblock print of Ivan the Terrible on the overhead (I had not forgotten the words of the well-meaning veteran from my first year). Then I asked the students, "What do you see?" I waited. And waited. And waited some more, as the class processed the print of Ivan on a rearing horse, holding a head on a pike, as three rotting corpses swung from the gallows in the background. I had decided to build my whole lesson around the print. This would build document analysis skills.

The students started by cautiously taking apart the document—the corpses, the unhappy head on a pike. Slowly, more hands went up as we analyzed the artist's point of view by examining not only the content of the print, but the manner in which it was framed. Why was Ivan's face so impassive, even as he carried his gruesome prize? What was the point of depicting him on horseback? What other cultural influences were evident in the picture? I held my own responses in check so as to keep up the momentum of the class discussion. Pretty soon, the students were talking to each other.

Then came the query: "What's that underneath the horse?" I squinted—and then gasped in shock. There, neatly framed by the horse's legs, was a rough outline of a naked baby dangling—by the buttocks—on a most unlikely miniature tree. "Oh, my goodness!" I must have said at least five times. I had never noticed the baby before. While I had found the print on my own at a public library, it was the gruesome head that had captured my attention. But now my class had come alive, and for the rest of the school year, the students scrambled to tear apart all manner of documents—they never knew what they might find.

My grandmother, an amateur landscape painter who fell on very hard times during the Great Depression, would use whatever she had at hand to keep her eye sharp. When she could not afford to buy paints, she would draw with pencils. Her circumstances thus helped her to remember what it really meant to "look"; in other words, she felt that a lack of resources actually improved her work by renewing her natural creativity.

For every classroom that has a SMART Board and a Proxima, there are far more that do not. But even as state planners and the "experts" argue that technology in the classroom will fuel an educational revolution, teachers struggle to meet evolving state and national learning standards. With or without high-tech equipment, those standards can be met with basic multisensory lessons that tap into the strengths of diverse learning styles and intelligences. Indeed, perhaps the best way to approach teaching as vast a curriculum as world history is to do just that.

Multiple Intelligences, Layered Learning

Traditional classroom learning has long stressed direct instruction. The role of the teacher is to offer information to be learned: the student adopts a passive role by taking notes and quietly absorbing information. Though in the last forty years American schools have tinkered with different models for the classroom, many teachers still rely on this method, particularly when (1) the information to be "covered" is perceived to be "too vast" for the students for the students to handle independently and (2) the teacher is concerned about relinquishing control of the classroom to the students.

The novice teacher quickly discovers, however, that classroom management is directly related to student interest. The challenge of teaching world history is its very scope. Where, exactly, to begin? What themes to hit? What major comparisons and continuities? These are, to a certain extent, defined by general curriculum. But just like the study of history, the teaching of history is a particular, unique experience. While teachers must heed, for instance, local, state, and national standards, their vision for the classroom is the guiding factor in determining student success.

That vision, then, takes into account the individuals in the room. Most teachers experience highs and lows in the classroom within the course of one day, though these peaks and valleys are smoothed out over time as the teacher moves toward mastery. Just as a lesson in one class might not be a perfect fit for another, so, too, the curriculum—and its teaching—can be tweaked to meet students' talents and abilities.

In 1983, Howard Gardner famously outlined his theory of multiple intelligences. These included: *linguistic*, facility in using verbal expression; *logico-mathematical*, the ability to use logical methods to solve problems; *spatial*, the ability to use and manipulate space; *musical*, the ability to create, perform, and appreciate music; *bodily-kinesthetic*, the ability to use one's body; *interpersonal*, the ability to understand other people's needs, intentions, and motivations; and *intrapersonal*, the ability to understand and reflect on one's own motivations and emotions. More recently, Gardner added to this list the *naturalist* type of intelligence, which he describes as the ability to recognize, identify, and classify flora and fauna or "other types of objects."[1] Multiple intelligences require teachers to use multisensory instruction, particularly when teaching history. At any rate, not all world history lessons lend themselves to direct instruction; even the most disciplined of high school students chafe at sitting still in a classroom. In addition, the body of curriculum we expect teens to absorb is so very vast that it is virtually impossible—not to mention unfair—to ask even the brightest students to sit still and take direct instruction day after day.

History—and the study of history—are living, breathing, and continuous. So the examination of the past needs to be layered in content and presentation. Each lesson should have objectives that go beyond mastery of content, seeking to build skills as well; each lesson should recall previous learning in some shape, way, or form. High-tech tools can then be dispensed with. While such tools can certainly enhance instruction, basic instructional methods that tap into diverse student intelligences work best.

Additionally, it is important for teachers to keep an eye on the dominant strain of intelligence in the classroom. For instance, each class tends to have student leaders, those who are willing to direct the course of instruction through their active involvement. Utilized properly, they will rally the group to mastery. The enthusiasm of student leaders tends to be infectious. It is so much more fun to learn from one's peers!

Such classroom leaders are not fixed; students take turns, depending on their confidence, much of which comes from an atmosphere of trust and comfort in the class. The key is to involve all the students, enabling all of them to lead at some point or other during the course of the year, and their own moment of discovery and feeling of brilliance will sustain them even as they venture into unknown periods of history. One of my quietest students became an outspoken, determined revolutionary as he role-played Pancho Villa during a simulated conference on revolutions. An athlete, this boy swaggered menacingly into the room on the day of the debate. He also dressed the part, wearing the largest sombrero that his classmates had ever seen. This shy kid *became* Villa. The other students were so stunned—as was he, I think—by his passion and fervor that the finer details of the Mexican Revolution stayed with them throughout the year.

Motivation and Reinforcement

From my first day of student teaching, my New York City mentor Joseph Nardi drilled into me the importance of a good motivation, a "hook" to the lesson. He had one rule in this regard: "Every single student needs to be *able* to participate." This hook is different from a "Do Now" that gets the class right to work. These can be quotes, music, documents, scavenger hunts, or controversial questions, depending on the lesson and the students.

But while a motivation may tap into one sense (e.g., sight), the actual lesson may tap into others (sound, touch) and thus spark the multiple intelligences that each student possesses, to varying degrees. All learning starts with the essential question: what is the lesson? The challenge of teaching world history is that there are so many ways to address the same issue.

In addition, there are basic skills that should be reinforced with each lesson. These include, but are not limited to, an analysis of sources, cause and effect, sequence of events, and interpretations (point of view). What is the source of our information on this particular period of time? Is it reliable? What other information is needed to provide an accurate portrayal of this time period? What other questions might we ask? This type of learning—a riff on the Socratic method—naturally appeals to students of strong linguistic and logical intelligence. Following are specific suggestions for using low-tech, multisensory teaching to reach out to even more students.

Apartheid in South Africa

The objective here is to initiate the students' analysis of the causes and effects of apartheid in South Africa, using Peter Gabriel's song "Biko," about the death of anti-apartheid activist Stephen Biko. First, give each student a handout containing the lyrics of the song. Ask the students to listen for the different instruments in the song, listing as many as possible, and to note the tone of the song. Then play the song for the class. Have the students answer the questions above. Keeping Bloom's taxonomy in mind, have the students interpret and analyze the song. That is, start out by asking what happens in the song, and clear up any questions about vocabulary and phrasing. Then use the song as a jumping-off point to discuss the causes and effects of apartheid.

World War I

The objective here is to enable students to analyze the factors leading up to World War I. As students file into the classroom, hand out to those with strong reading ability numbered cards containing quotations about the war. As the class discusses the sequence of events, call on these students by number to read their cards. These quotations will create an air of urgency and excitement, as though the students are directly involved in the events. Here are sample quotes:

Reader 1: "Today has been far too exciting to enable me to feel at all like sleep—in fact, it is one of the most thrilling I have ever lived through, though without a doubt there are many more to come. That which has been so long anticipated by some and scoffed at by others has come to pass at last—Armageddon in Europe!"

—Vera Brittain,
British nurse, writer, feminist, 1914

Reader 2: "One feels as if one were dreaming. Every hour brings fresh and momentous events and one must stand still and await catastrophes each more terrible than the last. All the nations of this continent are ready with their swords drawn."

—Vera Brittain, 1914

Reader 3: "The lamps are going out all over Europe. We shall not see them lit again in our lifetime."

—Edward Grey, British diplomat, 1914

Turning It Over: Reflection

Michele Forman, my AP World Summer Institutes instructor, suggests asking students to keep a reflection journal. Give them historical and cultural records such as literature, art, music, newspaper articles and instruct them to consider for each one: What is the source? Place it in the larger context of world history. Explain the point of view. Is it an accurate reflection of the times? What is the purpose of the piece? Who is the audience? To encourage reflection, the journals should not be harshly marked up.

DBQ Activities

Have the students "break apart" a document-based essay question (DBQ) by grouping and classifying the documents. Have them consider the DBQ as a puzzle. What trends do they see? Alternatively, have the students create their own DBQs, explaining their rationale. This assignment works best if students have ready access to computers and printers.

Religion, Philosophy . . . and the Meaning of Life

The objective here is to have students demonstrate a clear understanding of the basic values of different religious philosophies during the classical era. This works well as a Thanksgiving holiday lesson. The premise is that Confucius, Jesus, and Siddhartha Gautama are about to sit down for a Thanksgiving meal together. In groups of three, have the students write and perform skits that demonstrate the basic principles of each spiritual leader as he "gives thanks"— both words and actions should reveal his thinking. The skits should *not* directly reveal which is which—the audience needs to guess.

Art Analysis

This is a useful way to build DBQ analysis skills: whole lessons can be taught through the examination of a single piece of art. For instance, the Shiva Nataraja can be used to teach Hinduism.

Some questions to ask students as they examine any work of art:

What do you see?
Discuss the composition (how the work is "framed").
Discuss the reasons for the composition.
What materials are used? Why?
What is the point of view of the artist? Why?
Who is the audience?
To what extent does this piece serve as a reflection of the times? of the culture that produced it? To what extent is this piece relevant today?

Trials and Tribulations

Choose a topic that engenders controversy—or one you would like your students to examine in great depth. For example, students can put Hernán Cortés on trial for crimes against humanity. Was he guilty of the genocide of the Aztec Indians? Or was he a simple man, bent on pursuing gold, glory, and God? Stack the trial with witnesses you want the class to examine.

If time allows, have the students write their own affidavits and distribute them to the class. Otherwise, write short affidavits with key vocabulary terms (in boldface to reinforce learning). Affidavits should be limited to one double-spaced, typed page, since witnesses should be prepared to know all the content. Be sure to include some gray area—that is, witnesses should provide some shaky testimony.

While I am certain that my AP students who deconstructed the brutish print of Ivan the Terrible very much enjoyed that activity, it soon became clear to me that the image was seared into their minds. Although I recall the class a bit differently, those students noted that "everything they learned" had to do with Russia, and they were able to write extensively on Russian history for their state and AP World History exams. It took a little trial and error on my part to figure out what the students related to best; with a simple visual, they were able to anchor themselves to an event in time—and relate the world to it.

About the Author

Suzanne Litrel (BA, economics; MA, Chinese studies) is a secondary school teacher at Bay Shore Senior High School in Bay Shore, New York. She is also the author of *Jackie Tempo and the Emperor's Seal* (2007) and *Jackie Tempo and the Ghost of Zumbi* (2009), a young adult historical fiction and time-travel series (www.jackietempo.com).

Note

1. Mark K., Smith (2002, 2008). Howard Gardner and multiple intelligences, the encyclopedia of informal education, www.infed.org/thinkers/gardner.htm.

PART II

CONCEPTUALIZING THE COURSE

CHAPTER 5

The Human Web

WILLIAM H. MCNEILL

Human speech is a wonder. Words surround us from birth and, supplemented by gesture, link mother and child in a web of communication that grows more comprehensive and precise from day to day. Newborns catch on with amazing rapidity until, as full adults, they emerge with all the knowledge and skills needed to manage human affairs and reproduce their kind, generation after generation.

No other species relies so completely on such a means of communication or ever devised so many ways of supplementing speech by writing, drawing, map-making, and, more recently, by instantaneous worldwide telegraph, telephone, radio, and Internet. It is no exaggeration to say that the amazing success humans have enjoyed across the past 40,000 years or so was due to this web of communication and the way it propagated useful inventions and ideas far and wide.

At first, speech wove a complex array of agreed-upon meaning within human hunting bands whose members then proceeded to act upon shared hopes and expectations. When results were disappointing, they had to figure out why and often tried to do things differently next time. This process provoked ever-changing cooperative behavior, so that human skills soon became so great that older forms of genetic evolution were eclipsed for us and for many other forms of life by a far more rapid process of deliberate human innovation.

The first great landmark was control of fire for cooking, warmth, and protection from big cats, starting in Africa about 400,000 years ago, long before speech was perfected. Fire also allowed humans to expand their habitat literally around the world from their initial home on the savannas of East Africa. And wherever humans showed up, they altered existing plant life by burning vegetation deliberately to improve their hunting grounds.

About 40,000 years ago, humans also started to change the shape and increase the variety of their stone tools far more rapidly than before. This may signalize the full development of human speech, though no one can be sure when that basic capability actually came on stream. A more recent invention, the bow and arrow, is almost as mysterious since no one knows when or where it originated. But somewhere in Asia or Africa, sometime between 30,000 and 15,000 years ago, powerful bows and arrows were invented that could hit a target many yards away. Killing animals or human enemies at such a distance was far safer than coming close, so not surprisingly neighbors borrowed from neighbors to spread the new weapons in every direction. We know that arrowheads arrived in America across the Bering Strait by 500 CE, and they were still spreading southward when Columbus showed up in 1492. By then, North American peoples, Aztecs in Mexico, and Caribs in northern South America used bows, but further south the Incas did not.

This is the best attested example of how a superior device was capable of spreading across long distances among hunters and gatherers before settled agriculture multiplied human numbers, multiplied contacts, and magnified human impact on the environment. It shows that early human bands remained sporadically in touch with neighbors—both through conflict and through peaceable festivals when they met to sing and dance, exchange mates, and discuss novelties of every kind.

The resulting web of communication was worldwide, as attested by the fact that genetic exchanges sufficed to keep humankind a single species. Choke points kept Australia and America only slenderly in touch with the more closely interconnected continents of Eurasia and Africa. But we may plausibly infer that the human web remained a single even if tenuous whole, even though the bow failed to reach Australia before European ships discovered that continent.

Subsequent developments made the reality of a world-wide human web increasingly apparent. The shift to agriculture beginning about 10,000 years ago established half a dozen different forms of cultivation, with different crops and methods of work, each of which tended to spread to new ground wherever soils and climate allowed. The subsequent emergence of cities and civilizations in each of the principal centers of agriculture, beginning about 5,500 years ago, was sustained by organized trade and transport. Boats and ships began to traverse rivers, canals, and the open seas while animal caravans carried goods overland within Eurasia, but human portage remained predominant in the Americas and most of Africa. Trade was supplemented by raid whenever outsiders saw a chance of seizing what they could not acquire by peaceable bargaining. But both trade and raid disseminated goods, information, and skills, doing so, as transport capabilities improved, with increasing range and rapidity across the centuries.

At length, in modern times, as we all know, the worldwide web became obvious when sailing ships, based initially in Europe, began to visit all the coasts of the inhabited world, spreading diseases, crops, and novelties of every kind wherever their crews came ashore. Wholesale migrations—voluntary and involuntary—soon followed, mixing populations as never before, and the pace of change accelerated everywhere century after century. Instantaneous communication set in with the telegraph in the mid-nineteenth century and has since expanded to affect everyone, everywhere, in far-reaching ways. No one can doubt that a worldwide web exits today. But the claim that it has existed ever since humans emerged on the African savanna remains no more than a logical inference, and one I only recently came to accept.

* * * *

Let me explain how that happened. When first I began to think about world history, some seventy years ago, I paid no particular attention to communication nor to the critical role speech plays in human affairs. Politics and war were what historians had concentrated on ever since the time of Herodotus, and my schooling focused on ancient Near Eastern, Greek, and Roman history followed by medieval and modern Europe and America. Other peoples of the world were entirely left out until Europeans discovered them, thereby bringing them into the scope of history in variously subordinate, dependent ways.

I discarded this grotesquely distorted view of the human past only in 1939 when I read the first three volumes of Arnold J. Toynbee's *A Study of History*. His pages were a revelation to me for he roamed across the whole wide world seeking (and finding) patterns for the rise and fall of more than twenty civilizations, some arrested, some aborted, some fully developed, but all, he declared, "philosophically equivalent," growing, and eventually breaking down, very much as individual humans and other life forms do.

Toynbee explicitly dismissed the "unity of civilization" as a misconception and argued that significant borrowing among civilizations only occurred across time through "renaissances" and by succession—what he called "apparentation and affiliation." This was a view I rejected from the start for anthropologists had convinced me that borrowing attractive techniques or ideas from contemporaries was normal and indeed universal among human groups of every size and level of skill. But I did accept Toynbee's notion of separate and essentially independent civilizations as the principal actors of recorded history. Above all, he convinced me, close though I then was to a PhD, that my education was just beginning if I wanted, like him, to understand human affairs as a whole.

World War II then interrupted my academic career for five years. On returning, I finished my PhD and was hired by the University of Chicago in 1947 to join a college staff charged with constructing and teaching a new course in the History of Western Civilization. Needless to say, this task kept me firmly within the bounds of my training. But I profited from the expert knowledge of some of my colleagues, especially those who were exiles from Germany and Italy. So it was a stimulating experience.

Yet after seven years, repetition dulled my enthusiasm and I joined the graduate Department of History, where I had more freedom to teach what I wished, though there, too, I was expected to offer conventional courses in European history of the sort required of graduate students. But my ambition to improve on Toynbee's vision of world history remained alive. So, approaching the age of forty, which ancient Greeks reckoned the apex of a human life, I applied for a year's grant (1954–1955) from the Ford Foundation for "faculty enhancement," with the intention of starting to write my big book. I made good progress but found a whole year of reading and writing without normal contact with students and fellow faculty members very exhausting, so after a year's return to duty I applied to the Carnegie Foundation for a five-year grant (1957–1962) that allowed me to spend half of each year teaching as usual and the other half working on what became *The Rise of the West*.

Without these grants and without a library system that allowed me to withdraw books from the stacks and keep them on my desk as long as no one else requested them, I could not have finished my book in 1962 and published it the next year. I took no notes. Instead, when starting a new chapter, I read rapidly and extensively for six weeks, which was about as long as I could remember where I had seen a given bit of information, and then sat down to make an outline of what I had learned. That sometimes took several days of trial and error, but persistence allowed me to give each chapter what seemed a satisfactory shape and substance. The initial outlines sometimes raised new ques-

THE HUMAN WEB 25

tions that demanded further reading, but in all but one case I finished each chapter within three months of starting it, writing footnotes confidently by looking again at the pages of the library books still piled high on my desk.

Those months were the longest and most sustained intellectual effort of my life, and when *The Rise of the West* appeared it won extravagant praise and briefly became a best seller despite its 812 pages and numerous footnotes. The popular reception of *The Rise of the West* was partly due to the expansive self-confidence with which the United States emerged from World War II. Engaged in the cold war, Americans were more curious than usual about other peoples, and the title of my book seemed to promise success for their cause. Yet the book is organized around the notion that primacy among different civilizations shifted from time to time. It followed that the rise of the West since about 1500 was only the most recent such phenomenon, sure to change sooner or later. But most readers missed that message, briefly set forth in the last few pages.

In subsequent years I wrote other books, exploring themes only hinted at in *The Rise of the West* or entirely neglected, and little by little serious defects in my magnum opus became obvious to me as historians and anthropologists discovered new dimensions of the past. But by then I was too old to be capable of the extended effort needed to prepare a revised edition. Instead, soon after my retirement in 1987, I wrote an article, "*The Rise of the West* after Twenty-Five Years," which points out the book's defects as well as its strengths then apparent to me. This essay prefaces recent editions of *The Rise of the West* but falls short of reformulating its organizing principle.

Then, in 1997, my elder son, John Robert McNeill, professor of history at Georgetown University, invited me to collaborate with him in writing what we soon referred to as "A Very Short History of the Whole Wide World." John taught African and other exotic kinds of history and thought that students beginning such regional study needed a world history short enough to read in the first week, to put what they were about to learn into its larger setting. I was wary of collaboration but also flattered by his suggestion, so I agreed to write a short narrative account, correcting and

boiling down *The Rise of the West*. As he read and criticized my chapters, it soon became clear that he objected to my habit of writing about civilizations as competitive, more or less autonomous actors in world history. As he put it, "History is not a horse race," a comment that I felt was a miserable caricature of my approach, but he did convince me that civilizations were not persons and did not make decisions or act collectively and should not be described as doing so.

What we needed was a different organizing concept. The solution came suddenly one afternoon in 2000 as we discussed our book while waiting in the airport of Austin, Texas, after attending a conference about teaching world history, and the phrase "the human web" popped from my son's mouth. We both seized upon it as a promising substitute for my older vocabulary. Working out exactly how to use the term and what local and temporal variations to recognize within the overall web required much further discussion and careful adjustment of what each of us had written. But in due time we came to satisfactory agreement, and in 2003 our book—*The Human Web: A Bird's-Eye View*—was published.

This remains the best effort to conceptualize world history that my son and I are capable of. I believe it cuts with the grain of everyday experience and behavior, shaped, as humans are, by words and other forms of communication. Whether the term will catch on and become standard remains to be seen. There is little sign of it so far, but time, as always, will tell. At the very least, I am sure that the concept of the human web makes world history far more intelligible than rival, personalized civilizations as portrayed in *The Rise of the West* ever managed to do.

About the Author

William H. McNeill is emeritus professor of history at the University of Chicago. Among his many published works are *The Rise of the West: A History of the Human Community* (1963), *Plagues and Peoples* (1976), *A World History* (4th ed., 1998), and (with J.R. McNeill) *The Human Web: A Bird's-Eye View of World History* (2003).

CHAPTER 6

Conversations Between Past and Present

Thoughts on Teaching Current Events in a World History Classroom

TOM LAICHAS

Here is a memory that has stuck with me since grade school: taking scissors to the *Los Angeles Times* and, with long swatches of cellophane tape, affixing articles to notebook paper, writing the required summary ("in your own words") and opinion ("your *own* opinion").

Current events have been knocking around classrooms for a long time. One study tracked the demand for a "relevant" social studies curriculum all the way back to the 1890s.[1] Pushing even further into the past, Gary Hopkins found this helpful suggestion from an eighteenth-century editor: "Much has been said and written on the utility of newspapers, but one principal advantage which might be derived from these publications has been neglected. We mean that of reading them in schools."[2]

Two hundred years later, teachers are widely blamed for *failing* to teach current events. The most recent example is Richard Shenkman's book, *Just How Stupid Are We? Facing the Truth About the American Voter*. One small-town reviewer captured Shenkman's sentiments perfectly: "Our schools have been fundamentally derelict in their teaching of civics."[3]

These words sting all the more because, judging from a survey conducted by the National Council for Social Studies (NCSS), teachers *already* put current events near the top of their curricular agendas. Better than 90 percent of K–12 teachers consider current events "important" or "essential" to their work.[4] Putting aside for the moment the forces outside a classroom that would leach student attention from the news, there is a truth that all teachers know: while most of them *want* to integrate current events into their classroom work, they face considerable countervailing pressures.

What are these pressures? According to the NCSS study, "time constraints" rank first.[5] As the standards movement has gained ground in the last twenty years, teachers have seen a gradual accretion of mandated history content from local, state, and federal officials as well as from the College Board and other assessment developers. Time is particularly compressed for those who teach world history. Most schools, if they require world history at all, do so in a one-year course. This is also true of the advanced placement (AP) World History curriculum, whose deftly outlined curriculum guide recommends that teachers devote about ten days to the period since 1975.[6]

But the issue of time masks a deeper disquiet with the *legitimacy* of classroom current events. At one time, current events seemed to answer many concerns regarding student civic knowledge. The 1983 report "A Nation at Risk," for instance, called for three years of "social studies" in high schools in order to "enable students to fix their places and possibilities in the larger social and cultural structure; to understand the broad sweep of both ancient and contemporary ideas; understand the fundamentals of how our economic . . . and political system[s] function; and grasp the difference between free and repressive societies."[7] Current events assignments would easily meet these goals.

The report disappointed those who believed that students need more history, not more "social studies." For example, the Bradley Commission on History in Schools (1987) declared that "[h]istorical studies and historical literature have been widely neglected in the early grades" as well as in secondary schools, and it urged that history be returned to the center of the social science curriculum. Nationally, historians and history teachers organized (notably through the National Council for History Education) to pursue these goals. Meanwhile, at state and local levels, advocacy groups representing religious, ethnic, and political communities pressed school officials to demand that publishers incorporate their historical experiences into school texts. These developments led to calls for national history standards. While conservative critics lambasted those developed in the mid-1990s by the National Center for History in the Schools, too few observers, whether on the Left or Right, questioned the wisdom of holding instructors responsible for teaching from detailed inventories of essential historical knowledge.[8]

Few reformers intended to squeeze current events out of the curriculum. Yet such is the consequence. The phrase *current events* reminds many adults over a certain age of scissors and tape: a feel-good, hands-on assignment, but not one that is essential to a history classroom.[9] In my view, this is unfortunate. History simply cannot be taught at the high school level without reference to current events. Here is why.

Benefits of Teaching Current Events in a World History Class

Without Current Events, Historical Analogy Is Impossible

Among the Bradley Commission's reasons for privileging history is its capacity to illuminate the present. Yet, as Maris Vinovskis has noted, reasoning forward from the past can "mislead us." Selective evidence and politically charged argument can easily corrupt historical analogies. In fact, without a sense of the distinctiveness of current events, reasoning from history is downright perilous. It turned out, for instance, that the Gulf War was not Vietnam, just as Vietnam was not World War II, and World II was not World War I. Each successive analogy broke down because it privileged knowledge of the past over knowledge of the present. In a classroom, past and present must be in dialogue for students to reason historically.[10]

Without Current Events, It Is Hard to Take History Seriously

The most important fact about history is this: everyone in it is dead. This fact is far more important than the recent discovery that, in addition to dead white males, there are dead women, children, and men of all ethnicities and lifeways. In life, perhaps, such diversity matters. In death? Not so much.

The problem with parading the careers of dead people past our students is not that they are boring or irrelevant. Students are able to take enormous pleasure in fictional and virtual worlds, even though no novel or film or massive multiplayer videogame character has ever walked the earth. No, the problem is that the stakes are so low. No matter how history itself may fascinate, it fascinates in exactly the same way a novel or film fascinates. Students may be persuaded to construct intricate assessments of

individuals, nations, or cultures. Ultimately, though, these historical characters are already dead. Retrospective analysis is merely academic: student insights will not bring the dead back to life, and student misjudgments will not kill them. Students and teachers can both walk away from history's tragedies as easily as they put down a book.

More importantly, without current events, history classes can unwittingly nurture in students a contempt for the people of the past. Chapter and lesson titles (i.e., "The Coming of World War II") signal to students that a momentous historical crisis looms just a few pages or a few days ahead. Every subsequent event forges a link in a chain leading, quite inevitably, to the disaster. The result: an illusion of omniscience. *We,* students and teachers alike, *we* can see the train wreck coming. It's obvious. If the passengers or conductors or engineers can't, they must be blind. Moctezuma could have killed Cortez the moment they met. Couldn't he figure out what was going to happen? Why did German peasants rebel in 1521? Couldn't they *see* that they were going to get beat? Why did governments encourage heavy industry in the nineteenth and twentieth centuries? Didn't they *see* the environmental consequences?

Current events challenge these attitudes in two ways. First, the stakes in current events are sky-high: our collective poor judgment can bring death to the living (among whom, of course, we count ourselves). Second, since we cannot see the future, our solutions might make things worse. It is difficult, I think, to have real sympathy for the error-prone people of the past until we experience for ourselves the difficulties of fumbling for solutions against a harrowing and unknowable future. Current events allow students to understand that the past is more like the present than it is like a novel or film.

Current Events Correct History's Distortions

History is, of course, a form of memory. We imagine that historical memory serves reason—and often it does. However, history can just as easily deceive reason. This is because our minds draw upon memory not just to *recall* the past but *extrapolate* historical experience into the present. Paradoxically, the best history surveys often leave students with wildly distorted ideas about the contemporary world, distortions that current events can challenge.

Most world history classes devote considerable attention to the Atlantic slave trade, helping students imagine the "plantation complex" that dominated the Atlantic and Caribbean tropical coasts and archipelagos in the eighteenth and nineteenth centuries. Students will learn about Brazil's coffee plantations, Haiti's successful slave rebellion against the French, and the complicated interactions between slave traders and African coastal peoples. Usually, however, this is the last time that students will be asked to consider the Atlantic as a unit, Haiti as a country, or coastal Africa in its interactions with the Atlantic economy. Instead, students extrapolate forward from here: if they have never been to Africa, they imagine it as little changed from the photos and engravings their textbook or documentary films provide. They look at Haiti's contemporary problems and decide that current leaders have betrayed Toussaint L'Ouverture's revolution, though the two are two hundred years apart. As for the Caribbean coast of Latin America, it is terra incognita.

This is so because we devote lessons or units to particular regions, peoples, and ideas, only to abandon them entirely when they become less important to our narratives. What happens to Greece after the Roman conquest? Where does the Catholic Church end up in the five centuries since Luther's ninety-five theses? Is there any movement in Hinduism after the Rig Veda? In Judaism after the Talmud? In Islam after the Qur'an?

History classrooms can, quite unintentionally, reinforce a certain analytical laziness. If students do not know much about Irish history, then today's conflict between Catholics and Protestants is "caused by" the Reformation. If students do not know much Middle Eastern history, then the origins of the Israeli-Palestinian conflict date back, with a vague wave of the hand, "a thousand years ago."

Teachers cannot tie up every loose thread that history leaves hanging. However, they can emphasize to their students that when attention turns elsewhere, as it must, places and peoples already studied continue changing.

If History—and Especially World History—Corrodes Students' Faith in the Power to Act, Current Events Can Restore It

The scholars who have created the "new world history" are not shy in their ambitions. They call for "big history"—history that considers the impact of climate, of large-scale economic change, and of biological regimes at time scales in the thousands, tens of thousands, and even millions of years. It was this ambition that attracted me to world history in the first place: there is something extraordinarily exhilarating about teaching at such enormous scales.[11]

However, "big history" exacts a price. Implicitly, the new world history makes an argument: that human will does not matter. While vast scales and titanic forces delight and astonish students, they subtly encourage a certain detachment from students' own lives, which can seem small and insignificant by comparison. While I am a partisan of world history, I also know that some of the last century's worst political abuses grew out of a mechanistic determinism, a clockwork of nationalism or class conflict or religious millennialism so grand that its champions could feel justified in snuffing out those individuals who resisted the shifting gears.

What we call "current events" occur at the smallest of historical time scales: a few decades, months, or hours. Even the cold war, which dominated every bit of news that seeped into my classroom when I began teaching in the 1980s, lasted just under five decades. The decisions of individual political leaders, from Truman and Stalin to Reagan and Gorbachev, really did matter, as did the actions of movements such as SANE in the West and Helsinki Watch in Eastern Europe. Though institutions, legal traditions, and political culture constrained individual free will, none of these individuals was entirely imprisoned by big history. And so the cold war did not become a nuclear war. And so we all lived.

Thus people live in tension, as they always have, between large-scale conditions that they cannot change and the small-scale conditions that they can. Incorporating current events into the discussion can help students affirm their capacity for meaningful political engagement.

Reading a Newspaper (or Its Internet Successors) Really Is Important

We know that newspaper readership (both online and off) has declined over the last thirty years. We know that U.S. networks and cable outlets cover the world extremely poorly. Whatever the other arguments for turning student attention to the international news, this one should be blindingly obvious: if history teachers do not do it, no one else will.

Planning Current Events Instruction

In sum, I justify incorporating current events into my world history courses for five reasons:

- Historical analogies require a nuanced understanding of the present as well as the past.
- A study of high-stakes contemporary crises brings home the risks and uncertainties that faced people in similar straits in the past.
- History surveys can distort students' understanding of the present; current events can correct those distortions.
- Because current events foreground contingency, they highlight the importance of active political engagement.
- Only in world history classes are students likely to get *any* introduction to international news (and beyond that, to nonfiction writing).

Of course, a list twice as long as this will not alter the fact that few students get more than 120 hours of world history instruction. Nor does this list alter federal, state, and district expectations, not to mention those of students in AP World History courses.

Yet this rationale suggests a solution that can make the teaching of current events possible *within* the existing calendar. That solution is to plan current events instruction in advance, selecting contemporary issues that enrich student understanding of history and historical change.

How can one plan, months in advance, for current events? Most of what passes for news is perfectly predictable a few months or even a year before it makes the *New York Times*. I write this chapter in the summer of 2008. I know there will be a U.S. presidential election this coming November 4. I do not know who will win, but I do know the outline of the coming debates over international affairs.

I know, for instance, that revolutionary movements will remain in the news. Maybe Colombia's FARC will collapse (and maybe not). Maybe the Indian government will defeat the Maoist Naxalite rebellion (probably not). The Palistinian Liberation Organization (PLO), Hamas, and Hezbollah will still be around in June 2009, as will the Zapatista movement in Chiapas.

I know that the world's billion poorest people will not be getting any richer this year and that advocates of particular antipoverty policies (Bangladeshi microlenders, Brazilian peasant organizers, Bolivian indigenous activists, Chicago-trained free market economists) will not substantially change their proposed solutions.

I can predict that fault lines that now exist within and between major religions will persist. The Anglican Church may split along conservative-progressive lines, ostensibly over the issue of gay and lesbian clergy. In Iraq, Shi'a and Sunni identities will remain heavily politicized, regardless of the war's outcome. Tensions between the Buddhist Thai state and the southern Muslim minority will remain high. In Latin America, the Catholic Church will continue to face pressure from Pentecostalism.

I know that the environmental stories of the last year (deforestation, coral reef die-offs, the East Pacific garbage gyre, global climate change, and the rest) will remain in the news for the foreseeable future, as will debates over carbon sequestration, carbon trading, and carbon taxes.

I can predict that there will be natural disasters on a horrific scale that may or may not be related to climate change. In any case, I know that some of these natural disasters will provoke political crises.

I know that if I plan a lesson this summer on nineteenth- and twentieth-century technological change, I can, in the week before I teach that lesson, assemble a relevant list of articles from the *Economist*, the *New York Times*, ScienceDaily.com, *Discover Magazine*, and *Scientific American*. While I cannot foresee the perspective each of those articles will offer, I know that if a lesson on, say, Chinese research and development funding or Dubai's

desalinization schemes serves my purpose, I will be able to find timely articles.

I can, finally, predict that there will be events that I cannot foresee. I was no better than anyone else in anticipating the 1991 collapse of the Soviet Union or the September 11 attacks. Yet, such "surprises" are not surprising. Sometimes, current events radically alter history. I already know this. I can plan for it, keeping aside a couple of readings on the role of contingency and crisis in human history.

In short, I do not have to await the news to plan for it. I can pick and choose from as yet unwritten headlines, integrating them now into a sequence of units and lessons that I will teach in the coming year. Generally, I plan my course in three steps:

1. I divide the textbook into unit-sized readings that take about three weeks each. In this, I am very traditional. Not all world history teachers require a textbook or require that students read sequentially, chapter-by-chapter, cover-to-cover. When, earlier in my career, I taught U.S. history, I taught it thematically, taught it in reverse chronological order, and taught it without a textbook. I do not do this in my tenth-grade world history class because world history is inherently a more complex story than any national or regional narrative. I have found that tenth graders need a chronological framework—and frankly, so do I.

2. I identify a central theme from the readings. I look for a theme that will illuminate later units, prepare students for next year's U.S. history classes, and link to significant contemporary events. One such theme, for the period 1890–1914, is migration. A focus on migration illuminates concepts that are applicable to other periods (commercial and labor diasporas, cultural syncretism and hybridity, the transition from slavery to indentured servitude and wage labor). A focus on worldwide migration will also help students contextualize the "new immigration" they will encounter in their U.S. history classes, while exploding their preconception that migration is a specifically U.S. story.

3. I identify contemporary events that I can integrate into lessons drawn from each theme. Comparisons between the immigration debates of the late nineteenth century and those of the early twenty-first are obvious: I am gathering material about Turks in Germany, Africans in Spain, Palestinians in the Persian Gulf, Thais in Israel, Zimbabweans in South Africa, and Mexicans in the United States. I have pulled articles on Indo-Trinidadian calypso

(syncretism and hybridity) and political strife in Fiji between Indo-Fijians and Polynesian-Fijians (intercommunal conflict). I also have materials waiting, unprocessed, on the rural-to-urban migrations that have swelled nearly every major city in the world over the past seventy years. I may, however, reserve those materials for a unit on urbanization.

Current Events in Three World History Units

My plans for the 2008–2009 school year are very much in process. However, three units are nearing completion, focused on peasants, empires, and historical contingency (i.e., "heroes in history").

Finding Peasants in the Seventeenth and Twenty-first Centuries

> Behind the buzz over Brazil's cane-based ethanol production—the twenty-first century's environmental-friendly fuel par excellence—lurk enduring social problems . . . a day spent visiting cane production facilities of CBAA, a sugar and ethanol manufacturer, revealed the hardship from which these achievements were wrested. A cane field opposite an area overrun by landless peasants had been burnt in an act of arson.

—Roger Cohen, "Is Ethanol for Everybody?"
New York Times, January 10, 2008

Roger Cohen's article for the *New York Times*, filed away for use in the coming year, mentions, almost as an afterthought, a cane field burned by "landless peasants." Landless peasants? Who *are* these people?

Last year, at the beginning of a lesson focused on seventeenth-century peasant rebellions, I asked students the same question: what, exactly, does the word *peasant* mean? Most students, whether they know it or not, descend from peasants. Even so, their responses, written quickly on the whiteboard, came down to this: peasants are poor rural folk living in squalor. They are backward, illiterate, and (a few students said) stupid. This characterization, needless to say, offended some students in the classroom. But if I do not let students explicitly voice such preconceptions, I cannot challenge them.

And if I do not challenge them, I know that most of my students will grossly misread the history that awaits them in my class. From France's counterrevolutionary Vendée to Emiliano Zapata's militant Morelos state and the mountain fastness of Mao's Yunnan, students often will encounter the word *peasant* in their textbook and in original sources. In

some original sources, the word is used pejoratively. Sometimes, appearing as an adjective (as in a "peasant uprising") it substitutes for analysis. Many of those students who consider peasants ignorant find it easy to laugh at peasants who swelled the armies of China's Hong Xiuquan (who believed himself Jesus's brother) and Yemelyan Pugachev (who pretended to be Tsar Peter III). Reminding students of the bloodshed resulting from each rebellion does sober them up, but it also reinforces an underlying image of peasant rebellion as an act of nature: irrational, implacable, destructive, and animalistic.

In constructing this unit, I have to avoid replacing such misunderstandings with new ones. For one thing, students need to know that there is a long tradition of romanticizing peasant lives. If I am not careful, I will "correct" students' image of peasants as violently passionate rural bumpkins with an image of honest rural people, authentically human, closer to nature and the soil than we urban moderns. Any discussion of peasants also risks deteriorating into politically simplistic caricatures. Recruited by the Left, peasants become The People: heroically revolutionary cadres besieged by the behemoth of global capitalism. Conservatives tend to imagine peasants as religious traditionalists, defending their moral sensibilities against imperious, corrupt secular states. Finally, no matter what I do, I might leave the impression that "peasant" is a monolithic category, the same from one dwelling to the next within each peasant village, and the same from one world region to the next.

Thus, any assignment involving peasants must paint a more complex picture. One of the ways I do this is by offering students a set of brief excerpts documenting the many ways the word *peasant* has been used.

Current events can help students rethink their ideas about peasants, peasant economies, and peasant politics. Why is this? Because the people in contemporary rural villages, whether they are landless or smallholders, confront issues with which students are at least somewhat familiar: rising fuel and food prices, confiscatory taxes, and migratory labor markets. They also may find themselves taking advantage of growing economic opportunity, improved health and life expectancy, or a democratized political culture.

In the coming year, I will choose from among many headlines: localized peasant protests will continue in China, the Naxalite rebellion will grow in India, and Brazil's Landless Workers Movement will stage armed conquests of isolated rural plots. I know too that small-scale African farmers will reel from oil prices and that the Doha trade negotiations (which again collapsed as I was writing this essay) will fail to improve access to European Union and U.S. agricultural markets. I can count on rural migrants swelling the populations of Lagos, Nairobi, Shanghai, and Bangalore, even as they provoke political debate in Europe and North America. I know of some regions where government policy is grinding peasant economies under, and others—Brazil, for instance—which seem, on the whole, to be opening economic opportunity to peasantries.

I will begin my unit on peasantry when we hit the early modern period. The economic change sparked by the new Atlantic economy between the fifteenth and eighteenth centuries roiled local economies in ways that sparked peasant revolts worldwide.[12] At this point I will ask groups of students to define the term *peasant* and will record their responses on the whiteboard. Though students will come up with impressive ideas, I imagine that few responses will flatter peasants.

I will then distribute to students James C. Scott's description of an archetypal peasant village. We will read this together, aloud, in class. In Scott's telling, while peasant communities differ considerably both within regions and across the globe, all have developed complex systems of allocating resources, adjudicating disputes, and mobilizing in the face of natural disaster. These communities, Scott emphasizes, never were egalitarian or pacifist utopias. However, they were—and are—intensely localist and flexible, adapting on their own to conditions invisible from the national capitol. The policies of centralizing states ignore local conditions, replace customary arrangements with centralized legal codes, and frequently treat peasants as mere obstacles to progress or profit. Scott argues that peasants run considerable risks if they directly confront abusive landowners, overbearing states, or unfettered free markets. Instead, they employ "weapons of the weak" that gum up the works, rendering decisions from the top difficult to implement on the ground. My goal is to get students thinking about peasants as actors in their own right. Scott's point, drawn from research in Southeast Asia, has been illustrated in Indonesian writer Pramoedya Toer's novel *Child of All Nations*, from which I will read passages to my classes.[13]

I will then have students read contemporary news items dealing with peasantries. For this purpose, I am monitoring news from China particularly closely. In 2006, Chinese authorities acknowledged over *87,000* "mass incidents," ranging from petitions to demonstrations. If summer 2008's global economic slump ultimately hits China, unrest may deepen. In that case, I will narrow the current events focus to China itself, giving students an excerpt from Chen Guidi and Wu Chuntao's *Will the Boat Sink in the Water?*, an exposé of Chinese peasant abuses. A clip from the film *The Story of Qiu Ju* underscores Chen and Wu's point, though in ways far more favorable to Chinese authorities.[14] After reading the news items, students will discuss this question in small groups and in a class roundtable: *Do these news items support James Scott's description of peasants, flatly contradict Scott, or tell us something new?*

Having devoted class time to contemporary peasant societies, I can turn again to history. Last year, I introduced the Reformation with a lesson focused exclusively on the German Peasant Rebellion of 1523–1524. This year, I

will have each of several student groups take on one sixteenth- to seventeenth-century peasant uprising. I will ask students to again compare the peasants encountered in their sources to those in James Scott's account. I will have each group share its findings with the rest of the class, and then ask all the students whether early modern peasant communities differed from one region to another and whether peasant communities of four to five centuries ago differ substantially from those of the present.[15]

The time I devote to these issues, both in the present and the past, will pay dividends for the rest of the year, helping students wrestle with sharecropping, tenant farming, slavery, indentured servitude, Russian serfdom, the English enclosure movement, Stalin's anti-kulak campaign, and Che Guevara's idea of the *foco*. These lessons will also give them a first crack at the vocabulary they will need to debate twentieth-century agricultural and trade policy, global migration, and demographic change.

Is the United States an Empire?

> The Roman Emperor Hadrian (A.D. 76–138) came from a southern Spanish family of olive-oil magnates (the equivalent of a petroleum dynasty today). He ruled over territories that included forty modern-day countries, from Scotland to the Sahara, and from the Atlantic to the Euphrates. Parallels between Hadrian's Rome and today's United States are uncanny.

> —Paul Levy, "The Emperor's New Clothes: Hadrian in London," review of "Hadrian: Empire and Conflict," an exhibition at the British Museum, *Wall Street Journal*, July 25, 2008

If peasants get lost in world history narratives, it is because empires and other centralizing states loom so imposingly over their stories. That has never been truer than it is now. When even the *Wall Street Journal* indulges in a bit of Rome-U.S. analogizing, you know that the comparison has become conventional wisdom.

Of course, that analogy can cut more than one way. To the question "Are we Rome?" Cullen Murphy answers yes: the United States is the late Roman Republic, its institutions free-falling toward their doom. In *Empire*, Michael Hardt and Antonio Negri argue that America long ago did away with whatever shred of republican virtue it may have once possessed: it is not just a "hyperpower," it is a hyper-Rome, a hyper-empire. Niall Ferguson (*Colossus*) and Max Boot (*The Savage Wars of Peace*) wish that some of this were true; both believe that global stability and prosperity require that the American electorate embrace its imperial vocation willingly. Finally, there is classicist Victor Davis Hanson, a conservative commentator for the *National Review*, who, despite considerable sympathy for Ferguson and Boot, dismisses such analogies as "pop Romanizing" that ignores historical complexities and mistakes the past for the present.[16]

Having found another Rome-U.S. comparison on the op-ed page one Sunday last year, I read a couple of paragraphs to students and opened a discussion. At first pass, student definitions of *empire* were reasonable: a large territory under the ostensible control of an absolute (if often dotty) monarch supported by a well-trained (if often ruthless) army, exercising power over (and often a grudging tolerance for) the linguistic, ethnic, and religious diversity within imperial frontiers. Digging deeper, though, most students came up with descriptions heavy on psychosexual palace politics, lurid gladiatorial contests, and gory battle scenes.

I could have expected that. At fifteen, the word *empire* reminded me of Robert Howard's *Conan the Barbarian* serial, Talbot Mundy's *Tros of Samothrace*, and the BBC's *I, Claudius*. Not much has changed. The word now evokes a montage of videogames (World of Warcraft, for instance), films (Ridley Scott's *Gladiator*, George Lucas's *Star Wars*, Sergei Bodrov's *Mongol*), and television (HBO's *Rome*, History Channel's *Empire*). Students should feel no guilt in taking pleasure from the flotsam of pop culture. I never did. That said, it *is* pop culture flotsam and leaves the impression that Mongols, Mughals, Axumites, Safavids, Habsburgs, and Romans are just one costume change away from American citizenship.

If the problem of teaching students about "the peasant" is that they come to the subject knowing almost nothing, the problem with "empire" is this phony familiarity. The word positively creaks with pseudohistorical associations that, in my experience, subvert teaching at every turn. Rather than fight this battle directly, by analyzing what the word *empire* actually might mean, I will approach the question through the back door, via current events. Thus, in October, I will pose this question: *Why does anybody willingly pay taxes?*

Asked in an election year, the question is directly relevant both to national political debate and to several measures slated for the November 2008 California ballot. While student debates are standard fare in my election-year classroom, this year I will provide groups of students with data on taxation from selected countries: the types of taxes levied, the portion of individual and corporate income collected, and the incidence of tax avoidance. Each group will then consult materials I am gathering on the relevant national governments. Following two days of this work, groups will make their reports, provoking what I hope will be a lively roundtable discussion.

I do not expect students to develop a sophisticated feel for fiscal policy overnight. I do expect that students' comments will touch on public policy, political culture, political structure, each nation's economy, and its government's

legitimacy, bureaucratic efficiency, and transparency. The list itself is not important. It *is* important that students come up with a cluster of attributes that might explain the success of some states and the failure of others. Taken together, these questions will segue to a day of direct instruction: a lecture about just what the "modern state" means. It will highlight the connections between technological change and advancing government capacities throughout the world. To avoid grosser generalizations, I will compare national experiences within regions (Botswana and Sierra Leone, Thailand and the Philippines, Brazil and Venezuela) as well as globally.

With the election debates concluded, my classes will revisit premodern empires. I will begin with the Rome-U.S. analogy, but will turn it on its head. Rather than asking "Are we Rome?" I will ask, "Was Rome us?" The purpose is to encourage students to reason back from the present rather than forward from the past. I will divide the class into two groups, asking one to respond affirmatively, the other negatively. After a day and a night of preparation drawn again from materials I am gathering, I will sit the two groups on opposite sides of the room and let them have at it. If their preparation is sufficient, then the debate will not only reiterate the standard comparisons, but also remind students that Rome—and indeed any premodern empire—differs a great deal from any contemporary state.

This debate will become a model for comparisons later in the year: was the Qing Empire comparable to the European Union, as Alexander Woodside has suggested? What is gained—and lost—when William McNeill characterizes Mughal, Safavid, and Ottoman states as "gunpowder empires," a term now in every world history textbook? Does it make sense to characterize Periclean Athens, seventeenth-century Srivijaya, and the nineteenth-century British Empire as "naval empires," or does each have more in common with land-based polities of its own region and era?[17]

Students can pursue other kinds of analogies as well. For instance, empires such as those of Rome, the Mongols, Kanem-Bornu, and the Incas covered swaths of territory, every bit as extensive as modern states. By other standards, however (population, commercial production, labor productivity), most were relatively small. At its greatest extent, for instance, the Roman Empire was home to 45 million persons, with a per capita gross domestic product (GDP) of between $400 and $900. The ninth-century Abbassid Caliphate had a population probably in excess of 20 million and per capita GDP of about $600. I will ask students whether Rome and the Abbassid Caliphate might be compared to contemporary Sudan, Bangladesh, and Burma (which have comparable populations and GDPs) as usefully as they have been to the United States.[18]

I will employ current events in one final way: to explore the modern fetish for empire. As I said earlier, students' ideas of empire owe a lot to popular culture—a fact that is neither new nor unique to the United States. As brief conversation-starters, I will ask students to consider the following questions:

- Why have classical Mediterranean motifs (Egyptian, Greek, and Roman) appeared again and again in architecture and visual arts around the globe since the fifteenth century?
- Why did Reza Pahlavi, the last shah of Iran, spend $100 million in 1971 to celebrate the 2,500th year of Persepolis, despite enormous criticism?
- Why did the People's Republic of China destroy thousands of ancient monuments in the 1960s and yet, twenty years later, build impressive archaeological museums?
- Why do imperial names reappear in the modern states of Mali, Ghana, and Zimbabwe? What are these names intended to evoke, and are they successful in doing so?
- Why do the world's people enjoy films featuring empires? Why has the *idea* of empire and kingdom drawn Chinese audiences to *The First Emperor*, Thais to *Suriyothai*, and Indians to *Asoka*—all this in addition to the dozens of cinematic Romes?
- Why did Charlemagne call his state the Holy Roman Empire, tenth-century Bulgarian monarchs style themselves tsar, and sixteenth-century Russians call their country the Third Rome? Why did Ottoman sultans and African jihadists call themselves caliphs? Why is the upper house of nearly fifty governments called a senate? Why do so many republics house their heads of state in presidential "palaces"?
- Why does so much news and gossip focus on living monarchs—from Gulf state emirs and British royals to the imperial families of Japan, Thailand, and Tonga?
- Less than fifty years after the collapse of the last self-described empires, why does the *idea* of empire remain so significant? What does that tell us about ourselves? About our political cultures?

Heroes in History?

The long run is a misleading guide to world affairs. In the long run we are all dead.

—John Maynard Keynes
A Tract on Monetary Reform, 1923

A diet of current events challenges the environmental, technological, economic, and other determinisms implicit in many world history texts. Yet I do not believe that students are ready for the challenge until they have a good grounding in both micro- and macro-historical thinking.

Over the course of the first semester this coming year, I will introduce to students significant works of "big history," particularly Fernand Braudel, Jared Diamond, Cynthia Stokes-Brown, David Christian, John and William Mc-Neill, and Alfred Crosby. These introductions will consist of reading excerpts—just a paragraph or two—once every couple of weeks as discussion warm-ups: for instance, a bit of Crosby on the impact of cattle on the Argentine pampas to provide some context for discussing seventeenth- to nineteenth-century Latin America.[19] Around February, I will have students root around their notebooks and find these paragraphs again. Having reread the excerpts, they will begin preparing a response to this question: *Which matters more for creating the future: the legacy of "big history" or that of individual human action?*

Though current events will be crucial to the success of this essay and discussion, I choose to place it during a unit on "the long nineteenth century" (1790–1914). These twelve decades saw dramatic macro-level change, arguably the most significant in millennia (think industrialization, globalization, technological innovation, and the end of the "little ice age"). Yet political power became in this era more open to the pressures from organized individuals and groups. Political leaders (Otto von Bismarck, Juan Manuel de Rosas, Empress Cixi) met their match in the women and men who joined revolutionary movements, labor unions, antislavery societies, feminist organizations, corporations, and the like. Drawing solely from the nineteenth century, it is possible to make a case for either "big history" or heroic history.

A central figure in this discussion is Napoleon Bonaparte. Over time, Napoleon has retreated from the textbooks, overwhelmed by the Revolution and Terror that preceded him and the twentieth-century Communist and Nazi regimes that followed. Nearly two centuries after his death, we seem to regard Napoleon's Europe as an evanescent imperial experiment, an interruption to the story of nationalism, industrialization, and capitalism. While fans of military reenactment and historical novelist Patrick O'Brian still study Napoleon, most schoolchildren do not. Yet Napoleon played a direct role in the story of Haitian independence, the U.S. conquest of North America, and modernization debates in the Arab Middle East. Latin American caudillos modeled themselves after Napoleon, as did some military-political leaders in postindependence Africa. Ideas significant in the twentieth century—that the army represents the nation, that the leader embodies the popular will, that legal and educational systems must be centralized—were not original to Napoleon, but they were certainly identified with him. Well beyond Europe, "Bonapartism" became both an ambition and an epithet.

It happens too that Napoleon figures in the century-old debate between those who would stress individual will and those who would emphasize large-scale historical contexts.

When Thomas Carlyle argued that heroes and heroism make history, he called forth Napoleon to prove his point. Carlyle's theme resurfaced nearly a century later in the work of Sidney Hook, who (with intended irony) cited V.I. Lenin's career as evidence that individual initiative matters more than Marxist historical determinism.[20] To get at the question of whether Napoleon "mattered," I will have students read Adam Zamoyski's counterfactual essay assessing what might have happened through the late twentieth century had Napoleon defeated Russia. Zamoyski speculates that a Napoleonic Europe would have ultimately ossified, its commercial growth sapped by protectionist policies and government favoritism. In the end, Zamoyski writes, Napoleon could have done little to alter large-scale economic patterns that dominate the twenty-first century.[21]

I will then move from a hypothetical present to the real thing. Just before they actually respond to the heroes-in-history question, I will ask groups of four students to research a cluster of biographies significant to recent events in a particular region. For instance, a group investigating Pakistan would research both well-known figures (Pervez Musharraf, Benezir Bhutto, nuclear weapons scientist Abdul Qadeer Khan) and some less well known in the United States (lawyer and human rights activist Hina Jilani, Islamist militant Muhammad Adbdul Aziz, Supreme Court Chief Justice Iftikhar Muhammad Chaudhry). These students will also read news items and analysis available from the BBC, the *Economist, Foreign Policy*, and news databases at the school library, as well as relevant materials from earlier units. I will then require that the four students divide themselves into two pairs to debate this question: *Who has created contemporary Pakistan: individuals such as these or "larger forces"?*

After these debates, the entire class will return to the original question: *Which matters more for creating the future: the legacy of "big history" or that of individual human action?*

Conclusion

The three units above, out of perhaps six I will introduce in the coming year, have developed from my conviction that "current events" can do far more for a history classroom than motivate political engagement. They are, I believe, essential to historical reasoning.

About the Author

Tom Laichas, PhD, teaches world history at Crossroads School in Santa Monica, California, and is founding co-editor of *World History Connected*, an online journal for high school and college world history educators. He is the author of, among other works, *Infinite Patience, Indomitable Will: Ralph Bunche and the Struggle for Peace and Justice* (National Center for History in the Schools).

Notes

1. See Marlene Stone Cowan, *History of the Newspaper in Education Programs* (Washington: American Newspaper Publishers Association [now Newspaper Association of America], 1978).

2. *Portland* [Maine] *Eastern Herald*, June 8, 1795, quoted in Gary Hopkins, "Why Teach Current Events?" *Education World*, August 3, 1998, www.educationworld.com.

3. Richard Elrick, "Americans' Ignorance Endangers Democracy," *Barnstable Patriot*, July 24, 2008, www.barnstablepatriot.com. For Shenkman's argument, see Richard Shenkman, *Just How Stupid Are We? Facing the Truth About the American Voter* (New York: Basic Books, 2008).

4. Mary E. Haas and Margaret A. Laughlin, "Teaching Current Events in Social Studies Today," paper presented at the annual meeting of the American Educational Research Association, New Orleans, April 24–28, 2000, 12.

5. Haas and Laughlin, "Teaching Current Events," 25.

6. College Entrance Examination Board, "AP World History Course Description," www.collegeboard.com/student/testing/ap/sub_worldhist.html. The College Board recommends six weeks for the period from 1914 to the present.

7. "A Nation at Risk," in *The American Curriculum: A Documentary History*, ed. George Willis et al., 405 (New York: Praeger, 1994).

8. For the Bradley Commission report, see Bradley Commission on History in Schools, "Building a History Curriculum: Guidelines for Teaching History in Schools," (Washington, DC: Educational Excellence Network, 1988), available from the Educational Resources Information Center as ED 310 008. For an account of the fight for history standards, see Linda Symcox, *Whose History: The Struggle for National Standards in American Classrooms* (New York: Teachers College Press, 2002).

9. See, for instance, Marnie Hunter, "No Time to Study Timely Events," CNN, www.cnn.com/2003/EDUCATION/08/13/sprj.sch.current/.

10. Maris Vinovskis, *History and Educational Policymaking* (New Haven: Yale University Press, 1999), 241. For more on the problem of reasoning through analogy, see David Hackett Fischer, *Historians' Fallacies: Toward a Logic of Historical Thought* (New York: Harper, 1970).

11. See, for instance, David Christian, *Maps of Time: An Introduction to Big History* (Berkeley: University of California Press, 2004); Cynthia Stokes Brown, *Big History: From the Big Bang to the Present* (New York: New Press, 2007); Jared Diamond, *Guns, Germs and Steel: The Fates of Human Societies* (New York: Norton, 1999); John McNeill and William McNeill, *The Human Web: A Bird's-Eye View of World History* (New York: Norton, 2003); and Felipe Fernandez-Armesto, *Civilizations: Culture, Ambition, and the Transformation of Nature* (New York: Free Press, 2001).

12. It is difficult to say whether the seventeenth century really saw more peasant revolts than any other period. But many of those that occurred had serious political repercussions and, arguably, resulted (unbeknownst to the rebels or their opponents) from global economic change.

13. James C. Scott, *Seeing Like a State: How Certain Schemes to Improve the Human Condition Have Failed* (New Haven: Yale University Press, 1998), 33–36; James C. Scott,

"Normal Exploitation, Normal Resistance," ch. 2 in *Weapons of the Weak: Everyday Forms of Peasant Resistance* (New Haven: Yale University Press, 1985), 28–48; Pramoedya Toer, *Child of All Nations*, vol. 2 in *Buru Quartet* (New York: Penguin, 1996).

14. For a report on China's 87,000 protests, see Kristen Jones, "China's Hidden Unrest" in *Dangerous Assignments*, Committee to Protect Journalists, May 2006, www.cpj.org/. Chen Guidi and Wu Chuntao's *Will the Boat Sink in the Water? The Life of Chinese Peasants* (New York: Public Affairs Press, 2006); Yimou Zhang (dir.), *The Story of Qiu Ju* (Sony Pictures, 2006 [1993]). I join many reviewers in considering *Qiu Ju* too slow-moving to show in its entirety, though at 100 minutes it will take just two class periods. Excerpts, however, work well.

15. For more on the German Peasant Rebellion, see Keith Moxley, *Peasants, Warriors, and Wives: Popular Imagery in the Reformation* (Chicago: University of Chicago Press, 2004), a rich collection of sixteenth-century German woodcuts. For original source material, including the petitions of the peasant rebels themselves, see Tom Scott, *The German Peasants' War: A History in Documents* (Amherst, NY: Humanities Press, 1994).

16. Cullen Murphy, *Are We Rome? The Fall of an Empire and the Fate of the United States* (New York: Houghton-Mifflin, 2007); Michael Hardt and Antonio Negri, *Empire* (Cambridge, MA: Harvard University Press, 2001); Niall Ferguson, *Colossus: The Rise and Fall of the American Empire* (New York: Penguin, 2005); Max Boot, *The Savage Wars of Peace: Small Wars and the Rise of American Power* (New York: Basic Books, 2002); Victor Davis Hanson, "Pop Romanizing," review of Cullen Murphy, *Are We Rome?*, in Hanson, *Private Papers*, www.victorhanson.com. Also useful in the classroom is Robert Harris, "Pirates of the Mediterranean," *New York Times*, September 30, 2006. Harris compares Rome's response to an attack on the port of Ostia to that of the United States following 9/11.

17. For the Qing-EU analogy, see Alexander Woodside, *Lost Modernities: China, Vietnam, Korea, and the Hazards of World History* (Cambridge, MA: Harvard University Press, 2006), 10. For the "gunpowder empires," see William McNeill, *Age of Gunpowder Empires, 1450–1800* (Washington, DC: American Historical Association, 1990). The term *naval empire* was already applied to Greece and Britain in the nineteenth century; the term is now used widely, if casually.

18. These very approximate estimates, probably the best we can expect given the fragmentary nature of the evidence, may be found in Angus Maddison, *Contours of the World Economy, 1–2030 AD* (Oxford, UK: Oxford University Press, 2007), especially ch. 1 and 4.

19. Crosby, *Ecological Imperialism: The Biological Expansion of Europe, 900–1900* (Cambridge, UK: Cambridge University Press, 1986), 159–161. See also, for instance, Fernand Braudel, *Civilization and Capitalism, 15th–19th Centuries*, 3 vols. (New York: HarperCollins, 1982–1984); Jared Diamond, *Guns, Germs and Steel: The Fates of Human Societies* (New York: W.W. Norton, 1999); Cynthia Stokes Brown, *Big History: From the Big Bang to the Present* (New York: New Press, 2007); David Christian, *Maps of Time: An Introduction to Big History* (Berkeley and Los Angeles: University of California Press, 2004); John McNeill and William McNeill, *The Human Web: A Birds-Eye View of World History* (New York: W.W. Norton, 2003).

20. Thomas Carlyle, *On Heroes, Hero-Worship and the Heroic in History* (Lincoln: University of Nebraska Press, 1966); Sidney Hook, *The Hero in History* (New York: John Day, 1943).

21. Adam Zamoyski, "Napoleon Triumphs in Russia," in *What Might Have Been: Leading Historians on Twelve 'What Ifs' of History*, ed. Andrew Roberts, 79–91 (London: Orion, 2005).

CHAPTER 7

The Twenty-first–Century Classroom
Using Online Course Management Systems to Help Students Make the World's History Their Own

MICHAEL S. BROWN

In the next few years American public school systems and institutions of higher learning will face an interesting demographic milestone. For the very first time, educators will be instructing a student population that, from kindergartener to college senior, has no conscious memory of a time before the mass availability of the Internet. The influence of Internet-based technologies, though varied in scope due to socioeconomic inequities, has changed the way students interact with each other in a profound way. Their social world no longer remains confined to the family once the sun goes down and the streetlights glow. Social networking sites such as MySpace and Facebook, online console video gaming, and text messaging have made it possible to interact with peers, both familiar and new, regardless of geographic distance and time of day. For these students, the Internet is far more valuable than the passive mediums of radio and television—it is an active tool for understanding that they control. They are learning about themselves, each other, and the world in which they live by using a boundless, increasingly more interactive online component that could only be imagined a generation ago.

The manner in which students wish to have information conveyed is changing, and so too must the history classroom change with it. In order to take advantage of students' growing interest in online interactions, educators have developed course management systems (CMS). Educators can use a CMS to create interactive, online learning communities and provide students with an additional avenue to apply their knowledge in a public forum. Rather than the passive, traditional website where information is simply posted like notices on a cork bulletin board, a CMS allows teachers to provide a course website featuring a greater degree of support and interaction for students. A CMS-based website is far more interactive, giving students and teachers the ability to exchange ideas about course concepts and manage course information using online chat programs, message boards, and wikis. It is technology that absolutely belongs in a world history course!

The problem that many students have with history is that it feels cold and remote, with little bearing on the immediate experiences that children often hold in higher esteem. The impacts and themes of world history are everywhere, reaching into their lives at all times. Therefore, students deserve a course experience that teaches world history in a way that is not defined chronologically by tardy bells or physically by classroom walls. World history is everywhere, subtlety reaching into their lives at all times regardless of whether or not it is perceived. Teachers must seek methods of instruction that encourage students to stop thinking of history as a function of the classroom and strive to recognize its impact on their lives. History instruction needs to have elements that make it personal and fun to achieve this objective. The beauty of a world history CMS website is that it can bridge the gap between what students consider "schoolwork" and "leisure fun" by using a technology that imitates some of the same interactive elements that they use every day on their favorite social networking websites and in online games. While it has use in the classroom, a CMS website with activities that inspire students to think critically about history and share their own educated opinions can compel them to take the course *home*. It is easy enough to imagine students, guided by a teacher, discussing the concept of *hijab* and traditions of Muslim dress in a history classroom, but what about an online debate that has students posting ideas at 8 p.m. on Sunday? It happens. Students are excited about using these technologies, and an effective world history teacher can channel this enthusiasm in positive ways to enhance students' understanding of the world as it was, as it is, and as it may become in the future.

Why Use Course Management Systems?

Many public and private employers are in the process of incorporating online collaboration as a vital part of their workplace environment, and a growing proportion of postsecondary schools require student participation in online learning before graduation. As a result, the need to give secondary school students meaningful, interactive online experiences is all the more imperative. An interactive website, as provided by a CMS, is a tool that allows teachers to create an online component to their classrooms, preparing students for the learning and workplace environments of the future.

A thematic, globally minded world history course lends itself well to a CMS website. The ultimate goal is to create a virtual gathering point where students can interact with each other, exchange ideas concerning the major themes of world history covered in class, and obtain electronic publications from the teacher. Students typically interact with each other in a classroom, but rarely do students from multiple sections have an opportunity to share ideas. Each section of a single course has its own unique personality due to student diversity. While two sections of a course can follow the same general lesson plan and arrive at the same instructional "destination," the connections and ideas expressed along the way are often quite different. A CMS enables world history teachers to create consistent opportunities for students to use message forums, wikis, and optional teacher-moderated chat sessions that can encourage students' interaction across sections and entice normally shy students to voice their thoughts on course-related materials. In addition, a CMS makes it easier for teachers to provide students with an extra degree of support by posting assignments, electronic versions of documents used in class, a course calendar, and practice quizzes and tests. The CMS site should serve not as a second classroom, but rather as a world history "lobby" where students can interact in a productive manner that supplements the regular classroom experience.

How Does a CMS Work?

A course management system is an online, computer server–based technology designed to be used by multiple teachers in a single school or across a school division. While it is possible for a single teacher to implement a CMS alone, the degree of technical knowledge and the expense necessary to maintain it are prohibitive to most; therefore the systems tend to be managed by the institution's information systems (IS) department. Popular systems in use include Angel, Blackboard, Moodle, and WebCT. Blackboard and WebCT are commonly found at the collegiate level and for many teachers have served as their introduction to the technology.

Once the system is established, teachers, students, and parents can be assigned usernames and passwords to provide a closed, secure online environment. Regardless of the system used, the features available for creating an interactive website are essentially the same, differing from one another only in appearance and implementation. All CMS have website creation tools esigned for computer novices to use, thereby making the technology accessible to all. The website can be accessed and edited from any computer with Internet access.

Teachers have a collection of tools available to create an interactive online environment for their students, all of which conform to a hierarchy of interactivity. Teachers have the ability also to monitor, edit, or delete the postings and messages sent by students in the course. The teacher is technically in complete control of the website and the online environment created. The chart in Figure 7.1 outlines some of the most common tools and activities, with the most interactive listed at the top.

Ideas for Peer/Teacher Interactive Activity

Discussion and Debate Forums

The heart of an interactive world history website using CMS technology comes from initiating activities from the top of the chart, with proactive and passive activities used as support. Discussion forums can provide the backbone of the website's interactive experience. Discussion forums are virtual rooms where teachers and students post messages that can be read and replied to by anyone enrolled in the course. The best online debates begin as cursory discussions in class and may be further bolstered by outside readings. The debate can then be extended through the discussion forum, which the world history teacher can use as a means to encourage students to talk about a specific concept after class. All CMS allow teachers to add static notes that give clear instructions to the students, encouraging them to respond to at least one other student. Here is an example of a simple set of effective instructions based on the previously mentioned topic of *hijab* and traditional Muslim dress:

> Post your personal impressions of the Muslim practice of *hijab*, which requires modest dress for both men and women, in relation to women. Many devout Muslim women choose to cover their bodies with the exception of the face and hands when in public. What do you think of the practice?

For this assignment, you will need to post at least THREE times according to the instructions below.

1. Post your initial impression here.
2. Read the Internet article about *hijab* linked in the Readings folder. You may find the article at the following site: www.islamfortoday.com/hijabcanada .htm.

Figure 7.1   **CMS Tools and Activities**

Tools and activities	Description
Discussion forums	Allows student/teacher interaction through public message boards. Students can post their thoughts and react to the ideas of others publicly.
Virtual office hours (chat)	Students interact in a teacher-monitored chat room. This format lends itself to online study sessions where the students can interact with the teacher and their peers in real time.
Wiki (virtual glossary)	Students create and share their own wiki (course glossary) online. Definitions and concepts can expand as students increase their understanding of the course.
Lessons and webquests	Students use the CMS as a base for interactive lessons and webquests. These can be used in conjunction with discussion forums for a truly interactive experience.
Online assignments	Students access, complete, and receive feedback for assignments online. Allows teacher to readily incorporate online material in the assignment.
Online tests and quizzes	Students take quizzes and tests and receive instant, automated feedback; teacher receives grades and a detailed item analysis useful for course planning.
Online surveys	Students participate in opinion polls, automated surveys on course topics, etc.
RSS feeds	Teacher posts RSS feeds to podcasts and news services (e.g., AP, BBC). This feature can be used in combination with forums or chat rooms to facilitate discussion of current events.
Calendar	Detailed calendar of course events managed by the teacher. Students can create personal calendars for themselves.
Course news forum	Teacher posts course news that is automatically e-mailed to all users.
Resource posting	Teacher can post PowerPoints, Word documents, and other classroom materials that students can download at their leisure.

3. Write a second post after reading the article. Did the article change your opinion? Strengthen it? Be sure to explain your answer.
4. Respond to the post of another student. You are encouraged to respond to someone outside of your class section! You may respond more than once, of course.
5. Can you suggest additional sources for your peers to read?

The preceding example may be used as a means of expanding the cultural perspectives of students, especially non-Muslims, when introducing the history and religious practices of Islam. Students typically come to class with preconceived notions about *hijab* as it applies to women in the Muslim world, many of them negative. The initial post gives them an opportunity to express these preconceptions. The outside reading then provides what usually proves to be a very different view of *hijab* from a Canadian Muslim woman.

Figure 7.2 **CMS Pyramid**

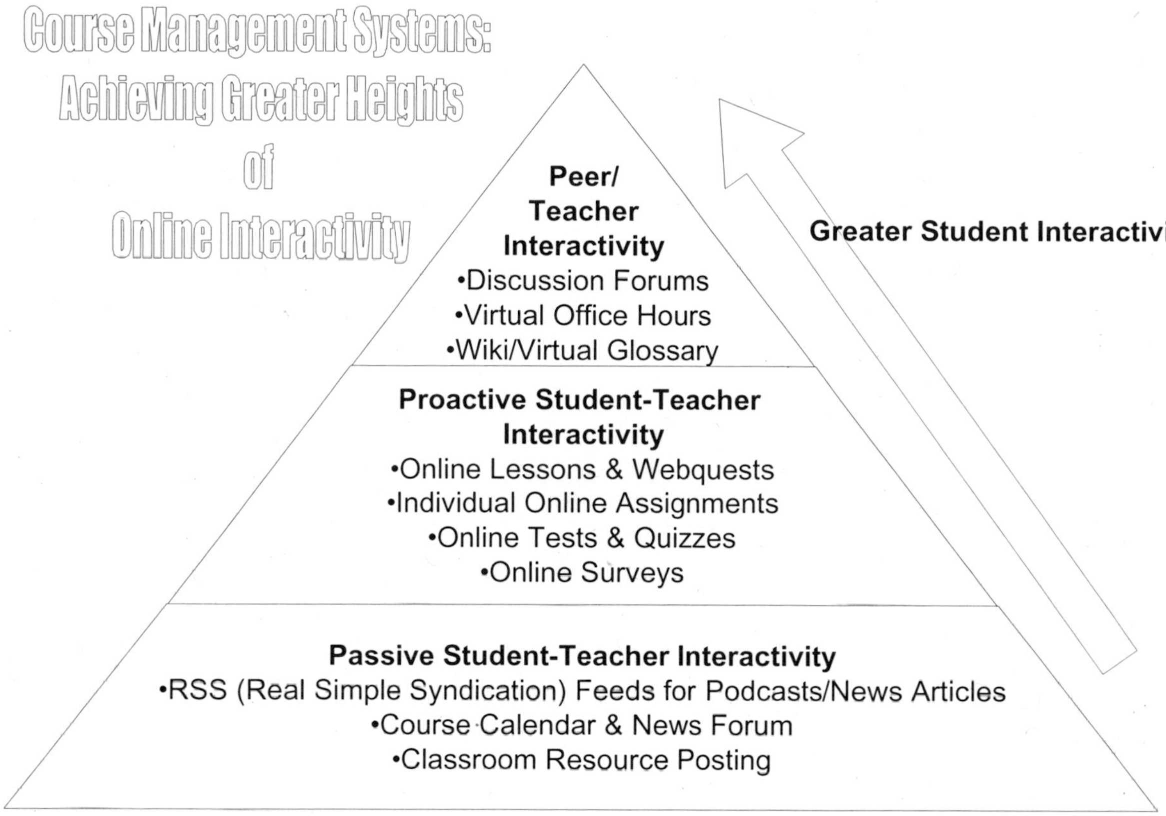

Course Management Systems:
Achieving Greater Heights
of
Online Interactivity

Greater Student Interactivity

**Peer/
Teacher
Interactivity**
•Discussion Forums
•Virtual Office Hours
•Wiki/Virtual Glossary

**Proactive Student-Teacher
Interactivity**
•Online Lessons & Webquests
•Individual Online Assignments
•Online Tests & Quizzes
•Online Surveys

Passive Student-Teacher Interactivity
•RSS (Real Simple Syndication) Feeds for Podcasts/News Articles
•Course Calendar & News Forum
•Classroom Resource Posting

The second post forces a reflection based on the new perspective, which may or may not change the student's initial opinion. It is most significant that students are asked to think critically about their opinions in a public forum first before replying to others. Students can be encouraged to bring in outside information and share sources. While this procedure may be a bit informal, the students are practicing the skills of a historian: to be conscious of their preconceptions, to explore potentially valid perspectives and synthesize them into a new conceptualization, and then to seek out additional sources that may further refine their understanding.

The main advantage of this type of assignment is that the bulk of it is completed outside of class under teacher supervision online, provided that a teacher allows students a week or more to make their posts so students without reliable access to the Internet at home have time to use school and public library labs. The time constraints that world history teachers must deal with during a typical unit make it difficult to strike a balance between the coverage of new concepts and the enrichment that comes with actively doing something with that knowledge. The *hijab* activity works well with a historical introduction to Islam. With students thinking and posting about Islamic traditions at home, the teacher can use the concept of dress in class as a means of marking change over time in Islamic society during the

postclassical era. Concepts of dress and the role of women changed as non-Arab converts to Islam joined Dar al-Islam and shaped the political and social transitions that marked the end of the Umayyad Dynasty and the beginning of the Abbasid. By reading the modern perspectives of Muslims concerning *hijab* and discussing the topic with their peers, students develop a conceptual shelf on which these historical transitions can be placed and retain meaning.

This technique can be applied to concepts throughout world history. Here are four additional subjects and historical questions that lend themselves well to this discussion and debate format (Figure 7.3):

• The wisdom of making the transition from hunting and gathering to agriculture during the Neolithic era
• The impact of the spread of proselytizing faiths on the declining empires of Han China and Rome during the late classical era
• Japan's relationship with the outside world: a simple case of copying others or the selective adoption and improvement of foreign innovations to strengthen national identity?
• Why didn't Ming China take on the mantles of exploration and colonization that Europe assumed during the early modern era?

Figure 7.3   **CMS Debate**

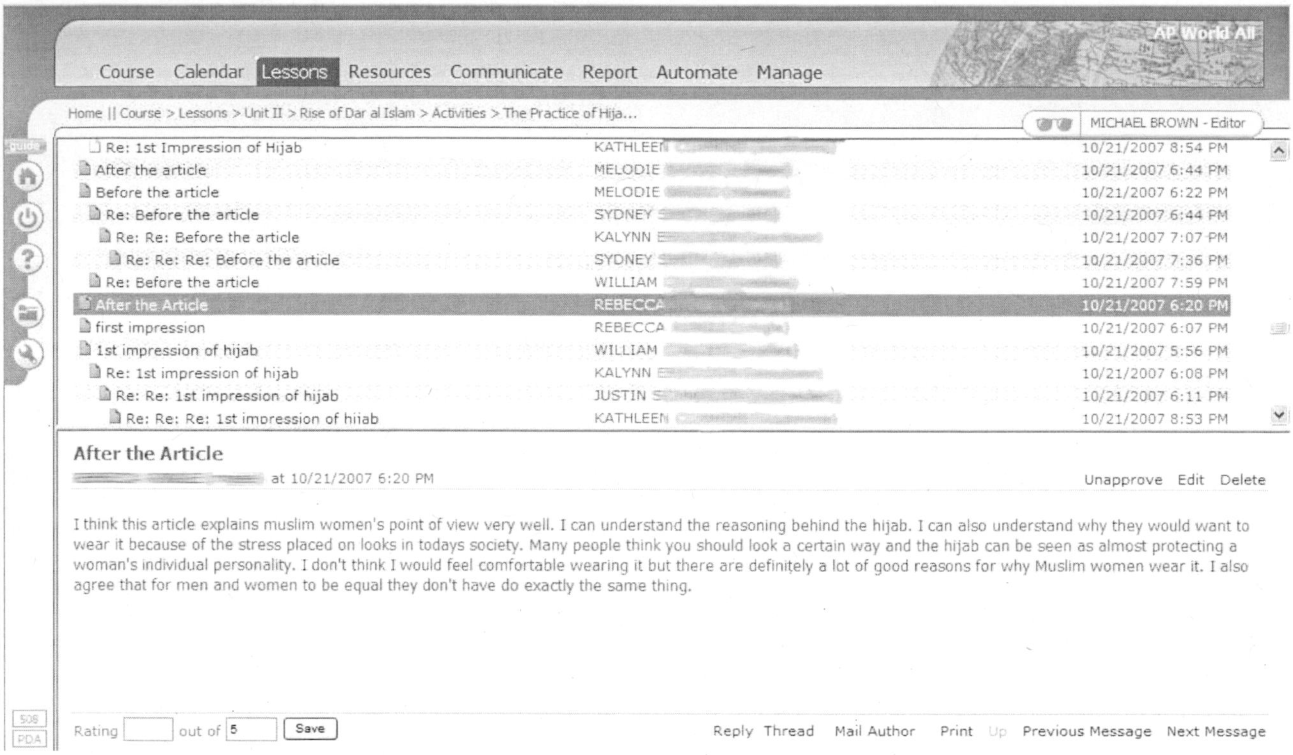

www.angellearning.com

Online Collaboration Forums

Forums have uses beyond discussion and informal debate. Another apt use for the discussion forums is to create places for online collaboration. This is especially valuable for group work and projects when it would be advantageous for students to share information across class sections. Most CMS websites give teachers the ability to group students into instructional teams. When creating a discussion forum, it is possible to make the forum exclusive to a particular team or group. While students outside the group may read the content, they may not post on the forum. This feature is useful when assigning the class graphic organizers to complete. Students can be grouped in class and on the CMS website into teams, each responsible for completing one particular part of the graphic organizer. Individual teams can collaborate in class and then post their portion of the graphic organizer online using a discussion forum. Other teams can look at the discussion board content, which in turn gives the teams another opportunity to collaborate outside of class in an effort to complete the graphic organizer.

In the world history classroom this collaborative CMS tool works extremely well for graphic organizers. Take a study of the classical era as an example. Given a graphic organizer (Figure 7.4) using the SPRITE organizational technique (*s*ocial, *p*olitical, *r*eligious, *i*ntellectual, *t*echnological, *e*conomic), students can be grouped into teams based on civilization or institution category. Students post their findings on the forum, and if given an electronic copy of the graphic organizer, they can copy and paste the findings of their classmates posted on the discussion forums into the chart. In this way, students work together to complete an organizer by sharing equally the workload and collaborating online—in this case, making an assignment that would require students three to five hours to complete individually achievable in a single ninety-minute class block. With the basic information organized and freely available to students (and, more importantly, *made available by students*), the teacher can spend a greater amount of time in class helping students make connections between civilizations by comparing institutions.

Virtual Office Hours

CMS websites provide opportunities for real-time online interaction between students and teachers using chat programs. One of the most popular applications comes in the form of virtual office hours. Teachers can establish a chat

Figure 7.4   **Classical Era SPRITE Graphic Organizer**

The Institutions of the Classical Era

	Qin Dynasty China	Han Dynasty China	Mauryan Empire	Gupta Empire	Ancient Greece	Roman Empire
Social						
Political						
Religious						
Intellectual						
Technological						
Economic						

room that students can visit at appointed times to ask about course-related concepts and assignments. Students log into the chat room, where the teacher is already waiting, and type in their question or comment, which is broadcast publicly for all in the chat room to see. Both the teacher and other students can reply to the messages. Compared to the detailed responses posted in a discussion forum, the virtual office hour chat session is designed for the rapid communication of relatively short statements, akin to instant messaging and text messaging via cellular phone. Teachers should schedule chat sessions for consistent times during the week or before major course assignments, such as exams, projects, and reading assignments, are due.

The most common problem that arises from scheduled chat sessions is that not all students will be able to meet at the designated time. Luckily, most CMS websites allow teachers to maintain detailed text logs of each chat session, which in turn can be made available to students and parents for download. Although students do not get the benefit of real-time interaction with the teacher, they can peruse the chat session for questions addressed that they may have had in common with other students.

Wikis and Virtual Glossaries

One of the most novel CMS tools at a teacher's disposal is the wiki. A wiki is either a web page or a collection of web pages that allows visitors to add and edit content, usually after registering with site owners. Most teachers are familiar with major online wiki projects, including Wikipedia, a site launched in 2001 to provide a free online encyclopedia, available in multiple languages, that constantly updates and expands itself through the submissions of registered and anonymous users. As of 2008, Wikipedia has amassed over 2 million articles in English alone, and it continues to grow in popularity.[1] Unfortunately, the same dynamic that encourages users to post valuable information also allows for the publication of inaccurate or inappropriate content contrary to the purpose of the site. Recent scandals have revealed how easy it is to anonymously use Wikipedia to report inaccurate, libelous information with little threat of legal recourse. As a result, the merits and pitfalls of large-scale open wiki projects continue to be debated.[2] This situation, however, should not deter a motivated teacher from using the same technology under more tightly controlled conditions.

When it comes to world history, few tasks can be more daunting to students than processing the scores of terms, people, places, and events necessary to achieve a mastery of the subject material. A wiki can provide the solution. Most CMS provide teachers with the option of making a limited-access wiki open only to authorized members of the class. Working together, students can then create a virtual glossary (organized by topic, unit, or chapter) of definitions and connections between terms as a study resource for summative assessments. It is best for the teacher to set up the basic structure of the wiki and model the definitions at first. The students then plug in the information where appropriate, ideally with each student responsible for a set of terms assigned by the teacher. This activity requires a fair amount of vigilance on the part of the teacher to ensure accuracy. It can last the entire academic year.

As a bonus, some CMS websites such as Moodle allow students to search the wiki and expand the definitions to other features. Using Moodle's glossary wiki function, students can establish hot words that will automatically link to the definition if used in discussion forums. For example, a student can compose a definition in the virtual glossary for the term *shogun* and set the term as a hot word. Then, any time a student writes the word *shogun* in a forum, the CMS automatically creates a link to the definition, which can be viewed either by clicking on the link or by hovering the pointer over the term. Although this feature is not available for all CMS websites, it is a useful tool that may be more widely available in the future.

Creating the Proper Environment for Collaboration

Considering the collaborative nature of most advanced CMS features, it becomes of utmost importance for the teacher to create the proper online environment. It is key to remember that today's students view the online world as their own and that many of them come to class with a plethora of online social skills that may be inappropriate for an academic setting. Students tend to communicate with each another online in a very relaxed manner, using slang terms and symbols that are unique to the medium. The anonymity of the Internet may accustom children to acting in negative ways that they would not dream of in "real life."

Students typically undergo a "Goldilocks period" when teachers establish their online environments. Like Goldilocks testing the temperature of multiple bowls of porridge, some students will experiment to see what elements of their online social networking skills are acceptable in this new, more academic environment. With a set of firm initial instructions from the teacher and a little trial and error on the part of students, it is possible to create a respectful online environment that encourages collaboration. On the first day of school, it is a good idea to set down a few simple rules as the basis for class online interactions:

1. Refrain from slang, "leet speak" (using alternate letters and numbers to spell common words), and excessive use of acronyms (LOL, ROTFLOL, J/K).
2. Be respectful at all times. You may disagree with someone, but please be courteous when you express your disagreement.

3. Refrain from pointing out misspellings, grammar errors, and broken links in the posts of others through a post on the message board. You can do so tactfully with a simple personal message to the author without cluttering up the message boards with a public plea for an edit.
4. You are responsible for proofreading your posts for accuracy, spelling, grammar, and civility. Poor posts are subject to deletion.

The fourth rule is perhaps the most important, and it will prove to be the most time-consuming task for the teacher at the beginning of the year. The students will make mistakes early, which can provide teachable moments in class if carefully managed. During the first assigned debate, it is best to compile inappropriate posts before deleting them. In class these posts can be anonymously presented in a tactful manner with an explanation as to why each was deleted and, ideally, a suggestion for a proper alternative. If the teacher is firm and vigilant, the online environment can be shaped positively in a matter of a few weeks.

Beyond establishing degrees of civility and post quality online, the other major issue that teachers must confront is just how involved to be in the online discussion. Teachers should not be bashful about deleting substandard posts or making posts of their own at first. In time, once the students begin to internalize the online rules, they tend to police themselves. If done in a positive, helpful manner, the teacher should encourage this behavior instead of handling all issues personally. In many ways the online experience with secondary school students is much like driver's education. Once the expectations for online conduct are established, there is nothing wrong with letting the students do the driving, provided that the teacher continues to keep an eye on the road and a foot on the passenger-side brake. Some classes will need a great deal of guidance, others only a minimal amount. Teachers should not be hesitant to post messages in order to shape the activity so that it better conforms to instructional goals, but the students need to feel as if they have a degree of ownership over the activities as well. Just as a driving instructor's goal is to produce a student who drives safely and proactively without being prompted, the goal here should be toward fewer teacher posts in order to give students the freedom to explore *their* discussion. The teacher should strive to let them drive, to let them talk, and above all, to let them learn from each other.

Proactive CMS Functions

While not as interpersonal as discussion boards and wikis, CMS websites employ several tools that allow students to interact with programs such as automated lessons, online assessments, and opinion surveys. Many world history textbooks come with test banks that can be legally uploaded to a CMS (provided that it is a closed, password-enabled system that cannot be accessed by those outside the division). Teachers can add their own questions to a master bank and then create online quizzes and tests that students can take for grades or review purposes. In addition to more traditional online assessments, written work can be submitted to teachers online using the CMS.

This feature typically ties into an online grading system of some kind. This evolving feature, found in all systems, in turn allows for the automation of grades. Students take an online assessment; then the CMS evaluates it according to standards set by the teacher. A grade is reported to both the student and the teacher, with the latter typically able to upload the assignment and grade to an outside grade book program. The grading feature supports the submission of essays and other assignments that require the teacher's full attention. Using the grading feature, teachers can grade the online submissions of students and provide detailed comments. It is possible to allow students to resubmit assignments as well.

Passive CMS Functions

Given the interactive possibilities of a course management system, it is easy to neglect its more passive functions. The passive CMS functions tend to be those that are more traditionally associated with a website, including providing class material downloads and posting class news and calendar dates. It is important not to neglect these important functions, for disseminating basic information about the course in a timely manner throughout the year is the surest way to encourage consistent usage of the website. Students should be encouraged to use the CMS website daily, and luckily these functions tend to be readily integrated into the system. Most CMS websites have a calendar system that is immediately available upon logging into the site. Angel, Blackboard, and Moodle allow students to customize their calendar systems, post their own events, and set their own automated reminders for due dates, special events, and assessments. All CMS websites give teachers the ability to organize their course materials, including outside web links, and make them available for download. A growing number of systems support RSS (Real Simple Syndication) feeds, which allow teachers to link to their own podcasts hosted on outside servers. Many news outlets (Reuters, Associated Press) maintain RSS feeds, which in turn can be integrated into the CMS website to provide students with links to current events that update hourly. In the past it took a fair amount of technological skill to include these feeds on a website. With the CMS websites, the process is greatly simplified.

Conclusion

Taken as a whole, course management systems provide teachers with a Web 2.0 solution to the passive websites of the last generation. It is exciting to think of the possibilities that this technology opens up for application in world history. A CMS website gives teachers the opportunity to use an interactive Internet technology that students normally view as their own. Just as students use social networking websites and games to exert some control over their social lives, so too can they use CMS websites to take control of their own learning. By interacting with their classmates and caring teachers in a virtual learning environment—helping, sharing, debating—students can be encouraged to act as historians, exploring concepts of history beyond the temporal and physical bounds of the classroom. When students still feel compelled to debate each other in the middle of the night on the causes of decline in classical empires a week after the graded portion of the discussion was finished, you know that history has truly come home. And the more history comes home, the more it comes alive in the hearts and minds of the next generation.

About the Author

Michael S. Brown (BA, history; MAT, social studies education) is an advanced placement world history teacher at Massaponax High School in Fredericksburg, Virginia. He is a lead curriculum teacher in AP World History and instructional technology for his school division.

Notes

1. Throughout the first half of 2008, Wikipedia consistently handled more than 50 million visits per month, posting a 26 percent increase in web traffic compared to the same point in 2007. For a snapshot, see wikipedia.org, June 2008, http://siteanalytics.compete.com/wikipedia.org/?metric=uv.

2. John Seigenthaler, "A False Wikipedia 'Biography,'" USA Today, November 29, 2005, www.usatoday.com/news/opinion/editorials/2005-11-29-wikipedia-edit_x.htm; "Will Wikipedia Mean the End of Traditional Encyclopedias?" Wall Street Journal, September 12, 2006, http://online.wsj.com/public/article/SB115756239753455284-A4hdSU1xZOC9Y9PFhJZV16jFlLM_20070911.html.

CHAPTER 8

Understanding World History
Some Frequently Asked Questions

THOMAS MOUNKHALL

In my thirty-plus years of teaching world history at the high school level and nine years of developing the next generation of world history teachers at the graduate school level, I have observed that new teachers tend to ask the same basic conceptual questions about the field. One of the main reasons for this is that history departments in our country generally do not emphasize world history in their course offerings, yet many of their graduates will be assigned to teach world history in their first appointment as secondary social studies teachers. Thus, the new teachers are taking on the responsibility to teach a subject that they are not prepared to teach well.

The primary purpose of this article is to improve both the pre-service and in-service professional development of secondary world history teachers. I hope that a review of the issues that so many new teachers grapple with will stimulate the design of more effective world history teacher training. At the core of the questions that follow is the problem of how to conceptualize the field, for, in order to teach world history well, one must understand the subject at the conceptual level.

Doesn't World History Challenge the Canon of History in General?

World history at its core is revisionist history. World historians focus on processes such as imperialism, long-distance trade, and cultural diffusion that go beyond national borders. The historical profession, even today, emphasizes the internal past affairs of countries. However, most world historians argue that the cross-regional connections of countries and empires have been an important change agent in the human narrative. For example, when Dominican priests introduced Roman Catholicism to Oaxaca, Mexico, in the sixteenth century CE, the mental worlds of the indigenous Zapotecs and Mixtecs

were fundamentally altered. World historians do not seek to replace national history, which they view as the base of the discipline. They do intend, however, to complement internal histories by placing them in cross-regional and sometimes global contexts. Would the history of Hawaii be complete without the inclusion of Captain Cook's voyages?

Doesn't World History as Presently Conceived Challenge the World History Canon of Eurocentrism?

The essence of this question deals with the place of Western Europe in the world history narrative. Since the 1920s Western European history has been at the center of world history's focus. This centrality makes sense in the context of the influence of Wilsonian thought in the United States after World War I. It was bolstered by the cold war modernization theories of the 1950s and 1960s. Consequently, for most adults educated prior to the 1990s, world history equals Western European history writ large. Many high school textbooks have kept the Eurocentric narrative and just added chapters on other regions of the world. Partly as a result of postcolonial and world systems theories influential since the 1960s, contemporary world history is challenging the Western Eurocentric nature of the discipline. Depending on the time period under consideration, Western Europeans may be portrayed as minor or major players in the human story. The Carolingian empire of medieval history pales in global importance compared to the contemporaneous Abbasid caliphate, Byzantine Empire, and Tang dynasty. However, new teachers should never take the idea of polycentrism to such an extreme as to leave the scientific revolution and the Glorious Revolution out of early modern world history story simply because of their Western European orientation.

Doesn't World History Challenge the Focus on Civilizations as the Primary Unit of Analysis for the Field?

The world history canon implies for some a focus on civilizations as the primary subject of study. A glance at many traditional world history textbooks makes this point with chapters on ancient Sumer through medieval China to the Western European Enlightenment. Contemporary world history challenges this approach. Groups of people without well-developed alphabets and classic literatures are being identified by world historians as major players in the global narrative alongside the so-called "great civilizations." The Polynesian migrations across the Pacific, the creation of the Mongol empire and its road system across Central Asia, and the Bantu migrations into southern Africa are examples of significant world historical developments that were not recorded in indigenous documents. The emphasis on "people without a history" is partially the result of the influence of anthropology and archaeology on world history since the 1960s. Most world historians do not omit important developments of the ancient Greeks nor changes in Tokugawa Japan. That would be ideologically driven and ahistorical. What world history demonstrates, however, is that people from nonliterate societies have also made important contributions to the human story. The practice of western African religions by slaves in the Americas in the seventeenth century CE and the early modern aboriginal history in Australia come to mind as excellent examples of this perspective.

How Does One Make Sense of the Variety of Approaches to World History?

The factual database for world history is broad and deep and it is growing at an exponential rate. Teachers need to work within a conceptual framework that will allow them to make some sense of the huge amount of data available. For example, if teachers adopt the conceptual framework of "great civilizations," they will emphasize the narratives of the Greeks, Egyptians, and Sumerians in ancient history and perhaps leave the Polynesian navigators out of the story.

The problem is which of the many competing conceptual approaches to adopt. This choice can be as confusing as trying to negotiate the maze of world history data. Marxists, world systems analysts, modernization supporters, Eurocentrists, and many others vie for the attention of world history teachers. While all these systems would serve to classify data and assist in planning a course, none of them is the master narrative favored by most contemporary world historians.

Taking their lead from the seminal work of McNeill, Stavrianos, Curtin, Hodgson, and other scholars from the early 1960s, most current world historians are using cross-regional connections as their primary conceptual approach to the subject. In other words, a major change agent in world history has been contacts between and among peoples in various regions of the world.

There is much variety among world historians in the detailed application of this conceptual frame. Nevertheless, new teachers should be encouraged to read a few monographs from this school of thought, such as those written by Jerry Bentley and Alfred Crosby, to become familiar with its application. Once a conceptual frame is familiar, new teachers should be directed in its use in planning, teaching, and assessing learning in a world history course.

Once the Cross-Regional or Transnational Conceptual Approach Has Been Adopted, Why Should Themes Be Used to Inform Teaching?

When new teachers adopt the conceptual frame of cross-regional or transnational connections as their primary guide for understanding the field, they have already chosen to leave a data-driven world history behind. This means no more fact-after-fact-after-fact history, which is deadly and self-defeating. As a substitute, new teachers need to be introduced to the learning theory of constructed knowledge.

Constructed knowledge holds that people learn new information best when they are guided by the teacher or themselves to see connections between the new data and previously learned significant concepts or themes in the discipline. Information about the Mughals, for example, probably will be new information for many world history students. If left at the data delivery level, students may remember something about Akbar and his religious toleration or they may not. If the same students are guided to connect their notes on the Mughals to such previously developed world history themes as imperialism, gunpowder empires, and ethnic diversity, the novel information gains meaning, facilitating the long-range retention of data. Factual data on the British Empire of the late nineteenth century can be another fine example of constructed learning theory if it is linked to such ideas as ocean-based empires, technological superiority, and long-distance trade.

Which Cross-Regional or Transnational Themes Should Be Used as Core World History Concepts?

The number of themes available to inform the teaching of a world history course is huge. However, a very large list of themes would be an inefficient planning tool. Themes are guides for both instructors and students. Consequently, the teacher is forced to choose. The selection process will make the teacher a much better world historian.

The choice of core world history themes must be based on a set of rational criteria. The list of selection criteria should reflect the basic approach that the teacher takes to the field. Marxist and Sinocentric historians would certainly have contrasting selection criteria, with the Marxist choosing themes of class struggle and the Sinocentrist selecting concepts of cultural superiority. Since world history students are being encouraged to take a cross-regional or transnational process approach to the discipline, the search for core themes takes place in this general category.

For the sake of classification only, I advocate the use of four groups of themes for course planning. Obviously, human experience is integrated, but I suggest categorizing the concepts in order to make selection efficient. Students should be encouraged to find four central themes in each one of these groupings: political, economic, cultural, and biological. Once this scaffolding is created, the task of selecting core world history themes may fruitfully begin.

Modeling of professional judgment is a very important aspect of teacher training. Therefore, it is important that teachers be shown a solid list of world history themes as an example of a core list of concepts. In addition, new educators should be exposed to the thinking that went into the creation of the core theme list. In short, why is a certain theme included in the core list and another excluded? Once this is done, the new teachers should be encouraged to develop their own list:

Core World History Themes

Political: imperialism, self-determination, cross-regional war, and exploration
Economic: long-distance trade, interdependence, multinational corporations, trade diasporas
Cultural: cultural diffusion, cultural synthesis, technology diffusion, and missionary work
Biological: flora diffusion, fauna diffusion, disease diffusion, migration

What General Understanding of World History Should Be Introduced to New Teachers?

There are general understandings of world history that all new teachers should be taught. Then teachers will have the necessary tools to conceptualize the field at an abstract level, which will enhance their ability to teach the subject.

Periodization should be introduced as a sophisticated thinking process, not just as a means of dating events. The notion that many world historians challenge conventional periodization systems as not being truly global in nature should be addressed. Some world historians begin modern world history with the Mongol empire rather than Columbus and Da Gama. However, there is little agreement among world historians concerning periodization. Does modern world history begin with the Enlightenment, the steam engine, or the French Revolution?

Do we keep the conventional date for the split between ancient and medieval world history? Is the fall of the Western Roman Empire in c. 500 CE the seminal event that marks the beginning of a new era in human experience? If so, the vertical line at 500 on a timeline is valid and should continue in use. However, were there other events, roughly contemporaneous with the demise of the western Roman Empire, that have more legitimate claim to the position of macro-change in human history? A fair number of world historians argue that the institutionalization of Islam in the mid-seventh century had much greater global influence than the destruction of Rome in the West. If so, the vertical line separating ancient and medieval world history should be moved from 500 to 650 or roughly 28 AH on the Islamic calendar.

Macro-change as a concept relates very well to periodization in that the vertical lines on a world history timeline should relate to significant alteration in human experience. Most professionals in the field would include the agricultural revolution and the industrial revolution on their lists of macro-changes. After these two, however, teachers should understand that a universally accepted list of world history macro-changes does not exist.

Does the creation of the first alphabets in c. 3000 BCE in the Middle East qualify as a macro-change? Was the Mongol road system in c. 1250 CE, which effectively linked the eastern Mediterranean and western China in long-distance trade for at least 100 years, a candidate for this category? Does the completion of the ancient Greek–medieval Islamic scientific synthesis by Newton and his seventeenth-century contemporaries represent a fundamental alteration in human experience? Do the French Revolution and World War I rise to the level of macro-change? The important point for new teachers is to allow them to construct and defend their own lists as they develop as scholar educators.

The fact that most world historians reject any school of determinism must be taught to new teachers. This knowledge will keep them vigilant about including any semblance of this ahistorical type of thinking in their courses. Most world historians do not hold that history had to play out the way it did. Nor is there support for determinism, the belief that some outside force, whether spiritual or secular, has shaped human experience. Examples of Judeo-Christian teleology and Marxist determinism should be studied. In addition, students should be introduced to the professional literature that challenges this type of historical reasoning.

The notion of human agency should be taught to new teachers as a counterbalance to determinism. This notion holds that human decision-making and action, which are obviously unpredictable, constitute a driving force in history. Alexander, Muhammad, Genghis Khan, Akbar, and Ataturk would all serve as excellent models of the important influence of human agency in the human narrative.

A second challenge to determinism is the idea of contingency. History is seen as unpredictable as a result of influential chance developments. The locations of Constantinople, Cape Town, and Manila would all be useful case studies of the influence of contingency on their development as centers of long-distance trade. The Spanish found silver in Bolivia and the Portuguese found none in Brazil. Saudi Arabia is rich in oil deposits and Jordan has none. This "luck of the draw" understanding should be emphasized to all new world history teachers.

World history's penchant for going beyond the conventional units of analysis in the field must also be taught. Most world histories in the past have focused on the so-called "great civilizations" to the exclusion of any other important developments in the human story. Teachers should be encouraged to consider such topics as peoples without a written history, the nature of borderlands, and wide geographical regions such as ocean littorals and steppe lands. Through this experience, novice educators will be introduced to the challenging breadth of the discipline.

The Mongols come to mind immediately as a "people without a history." They would serve as a fine example of this area of focus, but they also symbolize many other groups of people who have not made it into the world history narrative. Since most of these groups come from nonliterate societies, they have been considered "uncivilized"—proper subjects for ethnology and anthropology but not world history. The Celts, the Huns, and the ancient Polynesians all fit this category, as do most nomadic groups in the human story.

Borderlands, by definition, imply cross-regional contact and make very interesting world history subjects. The eighteenth-century border in modern Croatia, which was the effective line where the Austro-Hungarian and Ottoman Empires met; the contemporaneous eighteenth-century area between the Mississippi river and the Appalachian mountains, where French and English North America met; and the early modern Mekong delta, where Chinese and Indian cultures came together, are three borderlands that can be seen as novel units of world history attention.

Large geographic units, such as medieval central Asia and the early modern Atlantic littoral, are also drawing increased attention in the study of world history. New teachers should also be exposed to the potential of such units as the Indian Ocean, Siberia, and Pacific studies in world history.

What Types of Cognitive Skills Need to Be Developed in World History Students?

For many world history teachers and students, past and present, the only cognitive skill that matters is recall of factual information. This emphasis on memorization flows directly from the traditional data-driven approach to the discipline. It leads to only short-term retention and boring classes, which are two of the main reasons for challenging this method of teaching. New teachers need to be exposed to the realization that world history is an opportunity for understanding human experience through the development of sophisticated, important thinking skills.

For example, if students are taught new data about the Manila galleon trade of the seventeenth century, the facts themselves are pretty interesting. However, this level of learning should be the beginning of thinking about the process, not viewed as an end in itself. Students could be led to discern the similarities and differences between Manila and Cape Town as seventeenth-century centers of long-distance trade.

Constructed learning theory must be taught to new teachers. New data must be linked to already learned concepts in the field so that the new information is given meaning beyond the data level. As an example, if students learn novel information about the Manila galleon trade, their learning will be broadened by the connection of the data to previously developed world history themes such as imperialism, long-distance trade, colonialism, and the influence of the oceans in the human narrative.

The year for the Spanish establishment of Manila, 1571 CE, could be just a date to identify and memorize. However, considering relationships across time and place would allow the new teacher to see connections between Manila in 1571 and any one or all of these earlier events: the Crusades, the demise of the Mongol empire, the Ottoman conquest of Constantinople, the voyage of Magellan. Such connections would make for profitable discussion and thought.

In my view, multiple causation is History 101. For world history, educators should be shown how to address the nexus of internal and cross-regional dynamics in the causation of most important events. In reference to sixteenth-century Manila, for example, its proximity to China, its location on the Pacific wind currents, and its natural harbor potential all were indigenous factors in its establishment as an urban center. Magellan's voyage, Ming demand for silver, and the existence of a mountain of Andean silver in Spanish Potosi are three of the many cross-regional factors that contributed to the creation of the port city in the late sixteenth century.

New world history educators should also be taught how to address multiple perspectives in the discipline. The Spanish port in the Philippines was viewed in contrasting manners by many of its contemporaries. Peruvian silver merchants and Spanish Jesuits saw very different potential in Manila. The Portuguese saw the trade entrepôt as serious competition for their long-distance trading business in Macao. Chinese silk merchants saw Manila as a market where they could achieve higher status than neo-Confucianism allowed them at home.

Conclusion

In too many cases, new social studies teachers are asked to teach a high school world history survey course without the proper professional preparation. This can be a frustrating experience. The adjustment to teaching five classes a day, preparing lesson plans, and correcting written essays almost every evening is a difficult enough workload for a beginning instructor. Having to learn a conceptual approach to world history on the job is an unnecessary burden that can be avoided.

All the questions in this chapter are central to the pre-service and in-service development of world history teachers. Instructors teaching world history courses would do well to include these issues in the education of novice teachers. The answers along with the many specific examples can inform the construction and implementation of future world history teacher training programs.

About the Author

Thomas Mounkhall taught world history at Spring Valley High School in a New York City suburb for thirty-three years. Upon retirement in 1999, he completed his doctorate in modern world history at St. John's University in New York City. Since 1999, he has taught world history at the undergraduate and graduate levels and graduate courses on the teaching of world history at the State University of New York at New Paltz. He has also directed and co-directed numerous teacher-training workshops in world history at sites ranging from New Paltz and New York City to suburban Atlanta, Eau Claire, Wisconsin, and Honolulu, Hawaii.

Bibliography

Bentley, Jerry. *Old World Encounters*. New York: Oxford University Press, 1993. Premodern cross-regional connections.

Crosby, Alfred. *Ecological Imperialism*. New York: Cambridge University Press, 1986. Plants and animals as agents of imperialism.

———. *The Columbian Exchange*. Westport, CT: Greenwood Press, 1972. Three-way cross-regional exchange.

Curtin, Philip. *Cross-Cultural Trade in World History*. New York: Cambridge University Press, 1984. Long-distance trade as an important change agent in world history.

Lewis, Martin, and Karen Wigen. *The Myth of Continents*. Berkeley: University of California Press, 1997. Various perspectives on global geography.

McNeill, William H. *Plagues and Peoples*. New York: Anchor Books, 1977. Disease diffusion as a change agent in world history.

McNeill, William H., and J.R. McNeill. *The Human Web*. New York: W.W. Norton, 2003. Fine example of cross-regional connections as the organizing principle for world history.

Wright, Donald. *The World and a Very Small Place in Africa*. Armonk, NY: M.E. Sharpe, 1997. Cross-regionals in the Gambia from c. 1400 CE on.

CHAPTER 9

Integrating World History Themes

MORGAN FALKNER

Beginning world history teachers must, in addition to mastering the content itself and delivering instruction, imbue their students with a sense of the texture or fabric of history. This texture takes form, in the student's mind, upon the analysis of several discrete themes that, together, make for the study of history itself. The integration of the themes, which is the subject of this chapter, makes possible a kind of teaching that is perhaps more durable (in that the learning sticks to students long after the delivery of instruction) as a consequence of the integrated way in which the material is taught. The approach makes it more likely that students who might otherwise remain indifferent to the subject will form coherent understandings of history that are meaningful and relevant. All too often what passes for history teaching is the force-feeding of an unintelligible mass of disconnected events that, ultimately, means very little to the actual lives of sixteen-year-olds.

Many teachers new to high school–level world history despair of choosing what to teach. Instructors find themselves practicing a grim editing of history in an effort to make the entire story, from Mesopotamia to modernity, intelligible over a ten-month school year. What is perhaps an accidental victim in this attempt is the study of history itself: it can become superficial. It often lacks nuance and fails to make meaningful connections across the spectrum of themes.

As if historical incoherence were not enough of a problem, world history teachers must surmount considerable ideological barriers as well. Western-trained historians have long sustained a world history that tended to privilege political, diplomatic, and military analyses. The nation-state, that creature of the newly ascendant West, was, for most Western-educated historians, by the late nineteenth century the proper field of study. History, properly understood, involved the study of political or diplomatic figures and the events they shaped. That bias toward the political, it should be noted, often disparaged as trivial a great deal that is most accessible to students through the lens of, for example, social analysis, or cultural, or economic. We now know that political analysis, while undeniably relevant and vital, is by itself incomplete. A great deal of world history—the most part, almost certainly—does not get said in that narrative alone.

In this chapter I offer world history teachers, new ones especially, a way out of some of these problems. It should perhaps first be pointed out that the suggestions in this article borrow unapologetically from the Advanced Placement (AP) World History curriculum, which has identified five themes, or ways of perceiving and approaching history. Regardless of whether a world history teacher intends to teach AP or regular world history to a general audience of sophomores, it is important that the content be taught through several prisms and in an interconnected way that reinforces learning at every step.

The categories of analysis include: (1) the relationship between humans and their physical environment, which includes considerations such as technology, demographics, and migration; (2) cultural formation and interactions; (3) the creation, growth, and conflict of states; (4) the evolution of economic systems; and (5) the development and changes of social structures. Together these angles provide depth and dimensionality that the meta-narrative line—involving a preoccupation with political, diplomatic, and military considerations to the exclusion of other areas—simply cannot.

What follows is the application of this integrative approach to two historical analyses. The first example involves the Columbian Exchange; the second, regional analysis of the Indian Ocean basin over time. I chose the Columbian Exchange because it supplies several compelling and obvious examples of the merits of integrative analysis. The Indian Ocean was picked simply to illustrate that the methodology need not restrict itself to discrete phenomena such as biological exchanges (Columbian or otherwise), the French Enlightenment, or the Black Death. It will be shown that a thorough study of the Indian Ocean basin cannot help but be advanced by the sustained reliance on multiple analytical frameworks.

Before sketching a few of the obvious connections made possible through an integrative approach, it may be useful, first, to review the central narrative of an earlier paradigm: Spain and Portugal, in pursuit of national wealth and pride, sponsor voyages to the Western Hemisphere. Conquest of indigenous polities ensues, eventually paving the way to European colonization of the Americas and the articulation of these political entities as nation-states in the eighteenth and nineteenth centuries. And the narrative is true, as far as it goes. There is certainly no denying or minimizing the establishment and development of Iberian colonies in the New World or the importance of war and diplomacy in the conquests themselves. But notice how the history of the Columbian Exchange takes on depth and texture as we approach that historical phenomenon from a variety of angles—each informing the others and permitting a complex mental ordering of the history into one integrated whole.

Take, for example, the first theme identified above, the relationship of humans to their physical environment. One of the considerations typical of this theme concerns demographics. And here, quite obviously, demographics loom large in a discussion of the Columbian Exchange. First came hemispheric-wide die-offs of Amerindians (estimates vary widely, but perhaps 90 percent of the pre-Columbian population perished), a phenomenon of central importance to the future development of societies there. But the Columbian Exchange entailed a *second* demographic catastrophe as well, namely the African Diaspora (the system of trans-Atlantic slavery that violently resettled 8 to 12 million Africans throughout the Americas). The demographic implications of the Columbian Exchange do not end there. Domesticable plants and animals were taken from the Old World to the New, and vice versa. This eventually—once foods gained cultural acceptance in their adopted lands—played a significant role in the aggregate rise, on a planetary scale, of edible foods available for consumption. This in turn began to make itself felt by contributing to a global demographic rise by the eighteenth century. But the exchange itself was even more thoroughgoing than that. As the historian Alfred Crosby has brilliantly shown, the exchange entailed a massive biological takeover (invasive European strains of plant and animal life choking out indigenous ones) that, in a darkly poetic way, mirrored the spread of Old World humans throughout the Western Hemisphere.[1]

Against this environmental and demographic backdrop, the skillful teacher of world history will find it relatively simple to guide students to their own important discoveries: that these discrete categories are in fact connected to one another in important ways. Students can see for themselves, for example, that the sixteenth-century falling to pieces of pre-Columbian political systems (theme no. 3 above) is barely intelligible in the absence of a full discussion of demographics and, broadly, the environment. Similarly, the task of teaching the effect of the Columbian Exchange on existing *social* systems becomes easier in that the historical material is being presented, studied, and learned in mutually reinforcing ways—analysis of one of the categories informing students' study of the others. This kind of cross-theme integration and reinforcement is likely to have a much longer mental or intellectual shelf life than something studied in isolation, drilled into memory in such a way that may be fine in the short term (a solid performance on Tuesday's quiz), but which may not continue to burden the student's brain much past that, when a fresh crop of academic and nonacademic crises du jour make themselves felt.

An integrated approach such as the one being argued here makes possible an almost dizzying number of connections for the student. Studying the demographic ramifications of the Columbian Exchange informs the student's understanding of state breakdown in Mesoamerica, which in turn complements a class discussion on Mesoamerican social collapse, which squares with what our emerging students of history have begun to figure out for themselves: that collapse itself, at a certain point, implies breakdown across the categories. Indigenous economies, so our hypothetical students understand, wither when overwhelmed by demographic, political, and social stress—which, finally, permits the students to *get* what it means to speak of cultural collapse (theme no. 2). They understand it because they are able to articulate the intimate connections among the themes.

A thematic approach to the study of the Columbian Exchange may be a somewhat obvious example to demonstrate the method's virtues. The approach works equally well, however, for regional historical analysis. For this second example, the object of our inquiry will be the history of the Indian Ocean basin. Unless teachers' undergraduate training happened to include a survey in world history, Indian Ocean historiography probably figured peripherally, if at all, in their academic training.

What follows is a theme-by-theme examination of some of the noteworthy components of Indian Ocean historiography. It makes no pretence to completeness. Indeed, it is merely a subjective sketch that I myself, as a world history teacher, feel I must teach students if they are to understand the main contours of the region over the *longue durée*. Finally, it should be noted that the calibration of the themes by teachers will vary from one area of history to another, simply as a consequence of the intrinsic nature of the history itself. For instance, the political theme correctly receives greater attention in a French Revolution unit than in studies of the Industrial Revolution. Teachers of world history should feel no obligation to weigh equally each of the five themes when it comes to lesson planning. The broad outline of themes that follows reflects this inherent unevenness in the treatment of themes relative to one another.

Humans and Their Environment

Until the age of steam in the nineteenth century, the rhythms of the Indian Ocean's monsoons dictated the pace and flow of commodities and people from the western half of the basin (the Arabian Sea) to the eastern half (the Bay of Bengal). Students learn that the summer and winter monsoons in fact represent the pulse of the peoples along the Indian Ocean's vast littoral and that shipbuilding technologies varied widely around the ocean rim as a result of geographic considerations and available materials.

Human migration belongs to this theme, too, along with demographics and more obviously environmental considerations (e.g., the monsoons). In the Indian Ocean there are several critically important movements of people that must survive the teacher's winnowing of content. Almost certainly the oldest and for millennia the most important reason for migration within (or beyond) the Indian Ocean was economic gain (more on the theme of economics below). There exist to this day diaspora communities along the rim of the ocean that have existed for hundreds of years. South Asian merchant-families have long maintained diaspora communities along the Swahili coast, and Arabs have inhabited the Malabar Coast of India since before the birth of Islam. Indeed, many of the cities of the Indian Ocean were divided into quarters that belonged to different communities. Indian Ocean migration after the arrival of the steamship, however, tended to be a much different animal. Driven by global and industrial forces, the nineteenth and twentieth centuries saw massive migrations of peoples along the littoral. Thus, to this day the nation of South Africa maintains a large population of ethnic South Asians. Similarly, migrations from China to Southeast Asia have had a profound effect on the demographic profile of that region.

Culture

Broadly, cultural expression and diffusion throughout the basin have created over the millennia a littoral of great complexity. People from Sofala to Malacca have moved freely about the basin for a thousand years or more. There is not only a bewildering variety of cultures from the Swahili coast to the Arabian peninsula to the coast of India to insular Southeast Asia, but the frequency of sustained contact over a long period of time earned the basin the reputation for being cosmopolitan and rather tolerant of other peoples.

An interesting concept to share with students is the assertion that the peoples of the Indian Ocean had, over time, created a littoral culture that transcended, in an important way, those cultural bonds that linked port cities with their hinterlands.[2] Here lies a teachable moment for instructors, who can consciously, explicitly, tie migration (an element of theme no. 1) to the formation of culture (theme no. 2), allowing students to see for themselves the intimate nexus formed by migration and culture.

Spirituality, a subcategory of culture, figures prominently in students' studies of the Indian Ocean. Outside of the establishment of a handful of Jewish and Christian enclaves along the west coast of India, the first major change to the religious status quo in the basin was the formation and spread of Islam in the seventh century. That spreading of Muhammad's teaching reached the Atlantic Ocean and the Indus River, but it also embraced the east coast of Africa, which too underwent its own process of Islamization. The resultant Swahili coast, now more fully integrated into the Indian Ocean network, had achieved for its rulers and merchants a legitimacy and economic relevance throughout the basin. And it is important to note that Islamization did not end there. Indeed, by the fifteenth century, Islamization had spread across the eastern half of the basin. First Aceh converted, followed by island after island throughout the region over the course of several hundred years. The coastline of the subcontinent is itself home to huge numbers of Hindus who live side by side with Muslims, particularly along the coast of the Arabian Sea (Sind, Gujarat), along the Malabar Coast, and in Bengal.

Politics and Government

One of the first things a student may notice about the Indian Ocean is the absence of a single governmental model that held throughout the region historically. Moving clockwise around the basin, one can identify broad trends that hold, but only in geographically limited ways. Along the Swahili coast, the city-state is the form typical of polities. From the Arabian Sea down the west coast of India, some coastal governments had extensive hinterlands (from which to extract raw materials such as cotton and pepper), while others did not. Large or small, states were ruled by kings. What is of the first importance was rulers' attitudes toward maritime commerce. Like rulers along the Silk Roads, Indian Ocean rulers had long figured out that it paid to be attentive to the needs of merchants. Rulers who taxed merchant activity at a fair rate and who guarded against predators along the trade routes stood to profit handsomely from commercial revenues. On the other hand, rulers who got greedy and taxed commerce too heavily saw business redirect itself to more accommodating ports—of which there was never a lack. If rulers proved to be too casual about protecting ships and their cargos and crews, then again the end result was the same: the shifting of commercial lines toward ports and kingdoms with a better track record of vigilance.

It may be worth noting that what is perhaps most conspicuous about Indian Ocean statecraft is that it rarely, if ever—at any rate, not in a sustained way until the eighteenth or nineteenth century—witnessed the presence of a hegemonic power bent on forcing its will in the basin. (Perhaps the closest this came to happening before 1500 was the ephemeral appearance of a Chinese treasure fleet in the Indian Ocean in the early fifteenth century.)

Beginning in the sixteenth century, Europeans—first the Portuguese but in due time the Dutch and British—aimed to exert that very dominance over the region. The British finally succeeded, but not until they achieved an industrial breakthrough in northern England in the eighteenth century. The nineteenth and twentieth centuries have proven to be disastrous to the societies along the littoral. While they have received a measure of stature by virtue of being folded within the community of nation-states—everyone gets a seat in the United Nations General Assembly—cultures along the basin (or culture in the singular, if Michael Pearson is right) have suffered mightily in the age of industrialized and globalized economics. Cultural autonomy, perhaps even cultural viability, is now at risk there.[3]

Economics

It would be difficult to overstate the importance of thoroughly covering the economic component of Indian Ocean history, for the basin was, among other things, the most dynamic and wide-reaching trade network through most of history. It was once fashionable among Western historians to downplay the significance of Indian Ocean trade. Not until the arrival of Europeans in the sixteenth century, they argued, did anything approximating scale or sophistication come to the shores of the basin. We now know better. The Indian Ocean was an economic arena of vast scope and complexity that linked, albeit indirectly, the Mediterranean basin to China. It connected in a thousand places to the more northerly land network (known as the Silk Roads) that also largely followed an east-west axis.

Despite what earlier histories may have suggested regarding the nature and extent of Indian Ocean commerce, trade in the ocean has been robust for well over 1,000 years. Indeed, we have abundant evidence of vigorous trade between Mesopotamian merchants and those from Harappa, along the Indus River, dating back to the third millennium BCE.

From bulk everyday items to luxury goods, the commodities of the Indian Ocean ran an extraordinary range. Gold from East Africa, cotton from South Asia, rare woods from Southeast Asia, and perfumes from the Middle East

circulated widely throughout much of the Old World ecumene. But Indian Ocean economics entailed more than commerce in the strict sense. An array of financial services, including banking, investment, and insurance, was provided throughout the littoral, too.

New teachers of world history need to be careful how they handle modern Europe's domination of Asia. As it has been handed down, European hegemony dates to the first Europeans who plied the waters of the Indian Ocean. According to this narrative, Portugal monopolized the western Indian Ocean and, during the seventeenth century, the Dutch effected a similar control of the so-called Spice Islands. The narrative, though, is only partially accurate. Only the Dutch enterprise proved effective in establishing firm economic control. The Dutch did exert effective, indeed oppressive, domination over the spice trade that, for a time, amounted to a monopoly. But the polities and commerce of the Indian Ocean as a whole remained largely autonomous, despite the best efforts of the Portuguese, Dutch, and British. European maritime powers were players in the Indian Ocean, to be sure, but the game featured a great many participants in the so-called in-country trade conducted within Asia. The Europeans did not prove terribly exceptional in this arena until the Industrial Revolution.

Social Structures

In at least some areas of the Indian Ocean, gender roles were, perhaps, somewhat more fluid than elsewhere in the agrarian world. In Southeast Asia, for example, women often played key roles in the family business and, consequently, represented a certain empowering of women, at least in the realm of commerce. Given the often-limited scope of basin polities in the social lives of subjects, the family was the key economic unit. In South Asia we know of quite elaborate family firms managing diverse portfolios, with junior members of the family rising to positions of prestige on the basis of banking or commercial acumen.

Social relations in the basin produced at least one historically dramatic phenomenon: the Islamization of East Africa and Southeast Asia. Islam spread across the ocean by peaceful contact with captains and crews. The Qur'an, which sanctions just, fair commerce, proved an excellent companion to Islamic merchants throughout the basin. Carried by commerce, the values of the honest deal and, even more broadly, social justice spread through social contact along the littoral.

In closing, it is worth mentioning that there are further benefits to this integrative approach. For one, it lends itself to successful essay writing by students. For students to survive the comparison/contrast and change/continuity-over-time essays on the AP world exam, they must be able to confront the history in an integrated way. In a typical essay, students are asked to compare and contrast, for example, the economics and politics of two societies. Or students might be faced with a prompt that requires them to describe changes and continuities in a world region—say, the Indian Ocean—over a given period of time. In other words, students thrive or perish based largely on the degree to which their study of history has integrated the themes in meaningful ways. There may be yet another virtue to the approach: students find themselves thinking like historians when they see demographics impinging on economics, and social issues connected to the realm of culture. And finally, if nothing else, this approach lends itself to collaboration among students. By working in teams, they can explore the discrete categories of history such as culture, environment, and social structure and make their individual examination part of a larger fabric knit by the team. The notion of history as texture becomes reinforced in the very dynamic of the class structure itself.

About the Author

Morgan Falkner teaches world history and AP World History at Rio Rico High School in Rio Rico, Arizona. He has attended several AP world readings and written on border issues for *World History Connected*. He has a bachelor's degree in journalism from Southern Illinois University at Carbondale and a master's in journalism from Sangamon State University in Springfield, Illinois. He is credentialed to teach history, English, and journalism at the high school level.

Notes

1. Alfred Crosby, *Ecological Imperialism: The Biological Expansion of Europe, 900–1900* (Cambridge, UK: Cambridge University Press, 1986).

2. Michael Pearson, "Littoral Society: The Concept and the Problems," *Journal of World History* 17, no. 4 (2006): 353–373.

3. Kenneth McPherson, *The Indian Ocean: A History of People and the Sea* (New York: Oxford University Press, 1993).

CHAPTER 10

Teaching the Long Nineteenth Century (1750–1914) in World History
A Document-Based Lesson and Approach

CHRISTOPHER FERRARO

After nearly a decade of teaching world history in various formats, I have noticed certain obvious trends. The recognition of and approach to teaching these trends has allowed many teachers to survive and thrive in the often-grueling schedule that accompanies Advanced Placement (AP) World History on the high school level. The founding fathers and mothers of this course gave considerable thought to the necessary and sometimes controversial divisions of the material, which covers more than 10,000 years of human history. The time period that I found most intriguing and that will be the topic of this chapter is the long nineteenth century: 1750–1914. As with all the time periods covered in AP World History, it is the teacher's understanding of the trends that define the era that allows for excellence in teaching and better student understanding. When forced to cover so much ground in a course such as this one, a class can easily get lost in all the achievements, empires, philosophies, and conflicts that arise. Encapsulating or, more correctly, defining an era properly—whether Renaissance Italy or Imperial Japan—gives the teacher and the students a better framework for understanding.

The Era-Defining Concept: Revolution

In the long nineteenth century—as it has been established by the College Entrance Examination Board—it has become clear to me after many years and classes that a single concept, if properly understood, defines the era. The concept of revolution in all its permutations and variations is the axis around which the entire era revolves. Revolutions, be they political, industrial, or cultural, are the key to this time period. Of course, some historians will immediately claim that this approach is strictly a Western view, but a look beneath the surface of what a revolution is reveals that this concept is worldwide and omnipresent. Teachers of world history

must open their minds to a broader interpretation of revolutions. For example, the American, French, and Industrial Revolutions certainly frame Western history, but the inclusion of Latin American and Caribbean revolutions along with certain Asian revolutionary events that either opposed or favored change, regardless of their success or failure, provides a bigger picture of this era. In order to understand this era further, let us consider certain groupings.

Traditional Approach

In high school in the late 1980s, the aforementioned three Western revolutions were used as models to explain everything else that occurred. The American Revolution came first and founded a new nation, the French Revolution spelled the beginning of the end of monarchies in Europe, and, to one degree or another, the revolutions that came after followed its pattern in many respects. Lastly, the Industrial Revolution set the stage for the modern world, and all its major achievements and failures have been repeated, to varying degrees, in many countries since. Such an approach was perfect for understanding European or Western civilizations but it did not address greater world issues that were certainly interrelated.

Teacher Test

As teachers we are most comfortable giving tests, but in order to understand this era properly in a world history context you must first come to terms with your personal view by taking a test yourself. This short activity will go a long way toward establishing your philosophy. Consider the following chronological list of revolutions, rebellions, and uprisings and place them into categories of your own determination.

Revolutionary Events, 1750–1914

United States	1776
France	1789
Latin America	1800–1840
Industrial	1800
Haiti	1804
Mexico	1811
Opium War	1840
Sepoy Mutiny	1857
Meiji Restoration	1868–1912
Zulu War	1879
Boxer Rebellion	1900
Russia	1905
China	1911

There are many possible ways to categorize these revolutions. How did you do it?

I have found that teachers who are truly trying to bring a world perspective to their courses will organize their revolutions in the following way:

Group #1	Group #2	Group #3	Group #4
United States	Zulu	France	Industrial
Haiti	Boxer Rebellion	Russia	Revolution
Latin America	Sepoy Mutiny		
Mexico	Opium War		
	Meiji		
	Restoration		

While many arguments can be made for making changes to these groupings, the logic behind them, logic that took many years of trial and error, holds up.

The revolutions in Group #1 were all fought for independence and largely had similar successful results, at least initially. Those in Group #2 are all direct reactions to European imperialism and, with one exception, failed or had disastrous consequences. The first four of the group were all fought in hopes of removing European influence and returning to a time before European arrival, while the Japanese took a very different approach in the Meiji Restoration. The thought process that led me to the creation of these first two groups has a major effect on the way that I present these events to a class, as will be explained later. The last two groups are very small because of the uniqueness of the revolutionary events. While scholars and historians have made many comparisons between the philosophies that influenced the French and American Revolutions, it is their causes that I feel are most important and is why they are placed into separate groups rather than together. The Americans' desire for their rights led to calls for independence and eventually the creation of a modern democracy.

I make sure to stress this difference to my classes. The French and the Russians had to deal with a monarch and an aristocratic tradition that did not exist in North America. Finally, the Industrial Revolution as it occurred in England and Western Europe gets its own category thanks to the uniqueness of the event and the power that industrialization gave to European nations that was so vital during their imperialist quest.

Case Study #1: Industrial Revolution

It is impossible for students to grasp the long nineteenth century without having a good understanding of the Industrial Revolution; thus, it is critical that teachers spend significant time not only on what this revolution gave to Western European nations but also on what it enabled them to do on the world stage—namely, create empires and export Western culture. Of course, students must grasp mass production, the factory system, child labor, and the growth of unions, but to apply this event to world history students must also appreciate the drive for imperialism, the tools unique to Western society that enabled it, and the mind-set that developed as a result of industrialization; for example, social Darwinism and the White Man's Burden. Throughout my teaching of the Industrial Revolution and the scramble for empires that followed, I am certain to compare the technological and industrial haves to the have-nots. As a teacher I find it very useful to compare industrialized Europeans with preindustrial societies as they come into contact with imperialism because such a comparison further illustrates what a critical event the Industrial Revolution was and how it affected the world.

Case Study #2: Russia 1905

Perhaps the greatest example of a revolutionary event is the 1905 Russian Revolution. I use this in class as the crowning example of what this era is all about for a multitude of reasons. First, this revolution was a direct result of the Russo-Japanese War (1904–1905), a conflict between industrialized nations that had its roots in imperialism and was primarily fought in the Manchuria region of China over that country's vast resources. Second, it illustrates just how powerful industrialized nations of this period had become (use pictures of Japanese and Russian weapons for your students' benefit) and how powerless a preindustrial nation like China was to maintain its territory in the face of such technology. Third, its shows Russian horror and disbelief that an "inferior" Asian nation was able to defeat a Western power. When I was an undergraduate at Queens College (CUNY), my Russian history professor likened the Russo-Japanese War to Long Island declaring war on the United States . . . and winning. I have always liked that analogy because it underscores the vast geographic and manpower differences of the combatants, as well as paints an accurate picture of the new status of Japan as a result of the Meiji Restoration. Lastly, the 1905 Russian Revolution the followed the defeat reflects the Russian people's dissatisfaction with the tsar and their enlightened demands, surely a product of the French Revolution and the others that began the era. Russia was only partially industrialized in 1904 when compared to leading Western European nations and Japan, and the strain of fighting a modern, mechanized war proved too much for the people at home. The damaging terms of the Treaty of Portsmouth, which should be closely examined in class, caused mass protests and violent government reprisals and eventually forced the tsar to sign a constitution, which also should be examined in class. Here we have the perfect revolutionary event: an event caused by loss in an industrialized war fought for empire results in a revolution and transition from absolute to constitutional monarchy in Russia. Japan's victory solidified its status as an imperial power that would dominate the Asia-Pacific region for the next four decades, ending only with its defeat in World War II.

I have found that the best approach to teaching the 1905 Revolution is to allow some key documents to do most of the talking. Casualty figures from both sides, pictures of modern weapons of the day, a few maps, the text of the Treaty of Portsmouth, and excerpts from the constitution that the tsar was made to sign are usually all that is required. Student analysis of these documents in groups tends to provide the catalyst needed for this event to define the entire era. Students will typically ask how an island nation the size of California was able to defeat Russia, a nation of twelve time zones and vastly superior resources. I point to the Meiji Restoration. Typically, they wonder aloud at the implications of the Treaty of Portsmouth and my response usually includes showing a map of the Japanese empire by 1941.

The RTE is one of the best ways to approach teaching the 1750–1914 era. Each era in world history presents its own equivalent axis around which everything will revolve. When trying to teach a proper worldview, instructors will find it increasingly necessary to identify the era-defining concept that will be the key to success. This article provides only a framework for one era, but it is my hope that it can be used as a template of sorts for teaching other eras.

About the Author

Christopher Ferraro (BA, MEd, MA) is a secondary teacher in Spring Valley, New York, and a visiting lecturer of history at Arkansas Tech University. He has worked as a reader for the College Board and item writer for the New York State Department of Education.

PART III

TEACHING BASICS

CHAPTER 11

"I Can't Read This!"

Critical Thinking Strategies for Teaching Analytical Comparative Essays

DAVINA BAIRD

One of the many, sometimes unforeseen, challenges for new teachers is incorporating writing strategies within the framework of historical content. No question that history students must acquire skills to articulate logical, analytical arguments. The challenge often lies with the variety of skills that students bring with them into a history course. Many may not even demonstrate clear, thesis-based essay writing, let alone possess the skills to articulate a convincing, comparative argument. Such a situation is often overwhelming for new teachers and can be discouraging. At the core of this difficulty is another compounding issue: how to teach students to *think* critically and comparatively. However, after a few years in the classroom, with a bit of flexibility and some helpful strategies, even the new teachers can make a dent in their students' comparative thinking and writing abilities. Making such skills achievable takes a systematic approach, based on collaborative group work, consistent teacher feedback, and a willingness to borrow from related disciplines. Along the way, teachers can find much satisfaction and even surprises in watching their students grow.

Many new teachers arrive in the classroom assuming, sometimes incorrectly, that their students understand how to read their text, especially how to distinguish factual statements from analytical ones. Challenging this assumption seems like a decent place to start. Much frustration on the part of both teacher and students can be avoided simply by starting at the beginning. It might help to preface the following exercises by explaining to students that often their intelligence is not fully revealed in their current reading and writing performance. The teacher's goal is to clear the way, step-by-step, for students to fully demonstrate what they have learned about comparing various aspects of history. Most students will respond, at least begrudgingly if not enthusiastically, to the suggestion that they are going to improve their reading and writing skills.

Start by having students read the first chapter and identify which statements in the text are factual and which are analytical. Working in pairs makes this exercise a bit less daunting. Students will respond with a variety of incorrect answers, giving the teacher an opportunity to demonstrate what analytical means: a statement or phrase that gives a fact or facts significance to the time and place discussed. For example, the rise in population in towns in medieval Europe is well documented—a fact that can be statistically supported. But ask students why it matters? What does such a fact illustrate about the patterns of history?; about the "how" and "why" of world history? Such a cognitive connection takes the survey course out of the realm of boring and tedious and creates a bridge to the relevant—and to concepts that students can relate to. Students may come back with several different answers. Steer them to find a sample analytical statement in the text. Once they do, praise their progress—they have just made a small, but huge and significant step toward true historical thinking. Using a few sections of the text, and eventually entire chapters, to simply practice identifying factual and analytical statements (or, as often happens, phrases or parts of complex sentences—depending on the text) allows students to gain a clear mental picture of good writing. Reading good writing is a key first step to creating good writing.

Once students have begun to grasp the difference between factual and analytical statements, they can create their own. Success in this next step requires a bit of collaborative group work and some focused teacher feedback. It also involves the use of cause and effect—again, another aspect of historical thinking as a precursor to historical writing. Within the content area of the course, teachers should form small groups of three to six students and ask them to brainstorm a list of factual information about a given topic. For example, one simple content area in which this process works well is the fall of empires in the classical world (say, the fall of the Han, Indian, or Roman empire). Suggest that students go about this process by identifying aspects of decline—plagues, population decrease, political unrest, etc.—and then identifying either the corresponding cause or its related effect. It often does not matter which they see first—the cause or the effect—so long as students make that connection. Seeing causal relationships is a key cognitive skill in historical thinking. Cause and effect is a basic analytical tool for historians, one at the heart of the discipline. Many teachers assume that adolescents do this automatically. Some students do, but many do not. However, breaking down the thinking process into manageable steps is what makes for quality teaching—everyone can learn small steps, one at a time.

Watching students begin to articulate, even in small group settings, causal relationships between historical facts can be quite rewarding. Light bulbs go on all over the classroom as students begin to make connections. Suddenly, dry facts begin to make sense to them—and making sense leads to relevance—and to remembering! Of course, underlying this entire exercise is positive teacher feedback. It never hurts to praise the small successes. Teens often get less praise from adults than they ought, so a little can go a long way. In fact, this cycle of small success and praise, followed by directive instruction and more praise, can create an environment of intellectual enthusiasm—both for history and for the learning process. Despite what their faces may say, most teenagers do enjoy attending classes where they actually know that they learn something. Having students discuss causal relationships in small groups usually makes historical thinking less daunting for those students who might not come by it naturally. Once they experience this kind of brainstorming in a group setting, they can see what they need to do individually. So the next step is to have students do just that—come up with causal relationships of factual information.

Another simple way to break down almost any historical content is to create categories of political, economic, and social elements. Most students can identify key facts within these categories. Sometimes, especially early in the process, they will identify facts that they personally find interesting, rather than ones with obvious significance. Try to praise what does work while still suggesting or leading them to the key facts. For example, they may be fascinated by the gladiatorial games, but were the games really one of the key social factors or elements in the decline of Rome? Suggest to students that they focus a topic such as widespread poverty and urban crowding—aspects of Rome that were related to the popular games, but are most closely tied to the decline of Rome.

One interesting aspect of the teacher feedback throughout this process is the dialogue between teacher and students about which facts are significant. When they seem stuck on a particular fact—and whether it is indeed important to the topic—then challenge them to support it with other factual evidence. What causes (possibly short- and long-term) were behind the fact? What were the effects? Many a thought-provoking conversation, either in small-group or in whole-class discussion, has ensued from merely pausing to ask students why they think what they do. New teachers may be pleasantly surprised at the support students can suddenly find when challenged to prove their point. Opportunities like these conversations lead to the development of another key skill in historical thinking—providing acceptable evidence that any given historical phenomena are significant to the big picture.

At this point, students are ready to begin some individual homework involving facts and analysis. Have students construct a simple chart (Figure 11.1). On the left side of a page, list the categories of analysis: political, economic, and social, spaced evenly with room for ten to twelve lines between each category. Students draw a line top to bottom about one-third of the way across the page. On the right side, students will select the five or six most important facts about the category within the historical content. For example, they might list the six key political facts about the decline of the Roman Empire. Students should skip a line or leave writing space between each fact. They will later use the spaces in between each fact to write out analysis. The first few times students fill out this chart, they should bring it to class for feedback (from peers and from the teacher) that will help them properly direct their efforts. Once the teacher has verified each fact as key to the topic, students may proceed to create corresponding statements of analysis.

Although giving individual feedback on possibly fifteen or twenty factual statements per student adds considerably to the teacher's workload, it is one with a huge payoff. If students form the habit of correctly identifying key facts early on, the teacher will not have to waste time grading tedious essays containing mostly irrelevant information later.

Students may require several attempts at providing analytical statements that clearly correspond to factual evidence before being able to do it consistently. Like learning to ride a bike, they are often a bit wobbly at first. Again, the teacher's feedback can facilitate this process. Each time the student provides adequate analysis, the teacher has the opportunity to praise this small achievement. These seemingly small bits of positive feedback reinforce the students' confidence. Well-developed skills plus confidence leads to another generation of historians! When students grasp that historical analysis is within their ability, they will often show a new willingness to write about historical content. Sometimes, students will begin to transfer these skills into other content areas as well; the fields of literature and even science often lend themselves to this method of thinking and articulation.

Once students have the detailed side of the chart filled

Figure 11.1 **Facts and Analysis Chart**

Topic:	
A. Political	1. Factual statement here....
	1A. Analysis statement follows here...
	2. Factual statement here....
	2A. Analysis statement follows here....
	3. Factual statement here....
	3A. Analysis statement follows here....
	4. Factual statement here...
	4A. Analysis statement follows here...
	5. Factual statement here...
	5A. Analysis statement follows here,...
	6. Factual statement here...
	6A. Analysis statement follows here...
B. Economic	1. Factual statement here....
	1A. Analysis statement follows here...
	2. Factual statement here....
	2A. Analysis statement follows here....
	3. Factual statement here....
	3A. Analysis statement follows here....
	4. Factual statement here...
	4A. Analysis statement follows here...
	5. Factual statement here...
	5A. Analysis statement follows here,...
	6. Factual statement here...
	6A. Analysis statement follows here...
C. Social	1. Factual statement here....
	1A. Analysis statement follows here...
	2. Factual statement here....
	2A. Analysis statement follows here....
	3. Factual statement here....
	3A. Analysis statement follows here....
	4. Factual statement here...
	4A. Analysis statement follows here...
	5. Factual statement here...
	5A. Analysis statement follows here,...
	6. Factual statement here...
	6A. Analysis statement follows here...
Thesis Statement:	

out, instruction begins on the topic sentence (categories) side. Ask students to reflect on the key facts and the corresponding analysis and to identify a common theme or concept. For example, in the political decline of the Roman Empire, students might bring up concepts such as political corruption or outside invasion or both. Suggest that these concepts form the main idea for a paragraph in a future essay. For example, a possible topic sentence might read: "Politically, the decline of the Roman Empire was the result of internal factors, such as political apathy and corruption, as well as external factors, such as invasion." When students have the factual and analytical building blocks in place, creating the larger main ideas seems a more natural process. They are essentially working backward toward a larger essay, one step at a time.

With these category ideas in place, the time arrives for students to create a thesis. Certainly, most students can create simple thesis statements with relatively little instruction. For example, "There are political, economic, and social aspects to the fall of the Roman Empire" serves well enough for younger grades. Yet secondary students are capable of much more—despite their designation as regular or advanced students. Suggest that the basic thesis can be expanded, using the topic sentences, or main ideas of each category, as a roadmap. For example: "The decline of the Roman empire can be viewed as the culmination of political, economic, and social factors. Politically, decline involved apathy and corruption, as well as invasion. Economically, decline resulted from interruptions to corporate farming and trade networks. Socially, decline took a distracted and luxury-loving populace by surprise." While many teachers may advocate a single-sentence thesis, students will often need to begin by creating elaborate and analytical theses using multiple statements. With increased practice and skill development, students may then refine their writing into more concise statements without losing the elaborate analysis.

While this process of teaching analytical thinking and writing seems broken down into the smallest of steps, it does get results. Other content areas use small steps to build skills, and history should be no exception. Students are often surprised by their own achievements and the rapidity with which they can develop these skills. And yet there is still another way to enhance this thinking and writing process: building in comparative analysis.

When asking students to identify key facts on any given topic, suggest that there may be similar or contrasting facts on another related topic. For example, political corruption in classical Rome had similarities to political corruption in classical China. As they form analytical statements, direct students to do so using comparison and contrast. Start simple:

"While politicians in Rome became increasingly distracted and corrupted by status and love of luxury, bureaucrats in the Han dynasty struggled with the same issue." Explain to students that the strongest comparative statements include both subjects within the same statement. Simply juxtaposing facts of a similar or opposite nature does not make them comparative. Articulating the connection makes the comparison stronger and therefore analytical. Students will make modest progress with such statements at first—often finding similarities where there are none—but with adequate feedback they will become more consistent. Comparative statements make an interesting pattern when mixed with causal statements—leading to a more sophisticated essay.

Teaching comparative, analytical thinking and writing is a simple, step-by-step process that requires giving students lots of practice and patient, positive feedback. This investment by teachers early in the course brings months of rewards—for both teacher and students. New teachers gain confidence that both skills and historical content can be achieved simultaneously. History students begin to see themselves learning concrete and transferable skills in what is, unfortunately, a subject that is sometimes seen as lacking in relevance or interest.

One interesting by-product of this type of thinking and writing instruction is that students will eventually find the textbook and other source material easier to read, digest, and remember. Many will see these very patterns emerge within the text itself—and suddenly more light bulbs turn on. Students come to see the connection between critical thinking, critical writing, and critical reading—because they are doing it themselves.

Acknowledgments

Many thanks to Kathleen Hudzinski, secondary master teacher at Horizon Honors High School, for her patient direction and encouragement in this area. Thanks also to the many history students who served as guinea pigs for a new teacher seeking to make them better thinkers.

About the Author

Davina Baird has a BA in history from Arizona State University and teaches world history and global cultures to freshmen and sophomores at Horizon Honors High School in Phoenix, Arizona. She has also served as a reader for the Advanced Placement World History exam. Her passion for learning and teaching about different regions and cultures of the world has led her to pursue a master's degree in global history from American Public University.

CHAPTER 12

History or Hysteria
Teaching and Evaluating Discussion

JACK BETTERLY

Given the opportunity, most teachers of history find an energetic and dynamic student discussion one of the most glorious and invigorating experiences that can possibly decorate the daily round, flush the cheeks, and bring a new lightness to their plodding pace. Aside from being fascinating to follow, such a discussion can provide reassurance that a teacher has actually managed to transfer to students, perhaps, some of the excitement and pleasure of the discipline.

Most history teachers I have known have felt this way at one time or another and have argued that developing the ability to discuss issues is one of the major benefits students can gain from taking history courses. However, to say that a teacher "encourages discussion" is essentially a cliché of the profession. I have even heard it argued by teachers whose classes, I knew by experience, were devoted to lectures. Indeed, it is all too often that teachers forgo class discussion in the interests of what many know as "coverage."

Unfortunately, even when teachers do encourage discussion, the quality of the students' performance is rarely quantified and, as a result, just as rarely influences grades in the course. If it does, it is usually as some vague perception in the mind as the teacher reflects on the students' achievements, foibles, personalities, appearances, laughs, and other gateways to the comprehension of academic competence.

I must be honest and make it clear from the beginning that I strongly prefer to avoid giving number or letter grades altogether. Grading is apparently a practice that, according to Neil Postman, originated in 1792: "The first instance of grading students' papers occurred at Cambridge University in 1792 at the suggestion of a tutor named William Farish. . . . To say that someone should be doing better work because he has an IQ of 134, or that someone is a 7.2 on a sensitivity scale, or that this man's essay on capitalism is an A− and that man's is a C+ would have sounded like gibberish to Galileo or Shakespeare or Thomas Jefferson."[1] William Farish probably had no idea what havoc would ultimately be wrought by his innovation. Thus, I write this paper with immense trepidation, lest it prove to begin a similar descent into one of the darker underworlds of academe.

You see, between 1972 and 1984 I enjoyed the privilege of teaching all my courses with a final evaluation of Credit or No Credit, accompanied by extensive checklists and analytical comments. I still favor that kind of system. However, 1972 was quite a while ago, and this article assumes that most schools, including my former school, returned to conservative grading in the mid-1980s and remain firmly stuck there to this day. In fact, it would seem there is now even greater pressure from politicians around this vast nation—absorbed and obsessed as they are by intellectual and educational concerns and pastimes—to quantify performance and to standardize the results. Therefore, if a teacher believes that discussion is an important skill for students to master, the degree or nature of this mastery must be, in some fashion, integrated as part of a student's grade.

Discussion usually assumes small groups of students. My own sections at Emma Willard School in Troy, New York, consisted of anywhere from eight to eighteen students. I suspect that once sections go beyond twenty-five students, discussion as a disciplined activity becomes less feasible. However, some large lecture classes do break regularly into small discussion sections, and here this technique might be useful. One might divide classes of thirty or forty into half participants and half observers, switching the roles the next time around.

In most of the years following 1984 until my retirement in 2000, I was teaching a two-year required world history course. I loved it. I would argue that the two-year format is essential. The freshman year course was called Ancient and Medieval Worlds; the sophomore course was called The Rise

63

of the Modern World, which began at 1400 CE. I taught two sections of each course, as well as one section of an elective open to juniors and seniors. This course varied from year to year, but it was usually The Contemporary World, which was taught using student subscriptions to *The Christian Science Monitor*, as well as magazines and journals such as *Foreign Affairs*. I graded discussion in all these courses. The best way to describe where monitored discussions fit into grading is simply to reproduce what I handed out to students at the beginning of the course (Handout 12.1).

Handout 12.1   **Grading**

Your grade will be based on my overall assessment of your abilities as a student of history, as a historian, on your knowledge of history and the crafts and disciplines of history and of historical processes, and on your ability to function as a participant in the community of scholars. This grade will be relative not to the students in the section or the course but relative to the totality of students I have taught in the last forty-two years.

I will arrive at that judgment after giving equal and careful attention to:

Full-period essay tests—one or two each quarter
Daily quizzes
Monitored discussions—three or four each quarter
Class participation
Two- to three-page projects—prepared outside, one each
    quarter, usually a book review
Information from conferences

No grades will be "curved." You have both a right and responsibility to ask me for a reasonably accurate assessment of your ongoing grade at any time. That will ordinarily be given as a range; e.g., "B/B+."

You also have a right and responsibility to see me and contest any grade you feel is incorrect. I may disagree, but sometimes I am persuaded. One way or another, I will respect and applaud you for seeking redress.

I had obviously designed this system to allow students to compensate for their lesser skills with those that were stronger. As a result, it was fairly difficult to fail; at the same time, it was fairly difficult to get an "A+." I would average together quiz average, test average, project average, and discussion average, all of which were quantified, to come up with a single grade. Class participation and other information were not quantified, leaving me some wiggle room to shade the final grade one way or another. This grade I then converted from a number to a letter designation, which is what went on the transcript and was reported quarterly with a brief comment to the student.

When I designed the monitored discussions, I wished to avoid the most common problems that plague so many classes. By the time I did this, I had been teaching for more than twenty-five years, so I had many examples in mind. I wanted to produce a legitimate exercise, honestly presented, that would both interest the students, reveal more of their thinking to them, and train them in discussion.

There were two chief principles that guided me. The first was to treat discussion as a collaborative rather than competitive experience. In this age of free market theology, that may be pure heresy, but what can I say? I am an old relic of a semisocialist who believes people accomplish more by working with each other than against each other.

The second principle was truly daunting. It was that teachers talk too much and should shut up and listen. This would necessitate my depriving the students of my truly incredible expertise in a vast variety of historical areas, not to speak of my wit, my bon mots, my incisive vision, and my analytic precision. I could not make such decisions lightly or plan such sacrifices without weighty thought. After days and weeks of brooding over the tradeoffs, I decided that the urgent need for experimental innovation transcended even these prices to be paid: see Handout 12.2.

Handout 12.2   **Monitored Discussions**

Once every week, or once every two weeks, I will supplement your reading assignment with a topic position or question to be discussed by the class as a whole for all of the next class period and, as nearly as possible, to be resolved by that discussion.

History is not an enterprise for individual competition and achievement. History is a communal discipline in which the entire global body of historians pool their information, insight, and curiosity to attempt to find and refine at least the broadest current perceived truth about the past and to persuade their colleagues of its possible validity. That is why historians place such an emphasis on citations—giving credit to those who have come before and who have contributed to this ongoing struggle, and identifying the sources of alleged facts.

When the discussion takes place, I will ask for a volunteer to begin and then I will proceed to take notes. I will speak only twice—once halfway through to give my perceptions of how the discussion is going and to suggest what other routes might be explored, and once at the end to offer my evaluation and my perception of how it went and how you might improve the next one. Except for that, I will listen, watch, and take notes.

You will then tear out a small piece of paper and give yourself a numerical grade. Grade individually for both quality of listening and for quality of speaking and then average them. I will collect these, revise them as I see fit, add a comment or two, and return them to you the next day. Naturally, if you are dissatisfied with the revised grade, you should tell me immediately and I will consider your reasoning.

Silence is not an option. To draw in shy people, ask them for their specific opinion on a point under discussion. A monitored discussion is the opposite of a debate! It is not competitive! I subtract points if you are dominating the discussion and if you are withdrawing or waiting to be invited.

The mind of a single human being is a pitifully inadequate instrument. Only by collaboration, sharing, probing, questioning, and crosschecking have we survived as a species—such as we are. One may rely on passion and rhetorical skill to aid in persuasion, but once this becomes aggressive or domineering it misses the point entirely. Similarly, dominators often do not sense that they are dominating, and it is the responsibility of others to politely and laughingly point this out. Again, nudging those who are silent is equally in order.

You will be surprised at the degree to which your collective minds can refine, articulate, and clarify the issues being discussed.

The students came to love these assignments. At least, they *said* they did, and they kept nagging for more. It took only three or four monitored discussions for them to understand the process. After that, they focused on the topic quickly and were quite good at probing, reflecting, and maintaining a coherent thread rather than simply throwing out random statements.

Let me describe a typical discussion. For years before developing these discussions, I used the following format for full-period essay tests, handing out the description five or six days in advance to allow for preparation. Students then wrote the test in class without notes. In this example, their readings and study during the first half of the quarter had dealt with the period from roughly 700 CE to roughly 1000 CE:

> Defend, attack, or modify the following position with specific information:
> In this period of very gradual recovery from Roman imperial decline, West Asia and Europe inevitably reflected the influence of pastoral nomadic cultures from which the new peoples had come—Arabs, Celts, Anglo-Saxons, Franks, and Teutons, to name a few. East Asia, on the other hand, developed in a fashion much more reflective of a long history of urban civilization based upon peasant agriculture in extensive riverine basins. This difference would be reflected in both religious and political developments.

Because the students—at least those who had taken a course from me before—were used to being asked to take a position on a position, I decided to use the same format for discussion. At the same time, because it was on a single night's assignment, the topic would, in most cases, be briefer. Let us assume that the night's assignment was to be a document—Al-Jahiz's description of the arrival of the Seljuq Turks in Baghdad in 1055 CE and his description of these peoples in general.[2] In that case, I might have students take home the following topic to be used in discussion the next day:

> Defend, attack, or modify the following position with specific information:
> Al-Jahiz maintained that the Seljuq Turks were essentially similar to the original Arab Bedouins; in fact, he referred to them as "the Bedouins of the non-Arabs." This was really romantic, idealized nonsense. In terms of the kind of land from which they came and the cultural contacts that had influenced them, the Arabs and the Turks were radically different.
> You are free to utilize and bring to class any reference materials you might wish to use as evidence for your position.

In the years when I used a college text, most students would refer to it to review the original Arab Bedouins. In later years, I would keep several different college texts in my classroom and on reserve in the library. When the class met the next day, I would not be listening to determine who had used the most resources or how distinguished they might be. Although I never fully approved of it myself, students did spend much of their time outside of class completing, as well, assignments in math, science, languages, and other courses rather than mine alone. Some students were even known merely to read the document and then wing it on what they remembered or could cleverly make up.

I would read the position out loud and invite the first comment. You can well imagine what I watched for. Was the group listening carefully to each contribution? Was everyone being drawn in? How? Was it deliberate, and who was doing it? Were students able to articulate? Were they able to focus relatively quickly on a thread and to follow it out? Were there individuals with comprehension problems?

It may be difficult to believe, but for teachers to keep their mouth shut for extended periods is a monumentally difficult discipline. Once I discovered this, I tried doing it more and more because I could use the practice. I began discovering how very intelligent my students were.

At the midpoint in the discussion, my summary and suggestions for the class might run a bit like this:

> OK. You are all moving along well. Mary began with a qualified defense of the topic relying primarily on geographical factors. Did the atlas she brought get around to everyone? Paula moved on to cultural difference, and gradually you all spun off into that weird discussion of pastoralism. Andrea, you were very good to pin Jennie and draw her in, and her skepticism helped a good deal. You, Patty, Kit was good to shut you up!! Yes, I know, you are a very passionate young woman, but enough is enough. My suggestion for the second half is that you might move on to differences that would begin to reveal themselves once the Turks were truly settled and—the

leadership, at least—living in large urban centers. Think of Abbasid culture. Would you expect a Turkish urban empire to be similar? Iris, you are obviously the one student yet to speak. Sneaky. Why don't you start the group off?

All the time the discussion was going on, I was taking notes on students. These would be vital when I had to check the students' evaluations of themselves. They were also extremely useful for me to scan before making my midpoint or final summaries. In addition, taking notes *made* me pay attention. It is very easy, if student discussion is moving off in a direction of no particular interest to you, to find your mind wandering off and your eyes drifting toward the window. It is sometimes humiliating to discover how few truly important and worthy topics, if not in your specialty or stock speeches, can manage to hold your interest. You begin to wonder if students consider you a bit slow.

The second half of the discussion usually proceeded much as the first, and my final evaluation was often very similar to the one at midpoint. Students then graded their own behavior on scrap paper, with a simple numerical grade for speaking skills and one for listening skills, which they averaged along with a few words of clarification.

When I had a free period, I would flip through these scraps, looking at my notes and altering grades if I disagreed. If I did, I usually wrote a clarifying note on the back. I would return these the next day after recording them. The whole point was to keep the grading operation from becoming a major time consumer and yet keep it valid. I had enough stacks of tests and projects to be graded, and those required much more in the way of time, concentration, and analytical comments.

Notice that I deliberately avoided grading historical *content*. During a grading quarter the students were taking daily quizzes and essay tests and writing two-page projects, and thus I had plenty of opportunity to evaluate their historical knowledge. The monitored discussion was intended to teach them a great deal about what the *intellectual* craft of history is, to sharpen those abilities necessary to participate in a productive discussion, to make it clear that a discussion is something quite different from "all stating their own opinions," and that it should have not only direction but a sense of movement forward. At the end of a historical discussion, all participants should be able to feel that their opinions have been changed and improved, however minutely, from what they were when the discussion began.

For purposes of determining the students' course grades at the end of a grading period, I counted quiz average, project average, essay test average, and discussion average equally. This method tended to eliminate the extremely high and the extremely low, which I felt was quite realistic. As can be imagined, students who had difficulty with writing skills were often the most enthusiastically prepared when they came to discussion.

I believe I can say, honestly, that by the end of the year, my students were often conducting more enjoyable, focused, and substantial discussions than many of those I had endured in the school's History Division or, God knows, at the full faculty meetings. Students were not making speeches, nor seeking competitive advantage, and they were sensitive to the need for both direction and resolution.

In all fairness and with no substantiating documentation whatsoever, I suspect that part of the success was due to the fact that I was teaching young women exclusively. I taught coeducational classes for eight years and, frankly, prefer them to single-sex classes. However, I do suspect that teaching these skills to young men, while it would work perfectly well, would require a good deal more deprogramming.

I have tried to keep this chapter light, but do not make the mistake of assuming that the issue is not a crucial one for the discipline. Ask average people on the street how they felt about history courses. Count the number of times you hear "Oh, I hated history!" or "I was just terrible at history!" or "I don't remember any of it." And they mean it. The late and greatly missed geographer Jim Blaut and I had a running argument. He took the position that geography was the worst taught subject in America. I staunchly argued that it was history. We must do everything we can to overcome the public image that history is a matter of memorization and is vaguely irrelevant to the requirements of daily life in the real world. It is my experience that carefully monitored discussions have an important role to play. Given its immensely large and complex demand for making lucid connections over vast amounts of space and time, it would seem that world history stands to profit from such discussions more than any other course.

About the Author

After graduating from Yale University in 1955 and leaving the army in 1958, John Andrew Betterly spent his working life teaching history and fostering a love of learning at four private schools. He retired from Emma Willard School in 2000 and spent the next seven and a half years engaged in lively discussions and mentoring new teachers through H-World, AP World History, and other online listservs. He was a member of the board of *World History Connected*. He died on March 7, 2008, in Albuquerque, New Mexico.

Notes

1. Neil Postman, *Technopoly* (New York: Vintage Books, 1993), 13.

2. *The Human Record: Sources of Human History, Vol. 1: To 1700*, 3rd ed., ed. Alfred J. Andrea and James H. Overfield (Boston: Houghton Mifflin, 1998), 292–295, Document 75.

CHAPTER 13

Discovering Global Patterns

How Student-Centered Internet Research Can Build
a Genuine World History Perspective

RYBA L. EPSTEIN

When I began the journey from teaching Advanced Placement (AP) European history to AP World History, I realized that my ingrained habits of mind had to change. I discovered that as long as we try to teach world history in the same way we teach U.S. or regional history, we are doomed to failure: world history is too broad and complex to be taught using the same approaches we use for more traditional courses. As world history teachers, we must begin to adopt a big-picture perspective of history. We must examine and compare evidence gleaned from many geographical regions and across broad time periods, looking for patterns that reveal basic themes of human activity and development. To reorient ourselves to a world history perspective, we need to constantly ask ourselves big history questions: What are the major themes that we see painted on the world canvas? How are those themes encountered and elaborated in different cultures or in different time periods? (I developed the acronym SPICE™ to remind my students to look for and apply major themes: *s*ocial, *p*olitical, *i*nteraction between humans and the environment, *c*ultural, and *e*conomic.)

So how can we as teachers learn to think in terms of the forest, not the trees—the broad perspective needed for teaching world history? One way is to look at the world not as isolated regions or civilizations but as interactive systems. For example, looking at the Indian Ocean as a region, as in Linda Shaffer's essay "Southernization" or Janet Abu-Lughod's *Before European Hegemony: The World System A.D. 1250–1350*,[1] allows us to look at trade patterns, technology, and cultural exchanges across an entire region instead of examining each culture in isolation. In addition, one of the insights that this approach offers is the gradual broadening of trade contacts from local to regional and, ultimately, in the 1500s, to global. A teacher working from a world historical perspective would present the European entrance into the Indian Ocean trading region as one more development in a web of trading patterns that had been growing over thousands of years.

Another key concept in world history that helps break the patterns ingrained by traditional historical teaching is the use of multiple perspectives. To look at the world from a truly global perspective means trying to see the world through the eyes of other cultures instead of simply in terms of their relationships with the West. The creation of a multiple perspectives approach is aided by having students examine primary source documents and artifacts from members of various cultures and read works of fiction or nonfiction that are not written through the Western lens.

However, one of the most difficult feats in teaching world history is to balance the conflicting demands of content coverage with the need to engage students in active learning. I advocate the use of selective, creative abandonment to allow time for in-depth projects, primary source readings, debates, comparisons between societies, and student-centered discovery learning. Selective, creative abandonment involves reexamining content to distinguish topics that are truly essential from those that are more limited or peripheral to the major themes in world history. By consciously selecting what is to be included—and for what purpose—teachers can create new units that excite students and enable them to discover major patterns and themes across world history. Selective, creative abandonment constitutes a positive, fruitful approach to sorting and organizing the vast scope of world history into a well-integrated one-year curriculum. It is the reverse of the view that treats world history as merely the accretion of various regional and national histories. In this accretion view, there is simply too much material to cover, so, regretfully and somewhat arbitrarily, teachers have to trim this mass to fit into a year course. The accretion approach severely limits students' ability to discern significant patterns and make insightful comparisons.

Instead of arbitrarily cutting material to fit the time allotted, selective, creative abandonment starts by examining the available material in the light of essential questions and broad themes. For instance:

- Why do some cultures look outward and others inward?
- What technological innovations led to the great voyages of the Polynesians, Chinese, and Vikings?
- What are the relationships among the environment, trade, and technology across different time periods?

By analyzing such root issues, teachers can identify which content areas offer the most productive or creative teaching opportunities, while abandoning less central or more limited topics. Thus we selectively abandon the peripheral and make room for the central themes and comparisons.

In my personal journey, my new paradigm for understanding world history came to include the following elements:

- A big-picture view of history
- A comparative approach with the use of multiple perspectives
- A world or regional systems approach rather than focusing on discrete locations or events
- The development of integrative themes
- Selective, creative abandonment to liberate myself from the notion that the class needed to cover all possible content.

The next challenge was how to change the method of delivery of instruction to meet my new paradigm. I wanted my students to be active participants with me in looking for and describing patterns in world history, not passive note-takers. I wanted them to learn to "do" history, not just remember facts.

Creating Student-Centered Discovery Learning Projects

Alternative assessments, projects, discovery learning, student-directed learning—all these terms describe a fundamental shift from teacher-centered to student-centered learning. These activities engage students—especially more creative students—in ways that lectures or Socratic questioning may not. While the ability to understand documents and texts and to write clearly and persuasively is still the foundation of historical studies, today's students have many options available for acquiring information and presenting their knowledge. By using discovery learning, we give students ownership over their learning process. A carefully planned project can allow some students to soar,

while others may choose to do only the minimum. More importantly, we are teaching not just a specific set of facts, but a way to learn, to explore, and to discover that will remain with the student long after the course is over. In addition, by using a variety of ways for students to learn and show what they know, we will be able to differentiate for a variety of learning styles (e.g., right-brain or left-brain, visual or kinesthetic), foster creativity, and channel the exuberance that youngsters can bring to the classroom.

Setting up good projects requires thoughtful reflection. Even a well-designed project can be a syllabus buster—the brilliant idea that grows like a cancer to defeat your best scheduling and planning. Projects should encourage students to explore a theme, to make comparisons between cultures that may not be explicit in the textbook, to practice research skills, or to experiment with different methods of presenting and integrating information. A project requires hard work and should never be just a glitzy way to distract students or keep boredom at bay. Indeed, the knowledge and skills that students gain should be justifiable in terms of the class time allotted to a project—I use the mantra, "Is it important enough to take two days away from the Mongols?"

Since the Internet is a fact of life for students who often turn to it as a shortcut instead of reading the "boring" textbook, it is essential to teach students to use the Internet responsibly as a research tool. This task includes teaching students to evaluate the information they find in this new and growing medium. Too often, students click on the first page that comes up in a vague search, and are unable to distinguish between Sally Smith's middle-school web page and one from the Smithsonian—or, worse still, they accept a site with little scholarly validity or one that reeks of bias. It is vital to instruct students how to search the web efficiently, to analyze web information, and to evaluate the reliability and validity of a web source, just as they have learned to do with print sources.

Successful Internet Search Techniques

Many students, despite their familiarity with the Internet, have poor search techniques. They do not understand how search engines work or that the order and number of words they use as search terms affect the utility of the search results. Many students give up too quickly or accept the very first site they find after they input one or two very general terms. It is important to teach students both flexibility and precision in selecting their search terms. Assume that a student wants to find out how the ancient Chinese mined salt. Inputting the search term *China* alone generates an unusable number of hits for every meaning of the word: the People's Republic of China, porcelain, movie titles, and so on. The term *salt mining China* produces more usable results, while *salt mining China Han* is even more productive by limiting responses to those concerning a particular dynasty. Most search engines no longer require using the old Boolean logic terms such as AND to link all terms as part of the search (salt AND mining AND China) or NOT to exclude certain types of entries (NOT porcelain) or the + and – for mandatory or undesired results in the search string. However, sometimes an unwieldy number of responses can still be pruned by a judicious use of quotes in the search string. Using quotes around a phrase indicates that the words must appear together in this specific order (*"salt mining"* eliminates seasoning or metaphorical uses, for example).

Another useful tool is the "search within results" option, usually at the bottom of the page of a search engine. This option will allow students to narrow down results even further. Adding *provinces* to the search *"salt mining" China Han* reduces the number of hits from about 44,000 to 16,000. Then, if the role of the provincial bureaucracy in the mining of salt in the Han Dynasty is the real object of the search, adding *governor* to the search string will further narrow the results by about half (the string now reads *"salt mining" China Han governor*). If the technology that the Han used to mine salt is the desired topic, the search could be modified to *"salt mining" China Han technology*. Thus, in order to conduct a successful search, students must have a clear idea of exactly what area of information they are searching or they must learn to modify their search strings to follow interesting paths that unfold as they are searching. I compare the computer to a very literal-minded child: it will do (or find) *exactly* what you tell it to do. Do not rage against the machine; refine your directions. Incidentally, this process of narrowing the focus or increasing specificity is similar to the process of going from a general topic to a specific thesis in writing an essay. By teaching one skill, we are actually teaching the other as well.

Evaluating Online Sources

We assume that sources in peer-reviewed journals or books from reputable publishers meet accepted standards for scholarship and freedom from bias. In the past, all we had to do was to send students to the library, and they would return with acceptable sources to analyze. However, the Internet has changed that comfortable arrangement. In a situation not seen since the introduction of the printing press, huge quantities of information are now available without having passed through the screening that culls out much of the inappropriate print material available to our students. There is a heady feeling that anything can be found on the web—good, bad, brilliant, vindictive, untrue, suppressed—and far too often our students accept all the material as equally valid. They are unaware that anyone can post to the web, regardless of credentials. While some sites are self-correcting by the community that posts, there is a

lag time when incorrect, incomplete, or offensive material can be displayed—not to mention the hate sites. One beautiful opportunity is to teach point of view using a variety of sources: government-sponsored, academic, foreign press, splinter groups, and so on. This exercise is especially attractive if the students are older and have more experience in identifying tone and point of view. For younger or less skilled students, it is best to teach them what is acceptable and how to detect the unacceptable sites.

Here is a list of questions I discuss with my students to teach them how to determine the validity of a source:

- Is the page sponsored by an educational institution or academic journal?
- Is it peer-reviewed? (It is important to explain the academic peer-review system to students.)
- Is the source sponsored by a respected organization such as PBS, the National Geographic Society, or a major museum?
- Is it sponsored by an organization that might have a certain bias, such as an energy company discussing environmental issues?
- Is the page current? When was it composed? When was the last update? (This information is sometimes found in the small type at the bottom of the home page, perhaps in a copyright notice. If not, it can often be found by going to the option "page source" or "reveal source" under the view menu in most browsers.)
- Do authors have appropriate credentials or knowledge in the area under discussion? Do authors have academic training or job experience that would qualify them as expert witnesses in a court case? Do authors have any reason to be biased about the subject?
- Does the page cite its sources? Are those sources reliable? Do they reflect more than one point of view?
- Is the information on the page presented in sufficient depth?
- Can you corroborate the information given in the web page with material in reliable print sources or trusted web pages?
- Is the page free from obvious bias or slanting of information? Look for the rhetoric of distortion or hateful speech. Look for a circular trail of citation only to groups or sources in the same network. Look for common propaganda tricks such as bandwagon, sweeping generalizations, rhetorical questions, or invective.

Step-by-Step Guide to Planning a Web-Based Unit

Just as we need to teach students how to search the web effectively and evaluate the information they discover, we also have to design projects that will fit our teaching objectives, be feasible for students to complete in the time allowed, and advance their world history learning. These are the key steps I follow in designing web-based research projects:

- Identify the specific content, themes, and historical thinking skills you wish to develop.
- Decide what the outcome or end product will be. A travel brochure? A debate? A "meeting of the minds" discussion? An illustrated storyboard? An elaborate poster or chart? A short paper? A speech?
- Create clear guidelines and grading rubrics for the particular product you assign, and give them to the students in writing before they begin the project. The time you spend up front in teaching the standards and rubrics will pay off in quality of product (and will make grading easier).
- Determine what documents or other media are needed to supplement the online sources.
- Research the online materials to ensure what is actually available to your students. If possible, give the students a few good sites to begin with. Know what is available so that you can judge how well the research has been done. I offer extra credit to students who find exceptionally fruitful sites I do not know about—and I add them to my list for next year.
- Teach students, in advance, how to search for and evaluate online material the same way you would teach them to locate and evaluate printed material.
- Check for active links just before you begin the unit—the web is ephemeral. If possible, load suggested links onto the students' desktops or flash drives before students begin their research project. This will save students a lot of time and mistakes in typing the URLs.
- Do not allow students to substitute flashy products for critical, analytical thinking; this is especially a danger in PowerPoint presentations, which can lure students into using fancy fade or animation techniques at the expense of depth or insight.
- Weigh the time and energy spent on a web-based project against your overall course goals. Ask yourself if it is worth taking two days away from the Mongols.

Sample Project: Comparing Vikings and Polynesians

One of my favorite units is a comparison of the Vikings and Polynesians. The rationale: Much of the world history course concerns major cultures or civilizations, yet the history of the world includes many groups that are not part of one of the core cultures. These two cultures had significant impact on large regions of the world, but are often only a footnote in the standard world history course. Similarities between the two involve mastery of oceango-

ing ships and navigational techniques and a widespread area of exploration and settlement. Students discover the Viking sun-compass and that the Polynesians did not have a polestar to use for navigation, but did have the lateen sail. Students compare the Viking trade routes through what is now Russia to the Black Sea and the colonization of Greenland, Iceland, and Vinland to the Polynesian settlement of the Pacific Islands. The environmental theme is also related to both: Viking settlements on Greenland were abandoned when they failed to adapt to climate change, and the Polynesians drastically changed the environment of the islands they settled—most especially Rapa Nui (Easter Island)—sometimes with disastrous results. Both societies practiced sea-raiding and trading, exploration and migration to previously unknown parts of the world. Their expansion across the Atlantic and the Pacific prefigures the unification of the world's trade systems after 1500.

Handout 13.1[2]   **Vikings and Polynesians**

You will be randomly assigned to one of two groups: Vikings or Polynesians. After time to research the subject, the two teams will take part in a debate.

Debate topic: The Vikings' expansion had a greater, more long-lasting impact on their communicating zone than the Polynesian expansion had on the Polynesians' zone.

Use the following resources as well as the handouts to examine the development of Viking and Polynesian sailing and navigational technology and the areas explored, traded in, or settled by each group.

To be considered:
- Seamanship and types of ships used; diffusion of ship and navigational technology to other regions
- Time periods of expansion
- Geographical areas covered by exploration, settlement, and trade
- Trade—types of goods; impact on settled populations
- Environmental and demographic impact—types of plants and animals transplanted, effect on local ecosystems (including extinctions), effect of new climates and ecosystems on the settlers
- Short-term effects on indigenous populations, if any (trade, conquest, diffusion, assimilation, attitudes toward indigenous populations, etc.) Be specific!
- Long-term effects on indigenous populations, if any (trade, conquest, diffusion, assimilation, attitudes toward, etc.) Be specific!

Themes: economic (trade, technology) diffusion, environmental impact, migration

Thinking skills: comparison, multiple perspectives, change over time

Project timeline:

Before the project—Read and annotate before coming to class: "The Other One-Third of the Globe"

Day 1—View selections from NOVA film Vikings (PBS 2000)

Day 2—View the David Attenborough film *The Lost Gods of Easter Island* (BBC 2000)

Day 3—Media Center for Internet research[3]

Day 4—Work in groups to develop debate

Day 5—Debate in class

Note: The days need not be consecutive. It works well to allow extra time for students to work on their own to analyze their sources before coming together as a group.

Handout 13.2[4]   **List of Resources**

Print Resources

Bronsted, Johannes. *The Vikings.* Trans. by Kalle Skov. New York: Penguin, 1971.

Campbell, I.C. "The Lateen Sail in World History." *Journal of World History* 6, no. 1 (Spring 1995). www.uhpress. hawaii.edu/journals/jwh/jwh061p001.pdf.

Finney, Ben. "The Other One Third of the Globe." *Journal of World History* 5, no. 2 (Fall 1994). www.uhpress.hawaii. edu/journals/jwh/jwh052p273.pdf.

Vesilind, Priit J. "In Search of the Vikings." *National Geographic*, May 2000.

Vikings: Raiders from the North. Alexandria, VA: Time-Life Books, 1993.

The Vinland Sagas. Trans. by Magnus Magnusson and Hermann Palsson. Baltimore: Penguin, 1970.

Web Resources

Diamond, Jared. "Easter's End." www.greatchange.org/ footnotes-overshoot-easter_island.html.

Hale, John. "The Viking Longship." *Scientific American.* www. sciam.com/1998/029 8issue/0298hale.html.

"Introduction to Pacific Islands Archeology." www.arf.berke-ley.edu/~oal/background/pacislands.htm.

"Scandinavia: Finding Information." *ORB: Online Reference Book for Medieval Studies.* www.the-orb.net/encyclop/early/pre1000/viking.html.

"Secrets of Easter Island." NOVA PBS Online. www.pbs.org/wgbh/nova/easter/civilization/first.html.

Viking Boat Project. *ORB: Online Reference Book for Medieval Studies.* www.the-orb.net/encyclop/early/pre1000/v-boat.html.

"The Viking Network Web." www.viking.no/e/index.html.

"Vikings: The North Atlantic Saga." *Smithsonian Institute.* www.mnh.si.edu/vikings.

Films

"Easter Island in Context: From Paradise to Calamity." Films for the Humanities and Sciences, 2000. http://ffh.films. com/id/4697/Easter_Island_in_Context_From_Para-dise_to_Calamity.htm.

"Secrets of the Dead: The Lost Vikings." *NOVA*, PBS, 2000.

"Wayfinders: A Pacific Odyssey." PBS. www.pbs.org/way-finders/.

Handout 13.3   **Viking/Polynesian Debate Rubric**

Individual Accountability:

1. Each person must submit his/her notes (not print-outs of the websites) taken during the Internet research phase of the project. These notes must include an assessment of the sites' validity, reliability, and suitability for world history classes. Be sure to include URLs and titles of all web pages visited.

2. Each person must submit his/her one-page summary of the main points for two print sources (such as "The Other One-Third of the Globe" or "The Lateen Sail in World History").

3. A group may choose to divide the research into sections or topics, such as navigation or environmental impact. Each person must clearly identify his/her specific topic and contribution to the group project. Each person must also compose a preliminary argument and outline for his/her part of the debate and list several supporting facts or examples (citing the sources of the information).

4. Individuals may be awarded additional points during the debate for relevant questions or challenges if backed up by evidence.

5. Individuals may also be awarded points during the debate for relevant additions or support for their side if backed up by evidence.

Group Accountability

Each group will choose a captain to deliver the opening and closing statements. The captain will receive points for this position, since he/she cannot participate in the questioning or answers.

1. During the question-and-answer period, the captain will choose which team member will respond to a specific question posed by the opposite team.

2. Each side will submit a typed outline of its opening statement, including relevant support, prior to the beginning of the debate.

3. The debate will begin with an opening statement by each side to last no more than five minutes. Order of presentation will be determined by a coin toss.

4. A questioning/challenging period will follow. Each side will alternate in directing questions to the opposite side. Points will be awarded based on the level of insight and support for both questions and responses. No points will be awarded for silly or unsupported answers or frivolous or repeated questions. Good demeanor is expected at all times.

5. Each group will have two minutes for its closing statement and final rebuttal.

Handout 13.4   **Viking/Polynesian Grading Checklist**

Group Portion Grading Checklist

1. Opening statement and written outline _____ / 35 points

   - Coverage of topic

   Geography
   Environmental impact
   Demographic impact
   Social impact
   Political impact
   Economic impact (trade, etc.)
   Seamanship, navigation, and technology
   Short-term effects on region
   Long-term effects on region
   Other

   - Evidence of advanced level of research and support
   - Logical and persuasive argument

2. Team's responses to questions and challenges _____ / 10 points
   Must be correct and supported by reference to appropriate sources.

3. Closing argument _____ / 5 points
   Must be convincing and responsive to topic as well as to issues raised by opposing side.

4. Flair—Goes above and beyond the requirements in intellectual depth, presentation, etc. _____ / E.C.

Group Portion Total: _____ / 50 points

Individual Portion Grading Checklist

1. Before the debate _____ / 40 points

   - Notes taken during research reflect advanced level of work and time allotted for research
   - Handouts appropriately annotated and summarized
   - Argument and outline reflect appropriate depth of knowledge and use of sources

2. During the debate _____ / 10 points

   - Questions or answers during the debate are relevant, thoughtful, and appropriate
   - Conduct is appropriate for civilized discourse: no *ad hominem* arguments, no rhetorical fallacies, no shouting or interrupting

Individual Portion Total _____ / 50 points

Project Total _____ / 100 points

About the Author

Ryba L. Epstein teaches world history, Advanced Placement World History, humanities, and Advanced Placement English Literature at Rich East High School in Park Forest, Illinois. She is an AP consultant and question leader for the AP World History exam reading. Her MA and PhD are from the University of Illinois in Urbana-Champaign, and she received her AB from UCLA.

Notes

1. Linda Shaffer, "Southernization." *Journal of World History* 5, no. 1 (1994): 1–21; Janet Abu-Lughod, *Before European Hegemony: The World System A.D. 1250–1350.* New York: Oxford University Press, 1989.

2. Copyright © 2009 The College Board. Reproduced with permission. http://apcentral.collegeboard.com.

3. Many of my students do not have Internet access outside of school, so I need to devote a day for them to work in the lab during class. If students have access to the Internet at home, this day can be eliminated from the schedule.

4. This project aligns with Illinois Learning Standards 5A5a, 5A5b, 5B5a, 5C5a (language arts); 15C4a, 15D3a, 15D4b, 15E4c, 16A5a, 16B5c(w), 16C3a(w), 16C3c(w), 16D3(w), 16E3b(w), 17A4, 17A5, 17C5b, 17D4, 18A5, 18B5 (social sciences); and ILS Social.

Figure 13.1 **Debate Checklist for Teacher**

Vikings	Questions	Answers
Student name		
Student name		
Student name		
Student name		
Student name		
Student name		
Student name		
Student name		
Student name		
Student name		
Student name		
Student name		
Student name		
Student name		
Student name		
Polynesians		
Student name		
Student name		
Student name		
Student name		
Student name		
Student name		
Student name		
Student name		
Student name		
Student name		
Student name		
Student name		
Student name		
Student name		
Student name		

CHAPTER 14

Stimulating Through Simulating
Thinking Historically in the Classroom

DAVE CLARKE

If you want to scare history teachers, tell them that they will soon be as obsolete as stone wheels. They might rant about the importance of not repeating the past or owning our heritage, and those are valid points. But remind them that forty years ago, a computer that could simply do word processing (like the one resting on my lap right now) or do easy calculations (one of the dozens of functions of the cell phone resting in my pocket) would have taken up an entire room. Before most of us become pieces of history ourselves, denizens of the developed world will walk around with watches or phones that will voice activate on a search for any date, name, or geographic feature.

"Computer, when was the War of 1812?"

"Is that a trick question, Dave?"

"OK, Computer, where is South Korea, relative to North Korea?"

"I'm checking all your vital signs, Dave, and they seem quite normal. Are you feeling all right? Would you like me to play some soothing music for you?"

"Computer, what need do we have for history teachers?"

"That may take a while for me to compute an answer, Dave. Please be patient."

Rather than wait for that hypothetical answer, let me suggest the obvious: society will always need history teachers. While memorizing facts and data will become less vital in the future, there will be a correspondingly greater need for critical thinking skills and humans who understand other humans. History, as a part of the humanities, is always going to be crucial for fulfilling these functions.

The purpose of this chapter is to describe a means by which students, of world history especially, can learn these vital skills and more through historical simulations. In order to understand the power of simulations, however, we should first examine historical thinking.

Thinking Historically and Historical Thinking

One of the most earnest pursuits of teachers in the history field in this generation has been the instruction of students in thinking historically. What this means in layman's terms is that students need to learn to think like historians. We researchers of archaic lore gather sources of evidence, consider the validity of those sources, and seek primary accounts of diverse natures. When we examine events of the past, we consider their ramifications locally as well as regionally and globally and try to make comparisons across lands and time. We seek to understand the forces of change and tradition as well as economics, geography, and a host of other factors that can shape the course of events. We then try to impart these habits of mind unto our young wards. This is what we call historical thinking, but it is not thinking historically.

What I am suggesting is that historical thinking (i.e., thinking like someone at some point in history other than your own) can be taught through historical simulations. These exercises, when properly done, can bring students closer to understanding why a people removed from them by miles and centuries might have made the choices they made. What possessed some of Magellan's crew to mutiny—while others stayed at his side, even outliving him? Why did nomadic peoples have fewer children than settled farmers? Did they not love having children as much as sedentary folk? Putting your mind in the place of someone else (especially someone who seems radically different from you) demonstrates, more than any other exercise, the common nature of the human condition. Hutus and Huns, Mayans and Mongols were (are) more like us than different. In many ways, history is simply the study of different solutions to common problems. How do we find resources? How do we create justice? How do we get work done? How do we explain bad things happening to good people? The answers to queries such as these may seem exotic, but the questions themselves are quite rudimentary. Getting students to look past the exotic, however, is a difficult task. Simulations enable students to become historical actors and retrace the steps of bygone peoples. Within those parameters, teachers can introduce concepts that can be demonstrated or have students investigate scenarios that are totally new (to them). The end result is that students can benefit from simulations by thinking both critically and historically. They can learn to think both like historians and like the actual inhabitants of history themselves.

Two Types of Simulations

From the vantage point of a teacher, the biggest drawback to using simulations in the classroom is preparation. Creating simulations or even adapting existing ones is very time-consuming. In addition, having students go through a simulation is often a lengthy process, especially if the teacher is waiting for the class to come to certain conclusions that can only be reached through experience. Bearing these limitations in mind, teachers can use two general types of simulations.

The first type could be called the open outcome simulation. In this type of simulation, the ending is not predetermined and participants are free to make any number of choices. The other form is a fixed outcome simulation wherein the ending is a fait accompli and students are taking steps toward an inevitable conclusion. In this instance, the conclusion is an important element of the exercise, which is not necessarily the case in an open outcome simulation. This distinction is important since the end may never arrive in an open outcome exercise! In both instances, I would suggest that simulations in world history should be done as group exercises because it is the group dynamic that powers history. How these groups are formed and function is, of course, up to the teacher. Groups may be random, heterogeneous by ability, or homogeneous by ability. With the end products in mind, I often survey students in advance and match their roles in the project to their interests.

Let us first examine the open outcome version. One common type of such simulation is the *Civilization* series of computer games produced as an entertainment product. Players begin as nomads; their first goal is to find the right patch of earth to call home. Once said homeland is reached, the nomads instantly found a city and become farmers—literally with the click of a button. Those former nomads are now urbanites who work at manufacturing or growing food within the city to produce more citizens. A second nomad continues on to found another city at the players' desire. (Afterward, nomads can be generated by a city at the cost of some population, to found even more cities.) At this point, the choices for the players are pretty close to

endless. Where should the farmers be positioned? Should the city focus on growing food, mining gold, or procuring timber? Should they turn their energies toward advancing the society through art and architecture, or should they invest in a powerful military in preparation for the inevitable first contact with other people? Literally, what the group of students is creating in these embryonic moments is their own microculture. Will they be warmongers or philosophers? Will they be artists or merchants? Interestingly, students never realize that they are consciously making these choices because these decisions are reached simply through discussion. Yet the choices that are preferred, the beliefs that shape these choices, and the assumptions that underlie the behaviors are nothing less than nascent culture! It is a fascinating comparison to examine (after a few hours of real time) how diverse the cultures of different student groups will have become.

My personally favorite moment for examining the culture of any group is that initial encounter with other peoples. When "the foreigner" crosses the horizon, does the group seek to make contact or hide behind their city walls in fear? Do they reach out in friendship with offers of trade and diffusion of technology or do they simply reach for their ever-handy clubs? Imagine if your students played the simulation via the Internet with students who were from different cultures to begin with! How different might their choices be? How much might we learn about the culture which we are part of by reflecting on the ways in which it impacted the formation of our virtual culture? Did our culture lead us to be "clubbers" or "sharers"?

The software of the *Civilization* series keeps track of the myriad conditions that might impact the newly formed communities. How fertile is the land, and how hostile are the neighbors? How satisfied is the populace with the decisions of the leaders, and how quickly or slowly is that populace increasing? Are the trade goods valued by other peoples, and how rapidly is the study of technology expanding? Clearly this exercise could go on for weeks at a time. (Serious players can devote hundreds of hours and may start over many times, continuously perfecting their playing skills and/or experimenting with different decisions.) For the sake of making a point in class, however, four to five hours should suffice if the groups are functioning correctly. At that point, groups should have generated data over several centuries of game time and be able to examine changes and continuities as well as make comparisons to the experiences of other groups. Reaching the end of the game (if such a thing even exists) is hardly the point; besides, students may lose interest once the game becomes simply a matter of management after the initial challenges are over.

This open outcome simulation presents historical content that may otherwise be difficult to impart. Were some geographic features better for farming, mining, and other occupations? Which areas were the best? Why did some early peoples manage to conquer others? How important was technology? How important was trade? While the software that I have used with my classes was not specific to individual cultures (beyond names and some artistic styles), I would argue that human history from the Neolithic Revolution through the Iron Age might all be covered through the playing of this "game." (Teachers would have to augment the experience with specific knowledge about actual historical events, persons, and places as far as those facts were deemed necessary.)

One other example of an open outcome exercise might be necessary to demonstrate a more specific historical era. The software I have used is from a series of computer games called *Uncharted Waters*. The players begin as Spanish ship captains in the late fifteenth century, with tiny boats, some goods for trade, and a small crew. The software keeps track of dozens of ports around Europe and the world, including what commodities are for sale and the going prices. These prices fluctuate with the sales or purchases of the players in a simple but convincing demonstration of supply and demand. Political tensions between Spain, Portugal, and other nations would factor in at given times, as would the behavior of the players themselves. (Attacking those Turkish ships off the coast of Egypt could result in an embargo against the crew in need of supplies, upon reaching Azov!) There are also variables such as wind and water currents (changing by the seasons), storms, roaming merchants and rogues.

Again, my students work in teams as the crew, collectively making decisions. Although this is again an example of culture, group dynamics is not a component of the exercise. Instead, I give different students a variety of tasks and responsibilities within the game. The objective, however, is to experience the political and economic ramifications of the crew's actions and ultimately to explore the seas. This is always a fascinating element of the exercise: twentieth-first-century students, unlike their fifteenth-century counterparts, *know* that the Americas were there. When they set out to find the New World, they have no fear whatsoever of falling off the edge of the planet. Nonetheless, they generally underestimate the time it will take to cross the Atlantic so they begin the voyage undersupplied and undermanned. While the mariners of the 1400s and 1500s would have known to follow the currents along the coast of Africa and across to the Caribbean, my students generally head straight out of Lisbon or London for Virginia or Massachusetts. What happens when the food and water run out? Some members of the group urge a return to Europe—hoping to reach port in time to save some of the crew. Other students prefer to press on, certain that the verdant shores of Rhode Island lie just beyond the next horizon. Some groups manage to find land—in Nova Scotia! No ports beckon to them and no merchants rush to the shore to trade them exotic goods for the return voyage. While some groups are wise enough to protect themselves with technology such as sextants (for

latitude and longitude readings) and telescopes (which make any port on the screen pop up instantly), even these magical instruments failed to make fifteenth-century Maine the El Dorado of most groups' dreams.

Once again, if played to the end, the game could take hundreds of hours, but there was never time in class for more than five. Nonetheless, those hours were enough for students to learn about important economic elements such as supply, demand, scarcity, and opportunity costs. Geography and political machinations served as a backdrop to student exploration and the acquisition of crucial navigation tools. Different students were responsible for keeping track of the journey (creating a narrative "Captain's Log"), charts of sea and wind currents, tables of prices in various ports, and the ship's stores. For advanced classes, these activities could be accelerated to meet more rigorous expectations. What is crucial in these situations, however, is the experience of the students in the shoes and robes of their forebears. Like so much in education, the journey is the greater reward than the destination.

Both these simulations were computer-generated using commercial software. Because open outcome simulations require a great deal of depth to provide the limitless choices, they would be very difficult for teachers to create on their own. A modified version, which, for example, eliminated all the variables of *Uncharted Waters* except for the supply and demand component, might be relatively easy to employ with paper and pencil. At this point, however, students might have in fact created a fixed outcome scenario.

Simulations of the fixed type are designed with fewer variables and probably an ending that is a teaching point. One example is my Food Game Number One. In this simulation, students are broken up into five groups representing two farming communities, two sets of pastoralists, and a group of nomadic hunter-gatherers. The students in each group must allocate the various food-generating options available to them among their 100 citizens. They are required to use all the options but the emphasis is up to them. By trial and error, the groups eventually find the foods with the highest ratios of labor-to-return and then put as many people as possible into the high-return areas. Groups are rewarded at various benchmarks with increased population and technological innovations that will enable them to produce more food. The final requirement is that groups create line graphs of their population and food production. The resulting graphs are immediately recognizable as the demographic destinies of these three life patterns. Students quickly grasp the simple mathematical facts of rapid growth in farming communities versus pastoralists and especially nomads. The inevitable connections between food and population quickly become apparent to students. On to the next question: why don't the nomads take up farming? Descriptions of the various communities make it clear that farming is not an option in the forests where the nomads dwell; if they want a more sedentary lifestyle, they will have to migrate to more suitable lands. Who occupies those lands? Farmers. The game may be only a few rounds old, but already the farmers will have a numerical and technological edge over the invaders. The farmers' greater population seems obvious, but why would they have more technology?

Clearly, critical thinking quickly becomes a fundamental component of any decent simulation. Fixed outcome scenarios such as the Food Games (another version deals with the Columbian Exchange) are designed to demonstrate a principle that students' choices will not enable them to confound. Although they lack the awe-power of open outcome exercises, these fixed outcome simulations are both easier for teachers to create and less time-consuming in the classroom. They therefore are better suited to demonstrating specific concepts that students need to grasp. Most world history teachers are probably familiar with simulations involving the European plague, the Great Depression, and so on. Some of these exercises take less than a full class period, making them especially useful for teachers on block schedules.

Tailor-Made for Your Class

The final point worth discussing briefly is a quick primer on how teachers create fixed simulations for their own use. As noted above, open outcome exercises are too extensive for most teachers to have time to create themselves. There are, of course, a number of products available from the usual social studies supply sources, but cost, age appropriateness, and content might then become issues. How then to make one of your own?

The first step is to reflect on what the point or concept is that you want to get across. Do you want your students to understand how Siam was able to remain independent while all the rest of Southeast Asia was colonized? Are you hoping to have students comprehend how peoples of Southeast Asia might have converted to different religions over the centuries?

In the first case, the outcome is the independence of Siam, which could be represented by some students in the class while others portray the colonizers or other colonized peoples. Another option would be for the Siamese to remain unrepresented while groups of students representing other countries try to decide what courses of action they wish to take regarding its status. Either situation may require several rounds of conquest or decision-making as the process leading up to the decision of what to do with Siam. Students' choices would foster both competition and fear among the groups representing the various factions, again enabling the students to think *like* actual historical persons. Variables such as economics or individual leaders' charisma could be quantified and made a part of the exercise. The variables

would have to be designed by the instructor to ensure that the independence of the Siamese made the most sense to the various groups, but the simulation as a whole would then demonstrate why the actual nineteenth-century relationship between the various nations played out the way it did.

The case of Southeast Asia's changing religions represents a slightly more difficult task to quantify. Obviously, many converts to a religion undertake the transition because of the powerful call of the divine they hear in its teachings. Others, however, might convert for financial, legal, or status reasons. These latter issues can be quantified much easier than the spiritual attraction so by necessity they would have to become the focus of the exercise. Student groups would represent various Southeast Asian peoples, from the Khmer to the Mon or the Javanese and the Malay. The exercise could also be designed using fictitious religions in any part of the world. This approach might prove useful because it would prevent students from acting on preconceived notions about actual religions that might color their decision-making during the scenario.

Perhaps each team of students could aim to achieve a certain total number of points. Points are earned through increasing population (especially through conquest or hegemonic empire) and the worth of trade goods passing through the realm. Points might also be awarded for allying with more powerful nations, as well as for improving architecture in the kingdom. Each group will start out as polytheists and attempt to earn points through trade with one another or conquest. (Rolling dice might determine the outcome of these endeavors.) One by one, the world's great religions could enter the region. "Duinhism" could offer more opportunities for trade with a faraway land (not represented by a student group), as well as artistic inspiration and increased status for the ruler. These advantages might be reflected in bonus points won by this nation in dice rolls against other nations. Several rounds later, "Ubhudism" might be introduced from outside the region, again offering trade and status bonuses. A spirit of unity in the faith might help the people coalesce around its message and increase the nation-building force of the citizenry (i.e., more bonuses on the dice). Several more rounds pass before "Samali-ism" enters the region. Trade benefits are going to be huge. Soon after, an invading force takes over much of the region, bringing a fourth option, "Stricianity." By converting to this faith, nations might gain some points back from the conquerors in hopes of attaining independence. Will all groups convert? What will motivate them? Which options will be most attractive, and why?

The devil is truly in the details when it comes to simulations. How many points each of the various characteristics above is worth, how many groups there should be, and how many religions enter into the picture are all variables that the teacher needs to work out. Initially, creating simulations sounds like a lot of work, and it generally is. Where the benefit should outpace the investment of time, however, is in increased student understanding, critical thinking ability, and empathy for historical persons and situations. A number of simulations done throughout the school year should give students the skills and habits to unlock other historical case studies without having to engage in full-blown simulation activities.

Conclusion

In short, then, what society is going to need from history teachers in the future is a steady stream of students who can think critically and comprehend the human condition. History is full of the twists and turns brought about by technology—our age is but one example. In the future, however, technology is increasingly going to replace human busy work, including simple memorization of facts, leaving open the door for greater understanding and cognitive processing of the past and present. Simulations are among the best options teachers have for fostering these skills and habits of mind in their students. Through simulations, students can not only learn about, but also experience the issues dealt with by their ancestors and the ancestors of those who share this earth with them. Hopefully, this understanding and empathy will enable them to not repeat those mistakes of the past.

About the Author

Dave Clarke teaches Advanced Placement World History and a pre–advanced placement skills course at a public high school in suburban Milwaukee, Wisconsin. He is a National Boards Certified Educator with a Master's in history at the University of Wisconsin–Milwaukee.

CHAPTER 15

Improving Student Writing With Annotated Rubrics

BILL STRICKLAND

Be More Specific

It was Sunday night and I was grading yet another student's history essay that used nothing but vague generalities without a single, specific example that the class had supposedly learned while studying that unit. I wrote "Be more specific" in the margin, listed a few examples of the historical events that the student *should* have given as evidence, and gave the essay an appropriately low score. Sighing, I started the next essay and experienced the same frustration and disappointment yet again.

After I finished the class set, I realized that I had written the same advice on the same students' essays *all year long.* "Didn't these students ever make an effort to improve?" I wondered. Surely they did not like earning the same low score on their essays time after time. Why were they not using the feedback I gave them after every unit test to improve their next essay's attempt? I confidently blamed the students and attributed their low performance to factors beyond my control.

Certainly there is much truth in this diagnosis. After all, too many students simply make no effort to improve. They thoroughly deserve a mediocre grade. But after a few years of frustration, it occurred to me that while blaming the student works for many essays, it comes nowhere near explaining *all* of the lack of improvement by *all* students. Somewhere along the way I asked myself a dangerous question: "Are there any students who *are* making an honest effort to improve, but I am not doing enough to help? Could it just be possible that I am, however unintentionally, part of the problem?"

Perhaps I needed to be more specific than writing "Be more specific" on my students' essays? Great. That just put the blame back in my own lap. How could I possibly be specific enough for *every* student to be able to improve their writing for *every* question I *ever* as-

sign without driving myself crazy grading essays every waking hour?

So I went back to writing "Be more specific" on my students' essays for several more years. I consoled myself with the thought that this was as good as I do for my students, but I never lost the vague feeling that there must be a better way to teach essay-writing that would actually help a higher percentage of students.

A Vision of Something Better

In 2001, I began teaching the new Advanced Placement (AP[1]) World History course designed by the College Board. In 2004, I became an Exam Reader for the AP World History essays. Spending a week reading hundreds of essays may not sound like an enjoyable undertaking, but it was a truly enlightening experience. The College Board thoroughly trained Exam Readers in the proper way to consistently score essays according to an AP World History–specific rubric. There were three types of essay questions.[2] Each rubric contained five or six characteristics, depending on the type of question. Some of the characteristics were relatively easy to evaluate, while others were much more difficult because the difference between an acceptable and an unacceptable answer was subtle and easy to misinterpret. For those rubric categories, the official in charge of the essay reading distributed to the Readers sample essays that included scoring annotations in the margin. These annotated sample essays greatly helped, as Exam Readers could instantly see *which* specific sentences in the essay satisfied which rubric points. I began to wonder whether this valuable feedback of "how Exam Readers think" was ever reaching students and teachers in the classroom. AP students receive a final score with their overall grade, but no detailed information regarding each essay's score or which rubric categories they successfully fulfilled.[3]

Figure 15.1   **Annotated Rubric Sample**

Question: Compare the political and religious characteristics of ancient Egypt and Mesopotamia.	
Generic description with explanation and commentary	**Examples with explanation and scoring commentary**
Has an acceptable thesis *Addresses the issues or themes indicated in the question.* *Cannot merely restate the question.* *Must include BOTH a similarity AND a difference relevant to the question.*	**Unacceptable** There were many similarities and differences between the Egyptian and Mesopotamian civilizations. *This is too vague and merely repeats the question.* **Acceptable** Egypt and Mesopotamia were politically different but religiously similar. *This gives a minimal categorization to the thesis.* **Excellent** Although Egypt's political structure was more centralized than Mesopotamia's city-states, both Mesopotamian and Egyptian religion were influenced by the natural rhythms of their environment.

In the weeks following my reading experience, I realized that what students needed was sentence-by-sentence feedback on their writing. There was obviously no way I could provide that degree of feedback, but the College Board's AP Central website contained all the pieces of information that students needed:

1. an essay rubric;
2. a sample essay; and
3. commentary on which rubric points the essay earned or failed to earn.

Unfortunately, the pieces were scattered in separate files. What I needed to do was merge pieces of the scattered files into a single file. I called this creation an annotated rubric and used it the next year with my students.

An Annotated Rubric

Above is a sample of an annotated rubric (Figure 15.1):[4]

An annotated rubric will have certain elements (Figure 15.2). It is imperative that an annotated rubric contains these elements for *each* rubric category: Instructors should *not* summarize *all* commentary for *all* rubric categories at the end of the whole essay or students will not specifically apply each individual comment to the appropriate sentence in the essay.

So how does a teacher create such a resource?

Step 1: Create the rubric categories.

I have not found any universally accepted consensus for what is the "best" rubric. You will have to determine what characteristics you feel are important. One of the fundamental questions you need to decide is how much you will value historical content as opposed to formal characteristics such as spelling, punctuation, choice of vocabulary, organization, and footnotes. Below are listed several websites offering various rubrics that may guide your decision:

College Board AP World History Course Description (essay rubrics explained on pp. 31–45)
http://apcentral.collegeboard.com/apc/public/repository/ap-world-history-course-description.pdf

SAT Scoring Guide
www.collegeboard.com/student/testing/sat/about/sat/essay_scoring.html

Detailed Rubric/Checklist for History Essays (adapted from a rubric by Richard Weeks, professor of history, West Virginia Wesleyan College)
http://faculty.chass.ncsu.edu/slatta/hi216/

Figure 15.2   **Annotated Rubric Elements**

Rubric category and description	Examples of students' responses	Instructor's comment and explanation of score

Holistic Critical Thinking Rubric, by Peter A. Facione and Noreen C. Facione
www.insightassessment.com/pdf_files/Rubric%20 HCTSR.pdf

History Essay Rubric, John I. Brooks III
http://faculty.uncfsu.edu/jibrooks/FRMS/rubricessay .htm

Rubrician.com (provides links to rubrics)
www.rubrician.com/socialstudies.htm

Rubrics for Assessment (K–12 rubrics from University of Wisconsin–Stout School of Education)
www.uwstout.edu/soe/profdev/rubrics.shtml

English Essay Rubric (from University of Nebraska–Kearney)
www.unk.edu/academicaffairs/assessment/index .php?id=4897

Authentic Assessment Toolbox, by Jon Mueller (general advice for designing rubrics)
http://jonathan.mueller.faculty.noctrl.edu/toolbox /rubrics.htm

Step 2: Describe the standard by which an acceptable answer is determined.

Rather than simply instruct students to write an "acceptable" thesis, describe what characteristics make a thesis acceptable. (Does it have to address all components of the question? Does it have to be in the first paragraph?) Then complete these descriptions for all rubric categories created in Step 1.

Step 3: Give students realistic examples of an unsatisfactory, a satisfactory, and an excellent response for each rubric category.

Step 4: Give feedback for example responses in Step 3, explaining why each response earned or failed to earn the rubric point.

By the time all these elements are combined, each rubric category usually fills one page of paper, occasionally even more. The end result is a document several pages long that gives students detailed instructions on what their essay should look like.

Results of Using an Annotated Rubric

I used an annotated rubric with my students beginning in the 2004–2005 academic year. The results astounded me. Not only did my students' writing dramatically improve, but also it was my struggling students' writing that improved

the most. For years I had photocopied sample essays and critiqued them with my students. Only after I had created an annotated rubric did I realize how an annotated rubric helped students more than the traditional method of photocopying an entire essay:

Benefit 1: A spectrum of answers for each rubric category encourages students to incrementally improve their writing, rather than overwhelming them with entire sample essays with superlative writing characteristics.

Breaking an entire essay into rubric categories demystifies essay writing for students. Giving examples of attempts at each rubric category allows students to pick their own target for improvement. Poor students will concentrate their efforts at improving to an "acceptable" level, while students already writing at that level will focus on reaching the "excellent" level. Most students recognize their own level of writing ability and can set a realistic goal for themselves far better than I can.

Merely photocopying an excellent essay and showing it to the entire class is inadequate for this purpose. When poor writers see an entire essay brimming with superlative characteristics, they simply give up. "There's no way I can write that entire essay that well!" they say to themselves. By examining examples of individual sentences along the entire spectrum of quality, students can aim for incremental improvement and can focus their effort on a specific sentence. Entire essays can (and should) be used to model writing, but in my experience that technique works far better only after students have seen examples of individual sentence-by-sentence responses.

Benefit 2: An annotated rubric allows students to concentrate on preventing rather than breaking bad writing habits.

Rather than having to *unteach* bad writing habits, the annotated rubric *prevents* students from developing those bad habits in the first place. When I use an annotated rubric for the first time, I put several sample sentences on the board and ask students to rank them from worst to best.[5] Then I ask them to draw a line separating the acceptable statements from unacceptable ones. The trick is that *none* of the samples is acceptable. Students quickly see that quality writing is a challenging task and that lengthy fluff written on the page will count for nothing.

Benefit 3: The annotated rubric encourages students to think before writing because they can easily imagine how their reader or instructor will respond.

With apologies to Sun Tzu, I believe that "every essay is won before it is written." My experience as a classroom teacher and AP Exam Reader has convinced me that the vast majority of high-quality essays are well planned before the student begins writing. Students who have seen several annotated rubrics are likely to carefully plan their essay before they start writing the first sentence.[6]

Benefit 4: An annotated rubric can be used for multiple student learning styles.

Every teacher struggles with the question of how to balance the need for specific factual content versus transferable cognitive skills. The annotated rubric is ambidextrous is this respect. Students who think deductively (or "top-down") can read the annotated rubric beginning with the rubric category, and then move down to the more specific example. Students who think inductively (or "bottom-up") can start with the example and conceptually move up to the rubric category. The annotated rubric acts as a bridge between where students are now and where they should be, but students can cross the bridge beginning at either end, depending on their own learning style.

Benefit 5: An annotated rubric can enhance students' creativity.

Many students think that there is only one way to answer an essay question correctly and that any other response is wrong. Giving several examples of unacceptable, acceptable, and superlative writing helps break this binary mode of thinking. One of the potential weaknesses of an annotated rubric is that students might try to reflexively copy an example of acceptable writing. Showing multiple examples minimizes students' temptation to write essays according to any simple formula.

Conclusion

Although an annotated rubric will not make up for illogical thinking or lack of honest effort, it will help students to focus their efforts for maximum improvement. I hope it helps your students to think more clearly and write better essays and that it helps you to enjoy grading their writing more.

About the Author

Bill Strickland has taught at East Grand Rapids High School since 1997 and AP World History since the course began in 2001. A College Board consultant, he has led AP workshops and Summer Institutes since 2006 and served as an AP World History Exam Reader, table leader, and sample selector since 2004. He has authored or edited several ancillary materials for textbooks, contributed articles to *World History Connected*, and in 2007 served on the committee that defined world history and geography standards for Michigan's public high schools. In his free time he enjoys reading Great War histories, listening to Russian symphonies, and embarrassing his children with outrageously goofy puns.

Notes

1. AP is a registered trademark of the College Board, which was not involved in the production of, and does not endorse, this product.

2. A document-based question, a question involving continuity and change over time, and a comparative question. See http://apcentral.collegeboard.com/apc/members/exam/exam_questions/2090.html for more detail.

3. Each September school principals receive an Instructional Planning Report that gives some information about how students scored on each AP subject exam as a whole, but there is no detail for each individual student or each individual essay rubric category. See http://professionals.collegeboard.com/testing/ap/grades/reporting/for-schools for more information.

4. To see examples of the annotated rubrics that I use for my AP World History class, see www.egrps.org/moodle/course/view.php?id=97.

5. This technique courtesy of Angela Lee of Weston High School, Weston, Massachusetts.

6. I once asked a college professor who was also an AP World History Exam Reader to compare the overall quality of the AP World History essays (most of which are written by high school sophomores) to his own students' essays. He stunned me when he declared that AP World History students' writing is generally better quality than his own students' writing. I remarked that I found that extremely difficult to believe. The professor's response was that "the only difference between your students and mine is that mine are two years older."

PART IV

PLANNING

CHAPTER 16

The First-Year World History
Teacher's Survive-and-Thrive Guide

MIKE BURNS

Okay, so your administrator has just informed you that you will be teaching world history or Advanced Placement (AP) World History this school year—which begins next week! Your teacher certification program focused on things such as "methodology" and "assessment" and "classroom management." Your last college history course was The Woodstock Generation and you are thinking one thing: "I'm not qualified to teach this course." Congratulations. You have just joined the great fellowship of new world history teachers who have all felt the same way at some point. But with the right attitude and game plan you will survive . . . and thrive.

The teaching of world history has undergone a tremendous change over the past fifteen years. Many world history classes used to be "the West and the rest" or a series of area studies courses strung together to "cover" the world; some courses centered on a particular theme such as "conflict." Disappearing now are the classes in which the emphasis is on specific dates, individuals, battles, and places. Increasingly, courses are taught by teachers who ask students to compare and contrast different civilizations, to analyze change and continuity over time, to consider events in a truly global context, to deal with primary source documents, to examine and discuss point of view, and to think, write, and speak critically.

At first glance the task seems daunting—teaching about 10,000 years of human history in 180 days or less. Rome was not built in a day, but you might have to cover the 1,000 years of the Roman Empire in less than a week. Quickly disabuse yourself of the notion that you should be able to answer *any* student question related to history. In fact, you can turn this handicap into an asset and forge a bond with your students.

The goal here is to be practical. Time and money are important considerations. To that end, this chapter suggests five things you should do, five things you can read now,

and numerous resources that can help you keep your world history course real, and doable

Five Things You Should Do

Don't Panic!

You are to remain a student along with your students. Experienced history teachers will tell you that the person who has learned the most in their course is . . . themselves. Be up front with your students about this. It is not humanly possible to know everything about human history. Just remember: "Specialists know more and more about less and less until they know everything about nothing." Your job is to help students discover the "big picture."

Make a Calendar

This is especially crucial if you are teaching a course in which there will be an external assessment or in which you absolutely have to cover a certain amount of material. Even if your endpoint is more flexible, you will feel a lot better if you have a game plan and a timetable.

One of the most common questions I see on the AP listserv is: "Where am I supposed to be?" Let us assume that you are expected to "finish" the textbook by the end of the year (or exam date). Your first step is to create a pacing guide. This will go a long way toward reducing your stress level. Make a copy of your school calendar. (I do this on a whiteboard, which allows me to see the whole thing at once.) Calculate the number of teaching days you have based on your schedule. Cross out the days that you know will be lost to state- or district-mandated testing. Cross out any other days that you know in advance will be lost to other school activities. Also, subtract the number of days you anticipate losing for reasons unknown at this time, but that inevitably impact your teaching time: weather, assemblies, athletics, field trips, a school crisis, and so on. The number you have left is what you will plan around. If those interruptions do not materialize, you will always find ways of filling the time; creating more time is the problem.

It is helpful to start at the end and work backward. If there is a final or external exam, begin there. Allow some class sessions for review. If possible, work around school breaks, finishing units prior to a break. Set up units according to the textbook's periodizations:

Foundations–Agricultural	
Civilizations	8000 BCE–500 BCE
Classical Civilizations	500 BCE–600 CE
The Postclassical Era	600–1500
Making of the Modern World	1450–1750
A Long "Revolutionary" Century	1750–1914
The Twentieth + Century	1900–Present

Each periodization might be broken into smaller units, since six-week units can be a bit unwieldy and lose focus over time. For example, the Postclassical Era might include units such as "The Nature of Empires" and "Transitions and Transformations of the Indian Ocean Basin Trade" (please insert your own clever unit titles!).

The calendar is not a rigid timetable that tells you where you *have* to be and when. Rather, it is a map that shows where you *want* to be and when. This way, when you deviate from what you have planned, it is a conscious decision and you can make allowances for it.

Write Enduring Understandings and Essential Questions for Each Unit

If you have read *Understanding by Design* by Jay McTighe and Grant Wiggins, you are already familiar with the concept of Enduring Understandings (EUs) and Essential Questions (EQs). These are at the heart of each unit and should be the first thing you establish as you plan each unit. In essence, you are creating your assessment first. Teaching to the test is not a bad thing, provided that the test is meaningful and is actually assessing what is most important. You want your students to show understanding of what it is that you wanted them to learn.

Use the concept of backward design whenever possible. It will make your teaching a much more deliberate and conscious act.

Identify the key ideas or themes you want students to learn—say, three to five EUs and three to five EQs for each unit. EUs are the big ideas and concepts that you would hope students will recall ten years down the road. You have no real way of assessing these, but they do help you focus on what you feel is most important. What you can assess, however, are the EQs. EQs are those key questions whose answers help students arrive at EUs.

For example, for a unit on the long nineteenth century (1750–1914), you might formulate the following EUs. Start each with the key phrase "Students will understand that . . . " in order to emphasize understanding as opposed to listing skills).

Students will understand that there are various theories regarding the process of industrialization.

Students will understand that there are various interpretations of, and reactions to, colonialism and imperialism.

Students will understand that nationalism has played a key role in the evolution of modern states.

Then, formulate the relevant EQs:

How do nations industrialize?

What are the effects of colonialism and imperialism on both the colonizer and the colonized?

What "creates" a nation?

There does not have to be a one-to-one correlation between EUs and EQs. You might have two or three EQs that address one EU. Warning—more is not necessarily better. You will have to make some hard choices about the key points of emphasis for your unit.

Give Your Students Helpful Feedback

I know, I know: too many students, not enough time to give meaningful feedback. Yet how else will you be able to help your students improve their analytical writing skills? You would not expect your English Department colleagues to demonstrate expertise in a comparative analysis of the social, political, and economic aspects of the Roman Empire and the Han Dynasty any more than they should ask you to assist students in a comparative literary analysis of *Paradise Lost* and *Utopia*.

Professor John Hattie of the University of Auckland (www.det.nsw.edu.au/proflearn/docs/pdf/qt_hattie.pdf) has done extensive research supporting the conclusion that the *most* important factor in student learning is the teacher's feedback. It is more important than the student's prior cognitive ability, more important than class size, more important than homework or testing, more important than the quality of the teacher or the student's motivation to learn. So you need to give your students plenty of feedback by focusing on the skills you want them to develop. If you want students to write better thesis statements, then give them plenty of prompts to do just that.

Students do not need to write an entire essay every time; have them just write a thesis statement. This exercise works well as an entry task after an assigned reading: the statements can be read by you in less than a minute, they are easy to share with the class, and they are easy to critique.

Use rubrics. Decide what you want to emphasize and use rubrics. Collect exemplars to show students what good writing looks like. The College Board website lists the rubrics used on the AP exam along with exemplars as one resource. Rubistar.com is another resource available to you. Using rubrics makes evaluation easier because they allow students to know specifically what it is they need to do. And besides content you can also include conventions (spelling, grammar, etc.) as one of your categories. For a more detailed treatment, please read Bill Strickland's article on writing with annotated rubrics in this book.

Use groups to evaluate. After establishing the rubric and walking through the criteria necessary to meet a rubric point, allow groups of students to evaluate each other's essays. Designate one person to be the thesis checker, another to be the point-of-view analyst, a third to be the supporting-argument fact checker, and so on. The students read all the essays in their group, focusing on their specific task. Students are thus exposed to a variety of essays; they can see what their peers have done; they have to read and evaluate critically. Tasks can be rotated for each assignment. You can tailor the groups to meet specific needs; for example, sometimes making sure a strong writer is in each group, sometimes putting the strongest writers in the same group.

The College Board website has all the essay prompts from previous years' exams (www.collegeboard.com). Teachers must be registered on the College Board website to access this information. Another useful resource is the DBQ Project website (www.dbqproject.com). Using document-based questions is an excellent way to help students improve their critical thinking, reading, and writing skills. Students get better at writing only by writing more and getting feedback on their efforts.

Join Professional Organizations

Every world history teacher should be a member of the World History Association (www.thewha.org), which provides scholarly articles on developments in the world history field. If you teach AP World History, you should also join the AP World History listerv (http://professionals .collegeboard.com/prof-dev). Both groups provide lively discussion and a great deal of help for new and veteran world history teachers. This is a very active, helpful, and vocal online community.

Five Things You Can Read Now

Finding time to read is nigh impossible, I know. Here are five mostly short books that can provide grounding in world history along with ideas about how you might structure and teach your course.

This Fleeting World by David Christian (105 pages). Christian is one of the prominent voices of "big history." Be sure to read the preface, "A Teaching Tool for World History Teachers," by Bob Bain and Lauren McArthur Harris of the University of Michigan. Christian breaks this "short history of humanity" into three chapters: The Era of Foragers, The Agricultural Era, and The Modern Era.

What Is Global History? by Pamela Kyle Crossley (120 pages). Crossley addresses four key concepts in world history: divergence, convergence, contagion, and systems.

The Origins of the Modern World: A Global and Ecological Narrative from the Fifteenth to the Twenty-first Century by Robert Marks (208 pages). Marks provides one possible narrative for the modern world in the following chapters:

> The Rise of the West?
> The Material and Trading Worlds, c. 1400
> Starting with China, Empires, States, and the New World, 1500–1775
> The Industrial Revolution and Its Consequences, 1750–1850
> The Gap
> The Great Departure
> Changes and Continuities

World-Systems Analysis: An Introduction by Immanuel Wallerstein (109 pages). This is clearly the most difficult read of the group, and also on a topic many people know little about. Wallerstein discusses the structure on which the "world-system" is based, how it works, and where it is headed. It is not a theory, but rather an approach or framework for viewing economic development, social change, and analysis, albeit from a post-Marxist viewpoint. The book contains the following chapters:

> Historical Origins of World-Systems Analysis
> The Modern World-System as a Capitalist World-Economy
> The Rise of the States-System
> The Creation of Geoculture
> The Modern World-System in Crisis

The World Trade Created: Society, Culture and the World Economy, 1400 to the Present by Kenneth Pomeranz and Steven Topik (287 pages). Pomeranz and Topik have written a highly informative and accessible book. There are seven sections, each made up of short two- to three-page essays on a particular topic. For example, the section "The Economic Culture of Drugs" contains essays on chocolate, coffee, mocha, tea, sugar, opium, tobacco, and coca. These are interesting stories to share with students, easily accessible, and a great resource for jigsaw lessons.

Other Helpful Resources

The textbook is *not* the curriculum. It is but one resource. You need other resources as well—books and websites. Some are free, some inexpensive, and some are great to have if you have the budget to purchase them.

The Human Web by John McNeill and William McNeill

Maps of Time by David Christian

Big History by Cynthia Stokes Brown

Bring History Alive! A Sourcebook for Teaching World History by Ross Dunn, one of the progenitors of the World History for Us All project.

Navigating World History: Historians Create a Global Past by Patrick Manning

Historical Thinking and Other Unnatural Acts: Charting the Future of Teaching the Past by Sam Wineberg

The following five books offer excellent reading on fairly unfamiliar topics:
The Mongols: *Genghis Khan and the Making of the Modern World* by Jack Weatherford
Why the Columbian Exchange was so one-sided: *Guns, Germs, and Steel* by Jared Diamond
The environmental impact of Native American culture before Columbus: *1491* by Charles Mann
Modern Africa: *The Fate of Africa* by Martin Meredith
The Belgian Congo: *King Leopold's Ghost* by Adam Hochschild

World History Connected (http://worldhistoryconnected .press.uiuc.edu/index.html). This e-journal is rich in content, especially practical ideas for use in the classroom.

World History for Us All (WHFUA, http://world historyforusall.sdsu.edu). WHFUA is a web-based curriculum designed by San Diego State University and The National Center for History in the Schools at UCLA. It is indispensable and it is free. From the website: "This web-based curriculum has two major elements: (1) a logical conceptual framework of guiding ideas, objectives, rationales, themes, and historical periods, and (2) a rich selection of units, lessons, activities, primary documents, and resources that are linked to this overarching conceptual structure." The curriculum addresses recognized national standards and addresses key themes of history. The WHFUA site is a work in progress. There are nine big eras, plus prehistory and "the Future" units. Most of the early time periods (Eras 1–6) are complete; the more recent eras are still being developed as of this writing. Units come online as they are completed.

Bridging World History (www.learner.org/channel /courses/worldhistory). This is a free, twenty-six-episode, theme-based series. Topics include Human Migrations, Early Economies, Connections across Water, Ideas Shape the World, etc. The series is available for purchase or for free as video on demand. If used as VOD, it has to be streamed via the Internet and cannot be saved or downloaded. There are resource materials available online. Each episode runs thirty minutes and is broken down into three segments, aimed at a high school or college audience, and can be used in middle school in selective doses and with more teacher guidance. This site is a wonderful resource from the Annenberg Foundation, both for instruction and professional development and across the curriculum.

The Teaching Company: A Brief History of the World (www.teach12.com). This series of thirty-six lectures by Dr. Peter Stearns provides an eighteen-hour overview of the key themes and ideas in world history. It closely parallels his *World Civilizations* textbook, a commonly used book in AP world history. This course is available either on DVD or as an audio download for either MP3 players or iPods. Every course in The Teaching Company catalog goes on sale at least once a year, but usually more frequently. Many other interesting courses are available. Transcripts and a study guide are available as well. This would be an invaluable asset for both new and experienced world history teachers.

Teacher's Curriculum Institute (www.teachtci.com). There are some very interesting, useful, academic and student-centered units here. Students enjoy the activities and role-playing, but there is depth and structure to make it worthwhile.

College Board (http://store.collegeboard.com). This is a good source for world history units geared to AP world history.

Social Studies (www.socialstudies.com). The website's catalog lists many units that are very useful for developing analytical skills. Particularly, the Mindsparks collection puts the students into the role of historian, analyzing sources, debating points of view, and writing essays to support their findings. For example, "Africa's Slaves" looks at both the Atlantic slave trade and the often-overlooked East African slave trade; another unit looks at the impact of the printing press on both China and Europe.

Choices (www.choices.edu/). The Choices program from Brown University develops curriculum on foreign policy and international issues.

CNN: Millennium. This VHS is out of print, but copies surface from time to time. This is a ten-episode look at the last thousand years, appropriate for middle and high school use. Each episode centers on a century and a theme—for example, "The Century of the Stirrup." Each episode runs forty-five minutes and consists of five segments. The companion website (www.cnn.com/SPECIALS/1999 /millennium) contains study guides, focus questions, and other activities.

The New York State Education Department (www.nysed .gov) has many resources available to prepare students for the Regents exam. No reason you cannot use them as you see fit!

This is an exciting time to be a world history teacher, and there is a veritable banquet of information and resources available. You need to remember not to put too much on your plate at one time, to take small bites and chew well to aid in your digestion; you can always come back for more. It is obviously necessary to begin with what you know, but you must also be willing to extend yourself, to consider various points of view, to be willing not only to try new things, but also to refine them if they do not initially go as you had planned. Remember, always take a towel, and don't panic!

About the Author

Mike Burns (BA, Communications, Liberal Arts) has been teaching internationally since 2002, moving to Concordia International School in Shanghai beginning the 2009–2010 school year. Previous assignments have been at Shekou International School in Shenzhen, China, the American School of Doha in Qatar, and the Peninsula School District in Gig Harbor, Washington. He has taught AP World History since 2001 and is a reader of AP World History exams.

CHAPTER 17

Time Management and Student Ownership

How to Get Through Your Curriculum in the Time Allotted

CHRIS PEEK AND ANGELA WAINRIGHT

Why is it that some teachers can cover all the important content in the courses they teach within the time allotted and others cannot? The distinction seems to rest on the teachers' belief that they must be experts on all facets of their subject. Teachers believe that they must cover the entire curriculum and thus they fail at completing the task. Teachers need to remember that the reason they love social studies is the joy of discovery, which is what keeps them passionate about the subject. Teachers need to consistently share that feeling of discovery with their students, making them active learners. Telling a student "I don't know" is a great teachable moment. It lets the students know that history is not a finite subject and that there is always more to learn. Teachers will never know all there is to know about their subject, so they should not bother trying. What they need to do is to find a way to let the students get the most from the course in the time allotted. The issue is how to go about doing this.

As more constraints are added to a teacher's time each year, meeting course curriculum requirements becomes increasingly difficult. The following suggestions will help teachers create the time they need to cover the material effectively without worrying that they have missed something, even when they do. These suggestions also allow students to leave a course with the confidence that they can handle any assessment or related course in the future, while allowing the teacher time for a life outside the classroom.

One valuable way to accomplish your goals is to collaborate with another teacher who has a similar set of goals. Most teachers work in a school big enough to have more than one teacher teaching the same subject. If not, other social studies teachers have probably taught your subject in the past and can be most helpful. Collaboration will help you feel more competent in areas in which you do not have extensive knowledge, collaboration will cut your workload by allowing you to delegate responsibilities, and collaboration will produce higher-quality end products. For instance, when making up a new test, each teacher on the collaborative team can be responsible for questions on certain topics; that way the burdensome task of developing good test questions does not fall entirely on one person. Collaboration will especially aid you in deciding what is important when focusing on the big picture.

Teachers need to realize that they can also collaborate with their school's other professionals, such as the librarian and media specialist. That does not mean just consulting with them; most will come to classrooms and teach the particular task in which they specialize. The time of teachers autonomously teaching in their classrooms is at an end.

If you do not have a support system in your school, you need to focus on what you can do to streamline the work for yourself. Taking care of yourself is key to being a positive force in the classroom every day. Students enjoy classes taught by teachers who love what they do, show that they continue to learn, and enjoy sharing what they have learned. If you continue to pursue what you love, your enthusiasm will transfer to the students. Taking care of yourself means making sure that you do not take on more than you can handle. There are certain ways to accomplish this; planning effective lessons to reach students with multiple learning styles and grading efficiently are two important skills that take time initially but ease your workload in the long run.

I have a colleague who plans his lessons in the shower on the morning he is presenting them. He then rushes around school for an hour before the students arrive, throwing together whatever materials are at hand, many of them substandard. He then spends more time in class explaining what students are to do with these last-minute activities, causing more stress that could have been avoided with some planning.

Many teachers tend to rely on lectures and worksheets provided as ancillary materials. Also, videos and movies are often overused and tend to take more time than they are worth. Admittedly, some videos are well worth showing in their entirety; however, most are definitely not. So how do you get around these pitfalls? Learn how to effectively use the technology of PowerPoint or Flash Maker to merge your lecture with short embedded video clips (no longer than three minutes each). Someone with minimal technological skills can learn how to use PowerPoint in a few hours. Teachers who are more technologically challenged can take classes offered by school districts or get help from the school technologist. PowerPoint has gained a bad reputation from commonly being overdone and misused; however, when used correctly it is a major time-saver that can engage students far more than a traditional teacher lecturing. The problem with the traditional lecture is that it reaches only the auditory learner. A well-done PowerPoint will engage the auditory learner with sound, the visual learner with pictures and video, and the kinesthetic learner will take notes and do embedded tasks during the lesson.

It takes Ms. Jones longer to teach
World War II than it took to fight it.

"Time bandits" are those favored topics that are given more time than they warrant. Letting go of those lessons will free up time to devote to a more balanced curriculum. These time bandits are often the topics that either the instructor or the students find most interesting. Why are they interesting to the students? Because the teacher is excited about teaching those topics. Ultimately, however, the student loses out when other topics are lost to these time bandits. In secondary history class some of the most common time bandits are ancient Egypt, ancient Greece and Rome, medieval Europe, the Renaissance and Reformation, the French Revolution, the Great Depression in the United States, and World War II. In our world history course most of these topics are covered in two to three days plus an outside student reading instead of the week or more that each topic could easily steal from the course. It is fairly common for teachers to finish the school year no farther along than World War II; this is a disservice to the student.

When studying the Civil War in U.S. History,
I had to memorize fifty battles, the generals
on each side, and the outcome of each;
do I remember any of that now? No.

Focusing on the big picture means that causes, effects, and analysis are more important than memorizing trivial facts. Too many students, reflecting back on history class, see it merely as systematic memorization of dates and names without express purpose. Students get the wrong idea about what history is really about and thus begin to avoid history.

By remaining focused on the big picture, the teacher can easily get to those topics that might otherwise be dropped from the curriculum due to a lack of time or knowledge. The topics most commonly neglected by stressed teachers include India, sub-Saharan Africa, Southeast Asia, Latin America, environmental history, Ethiopia and East Africa (600–1750), imperialism in the Middle East, the fall of communism, globalization, and ideologies of the twentieth century. As mentioned earlier, teachers should not be afraid to teach outside their comfort zone. Although it is common in college to specialize in a historic period, it is becoming more common and more acceptable to be a generalist. High school teachers who see themselves as generalists will better serve their students and will be more willing to give up those time-bandit habits, discussed earlier, in favor of a more balanced curriculum.

A final goal that will help teachers get through the curriculum is to get the students to buy into the course and see that ownership of their learning will enhance their classroom experience. An important way to make sure this happens is to devise assignments that force the students to manage their time in a way that effectively helps the teacher cover the material. Repetitive assignments that can be adapted to different time periods and used consistently during the year can help a student focus on curriculum rather than on shifting assignment types. This allows students to improve the skills being emphasized by reflecting on past assignments. Also, by doing the same types of assignments, students build confidence as they see their success increase during the year. This keeps the students focused on the big picture of learning the material and not the memorization of trivialities. Most tasks should be cumulative in some way; if students know that what they are doing is going to lead them to a task focusing on the big picture, then they will make those connections in their head during the unit in anticipation of the final task.

Some small tasks to get the students started toward the big picture are weekly reading quizzes and discussion. The point of weekly reading quizzes is to make sure that the students comprehend those aspects of the topic that you do not cover in class. To effectively do this takes long-term planning. You need to dissect the textbook into its topics. Pay special attention to topics that you will not cover in class and topics that you are not comfortable that you will cover effectively. Give the students reading assignments averaging twenty pages a week (we do this six weeks at a time). Then consistently quiz the students on these reading assignments; for example, each Friday give an oral quiz that consists of five questions and a bonus question. When making up questions, remember to focus on the big picture and not trivialities. Never ask dates or names unless they are milestones. Give a different quiz to each class you teach. Assuming you teach five classes, you need twenty-five questions (plus five bonus questions) covering each reading assignment. If you work with a collaborative team, this is a good place to divide up the responsibility. Do not be shocked when the quiz grades start very low. This is one of those repetitive assignments for which students figure out how to prepare more effectively as time progresses. If you allow students to bring in handwritten notes, limit the notes so the students learn to take effective notes instead of merely copying from the textbook.

It is also important to get students to analyze primary sources and other scholarly works. This is a life skill that will be valuable in later academic and professional environments. To do this effectively, use guided discussion. Assign articles to the student ahead of time, usually in packets that contain three to eight readings on a topic. Include activities and questions to guide the students toward the big picture. Allow several days for the students to read the articles. Then dedicate one class period to the discussion of the articles; this is the basis for most of the class participation grade. These discussions can be teacher-led or student-led (like Socratic seminars or inner-outer circles). Students are responsible for their own participation in the discussion. It is not the teacher's responsibility to call out students who have not read the materials; this will be evident in their cumulative participation grade. Obviously, many other types of assignments, such as student-created graphic organizers, can get the students thinking about the major themes, but we think that the two discussed here are among the most useful: "snapshots" and "mental maps."

At the end of each unit, assign a task that forces the student to put all the pieces together and create a finished product that is comprehensive as well as a good short-term and long-term study tool. Two assignments that have gained positive feedback from the students are period snapshots and mental maps. Period snapshots allow students to take a look at various empires or regions and compare them socially, politically, economically, and culturally. For instance, for a comparison of the Han, Roman, Persian, and Gupta/Mauryan empires, students take detailed notes on the *s*ocial, *p*olitical, *e*conomic, and *c*ultural (SPEC) aspects of these societies and then come up with main-idea sentences encompassing the notes for each category. In essence, the student is preparing for an objective and subjective assessment.

Mental maps are another comprehensive assignment. Students can complete this task in various ways that suit their individual learning style. To create a mental map, the student takes visual notes on a map background. The focus of the map is connections between societies (both positive and negative) across space and time. Using a given reading assignment, the student transfers the information onto the map in a series of drawings, symbols (necessitating a key), and text boxes. This assignment is especially good for learning trade patterns, interaction between humans and the environment, and cultural diffusion. The students should not focus on SPEC issues on this assignment.

Many teachers find research papers a daunting task, but it is imperative that you assign at least one during the allotted time of the course. First a teacher must design a list of thesis-directed prompts that are appropriate to the course. Student choice is essential to get buy-in on a topic that interests the learner. Students, however, cannot have total freedom; that would result in hundreds of papers about the history of rock and roll or the civil rights movement. Topics should be ones that will not be covered in class until after the due date of the paper; it's no good having the teacher lesson parroted back. Then the focus should be not the length of the paper, but the quality and the skills mastered. A three- to four-page paper is an appropriate length for a high school student.

The teacher must then clearly explain what the parameters of the end product will be. This takes time away from teaching content; but the teacher will find that the writing the students are prepared to do is usually not what is desired in a finished historical research paper and the students writing must be shaped to be more analytical, critical, and persuasive. Include a detailed grading rubric when you assign the task. Students who know up front what their grade will be based on will write a paper toward that end.

Give the students four weeks (including four weekends) to complete the task, but have a project check up after one week where you inspect the student's thesis paragraph and list of sources. Give the students some small grade for this. Then have a rough draft due one week later, also with a small grade attached. In most cases, this first rough draft will be very poor. Make copious comments to ensure that the student understands what to correct. This is also the point where the instructor will catch that small group of students who have not started their paper and the teacher can take appropriate action. Have the final draft of the paper due on a Monday; this gives students a final weekend, but offer some extra credit for students who have finished the Friday before. Require that an electronic version of the paper be emailed to the teacher or directly through a website that checks for plagiarism and other forms of cheating.

Grading the papers will now be faster for the teacher because of the effort put out to ensure higher quality essays; and the students will have completed a very complicated task by taking it one small step at a time and creating a much less stressful atmosphere.

Once you have your assignments in mind, it is time to plan how to assess them in a timely fashion. When it comes to grading, it is more important that students get constructive feedback on a few assignments than to continue putting effort into tasks whose results they will not see. First, let us look at assignments that are fast for the students to complete and easy for the teacher to assess.

Students need to do homework, but teachers do not need to grade everything that is assigned. There are other ways to assess these assignments. One way is called "stamped" assignments. These began as a substitute for a notebook grade, since no teacher wants to carry 150 notebooks home to grade. Although teachers give up the old notion that every student needs a notebook, stamped assignments reinforce the bigger idea that students need to be responsible for their own organization. Stamps allow the teacher to quickly assess whether homework has been done. An entire class of stamped assignments can be graded in a few minutes. The teacher uses a rubber stamp to stamp work that is done on time. Students who do not do the work do not get a stamp. The responsibility of keeping track of the stamped work falls on the student until the end of the grading period when it is turned in for a major grade. The grade is assessed by simply counting the number of stamps and not by checking the accuracy of each task attempted. Each stamp is worth a portion of the total grade, which usually works out to being the equivalent of a test grade. Stamps are most useful when doing preparation for a discussion, guided reading, video questions, graphic organizers, reviews, and so on. The topics covered in the stamped assignments are then assessed on the tests or other assessment methods to make sure that students understand that all assignments are relevant and that the teacher does not fall into the habit of assigning trivial work that will not be useful in the future.

One problem with grading is that teachers often have a good idea for a project or assignment, but have trouble conveying to the students what is expected from the work. A rubric, provided to students when the assignment is given, will ensure that both teacher and students stay focused on the skills and materials to be learned; this will allow students to create better products and, in turn, will make grading faster and more efficient. Rubrics can be as simple or complicated as the teacher wants, but the clearer the rubric, the fewer explanations the students will demand. Students need to understand what each assignment requires. A rubric will also help the student understand exactly where they earned points or did not. Rubrics additionally improve consistency and standardization in grading, thus creating a climate of fairness in the classroom.

We had a student who once wrote a seventeen-page dissertation when the directions clearly asked for a three- to five-page essay. The student added so much extra information that it was difficult for the teacher to determine whether the task had been completed. The student learned a valuable lesson about following directions and providing quality over quantity.

Teachers should consider carefully the required length of each written assignment. Topics should be narrowed so that comprehensive student work can be achieved in as few pages as possible. There is no need to assign a ten-page paper when three pages will adequately address a topic. Students learn to be succinct and make clear arguments when given limited space to do so; students tend to be verbose when they feel the need to fill pages. This is also true for the teacher who creates an assignment that is unnecessarily complicated for the learner and unwieldy for the teacher to grade. The longer and more complicated the assignment, the more time it takes to grade that assignment. An assignment should not be so long that the student will have forgotten much of its content before it is assessed and returned by the teacher.

Peer grading is another strategy that will save a teacher time. When using peer grading, rubrics are especially helpful as they provide a concise guide for keeping the student grader on task. Peer grading is a reteaching tool that is most effective when used on assignments that have concrete answers that cannot be argued (trade-'n'-grade) or when you are checking for understanding especially in regards to teaching writing skills. For example, when teaching students to write a proper body paragraph for a historical essay, you first have students write their own paragraph. Two students then exchange paragraphs and locate the essential parts of a properly written paragraph in their classmate's work (topic sentence, evidence, analysis, and transition). By writing their own paragraph and then recognizing and critiquing the required parts in their classmate's paragraph, students become more aware of their own strengths and weaknesses when writing.

For many teachers, grading is the most unpleasant aspect of teaching. It can be extremely repetitive and take a great deal of time. Since it must be done, the key is to make the task less onerous by using rubrics, peer grading, and other time savers at your disposal.

Teaching well takes time and dedication. One key is to take those shortcuts available to you without sacrificing the essence of what the students need to learn. To stay at the top of your profession means continuing to take courses, attend workshops, and go to lectures that inspire you to keep your curriculum fresh. To stay on top of your classroom means being efficient and organized in order to create a smooth-running class that challenges students and that they nevertheless enjoy. Remember that, although teaching is a job, teaching well is a vocation and teaching efficiently will maintain enthusiasm.

About the Authors

Chris Peek (BA), a secondary teacher with over twenty years' experience, currently in Houston, Texas, is a Project CRISS trainer, a question writer for the ETS Texas Teacher Certification Exam, and an AP World History reader and table leader who has been writing and editing curriculum since 1990.

Angela Wainright (BA) is a secondary history teacher at an independent school in Houston, Texas. She has served on the SAT II World History Test Development Committee and is an AP World History consultant, an AP World History reader, and a table leader. She is also currently on her school's curriculum mapping committee.

CHAPTER 18

Nuts and Bolts

MONTY ARMSTRONG

Why do I teach world history? I teach world history because I work in a school that is 65 percent nonwhite. I got tired of being unable to teach my students about where they came from, since the California standards for world history are not the best in terms of that process. The California standards are Euro-centric and deal only with rest of the world, if at all, in terms of European contact. India, for example, is dealt with (but not mentioned specifically) only in terms of the New Imperialism. What have I learned? I have learned to take a different look at all history. I have learned how to put things into a large framework and to think comparatively and over a long range of time.

Despite these personal gains, I still face the challenge of the day-to-day operation of my classroom. What follows are some basic ideas to help other teachers with that task. What I hope to present is this short opus is the nuts and bolts of teaching world history—not the elevated though still very important issues of contending historiographies and new research, but the basic question of how to survive from day to day.

While we are correct in assuming a goodly measure of success, especially for world history at the advanced placement (AP) level, we must continue to confront major issues. The first is keeping current with the expanding scholarship in world history. The second is how to move that scholarship from the intellectual realm into the world history classroom. At the same time, we have to prepare AP students to score well on the AP test and non-AP students to take state standardized tests. As much as we would like to spend a semester delving deeply into *Old World Encounters* or *Guns, Germs, and Steel*, as world history teachers, non-AP and AP, we are driven by both the age of our students as well as those inevitable test dates. At all levels we are also forced to deal with issues outside the scholarship and the texts, not the least of which are essay writing and analytical skills.

This chapter is not based on any particular textbook, but rather is presented as an overlay to be used with any text.

The Calendar

As simple as it may seem, the calendar is a crucial item. Starting with the date of the AP test in May or the dates of the state tests and setting aside two to three weeks for review, you work backward to the start of school; and then you stick to that schedule. We all have our favorite topics and subjects, but also we understand that there is a body of information to be covered. Life being what it is, there will be fire drills and snow days, and adaptation will always be necessary, but staying on schedule is part of getting done what you need to do.

The other thing required is the constant revision of the schedule from year to year. You need to include testing in the schedule. Your testing schedule is more dependent on your students than on your book. If you are teaching sophomores, you should schedule, at the very least, a brief test at the end of each chapter and a larger test for each unit in the text. And if you are an AP teacher, you need to schedule a test covering each of the major AP World History periods. (Many AP students are convinced that they can get through this class without reading the text!)

You also need to make space in your schedule for document-based questions and essays. This includes not only the time for the students to write them, but also the time for you to give both training and feedback to the students.

I like to equate world history to a plane flight across a continent. Sometimes you land and get to talk to people. Sometimes you land and take some pictures, and sometimes you just get to fly low and look out the window.

Your Classroom Day to Day

Video Notes (Or DVD Notes, Depending on Your Technology)

There are many excellent world history videos available; the question becomes how to best use them. I like to have my students use a modified form of Cornell notes. After watching a video in class, the students split their paper into one-third on the left and two-thirds on the right. On the right-hand side the students take what could be called "normal" notes—basically, answering the question "What does the video tell you?" The students then complete the notes at home by filling in the left side with their thoughts about and reactions to the video. They put in references to the text with pages numbers. I have my students highlight the page references in yellow. They also mention other videos they have seen in class, movies they have seen, books they have read, and anything else that they can connect to the video. These references are highlighted in blue. The colors are your choice; they simply make it easy to separate out the information when you are scoring the notes. The finished notes are due the next class day. This method not only re-enforces the students' reading of the chapter; it also makes them consider the information in the video and in the chapter in a larger context.

Now, I know what some of you are thinking: "The students will just copy the notes from their friends that afternoon." The answer is simple and it is the same method, in a sense, that I use for in-class essays and lecture notes. On a random basis you collect the notes at the *end* of the period. You read through them very quickly and use either a marker or a rubber stamp to mark where the notes ended. You then hand them back the next day so the students can finish the second part of the assignment.

Lecture Notes (Yes, Current Pedagogy Aside, Lecturing Is Sometimes the Best Way to Deliver Information)

I ask students to set up their lecture notes much like the video notes, with the paper split vertically. On the right, students take notes on what I actually said. On the left, they write their thoughts, connections to other chapters or videos, and so on. I usually collect their notes on a random basis rather than after each chapter. This makes for less to read and the students still know I am checking on them. I also use the same method of stamping the notes with one of a rather strange collection of rubber stamps that I have. (For example, one is a man with his head in his hands saying, "Why me?" Another asks, "Are you making this up as you go along?" What you look for are stamps that the students will not be able to find easily.)

Notebooks (Because Organization Is Sometimes Survival)

Because world history is so vast and different textbooks present the material in very different orders, you can help your students by insisting that they get organized. Each of my students has a notebook specifically for world history, broken into sections for tests, lecture notes, charts, maps, video notes, quizzes, and miscellaneous. If the students keep their work in each section in date order, they will easily be able to locate a particular item, and review will be easier. The notebooks are collected on a regular basis and checked for order and completeness.

Charts (Because Students Learn in Different Ways)

I have had very good luck using various types of charts both in groups as well as single-student projects. I find charts especially helpful when done in groups with classes that are mixed in English proficiency (90 percent of my students have parents who were not born in the United States).

I find charts useful to connect chapters to each other. Texts that are organized chronologically usually deal with a given country in separate time periods without showing any connection between them. China, for example, might be covered in Chapters 8, 15, and 27. It is very difficult for students to keep track of that information both because it has been weeks or months since they have contacted that information and it has been dealt with in chunks, not a consistent whole. What if, when you finished Chapter 27, you asked groups of students to fill in a chart covering those three chapters? Or, if you are using the notebooks, perhaps you might want to give your students the chart during Chapter 8 and have them fill in information as each chapter is dealt with and then have them do a summary using a compare and contrast or change over time model. The material to be detailed in the chart could be organized according to the five world history themes that were originally developed for AP World History, but which also work very well as an organizing basis for any world history class.

1. Interaction between humans and the environment • Demography and disease • Migration • Patterns of settlement • Technology
2. Development and interaction of cultures • Religions • Belief systems, philosophies, and ideologies • Science and technology • Arts and architecture
3. State-building, expansion, and conflict • Political structures and forms of governance • Empires • Nations and nationalism • Revolts and revolutions • Regional, transregional, and global structures and organizations

4. Creation, expansion, and interaction of economic systems
   • Agricultural and pastoral production • Trade and commerce • Labor systems • Industrialization • Capitalism and socialism
5. Development and transformation of social structures
   • Gender roles and relations • Family and kinship • Racial and ethnic constructions • Social and economic classes

So now you have a chart on China with three chapters across the top and five themes listed down the left side. If you want students to go deeper, you could add another row dealing with comparisons and contrasts or the changes over time. (If you have a hard time creating the chart on your computer, the answer is the same as for any tech question: "Ask the students for help.")

To make the spaces on the chart large enough for students to write in them easily, I have devised a simple method. You create your original chart on legal-size paper (8½ x 14 inches) with the chart running on the long axis. Then you copy this original to 11 x 17 ledger paper, usually 125 percent on most copiers. There are two advantages to this method. First, the students have plenty of room to write. Second, if you punch holes along the left-hand edge and have students fold the chart so the right-hand edge just touches the holes, the chart fits nicely in their notebooks and they can easily fold it out. (I also use the same system with maps.) You can add a title on the back of the right-hand side and that will appear on the front of the chart when it is folded over.

Timelines (Because This Many Years Are Tough to Keep Track Of)

Given the scope of world history, many students lose track of not only when things happened but also how those events appear in relation to other events. You can use the same 11 x 17 format to create timelines. You give your students a chart with three or four timelines, one for each chapter in a unit. These timelines will allow students to see how events relate to each other. You can also provide a chart with three or four timelines (200 to 500 years long) and have students work with just one country or area.

National Anthems ("La Marseillaise" Really Says That? But It Sounded So Good in Casablanca!)

I have students pick four national anthems. The first has to be the one that they most closely identify with and they have to tell why. (Bear in mind that in some cases this explanation could be negative.) They then have to pick three others and research the following information for each one:

• Who wrote it?
• What is the historical background?
• Did it replace an earlier song and, if so, why?

If you like to have the students do presentations, ask them to bring in a recording or DVD of one of the anthems and give a brief presentation.

Maps (Where the Heck Is Nauru Anyway?)

One thing that I have discovered about maps is that unless students have taken a geography course before they get to you, they are woefully ignorant of the world and where things are. To remedy their ignorance, start small and build outward. Find a current map of your city and then see if you can locate one that is thirty years old. You might try the Chamber of Commerce or do some Internet digging. (I found mine at city hall, but our city hall is small and right across the street.) Ask the students to locate specific places on the old map, starting with where they live. Then have them examine the new image. What has changed, what is the same? Why? Then repeat the process with old and new maps of the county, then the state, then the United States, and finally the world. If you start with something familiar, you then go from there with greater success.

I try to use map assignments as often as possible and in the same 11 x 17 format. Put the map on one side of the page; write the assignment on the back right and the title on the back left. And we all know that even seniors love to color, so let them color away.

You can have students use the maps to investigate any number of items:

Trade routes
Muslim expansion
The Bantu Migrations
World exploration
Winds and their effect on travel and trade
The travels of famous people such as Marco Polo and Ibn Battuta
The expansion and collapse of empires and the overlapping of empires

There are two exercises with which I have had particular success, both dealing directly with the backgrounds of the students.

The first exercise I assign in the first week of school. I give students a large map of the world and have them trace back the homelands of their parents, grandparents, and so on, as far back as they can. They locate where each person came from and try to attach some dates. Students can color the maps and attach pictures of their relatives. This exercise will also give you some insight into your students.

The second exercise, which I call the Columbian Exchange Cookbook, is scheduled after the class studies the events of 1492. The students find a recipe with five or more ingredients that is typical of their culture and trace back where the ingredients came from. They then discuss how those ingredients might have arrived in the country of the recipe's origin. On the back of the assignment sheet you put a world map on which students trace what they think is the course of the ingredients. If it is possible, have them prepare the dishes and have a "Columbian Exchange Lunch."

Both of these exercises exemplify the idea of starting with something the students know well and moving out from there.

Using Music and Poetry as a Memory Aid (Why Can't I Get That Song Out of My Head?)

Although I would like to give credit to the original author of the Dynasty Song, I fear that information is lost in the mists of time. It is set to the tune of "Frère Jacques" and goes like this:

> Shang, Zhou, Chin, Han
> Shang, Zhou, Chin, Han
> Sui, Tang, Song
> Sui, Tang, Song
> Yuan, Ming, Qing, Republic
> Yuan, Ming, Qing, Republic
> Mao Zedong
> Deng Xiaoping.

If you search YouTube, you will find a number of renditions of varying quality and you can have your students record their own. You can also ask your students to create other sorts of mnemonic songs for whatever items they want to remember, bearing in mind that some will be great and others will be something to give points for and then leave on the shelf.

Students can also try writing mnemonic poetry because it works as well as music. Just think about how we keep track of the number of days in each month. Again the idea is to have the students create and share their poems.

Essays (You Have to Assign Them)

If your students are going to become better writers, they have to practice. If they are going to be better writers, they need feedback. In order to give them feedback, someone (guess who?) has to read the essays. In the category of

time-consuming tasks, this can be a big one. There are some simple things that you can do to not only help your students become better writers, but also speed up the grading process.

Of course, the first step is to find useful essay questions. This is the easy part. Your sources are other teachers, AP test questions (these even have the answers and scoring rubrics!), and text ancillaries, or you just make up your own.

The next step is finding scoring rubrics. They can be generic from your district office. They can be created by your department. You can borrow them from AP tests. You should bear in mind that rubrics stay the same throughout the school year. To constantly be changing rubrics is self-defeating. You can increase your expectations for students' essays, but use the same rubric to evaluate them. The other advantage of using the same rubric is that as you internalize it, scoring goes faster and faster.

The next step is scoring. You are going to use much the same method that you used with students' video and lecture notes but for a much different reason. After you assign them an essay, you collect the essays, run through them quickly, and put your stamp or a marker line where the student stopped writing. The students then take the essays home (either that day or the next, depending on how quick you are) and type them exactly as written. Reading and scoring typed, double-spaced essays is much easier.

Last But Not Least (Because I Have Been Allowed Only So Many Words)

Keep trying new stuff and do not toss it because it does not work the first time. Tweak it and see what happens on the second try.

About the Author

Monty Armstrong is currently a teacher and the social science department chair at Cerritos History School in Cerritos, California, and the moderator of the World History ListServ. His teaching experience includes both AP World History and AP European History. He has served as a sample selector and table leader for AP World History reading since 2002 and has presented world history institutes throughout the country. He is the lead author for the *Princeton Review*'s *Guide to Cracking the AP World History Exam* and has served as a reviewer for a number of world history texts.

CHAPTER 19

Common Pitfalls in Teaching AP World History and How to Avoid Them

STEVE CORSO

In the interest of full disclosure, let me begin with a couple of disclaimers.

The first concerns expertise. Although I believe I am very good at what I do—teaching world history—I would not claim to be a genius; I am, however, certainly a well-qualified expert on the topic of this essay. I have probably made every mistake and fallen into every pit imaginable in my journey to create a vibrant Advanced Placement (AP) World History course—one that gives my students a rich experience while simultaneously preparing them not only for the AP exam, but also for our own New York State assessment (the Regents exam) in global history.

The second disclaimer is about originality. Someone once said that there are four basic story plotlines, and one could certainly say something similar about teaching. Any teachers who have been around long enough will have borrowed much of their repertoire from someone or somewhere else. Many of the techniques I use and will mention here I actually owe, at least in their original form, to colleagues, and I am grateful to them for helping me to build my own pedagogical bag of tricks. That includes younger colleagues, whose ability to weave a variety of media and perspectives into their teaching is both instructive and a validation of my own, similar practices, many of which were once frowned on as rogue departures from the chalk-and-talk approach.

My experience teaching AP classes goes back several years. During most of my career I taught the at-risk students, with a fair amount of success. Then, the person who had been teaching AP European history left our district to take a promotion elsewhere, and I got a phone call in late August informing me I would be teaching the course. The last time I had even thought about European history was back in the tenth grade, and that was in 1969. Now, not only did I still have the at-risk classes, but I had this monster of a course

dealing with subject matter I was not well versed in, had no time to adequately prepare for, and, honestly, found quite tedious before the twentieth century. Fortunately, the teacher I replaced had left her notes and files behind, and I was able to get a running start on the textbook, staying a chapter or two ahead of the students. I found many helpful resources online, and I managed to piece together a decent course from what I had. My students did reasonably well on the exam. Yet it became an all-consuming preparation, and I felt nauseous before each class.

Another problem was that the students were sophomores, and New York State has a mandatory Regents exam in global history for sophomores, which is a graduation requirement. That meant that, after the AP exam in May, my AP European students had one month to cram the entire non-European history of the world from about 1500 CE to the present day in order to be prepared for the Regents exam. The AP European course was not a good fit, so we changed our sophomore offering the following year to AP World History. We split the AP World History course over two years, ninth and tenth grade, as our state-mandated Global History course does and offered AP World History as the advanced placement alternative in place of AP European history. At least I now had control over the selection of a textbook and some say about the course curriculum. I thought I could teach AP World History as a sort of super-charged honors class and get my students through the Regents exam.

The first year we had mediocre results, with about 55 percent of the students earning AP college credit. Then came the second year and the beginning of my realization of just how very wrong I had been in my assumptions and my approach. In 2003, only 28 percent of my students earned college credit, and twenty of my fifty-five students scored ones. Yes, that is one out of a possible score of 5, the lowest score one can achieve on the exam. No matter how depressed or discouraged you ever feel about your students' exam results, please remember that the person who was asked to write this chapter once had nearly 40 percent of his students earn a score of *one*. Some of these were really good students, so I let go of the "it's not me, it's them" excuse very quickly. The problem was me, and it was, therefore, up to me to do whatever I needed to do in order to turn things around.

So where did I go wrong, and how can you avoid the same mistakes?

Tip Number One: Get Thee to a Five-Day, Two-Day, or One-Day College Board Institute and Take Copious Notes

I do not mean just take notes on the presentation; take note of the suggestions you hear around you. Be willing to admit that, no, you do not know it all and, yes, someone with far less classroom experience than yourself may have a stupendous idea that you should try out. I had already been teaching for twenty years when I attended a one-day institute presented by veteran AP World History teacher Bob Nuxoll, who has forgotten more about how to teach this course than I will ever know, and I credit many of the ideas and techniques I learned in that workshop for the vast improvement not only in my own delivery of the course, but in my students' performance. A problem that has arisen, however, is the high cost and infrequency of institutes offered by the College Board for world history. In the absence of an institute, I strongly recommend becoming part of the World History AP listserv and gleaning as much teaching wisdom as you can from the dozens of truly dedicated professionals who participate. It really is not a substitute, but it is the next best thing.

Tip Number Two: Get Thee an Acorn Book and Read It Several Times

An "Acorn" book, so named for the College Board's trademark acorn symbol that appears on its cover, is a complete guide to the AP World History course. This is your single best source of information about the course, the exam, and everything else you need to know about the College Board expectations regarding AP World History. You need to ingrain those habits of mind in your students from day one and get them to internalize the generic versions of each of the three free-response rubrics as soon as possible. You should construct most (if not all) of your essays in one of the three formats, and you must utilize the rubrics to grade your students. Your goal is to train students to deliver a specific set of points in their essays. The more they practice during the school year, the better they will perform on the College Board exams. There are numerous sources for this information available at AP Central—

http://apcentral.collegeboard.com—the College Board's site for all of its AP offerings. In addition, if you would like access to any of the resources I use myself, please feel free to contact me. I will point you to a pretty formidable trove of resource materials that I have collected, some of which are of my own creation.

Tip Number Three: The Course Is the Course

The bar is set where it is set and it is up to the students to reach and clear the bar; it is not up to you to lower that bar (or raise the floor, for that matter). You either already have completed or, if next year will be your first year teaching the course, soon will complete the College Board audit process for AP World History. This will entail your submission of your course syllabus, which will be evaluated by a college professor who will determine whether or not your offering presents sufficient rigor, meriting the AP designation. In addition, both you and your principal will complete and sign the audit form, which is a signed contract of sorts indicating that you do present the course in the manner described, use an approved textbook, and adhere to other requirements. There is no deviation from these requirements. Whether your school has a completely open-door policy regarding placement in the class or presents some limited restrictions for admission, you must teach this course at the level warranted by the advanced placement designation. Now, that does not mean that you cannot bring your students up to speed gradually. I tend to give generous curves at the start of the course and tend also to be very generous in the time I allot for completion of written assessments, but the content and nature of those test and essay questions are *always* at the advanced placement level. I explain to the students at the start of the year that it is not where they are at the beginning, but where they arrive by the end that counts. No one except their parents will see their first-quarter grade in the course. All that colleges will ever see on a transcript is the grade for the entire course. If students earn a C+ in the first quarter, but end the year with a B+ in the course, that B+ is all that matters. At the beginning of the course I grade my students strictly while reassuring them that everything will work out in the end—and, by the way, reassuring their parents as well. It is a good idea to meet with your AP students' parents early in the year to explain the requirements of the program and recruit them as assistant "encouragers" who will reinforce what you say in class. They need to realize that their children have undertaken a major challenge and need as much support as possible. I would also offer a subtitle to this section: *pssst . . . they're only fifteen years old* (78 percent of the exams are taken by sophomores). When I remember myself at fifteen, I doubt that I would have been able to do what many of my own students have done in this course.

Tip Number Four: Do Not Spoon Feed

Despite the students' relatively young age, it is crucial that you demand intellectual rigor from them right from the start. I tell my students, "I'll set the table, you bring the food, and then, together, we'll figure out what goes on which plate." They have a textbook. Whichever text you use, it is rich with content. The Internet is both an endless source of information while simultaneously being a wasteland in many respects. I do searches and verifications of reliability for dozens of websites for each unit I teach, and then post them, sometimes as a web-quest, for my students. Between the text and the web, there is more than enough raw content available to them, and they need to know it. The connections between events, individuals and time periods and the historical significances of those connections are what my classroom discussions are all about. Of course, if students need me to explain a particularly difficult concept, I will. But they still have to have done the assigned reading to even know *what* requires explanation. Emphasize the reading. Give chapter quizzes on basic content from the reading *before* you discuss the chapter, in order to make sure they have done the reading. An AP World History course cannot be just about you writing copious notes on a chalkboard or creating endless streams of PowerPoint presentations while your students write down exactly what is already available in their textbooks. That pattern makes you the source of all information (you are not—none of us are) and completely absolves them of any responsibility for their own learning. Yes, the course is, to a large part, about preparing students for the AP exam, but you are also preparing them to be active learners, something they will be expected to shoulder more and more of the responsibility for as they proceed through high school, into college, and beyond. It is a balancing act we all have to try to master and it is not easy. It is, however, essential.

Tip Number Five: If Possible, Attend a College Board Reading at Least Once

The "Reading" is actually the grading of the essay portion of the AP World History exam. Each June, a combination of roughly 700 high school teachers and college professors congregate at a site and spend seven days, eight hours per day, grading all of the free response questions from that year's exam. Someone suggested attending one of these to me a few years back and I think my reply had something to do with all the things I would endure rather than spend eight days away from my family in an essay-grading gulag. I have rarely ever been more wrong about something. I participated in my first reading in 2007 and was able to repeat the experience this past June. It was, both times, the best professional development I have ever received. It was hard work (I think I graded over 1,300 change-and-continuity essays last June), but it afforded me an inside look at what my students need to do to succeed on the free-response portion of the AP exam. That kind of experience gives you a baseline for assessing your own classes—how strong were your own students' essays that you read all year long in comparison to the essays you are reading now by students from all over the country? You might be pleasantly surprised, whereas continually limiting your exposure to your own little bubble might cause you to be less sure of what you are doing. It is empowering to know for yourself what students need to do and that you are getting your students to do it. When the quality you expect from your students' writing equals or exceeds the level that the readers who grade the essays expect, it builds not only your confidence in what you are doing, but also your students' confidence in you. If you are unable to attend a reading, I would strongly recommend that you make contact with teachers who have, and try to get as much insight and information from them as possible. Check with your local professional organizations to see if any similar experiences are available to you.

I would also suggest very strongly that you invest in the Advanced Placement World History Lesson Jamboree DVD. This is a massive collection of lessons and best practices from teachers all over the country, and you cannot help but find several items therein that will be absolute treasures for you in constructing your own lessons.

I hope this brief list of lessons learned the hard way will be both encouraging and useful for you and that my mine-sweeping here will allow you to navigate the terrain a bit more safely. Prepare yourself, be confident, and remember—where you are now does not matter; what counts is where you end up at the finish.

About the Author

Steve Corso (BA, political science; MA, liberal studies, social studies education) is the lead social studies teacher at John H. Glenn High School in New York's Elwood School District. In his twenty-seven years as an educator, he has taught everything from special education inclusion classes to advanced placement classes.

CHAPTER 20

Year Two
Moving From Survival to Fun

SIGRID S. REYNOLDS

Last year you were assigned to teach world history. Your content knowledge may have been limited to one or two non-Western courses and you may not have taken a truly global history course. You talked to the teacher who previously taught the course or maybe you are the first to embrace the challenge. You have an inherited textbook or you selected one that kept you one or two pages ahead of the students all year, and you have dutifully taught the first year of a massive course to thirty or 120 students. Chances are that you did lots of lecturing since you had all those notes you took from the text. You have many ideas for improvement, but you do not believe that you will ever own the course. The trick is to find your passion and reveal it through the course. Your students may not remember the historical facts, although you certainly hope they develop skills such as reading, communication, and analysis well enough to incorporate them regularly into their future lives as they follow the news, pursue disparate careers, and vote in elections. Yet what the students will always remember is your enthusiasm for the subject. Thus, you have to figure out how to incorporate your hobbies and passions into the course. I can assure you that world history is the perfect vehicle to explore your interests and motivate your students.

Do-it-Yourself Approach

I am a passionate advocate of designing your own lessons because you can never teach someone else's interests as well as your own. This takes additional work but invigorates you and enlivens your teaching every year, making your classroom more stimulating for the students. If you are any sort of perceptive teacher, you know that the students can sniff out canned lessons and worksheets as well as educational films. These are recipes for boredom in the classroom. With the Internet, you do not need a master's in curriculum

development to dream up your own projects; a hefty dose of curiosity, some extra but interesting research, and new approaches that you can find in this book will give you all the expertise you need to own the course.

Familiarity With the Material

After one year, you do have some knowledge but also huge gaps, as specialization was the goal of college history departments. So assess the gaps in your knowledge and work toward amending them. I make a practice of reading several books that focus on a single global region each summer, fiction or nonfiction. As I tell the students, browse the shelves of your local library, college library, or bookstores to find a couple of palatable books. My own areas of lesser knowledge are South Asia and South America, so I have taken special interest in reading some of the literature of each. Modern authors are writing wonderful books that will give you cultural knowledge that you need. Do not forget to check out the travel shelves as well. You can glean all kinds of useful history and culture from Fodor, the Rough Guides, and Michelin guides while picking places for future or potential travel. I have had the advantage of living in Europe and Asia as a child but have visited Africa, South America, and South Asia by armchair. I can work up as much enthusiasm for Cuzco, where I have never been, as Jakarta, where I lived for two years.

Travel Interests and Experiences

Trade connects the regions and eventually the globe, so I used my interest in foreign languages to explore the topic of trading languages. Simple language phrase books offer tidbits of history and demonstrate cultural values that have persisted for centuries. With the help of these guides, I designed a three-day lingua franca unit on Latin, Swahili, and Malayan. I had only studied Latin, but I knew a bit of the Indonesian Bahasa, an outgrowth of Malayan. Then, with the help of an African student at school, I incorporated Swahili into the scheme. I used vocabulary from Swahili and Bahasa phrasebooks to demonstrate the incorporation of European words into each language. The Latin words for animals provide a lesson in the foundation for the romance languages and English. Now, I am looking for a source of Sogdian, the lingua franca on the Silk Roads. I may yet find that in a former student who has a Fulbright in Central Asia.

Useful Books and Journals

Of course, the point is that you are teaching global history so you cannot dawdle too long in any one region. Global history as a discipline is hard to grasp in its entirety, but it has its breakthrough tomes such as Kenneth Pomeranz and Steven Topik's *The World That Trade Created: Society, Culture, and the World Economy, 1400 to the Present.* I have found books such as *The Human Web: A Bird's-Eye View of World History* by Robert McNeill and William H. McNeill invaluable for providing the big themes chronologically. And although it is controversial in world history circles, *Guns, Germs, and Steel* by Jared Diamond certainly popularized global historical themes.[1] Join the World History Association or worldnetwork.com for the most current work as well as ideas for lesson plans. *The World History Association Journal* holds an annual contest that publishes the best world history lesson for high school classes that is submitted. I have found comparative studies and other articles over the years that I have been able to distill down to PowerPoint or lecture notes—with full attribution to the source, always. *World History Connected*, an online quarterly journal, is a wonderful source that distills current world history issues into classroom-appropriate usage.

Without a doubt, the current vogue in commodity histories for a popular audience has made grasping overarching themes even easier. The first book of this genre that I read was *Oranges* (1975) by John McPhee, which is still in print. At an Advanced Placement (AP) session in 2001, a group of us designed a primary document and geography lesson that continues to generate fun and learning in my classes today. Three more recent books are *Cod* and *Salt*, both by Mark Kurlansky, and Barbara Freese's *Coal*,[2] but I would also pick up any other book that offers insight into global and regional history as well as cultural values through one commodity. The books are short, well researched, and entertaining since they are written for a popular audience. After you have read them, take a few documents, some stories, and a map and design your own geography and trade lesson, with author attribution, of course.

Films

Most teachers have little time during the school year to do more than follow the news on television. And since all history teachers have had students and their fathers who expect the teacher to know the minutiae of an historical event that was the topic of a public television or History Channel show, I save these longer series for summer viewing. Few teachers have time to show entire films in class, but DVDs often include a short documentary on the making of the film that can provide insight into the era for you and your students. For example, despite my dislike of the historical inaccuracies of *The Last Samurai*, with its slant toward the glamour of bushido, the DVD includes an interesting comment by the director, Edward Zwick, on the class system of early Meiji Japan and the very real threat and nuisance that the samurai presented to a modernizing Japan.[3] That short comment triggered my students' exploration of the social and political challenges facing the Meiji emperor, beyond building a modern industrial base, a discussion that extended even to Japanese militarism of the twentieth century.

Other Textbooks

In my classroom, I keep sample textbooks and previous textbooks for my students' use. Since research is a primary skill for history, the additional textbooks provide insight into many issues that neither my students nor I can tease out of our own textbook. Early in my world history teaching, I had trouble with the evolution of Hinduism. It has neither historical nor composite founder, and somewhere between the first chapter on South Asia and the next, Hinduism appeared in its fully complex modern form. It took multiple readings in several books to flesh out the development of Hinduism for my students. Now I have my students do this as an annual exercise. By the way, I am not the only confused teacher. One thread on the AP World History listserv argued Hinduism's categorization as a mono- or polytheistic religion for over a week in 2008. Be warned, though, that students always prefer their own textbook, so I tell my students to leave their copies at home, and I store extra copies of their textbook in the classroom.

Your Interests

Discern your own modern passion and make a global study of it. You will find adequate historical information on the web for any of the following: sports, music, the visual arts, and cooking. Ball sports can be inserted into the study of most cultures and provide a study of rubber as a commodity as well. What fifteen-year-old does not want to hear of the ball games played in classical Mayan cities? You can discuss religion, culture, and warfare through a game. If you like the martial arts, East Asia is the most familiar venue but do not discount the martial arts of South America and Central Asia. What about falconry? Yes, it was a favorite of the nobility of Europe, but to this day, the descendants of the ancient Mongols use golden eagles to catch large prey such as foxes. Archery has a long past that spans the globe, transcends gender, and brings together domestic life with warfare. Did you know that some Americans still practice horse archery and compete in a festival in Iowa every September? If you have not used the longbow battle scene at Agincourt in the 1997 movie *Henry V*, you should.[4] And it goes without saying that global history can be taught through the lens of armament technology.

Music

Today you can download world music from numerous sources or search in the world music sections in stores. You should look for the Putumayo recording label that focuses on world music. In a presentation at the National Council for Social Studies conference in 2003, Tom Laichas described the music of revolution that he uses in his classes. Students do not need to understand the lyrics to get the fervent tone. On YouTube, if you are looking for a youthful genre to use as an example of globalization, you can now find Mongolian rap. Or you can compare the idea of the haunting vastness of Central Asia in the authentic throat singing of traditional Mongolia with Russian composer Alexander Borodin's romantic interpretation of the region: *In the Steppes of Central Asia*. I have found lullabies to be enormously accessible to teenagers as simple music, and the translated lyrics allow insight into the traditional values of societies. Lullabies often reveal gender roles and even break the stereotype of women as sole baby tenders.

Art and Architecture

It goes without saying that there are many wonderful websites for architecture and art history, although the analysis of sources beyond the European Renaissance may seem difficult without an adequate art history background. Nevertheless, anyone can look at art to determine the values and daily life of a culture. The French Duke of Berry's *Book of Hours* shows medieval work roles while the woodprints of Tokugawa Japan do the same. West African art of the period of European contact nicely demonstrates the arrival of the gun while retaining traditional motifs. How would you depict sports or instrumental music without art? You can even follow the evolution of dance forms through artwork in many cultures.

Games

There are board games available that can be used for education and rewards. I know a teacher who allows those students who have completed their homework to play mahjong at the end of class. Dice and card games are available at historical sites and art museums in major U.S. and international cities. While looking for souvenirs when traveling, I often opt for packs of cards with the visages of kings such as Guillaume the Conqueror, Napoleon, and Louis XIV. The German company Klaus Jurgen manufactures games such as Carcassonne, The Settlers of Cataan, and Puerto Rico, which require players to make economic decisions about land, resources, and cities in medieval Europe and colonial American settings. And you can require that the students research topics and locations before playing the games. Once the students have mastered the games, a final project in a world history class can consist of the design of similar games for different locations and time periods. Online games exist as well, although unless your classroom has total computer access and you have some control over the students, these may be problematic. It is certain that more computer savvy teachers than I have used online games with excellent results.

Technology

Of course, if your passion is technology, the world is at your fingertips, but be aware that students would rather create their own productions and presentations than listen to your PowerPoints in a darkened classroom for days on end. Why not let the students at least take turns running your PowerPoint after they have read the chapter? Or have you used Google maps in the classroom? For world history, what could be more exciting than showing the Great Zimbabwe site from a satellite today? For preparation, assign research to make a site map identifying the structures and then let the students see the real place in real time.

Cooking

The history of food is fascinating and accessible in books and on the Internet. Tom Standige's *History of the World in Six Glasses* provided the foundation for a lesson plan by Deborah Smith Johnston in *World History Connected*.[5] World history classes can study vegetarianism in South Asia and the movement of vegetables in the Columbian Exchange. Collaborate with a biology teacher in your building to collect and eat some common weeds, such as dandelions or purslane, which were brought from Europe. Famine diets in China represent a fascinating adaptation to life in a harsh climate. Bring foods to the classroom and give extra credit to students to do the same. I used to have a box of cereal called Ancient Grains in my classroom. It disappeared from store shelves due to its absolute tastelessness, but now I find quinoa and spelt easily available at the supermarket. Why should foreign language departments own the yummy smells in the halls? Have the students make dishes from these ingredients. At the very least, go to ethnic restaurants and request their menus to share with your class. Then have the students look up the ingredients to determine which are indigenous and which are borrowed and when.

Collaboration

Do not forget your colleagues in other departments; collaboration with foreign language and English teachers can enhance both disciplines even if your curriculum does not correlate. I have one friend who teaches next door to an English teacher. Thanks to flexible administrators, they have managed for years to arrange their sophomore schedules to correlate their content. Teaching next to Spanish, Japanese, French, and Arabic teachers has allowed me to use similar cultural resources. I have encouraged their use of historical films, while they have lent their considerable knowledge as well as artifacts to my classes. As I accumulated numerous sugar products now found on our local grocery shelves to discuss sugar production as well as globalization, the Spanish teacher was able to identify the uses of cane juice, Mexican sugar cones, and the cane itself. She later borrowed the items from me and they moved through the Spanish Department. With the advent of an Arabic teacher and Middle Eastern restaurants and groceries in our community, we have been able to stage a falafel-tasting contest with boxed and restaurant falafels. By encouraging your students to share their own cultural knowledge with the rest of the class, you make them, in effect, the expert on current life in those regions.

Conclusion

The essence of teaching this massive course is to use your own interests to foster curiosity and enthusiasm among your students. It follows that you should encourage students to pursue their interests as well with projects that allow them the latitude to do the same. For example, when assigning a monograph, allow the students to select from a list rather than require all students to read the same book. Thus, it was through Dava Sobel's *Longitude: The True Story of a Lone Genius Who Solved the Greatest Scientific Question of His Time* that one of the most science- and math-oriented students I have ever taught discovered an enthusiasm for history. [6]

About the Author

Sigrid S. Reynolds (AB, Duke University; BA, Coe College) was a public high school teacher in Cedar Rapids, Iowa. She serves as a table leader at the AP World History reading and as a member of the SAT Subject Test in World History Development Committee.

Notes

1. Kenneth Pomeranz and Steven Topik, *The World That Trade Created: Society, Culture, and the World Economy, 1400 to the Present*, 2nd ed. (Armonk, NY: M.E. Sharpe, 2005); Robert McNeill and William H. McNeill, *The Human Web: A Bird's-Eye View of World History* (New York: W.W. Norton, 2003); Jared Diamond, *Guns, Germs, and Steel* (New York: W.W. Norton, 2005).

2. John McPhee, *Oranges* (New York: Farrar, Strauss and Giroux, 1975); Mark Kurlansky, *Cod: A Biography of the Fish That Changed the World* (New York: Penguin, 1998) and *Salt: A World History* (New York: Penguin, 2003); Barbara Freese, *Coal: A Human History* (New York: Penguin, 2004).

3. "History v. Hollywood: The Last Samurai," *The Last Samurai*, DVD, directed by Edward Zwick (Burbank, CA: Warner Home Video, 2003).

4. "Battle of Agincourt," *Henry V*, DVD, directed by Kenneth Branagh (Los Angeles: MGM, 2000).

5. Tom Standige, *History of the World in Six Glasses* (New York: Walker, 2006); Deborah Smith Johnston, "Research and Teaching: A History of the World in Six Glasses," *World History Connected* 3, no. 2 (2008), http://worldhistoryconnected .press.uiuc.edu.

6. Dava Sobel, *Longitude: The True Story of a Lone Genius Who Solved the Greatest Scientific Question of His Time* (New York: Penguin, 1996).

PART V

TEACHING SKILLS

CHAPTER 21

What Should Happen on the First Day in a World History Class?
What Do You Want to Do and How Do You Want to Accomplish It?

HELEN GRADY

What a wide-open question and what an intriguing oppor-tunity! I have been teaching world history for about twenty years, and it is a labor of love. It also can be confusing both for teacher and student if there is no coherent vision to direct the venture or adventure. Please know that I rethink this first-day scenario every year, and each year I make revi-sions, additions, and deletions. What I have tried to do here is to distill the elements that remain constant and that I feel are critical for establishing the foundations of an effective relationship between my students and me.

Because world history requires some adjustments to the lenses through which we view history and some expansion of the skills we use to analyze the historical materials that are the fabric of the course, it offers opportunities and pres-ents challenges that stimulate both teachers and students. As history teachers, whether neophyte or veteran, we plan that first day with a great deal of thought and an eye to our goals. Why? Because its function is to set the tone we want to project, establish the credibility we embrace for our topic, and engage the students in our shared venture. In order to communicate our vision to the students, we must have a fully developed, coherent, metacognitive narrative. This means we must aim to define our topic, explain why it is important, describe our organizational plan for the course, discuss how we intend to approach the goals of the course, and elaborate on the expectations we have for our students.

First and foremost, we must define our topic. What is world history? Here we need to stress that it is a new kind of history we are talking about, one that demands a wide lens and an increased sense of the interconnected nature of global societies. It involves looking at the past in a different way than the studies of national or even continental histories demand. It highlights the idea of the whole world, a macro view that is important for reshaping our vision of the world;

at the same time, we must acknowledge the need for the micro or more local examples to enrich the discourse and ensure students' understanding by giving them the details necessary to help tell the story.

Our aim is to develop an interconnected framework rather than a series of parallel existences, a genuine world history dynamic that underscores large-scale patterns, long-term changes, interconnections, and interactions. To a certain extent, we want students to realize that one of our aims is to examine continuities and changes that have brought the world to where it is today. We can accomplish this goal by focusing on global themes and trends, by asking those questions pertinent to all human societies. In other words, world history means just that; it stresses the need to relinquish the perception that Western ideas (or any other culture-specific ideas) can be used as the standard by which all others are tested, thus promoting a more open perception of other cultures and value systems and inhibiting any perception of exceptionalism for any specific cultural identity.

Why do we want to teach world history? My enthusi-asm for the subject as a teacher of history stems from the idea that we are constructing a unified narrative of human history. For our students, world history will provide an essential context for understanding the world today. This goal cannot be overstated. Without a doubt, we live in a global society. To prove it, challenge students to name all the places that produce or provide the goods and services they use in their daily lives. Our schools educate students from various areas of the globe; this fact alone suggests how vitally important it is for each student to have a basic understanding of the cultures that helped shape their class-mates' worldviews. Additionally, our students are global citizens in training, so it is essential for them to begin to be aware of how public policy and political positions reflect a state's values and priorities. These explanations allow students to see world history as meaningful and useful for their present and future, as something more than a block of time during which they "go to history" each day. This purpose challenges them to think about the material and possibly to do something more than merely learning information.

So rather than a series of civilizations or a collection of regional studies, the scholarship of this course in world history is concentrated on developing a comprehensive study of human history across time and place. A global perspective is the framework for this course, and our students are embarked on a mission to understand the non-Western world, to see the West in a broader context, to explore the global interactions among the world's peoples, and in this time of interaction, diversity, and global change to make more informed decisions as U.S. citizens in the twenty-first century. Each of these points is an important one for that first-day encounter.

Next it is important to outline the scope of the course and its organizational framework. Here we want to emphasize the need for longer periods of time to embrace the expanded regions under examination as well as the global themes and processes that will shape the guiding questions for each region and time frame. Most of the current texts for world history are structured around the periodization that has been adopted by the Advanced Placement (AP) World History curriculum guidelines; I have used this structural format for a number of years and find that it works very effectively. Give students an outline of this structural framework and explain that as you move from era to era you will be eliciting from them their best guesses as to why a specific period begins and ends when designated. The periods that seem to work well are as follows:

1. c. 8000 BCE to c. 600 CE: Here it is quite possible to examine the early part of this period by investigating the emergence of agricultural societies among these early peoples and exploring interactions and comparisons between early settled or urban societies with earlier hunter-forager societies as well as with contemporary pastoral societies. The second part of this period is dedicated to an examination of the developments and interactions as early societies became increasingly more complex from about 600 BCE to 600 CE.

2. c. 600 CE to c. 1450 CE: In this era some of the themes to highlight are the emergence of Islam, the role of nomadic peoples, the expansion of empires, and the increased nature of cultural exchange.

3. c. 1450 to c. 1750: Emphasis on the emergence of a fully dynamic world economy as well as on the increasing complexity of human societies underscores this era.

4. c. 1750 to c. 1914: Exploration of industrialization, revolution, nation-building, and imperial designs occupy this era of study.

5. c. 1914 to the present: Themes and trends of global warfare, global polarization, and globalization take center stage in the examination of the twentieth and early twenty-first centuries.

As you itemize the time frames, it is important to make clear that the questions guiding each will revolve around those issues that give insight into an examination of all human societies. Here is the course description I give my students:

This is a course designed to project a global perspective, which means that we will be discussing global processes and focusing on the "big picture." At the same time, we will be unpacking common principles within each major society we study. We will look at the major political and economic developments in Asia, Europe, Africa, and the Americas. We will examine the social and cultural values that shaped these societies with the intention of developing greater understanding and appreciation for the differences and similarities that inform all human societies. A study of our world today demands an understanding of cultures beyond those shaped by Western ideas and values. Interaction among nations is a fact of life in our world today. We will discover that societal interaction has been a reality since the early days of written history, and we will explore the nature of those interactions and the ideas, technologies, and products that were exchanged. We will begin to see the cultural traditions that inform the way peoples respond to situations, and we will begin to understand how easy it is to misunderstand actions and responses if we are ignorant of the cultural traditions shaping and informing them. We will be dealing with three main approaches in our investigation of world history: the first involves asking about the role of culture in individual and social behavior; the second approach is a comparative one where we will compare societies in different regions using the same specific categories of analysis to discover patterns of similarities and to account for differences; and the third is to pursue the question of change over time—how things change and what remains the same.

On this first day, I also want to do an activity with students to reinforce the idea that my intention is to help students construct a global perspective. I project a variety of map perspectives on a SMART Board or on an overhead projector depending on the technology available to lead students in a discussion of how maps reveal cultural values, how they imprint political points of view, and how they impose priorities that are not necessarily geographically accurate or politically sound. Then I display a Dymaxion or Fuller map projection, a flat map that projects the earth's landmasses as almost contiguous in one continuous body of water. This allows students to visualize how a reconfiguring of the landmass of the earth can shift their perceptions of the world. This usually provokes some very interesting conversation as well as affirming the idea that their world-view can be altered and that the study of world history will force students to ask more pertinent and probing questions about the societies under examination.

Following this discussion I hand out sheets of 11 x 14 inch paper and have students construct their own mental maps illustrating their own perception of the world. I keep these maps and give them back to students at the end of the course to amend and expand. This is an exercise that I have refined over the years thanks to Deborah Johnston's excellent, insightful advice. Deborah Johnston is a world history teacher with whom I have had the pleasure of working for a number of years.

Lastly, during this first session I want students to have a strong understanding of my expectations of them. This gives them the opportunity to be self-reflective and to commit themselves both to studentship skills and scholarship. Here is the relevant part of the course description that I hand out to each student:

Handout 21.1 **Expectations and Student Responsibilities**

I expect each of you to be committed to the duties of studentship. This means that you will:

- read all assignments carefully and employ active reading techniques to help you learn relevant information and relate the story accurately. This means paying attention to annotation as you read text and source material and taking conclusive notes to help you participate in the discussion about the material read.
- remain on top of assignments—be punctual and prepared for class. If something interferes with your completing an assignment, let me know and realize that you will have to double your efforts the next night.
- participate in class dialogues by asking questions, sharing ideas and/or confusions, defending your positions, and exploring ideas of history

- work on your writing to improve legibility, clarity, cohesion, and conclusive support
- work to determine point of view when reading documents, etc.
- memorize facts to help you to own the material, understand cause and effect, see connections, and draw your own conclusions
- take effective notes in class during discussions and from reading assignments
- remain current about what is happening in our world—ten minutes listening to or reading news daily
- keep a timeline section in your notebook and update it regularly. Often this works most effectively if you block it by centuries and countries
- hand in all written assignments on time
- open your thinking to see all sides of a situation to help you better understand the past and the present

---

As in all history courses, world history rests on the teacher's awareness of and ability to integrate content, skills, and pedagogy. It is absolutely a large order, but the more transparent we are at the very beginning, the more dynamic will be our class discussions, the more engaged in the questions of history will be our students, and the more rewarding their study of world history will be. We want to inspire energy for the ideas of history, encourage dialogue to provoke interest in the analysis of historical issues, and generate trust so that we can have an interactive classroom where students are genuinely involved in their own learning.

About the Author

Helen Grady (BA, MA) is a recently retired secondary teacher from an independent school in Philadelphia who has published articles, presented at national conferences, and served on numerous panels focused on teaching history and curriculum development for world history. She currently serves as a consultant for the College Board for AP World History and AP European History.

CHAPTER 22

Bell-Ringers

JANET MARTIN

"First," said the farmer in the old story, hitting his mule on the head with a stick before giving it a command, "you have to get his attention." In the classroom, bell-ringers serve a similar function in a less painful way.

Bell-ringers focus students' attention in those awkward first few minutes of class. I write a short warm-up question on the board before the students arrive, and I require them to write a short response to the question. I view the element of unpredictability as part of the appeal of this activity, though unpredictability is not essential. I sometimes play music or project a cartoon or painting. I may place an artifact on the table and ask what it is. At other times, I ask who is familiar with a current event and share a newspaper article or short video clip. On the day of a test, I may ask a short review question or tell students to draw a mental map. When I have warned students that they will be writing an essay, I may ask what their topic sentence will be.

Music

I like to use music from the period, or at least the region, we are studying, but occasionally I use a modern song that relates in some way to the day's topic. Students are sometimes fascinated, sometimes displeased, but rarely bored. The teacher next door has told me that sometimes my "alumni" in his class hear one of my songs through our regrettably thin walls and tell him what topic I must be teaching that day. My writing prompt for music is usually "Name that tune." If I already have another warm-up for the day, I may just play "background music" as the students arrive.

I began this practice by using music that was mentioned (or music by composers who were mentioned) in my textbook, gradually broadening my repertoire with songs I happened to hear on National Public Radio, songs mentioned on the Advanced Placement (AP) World History listservs,

and sometimes songs suggested by students or colleagues. Although I am far from being an expert on music, I scanned the shelves of our school library and checked out every possible CD, saving many songs onto my classroom computer for later use. Sometimes music encourages a usually quiet student to speak up in class. Once when I played a selection from Yo Yo Ma's "Silk Road Journeys," a girl from Bangladesh, who rarely spoke a word in class, exclaimed, "Why, that's the music we listen to at home."

Some selections seem obvious. "A Mighty Fortress Is Our God" by Martin Luther introduces the Protestant Reformation. I play the "Marseillaise" as we start to study the French Revolution and Tchaikovsky's "1812 Overture" when Napoleon is about to invade Moscow. Stonewall Jackson's "Where Will You Meet Your Waterloo?" while not a period piece, is usually a hit. "Rule Britannia" and Noel Coward's "Mad Dogs and Englishmen" are both good mood music for imperialism. After I learned at a recent National Council for the Social Studies convention that the lion in "The Lion Sleeps Tonight" refers to Shaka Zulu, I played it when we discussed the Zulu wars. "Nazom Ras Baratu," a Ukrainian rap song celebrating the post-communist Orange Revolution, is popular every year. (This one prompted several colleagues and my assistant principal to pop their heads in to find out what I was doing.)

Pictures

Students can always benefit from an opportunity to hone their visual literacy skills. I remind them to follow three steps: describe, identify, and interpret. When they offer an interpretation, I prod them with "How do you know?" Often a student will notice a detail I had not seen, even in a picture I thought I knew well. For example, when I projected the title page image from Hobbes's *Leviathan* to illustrate that the state is made of people, one student observed that at the bottom of the page there were "church" pictures on one side and "state" pictures on the other.

How to use pictures depends on the technology available in your classroom. The school library or a colleague may have posters available for borrowing. Many paintings and cartoons are available on overhead transparencies, often in a packet of textbook ancillaries, and it is not difficult to print your own transparencies. If the classroom is set up to project images from the Internet, either on a television or a SMART Board, a nearly infinite array of images becomes available.

My standard writing prompt is "Tell me about the picture." I might also ask the students to write a caption for a cartoon or to create their own quick sketches of the same subject or in the same style. I can always ask more specific questions during the brief follow-up discussion: How do you know the men in the picture are soldiers? How do you know it is spring?

Artifacts

It is as much fun to search for potential artifacts as it is to present them to the students. You must simply open your mind to the possibilities. Objects from around the house are often relevant to the topic of the day. To introduce the river valley civilizations, I brought in a tabletop fountain and asked, "Why does she have that thing on the table?" (Because often the control of water was the beginning of civilization.) For the European voyages of discovery, I used cloves and sticks of cinnamon. Museum gift shops are a fruitful source of artifacts, though they are not always cheap. I use a replica of a Tang horse, purchased from a museum shop, both to illustrate an artistic style and to remind students of the proverb, "You can conquer China on horseback but you cannot rule on horseback."

I always look for interesting artifacts when I go on vacation. Now that they know that I am in the market, friends and family sometimes bring me unusual things. My son found me a piece of sugar cane over six feet long to introduce the history of Caribbean sugar plantations, and he brought me a set of Russian nesting dolls—Lenin to Putin—back from a trip to Russia. After a colleague loaned me a pair of shoes for bound feet, purchased on her trip to China, I found a pair of my own on eBay. At a Smithsonian Folk Life Festival one year, I found a small basket of frankincense, which I used to introduce Indian Ocean trade routes.

Current Events

Most social studies teachers make use of current events with some regularity. The warm-up gives me a handy niche for them, especially for events unrelated to the main topic of the day. My writing prompt for current events is "Why is (location X) in the news?" Usually I am pleasantly surprised to find that at least one student in each class has heard about the news story I am about to introduce.

Almost every year, the world cooperates by giving me news stories related to the curriculum—the fiftieth anniversary of Ghanaian independence in 2007, for example. When we come to that topic in the curriculum weeks or months later, I can remind the students of the news story. Even ancient history appears in today's news surprisingly often, for example, when a new archaeological find is announced or when some modern disaster overwrites the tracks of the past—Mesopotamian artifacts stolen from Baghdad during the Iraq war, for example.

Printed articles are one source of current events. If your classroom technology permits, you can also show short segments (about three minutes long) from a ten-minute, commercial-free program called *CNN Student News*, available on the CNN website, as a podcast, or you can record it when it is aired. This is only one of many websites that provide video clips; short clips from DVDs or tapes might also be relevant. For today's students, children of the television age, seeing something on television seems to confer a stamp of authority—it really DID happen.

Review Questions

These are helpful on many occasions— the day of the test when I want to start quickly without a long digression, the day when I want to go over something missed by many students on a recently graded test, the day when I realize, as the bell is about to ring, that I have forgotten to prepare a topic. The review warm-up can be planned or impromptu— "Name the first three Chinese dynasties"; "Draw a mental map of the three gunpowder empires." For map drawing, I circulate to make sure that everyone is really drawing, since there is always a subset of students who protest that they cannot possibly draw a mental map. When everyone has drawn something, I select a volunteer to draw one on the board, or I draw it myself. Usually everyone has a good laugh at my maps, which look like elephants or cars. I hope this convinces at least a few students that a map is a tool that need not be perfect.

Assessment

After some experimentation, I have found that the method that works for me is to collect warm-ups every two weeks and give students two points for each response or for each day that the student has taken the time to write the date and "absent." (In case of a suspiciously large number of "absent" entries, I can check attendance records.) Another possibility is to tell students that they are required to have their warm-ups with them at all times; I then call for a particular one to be turned in from time to time. I give credit for completion rather than correctness, but I do not give time for students to copy their friends' warm-ups when I call for them.

Challenges and Rewards

The presence of a bell-ringer every day is an element of structure, while the unpredictability of its content provides a bit of suspense and keeps students on their toes. A few of these bell-ringers require moderately elaborate planning, though usually their simplicity is one of their virtues. The bell-ringer activity must flow directly, smoothly, quickly into the first "real" activity of the day, or it must be a brief, self-contained digression before embarking on the main topic of the lesson. I had to learn this by doing it wrong. The challenge of ensuring that the students will, at a minimum, record a written response daily is met by rewarding each warm-up as a two-point assessment.

One of the rewards of the bell-ringer activities is that they often draw comments by students who tend to keep a low profile in class; if the warm-up for the day touches on some aspect of their background knowledge or family heritage unknown to most of their classmates, they have an opportunity to enjoy a moment in the spotlight. Occasionally I plan this result deliberately, but more often it is serendipitous. Usually both the students and I enjoy opening the class with a non-threatening but unexpected introductory moment.

About the Author

Janet Martin (BA, MPhil, PhD) teaches AP World History and AP European History at W.T. Woodson High School in Fairfax, Virginia. She has a PhD in political science from Yale University and has participated in three AP essay-grading sessions, made three presentations at National Council for Social Studies annual conventions, and contributed to four editions of the AP Lesson Jamboree CD. When her third and youngest child entered school, she quickly tired of doing office temp work, asked herself how she wanted to spend the rest of her life, and went back to school for a teaching certificate.

CHAPTER 23

Get 'Em Up!

Kinesthetic Learning for World History on Block Schedules

BETH WILLIAMS

Conundrum: Teaching the history of "the world" in less than ninety days? A daunting task indeed! It is difficult to meet our curriculum objectives with any bell schedule, but the block format can be particularly challenging for heavy content areas such as world history. Block scheduling typically reduces instructional time by twenty to twenty-five minutes per week compared to a conventional yearlong format. Teachers already lose chunks of instructional time to the chronic interruptions in the regular school day—intermittent assemblies, pep rallies, and the weeks of spring that go missing due to standardized testing.

So how do you grin and proceed?

- by invoking the deities of high-interest learning
- by making every minute that you have with your students count
- by making them eager to be ready for class, and by engaging their brains *and* bodies.

When students are turned on in your classroom, most of your work is done. Great lecturers can mete out content and provoke interest in their courses, but lecture, discussion, and seatwork as a steady diet can quickly turn into an intellectual guillotine, making even the French Revolution tedious. *Liberté, s'il vous plait!*

While there is no magic formula for all situations, adding a few simple strategies to your bill of fare can make your classroom an appealing and effective place to learn social studies. Research shows that music and movement engage students deeply and holistically. I have used the following techniques in both low- and high-performing high schools. They are certifiably field-tested and mostly homegrown strategies I developed from a need to reach students and enjoy my job. Take what you need and make it your own. Powerful teaching happens when the approach is authentically yours. Let these ideas inspire and nurture your own creativity.

The Human Timeline: A Chronology Review Game

The Human Timeline is a competitive, large-group game easily modified for any classroom setting. For this game, you need a completed unit of instruction, cardboard, markers, and your own rules about points or rewards for winning the game. Before the lesson, cut poster board into a size suitable for writing historical dates from a particular era on one side and key events and persons connected to that date on the other—basically, you are creating large flashcards. Make sure both sides of the cards can be read from the back of the classroom.

Divide the class into groups. Distribute equal numbers of placards—at least five—to each group; each student gets one. Choose the team that goes first. Those students go to the front of the class and mix themselves up chronologically, forming an incorrect human timeline. They hold up the placards, showing the persons and events to the other groups of students; the dates on the back of the cards are hidden. The competing groups take turns trying to arrange the events in the correct chronological order, forming an accurate timeline. Obviously, the first group that tries is at a disadvantage because they have not seen any ordering of the dates and will make the first attempt. The mistakes they make in arranging the human timeline will not be made by the second group. Similarly, the mistakes already made by the first and second group will not be made by the third and so on. Hence, you may have to rotate "first" groups each time. I award bonus points on unit exams or final exams on a descending scale depending on how many tries it takes to achieve the correct arrangement. But this is a win-win strategy because the students see, hear, and move with the material, reinforcing their learning. This is both a formative assessment and a review game. The Human Timeline can take an entire class period depending on the material you have covered; the placards can be used again and again. The game can easily be modified; for example, each group can create its own placards, although there is a certain risk of redundancy here. Students can also use charades, not placards, to depict an event, which is fun, but noisier!

Musical Scavenger Hunt (Remember the Old Cakewalks? Musical Chairs?)

This musical pair-share is both a review strategy and a formative assessment that works well at the end of a challenging lesson. It involves both an informal assessment through participation and a quick pen-and-paper pop quiz that assesses the lesson's content. It is a formative assessment because it lets you know how well the content was learned.

You need a well-spaced classroom, high-energy, upbeat music (James Brown works great!), a CD/MP3 player with a pause button, and a teacher-prepared quiz or set of questions for each student. Play ten to twenty seconds music. Students walk around the room when they hear the music and stand still when the music ends. When the music stops, pairs are formed by proximity. You need to monitor the partnering at each interlude in order to prevent the same student clusters from forming. Each time the music stops, you present a review question to the class. The pairs discuss the question and raise their hands when they have the answer. You call on any pair with their hands up until you get the correct answer. If no one answers correctly, start the music again, shuffle the class, and ask the same question this time providing a cue or clue. Call on pairs with their hand up until you get the correct answer. Continue to provide cues this way until at least one pair answers correctly. Then repeat the process for the next question. Monitor all pairs, check the room for accuracy, and start the music again, playing it long enough to shuffle the class thoroughly. The activity continues until all the review questions have been heard and answered. The students return to their desks and take a pencil-and-paper quiz prepared ahead of time. The entire activity, including paper quiz, can be completed in less than thirty minutes. Here is a tip: Do not make this game a routine. Keep it special.

Other Practices

Successful strategies are those that keep an eighty-five- to ninety-minute block vibrant and effective. So, remember, when suitable, get 'em up! Remember to vary these activities; do not overuse any strategy or it will become mundane.

Start each class with a bit of music. While students are entering and settling into the sponge activity, music can energize the class, reflect the historical period you are covering that day, or set a cheerful mood and makes your "place" special.

Take regular "brain breaks"! After a seated activity, such as a test or lecture, have your students stand and stretch their bodies. Breaking together helps ensure that they are paying attention together. You can be very creative here. This is an unlimited area that can be matched to your teaching style; you can find lots of ideas with a quick Internet search.

- News swap: Students have two minutes to discuss with a neighbor a current event topic. On their exit pass (see below), students write the topic of the news story they discussed.
- Five-facts posters: Tape large, blank paper on different walls in your room. Students walk to the nearest poster and write one fact they learned; then rotate to the next poster, writing a new fact not previously recorded by another student. Continue until each poster has five different facts about the lesson. Feel free to play music!
- Vocabulary relay race: Get a copy of Rimsky-Korsakov's "Flight of the Bumblebee" to play during this activity. Divide the chalkboard into sections. Write a key term or concept *vertically* on each section of the board. Using the acrostic poem method, have student teams write characteristics of that term *horizontally* in relay-race style. For example, you write REVOLUTION down the left side of the board; students write associated terms across—for example, R = reform (or another "r" word), E = eclipse of the old regime, V = vacuum of power, O = oath, L = liberty, U = unemployment, etc. . . . First team to finish wins!
- The Hokey-Pokey: Yes, that is what it's all about sometimes. Even my seniors like this exercise on that rare occasion. In this adaptation, student volunteers lead their classmates in doing the Hokey-Pokey in the style of a historical figure, according to their creative imaginations. A student playing Genghis Khan might say, "You put your right arm in and I twist it all about." For Henry VIII, a phrase might be, "I put the chicken leg in, and I chew it all about." Let the class choose the character, and your volunteer student make up the song. It's a hoot!
- Stand and deliver praise! Each student stands and offers an affirmative statement to the group or another individual student. Everyone takes an appropriate bow.
- Informal regroup: Students have two minutes to sharpen pencils, borrow paper, see you about an assignment, or use a hall pass. (When they know this chance is coming, they keep individual requests to a minimum.)

As a wrap-up activity at the end of class, allow one or two minutes for students to write exit passes. Students list five things they learned in class that day, noting what worked and what did not. They also can write questions they did not get answered in class. This is a formative assessment that gives the students a voice in their learning. Students place their exit passes in a basket as they leave. I read them at the end of the day and give check marks for completion as a part of a notebook grade.

About the Author

Beth Williams is the chair of social studies for DeKalb School of the Arts (DSA), a magnet school for performing and visual arts in the DeKalb County School System in Atlanta, Georgia. DSA is a Georgia School of Excellence, an AP Honor School for Access and Support, is currently ranked #380 out of *Newsweek* magazine's top 1,500 high schools in the nation, and was chosen in 2009 as a No Child Left Behind Blue Ribbon School. The Blue Ribbon Schools program honors public and private elementary, middle and high schools that are either academically superior or that demonstrate dramatic gains in student achievement to high levels. Ms. Williams teaches Advanced Placement World History, Accelerated World History, and Advanced Placement Psychology.

CHAPTER 24

Using Your Community in Your World History Course

NANCY JORCZAK

In teaching world history we are constantly relating local to global developments. We are also always aware of making any history course interesting and relevant to today's teenager. One technique to consider is a symposium of community members discussing a topic of concern for your students. Here are two ideas that worked well for my world history classes. The first was a religious symposium held early in the year after the students had studied the basic tenets and development of the major world religions. The second was a symposium on how globalization has been changing the careers that my students may be considering. The intent of this chapter is to share the process of developing a symposium and the results of the two mentioned.

If you live in a diverse community you may be able to convene a fairly large but manageable group of religious representatives. Your students may be some of your best contacts for participants. It was through my students that I was able to locate a representative for Hinduism, Sufism, Sunni Islam, Orthodox Christianity, and Protestant Christianity. The Asian Society of Philadelphia was helpful in locating an expert on Chinese religions. Some Internet research located a local Buddhist group and a Baha'i congregation. Representatives of Roman Catholic Christianity and Orthodox and Reformed Judaism were found by calling local churches and synagogues. With a little work you can probably convene nine or ten people from your community to participate. If you have the capability, it would be a good idea to videotape the proceedings. Your district might require a disclaimer from the participants in order to videotape them. Some of my participants wished to see the edited video before allowing it to go public. This proved to be a wise decision because the student media class that was doing the video edited in the name of the Reformed rabbi while showing the Orthodox rabbi on the screen. This error had to be corrected. The questions were

student-generated from classroom brainstorming sessions and submitted to the symposium participants ahead of time. Student moderators were used to give them public speaking and leadership experience in a familiar environment, the high school library, where the symposium was held. I cautioned the student moderators to politely not allow any one participant to dominate the discussion. The participants were very cooperative and considerate of the students who were learning to facilitate discussion.

Student feedback on the symposium was very positive. The students were most impressed by how the participants respected each other and valued their different belief systems. Students too often see religions as areas of conflict rather than as a means of mutual understanding and cooperation. To witness this cooperation in their local community was an eye-opener for them. They also appreciated the chance to speak with the participants informally at a reception following the symposium to learn more or ask individual follow-up questions about the religions.

In addition to attending the symposium, small groups of students were assigned the task of creating a PowerPoint presentation on past and present religions. These Power-Point presentations were also located in the library and open to other classes who wished to attend. It pays to find out the religions of your students and not make assumptions based on ethnicity. For example, in my class I had an Indian-American and an Egyptian-American who were both Christian. They collaborated on a PowerPoint presentation about being a Christian in a society where the majority of people are Hindu or Muslim. This led to discussions in class on minority religions and the spread of religions.

The autumn symposium worked so well that we staged another one in the spring. Inspired by reading Thomas Friedman's *The World Is Flat* and *Tough Choices or Tough Times*, The Report of the New Commission on the Skills of the American Workforce from the National Center on Education and the Economy, I decided I needed to do more for my students than just to teach them world history. I had to be proactive in making them aware of our rapidly changing world. The spring symposium would be on globalization and careers. My aim was to convene members of the community from a variety of careers to discuss the changes in their careers caused by globalization and the preparation that students today need for the careers of tomorrow.

To find my panel, I started with personal contacts, people I knew and contacts of friends. I got quicker, more positive responses from a potential panelist if my contact notified the person first that I would be calling or e-mailing. Taping and press coverage would allow a larger audience to benefit from the discussion. The invitation letter for the symposium included the questions on globalization and careers the panelists were to discuss. The five questions they were asked were:

1. How has globalization made getting a position in your field more competitive?
2. How has outsourcing changed what you do?
3. What expectations do you have of students coming into your field in regard to world languages, science, math, social sciences, communication skills, and technical skills?
4. What do students have to do to prepare for an occupation in your field that may be different from what you did due to more globalization?
5. How has globalization provided more opportunities in your field?

The panel consisted of Mr. Sean Dukes, a director of Systems Engineering, Integration and Testing at Commercial Space Systems of Lockheed Martin; Professor James Freeman, author and language and literature professor; the Hon. James C. Greenwood, president and CEO of Biotechnology Industry Organization and former congressman in the U.S. House of Representatives; Lt. Col. Steven A. Kelly, USMC helicopter pilot and staff officer at the Naval Control Point; Professor Harris Sokoloff, co-director of the Franklin Conference of the Penn Institute for Urban Research; Professor Nelleke Van Deusen-Scholl, director of Penn Language Center; Dr. Deidre V. Walsh, director of nuclear cardiology at St. Mary Medical Center; Mr. George N. Luciani, president and founder of Capital Planning Advisory Group Inc.; Mr. Kevin McCarthy, chief information officer for Glatfelter, INC., responsible for global information technology systems, software and infrastructure, and Mr. Christian Seiler, U.S. sales manager for Finish Line Promotions and Manufacturing, a Chinese manufacturer. Although their résumés were very different, their advice to students was often very similar.

Figure 24.1   **Symposium Invitation Letter**

Dear Sir or Madam,

Council Rock School district is committed to involving the community in our efforts to prepare students for the world they will face upon graduation from high school and college. We as educators understand that, in a world that is rapidly changing due to technological innovation, we may not be able to keep up with the changes you face daily. Therefore we are inviting experts in many occupational fields to participate in a symposium at Council Rock High School North on May 23, 2007, from 9 a.m. to 11 a.m. We would be pleased if you could join us for a roundtable discussion on these three questions:

1. How has globalization impacted your occupational field?
2. What challenges and opportunities might our students face as they enter careers in your field In this new century?
3. How would you advise our students to prepare themselves to meet those challenges and take advantage of those opportunities?

The roundtable discussion should last about one and a half hours with a half hour for students' questions at the end. As it is not possible to bring the entire student body into the symposium, we will have a selected representative student audience and will tape the symposium for later use in the classroom. There will be a reception in the Council Rock High School Library following the symposium for the members who can stay longer to talk with students in a more informal atmosphere. If you are able to participate in the endeavor, please respond to me by e-mail or by mail at the above address. Thank you for your consideration of this request to help our students prepare for their futures.

Nancy Jorczak
Social Studies Department

No matter what career students may think they want to follow, chances are that their choice will change at least once, often due to the realities of globalization. Mr. Seiler explained that in high school he thought he was going to be a professional baseball player and even played in the minor leagues, but now he works for a company based in China. He needs to understand Chinese business and social relationships as he deals with them every day; his job is to facilitate the interaction between the Chinese manufacturer and the American customer ordering the product, which requires an understanding of the thought processes of both groups. Mr. McCarthy, an IT specialist, lived in China. He explained to students that no matter what they did, they would be dealing with global diversity. People do things differently and learn things differently overseas and it is important to be aware of that difference, he told the students, in order to be successful in any career. If you are creating software for a Chinese firm, you must understand what they want on their terms, not yours, he said. You are working for them. Study their history and culture. Lt. Col. Kelly, the marine, said that you need to know how other countries evolved to be able to get into their heads. Mr. Greenwood added that as you walk down the hallway of a biotech lab you will notice all the different ethnic names on the doors. The people you work with will be from many cultures and you need to understand those cultures in order to work together.

Globalization impacts every thing, from the clothes you wear to the drugs you take. According to Mr. Luciani, you cannot advise people on investing if you do not understand how the global economy works, and even if you do not advise others, you should understand it for your own investment decisions. Moreover, projections are that by 2050 China and India will own more than half our capitalization and Americans will own only 16 percent, so you may be working for another country without ever leaving the United States. Dr. Walsh mentioned that many of the drugs she prescribes are manufactured in other countries so she must be aware of studies on cardiology in different countries. Moreover, doctors diagnosing a patient must be aware that people bring back illnesses from foreign travel or contact with those who have traveled. The local hospital often has patients who do not speak English, and the doctors cannot count on having a family member around to translate when trying to communicate with a patient. Hospitals are required by law to have international telephone lines for translators. Indeed, many of the panelists advised the students to learn world languages—the more, the better. The three trends seen at the Penn Language Center are students learning a language due to family connections, business majors learning languages to improve their future career opportunities (at Wharton Business School at the University of Pennsylvania, majors study two or three languages, especially Japanese, Korean, Chinese, and Portuguese), and professionals with a diverse clientele needing more language skills, particularly Spanish and sign language. According to Mr. Dukes, if you are applying for a job at Lockheed Martin, math and science are not enough. Can you read Japanese? Can you write Japanese so it is clearly understood? Studying world languages helps you learn different ways of thinking. Moreover, the more languages you study, the more you understand your own language.

All the panelists gave advice regarding the huge importance of good communication skills. Speak and write your own language well. Résumés with grammatical errors go right in the trashcan. Text messaging is not acceptable for formal writing. If you are communicating with people from another country and they write your language better than you do, they are not impressed. High SAT scores are not sufficient if you cannot write well. Members of Congress do not wish to send their aides to grammar school to learn how to spell or punctuate properly. Be a well-rounded student in your pursuit of knowledge no matter what career you wish to pursue. "A study of religion, philosophy, and literature can help you navigate a lifetime," Mr. Luciani remarked. Math and science are important if you wish to pursue a career in economics, technology, the military, or medicine, but if you cannot communicate well, you will end up in some back cubicle doing grunge work.

After establishing how important it is for students to learn world history, world languages, and English well, the panelists discussed what skills the students should work on over the next few years. Since you cannot predict the future, it is important to be well rounded in your education so you can be flexible and versatile and open to change. The military is also looking for well-rounded individuals. Research is an important skill. In today's global economy, Americans without information skills are the losers. Professor Sokoloff asked the students to consider what turns data into information, information into knowledge, knowledge into understanding, and understanding into wisdom. Technology provides the data, but learning and experience do the rest. Social skills are also important. Most occupations require collaboration with other people, and thanks to technological advances that means other people around the world. Professor Sokoloff noted that students in the Pacific Rim do better on standardized tests than Americans do. Those nations' average students match what our best students achieve on those tests, so why do those countries want American educators to evaluate their schools? The answer is that our current edge in the world is due to development of creative thinking. Governments in other countries want their students to excel in that too. Sokoloff believes that the two most important skills are learning how to learn and learning how to ask questions.

The panelists offered students useful recommendations to prepare themselves for their future. Do not waste your summers. Surround yourself with educated, interesting people. When you go to college, develop relationships with students from other countries. They may help your career. Explore opportunities to travel to different countries, such as mission work abroad. Live with a family in another country for a while. Do not go on the same semester-abroad program as all your friends. Choose a more unusual place, which may give you an edge as you apply for a job. For example, Lockheed Martin trains its employees how to interact with Vietnamese, Saudis, and other peoples. Having some experience in dealing with other nationalities may help you in any job.

How did the students react to all this advice? This symposium took place in the spring, after the advanced placement exam, a time to relax, they thought upon entering the symposium room. As the symposium ended, the students looked a bit shell-shocked by the recognition of how important all their classes were. They took some deep breaths as they realized that all this was important for them to know. Although some students were sure that their current career choices would never change, even they related to the rest of what the panelists said. This material was relevant. They will remember many of the panelists' suggestions.

About the Author

Nancy Jorczak has been active in world history teaching circles, with a special interest in integrating art and writing into the world history class. She has retired from teaching at Council Rock High School North, Newtown, Pennsylvania.

CHAPTER 25

The Importance of Teaching About Religion in the Classroom

Barbara Brun-Ozuna

Teaching about religion in the classroom is at once one of the most controversial aspects of the profession and one of the most important lessons we can teach our students. Along with celebrating racial and cultural differences, respecting and understanding various religious traditions is crucial to the future well being of democracy. There are clearly pitfalls, however, for if teachers stray into teaching religious dogma rather than religious traditions, they could find themselves in direct conflict with the First Amendment's establishment clause. Teachers should thus educate themselves on the laws regarding the teaching of topics containing religious components and think proactively about communicating that knowledge to parents and even to students. Another serious concern is presenting course materials without unwittingly reinforcing students' preconceived notions and thus contributing to stereotyping of religions. Teaching religion in a cultural context rather than from an orthodox practices approach should reinforce the concept that that religion is a component of a society's culture and thus varies from place to place. The teaching of a variety of religious traditions in a cultural context is crucial if we wish to help students not just tolerate differences, but embrace them.

The United States is one of the most diverse countries in the world, both ethnically and religiously. Its citizens have long embraced the notion of being a nation of immigrants who have voluntarily chosen to interact with one another. The process of integration is strong, for within a generation or so, the children of immigrants become assimilated into American culture, while remaining proud of their ancestral heritage. This diversity comes with a price, however, for it can create tensions and factions if pluralism is not truly embraced. The goal, therefore, is not merely to tolerate each other's differences, whether racial, linguistic, or religious, but rather to truly respect them. Respect for difference, and thus true pluralism, will come about only through education. We must seek to eradicate illiteracy of every type, not just academic, but also cultural and religious.

The difficulties inherent in teaching religion stem from the fact that many individuals equate the teaching of religion with the teaching of devotional practices. Thus, teachers tend to teach religion from a series of PowerPoint slides that quickly explain that Christians and Jews follow the Ten Commandments (with Christians accepting the divinity of Jesus while Jews do not), Muslims follow the Five Pillars, Buddhists look for the eight-fold path, and Hindus believe in reincarnation and the sanctity of cows. Not only does this approach reduce religion to the esoteric, but it also inadvertently strengthens the power of the orthodox practitioners and advocates of a religion, for it indicates that there is only one way to truly be a good Christian, Jew, Muslim, Buddhist, or Hindu. This approach tends to reinforce stereotypes, dehumanizes the individuals who practice the religion, and does very little to foster true respect for diversity. In order to teach religion appropriately, we must do so from a cultural perspective that clearly shows how vastly diverse religious practices are and how a society's culture molds religious practices and beliefs.

This focus on the cultural aspects of a religion not only makes the teaching of religion more multifaceted, but also reduces the likelihood of opposition from parents and fellow educators. The establishment clause of the First Amendment to the U.S. Constitution clearly states that the government can do nothing to promote one religion over another, nor can it prohibit the free exercise of religion. This means that teachers must be scrupulously neutral in teaching religion and must know the laws of their own state education agency. Texas law, for example, provides an opt-out clause that allows students who object to the content of a lesson to ask for an alternate assignment. Acknowledging that right and having such alternate assignments readily available will cut down on the tension and stress that these situations often involve. Furthermore, teachers' in-service training should focus on the legality of teaching religion in a public school context. Several websites help establish these dos and don'ts:

www.teachingaboutreligion.org
www.adl.org/religion_ps_2004/teaching.asp
http://www.pewforum.org
www.firstamendmentcenter.org

Teaching that religious practices are culturally determined not only accentuates the vast spectrum in which religious devotional practices are adhered to, but also makes religion seem truly multifaceted by emphasizing the cultural and societal roles that religion plays. However, unlike the traditional tour of devotion that students tend to produce, putting such genuinely cultural lessons together takes quite a bit of time, expertise, preparation, and creativity on the teacher's part. Furthermore, these lessons should be integrated into the curriculum of the course throughout the entire year, not just in the foundations section of the Advanced Placement (AP) World History course. One program that helps teachers do just that is Bridging World History, an Annenberg Media program whose streaming video segments teachers can access through the website www.learner.org.

As teachers of the world history course know, religion and spirituality have strongly influenced human beings since the dawn of time. There is pictographic evidence that spirituality and animism began extremely early in human history and that many of the symbols of spirituality were the same whether in aboriginal Australia or pre-Columbian America. A common religious and spiritual experience was clearly manifested in the rock art of various indigenous peoples. These commonalities within religion continued as humans settled into agricultural areas and devotional practices became more complex. Teachers should focus on these similarities.

One way to do this is by focusing on sacred sites found in various religions. Mountains, for example, are sacred in various areas of the world, including Japan, China, India, and North and South America. Why? Looking at that question from the viewpoint of various religious traditions is fascinating and with a site like www.sacredsites.com can be done relatively easily. What we learn is that mountains represent a life force because they are seen as being close to the sky. In many traditions, mountains serve to hold up the sky and are thus dwelling places of the god(s). Many mountains have thus become pilgrimage sites, from Machu-Picchu, located high in the Andes Mountains, to Mount Fuji in Japan.

Mount Fuji, Japan (http://en.wikipedia.org/wiki/File:FujiSunriseKawa guchiko2025WP.jpg)

Sacred Mount Tai Shan, China (Courtesy of Brianna Laugher; http://commons.wikimedia.org/wiki/File:Sunset_at_Mt_Tai.JPG)

Mount Kailash, Tibet, sacred to Hindus, Jains, and Buddhists (Courtesy of Ondřej Žváček. Permission is granted to copy, distribute and/or modify this document under the terms of the GNU Free Documentation License; http://en.wikipedia.org/wiki/File:Kailash_north .jpg)

Sacred Kachina peaks, Arizona (Courtesy of the Forest Service of the United States Department of Agriculture.)

Mount Olympus, Greece (http://en.wikipedia.org/wiki/File:Olympus _Litochoro.JPG)

Lake Titicaca, Bolivia, with sacred mountains of Ancohuma and Illampu in the background (www.flickr.com /photos/55628743@N00/134322120/)

Zoroastrian shrine of Chak Chak near Yasd, Iran (http://en.wikipedia.org/wiki/File:Chak-chak.jpg)

Carthusian monastery in France (Courtesy of Arne Eide; http:// en.wikipedia.org/wiki/File:La_Grande_Chartreuse.jpg)

Holy sites are not just nature-based, but also architectural. Sacred architecture all over the world has many common features. For example, sacred architecture often involves the use of perfect proportion; whether a Christian church, a Muslim mosque, or a Buddhist temple, the defined space is usually highly symmetrical and well proportioned. Holy space usually faces a specific direction—for example, the rising sun, Mecca, or significant constellations in the heavens. Many sacred buildings incorporate towers or high domes, again harking back to the mountains and the idea that the divine is celestial. Thus, Hindu temples at Angkor Wat resemble the Hindu Kush, whereas the Buddhist temples in nearby Burma, which look very similar, re-create the mountains where the Buddha ascended to enlightenment.

Mahabohdi Temple, Bagan, Burma (This file is licensed under the Creative Commons Attribution ShareAlike 2.5 License; http://en.wikipedia.org/wiki/File:Mahabodhitemple.jpg)

Pilgrims on the river Ganges in front of the temple compound, Banaras, India (Courtesy of Steve Evans; www.flickr.com/photos/babasteve/3267702/sizes/o/in/set-781175/)

Cathedral of Santiago de Compostela, Santiago, Spain (Courtesy of Niels Bosboom. This file is licensed under the Creative Commons Attribution ShareAlike 3.0 License; http://en.wikipedia.org/wiki/File:Cathedral_square_Santiago_de_Compostela.jpg)

Bayon Temple, Angkor, Cambodia (Courtesy of Charles J. Sharp. Permission is granted to copy, distribute and/or modify this document under the terms of the GNU Free Documentation License; http://commons.wikimedia.org/wiki/File:Bayon-temple.JPG)

Of course, religions do not develop in a vacuum. Rather, they are influenced by peoples and ideas traveling the many trade roads. Thus, architecture and architectural styles, as well as devotional practices, religious paintings, and statuary art, show the influences not only of the culture in which the religion originated, but also the culture to which it came.

This relationship can best be shown to students using a case-studies approach—for example, how Islamic mosque architecture changes as it moves from its place of origin to the outer edges of Dar-al-Islam. Mosques contain three fundamental components: the courtyard, the *kiblah* wall that faces Mecca, and the mihrab—a niche along the Kiblah wall that signifies the presence of Muhammad. The way these three components and other, optional components are put together is clearly influenced by preexisting cultural traits. In Spain and Morocco, the mosques have very strong quadratic lines and sturdy minarets, reminiscent of Romanesque architecture. The arches within the covered prayer areas also are strongly influenced by both Byzantine and Romanesque architecture. Further south in Africa, where sand and mud were more readily available than stone, the builders of the mosque at Timbuktu created a beautiful building that incorporates the essential building blocks of the mosque—the courtyard, the mihrab, and the kiblah—but does so in a fashion unique to the desert.

Front entrance, Great Mosque of Cordoba, Spain
(Mohammad Al-Asad, 1986. Courtesy of the Aga Khan Visual Archive,
M.I.T. This material may be protected under the copyright law [Title 17
U.S. Code].)

**Interior of the Great Mosque of Cordoba, Spain, with
distinct arches** (Maryalice Torres, 1990. Courtesy of the Aga Khan
Visual Archive, M.I.T. This material may be protected under the copyright
law [Title 17 U.S. Code].)

In Turkey, minarets tend to be pencil-thin and numerous, surrounding mosques with multiple domes. Mosques in Iran, on the other hand, tend to have one very large, ornate dome, covered in either blue or gold mosaic tiles. Often the entrances to the courtyard space, known as Iwan, are very big and imposing. In China, mosque architecture takes

Mosque of Al-Qarawiyyin, Fez, Morocco (Ahmad Nabal, 1990.
Courtesy of the Aga Khan Visual Archive, M.I.T. This material may be
protected under the copyright law [Title 17 U.S. Code].)

on a distinctively Asian flair. Although the basic mosque structure is still there, the building looks more like a Chinese pagoda than a mosque. Yet the Great Mosque of Xi'an serves 60,000 Chinese Muslims.

Meanwhile, architecture in India blends the influences of Hindu and Persian architecture into the famous tomb of the Taj Mahal and also the beautiful Friday mosque of Fatehpur Sikri. The presence of onion-shaped domes in mosque architecture continues in Indonesia and other areas of Southeast Asia. Minarets also take on distinctive forms, somewhat reminiscent of Hindu and Buddhist temple architecture.

Thus, through architectural representation or similar statuary or pictorial examples, teachers can easily show students that a religion changes as it is practiced in different areas of the world because religious beliefs blend with local traditions, just as religious sites are often erected on previous religious sites and blend local architectural styles with those traditionally found in the cultural center of the religion. These images reinforce the idea that any given religion is not unidimensional. On the other hand, emphasizing the commonalities in all religions reinforces the notion that human beings commonly seek answers to the same big questions and that those answers tend to be remarkably similar.

Djingabeyer Mosque, Timbuktu, Mali (Courtesy of Sian Kennedy/Aga Khan Trust for Culture)

Fatih Mosque, Istanbul, Turkey (Walter Denny, ca. 1960. Courtesy of the Aga Khan Visual Archive, M.I.T. This material may be protected under the copyright law [Title 17 U.S. Code].)

Shrine of Imam Reza, Masshad, Iran (Permission to copy, distribute and/or modify this document under the terms of the GNU Free Documentation License; http://en.wikipedia.org/wiki/File:RezaShrine.jpg)

Gate to the main courtyard of the Great Xian mosque, Xian China (© BrokenSphere/Wikimedia Commons; http://commons. wikimedia.org/wiki/FIle:Great_Mosque_of_Xi%27an_Wooden_Memorial _Archway_1.JPG)

Friday Mosque, Fatehpur Sikri, India (Michael Brand, 1984. Courtesy of the Aga Khan Visual Archive, M.I.T. This material may be protected under the copyright law [Title 17 U.S. Code].)

People look at religion in various ways. One way of thinking is exclusionist. These people believe that only they have the right answer. Relativists understand and tolerate other viewpoints on religion without embracing them or accepting them as legitimate. Pluralists believe that there is one truth and that various religious traditions understand

Minaret and Mosque, Kudus Indonesia (Jeffrey Westcott and
E. Padmodipeotro, 1981. Courtesy of the Aga Khan Visual Archive, M.I.T.
This material may be protected under the copyright law [Title 17 U.S.
Code].)

parts of that truth. Inclusive pluralists believe that their truth
is completely within the larger truth, but also acknowledge
that other religions understand that truth, which is larger
than any one religion can explain. Thus, pluralists embrace
difference in religious traditions and respect religious diversity because they understand that even though their truth
might be completely accurate, so are other people's. In order
to maintain democracy in the United States without degen-
erating into the conflicts we have witnessed in so many
other countries, we must embrace this pluralistic vision.
This can only be done through education. Thus, teachers
need to fairly and accurately teach about religion in the
classroom and put religious practices in a cultural context
for students. Only then can we move toward fundamental
understanding and thus true respect.

About the Author

Barbara Brun-Ozuna (MA, history) has taught in the Fort
Worth independent school district in Texas since 1990. She
began teaching world history to tenth graders at Paschal
High School in 2001 and currently serves as a table leader
at the annual AP World History reading. She has been a
consultant in world history since 2003 and has worked
as an AP Summer Institute consultant since 2005. She
is a member of World History Association, the National
Council for the Social Studies, and the Texas Council for
the Social Studies.

CHAPTER 26

Leaders' Forum
Learning About Leadership in World History

STEVEN L. BUENNING

Most men and women go through their lives using no more than a fraction—usually a rather small fraction—of the potentialities within them. The reservoir of unused human talent and energy is vast, and learning to tap that reservoir more effectively is one of the exciting tasks ahead for humankind.

Among the untapped capabilities are leadership gifts. For every effectively functioning leader in our society, I would guess that there are five or ten others with the same potential for leadership who have never led or perhaps even considered leading. Why? Perhaps they . . . have never sensed the potentialities within them . . . or have never understood how much the society needs what they have to give.

We can do better. Much, much better.[1]

—John W. Gardner

Preparing our students for the responsibilities and rights of citizenship is our most important job as educators. The myriad tasks we perform daily are all directed toward one overarching goal: to help young people become better human beings who will, one day, take over for us when we are gone. As historian Peter N. Stearns has written, "studying history encourages habits of mind that are vital for responsible public behavior, whether as a national or community leader, an informed voter, a petitioner, or a simple observer."[2]

In our classrooms, teachers are leaders—and we have the dual opportunity to model and to teach about good leadership. Leaders' Forum—an activity in which students do research on historical leaders, impersonate them in a role-play, and write essays on them afterward—is designed to foster reflection about leadership in four ways:

- by introducing individual leaders in world history
- by creating original written and oral presentations on the theme of leadership in history
- by comparing and contrasting the contributions of leaders in history
- by considering how examples from the past may influence attitudes toward leadership in the present and future

While a total of seven class days are allocated for the Leaders' Forum activity, these are not consecutive; Leaders' Forum days can be interspersed with days spent teaching a "regular" unit. On the first two Leaders' Forum days, students choose historical figures for impersonation and start their research. "What Do I Do Now?" is the theme of the third day. Day four is set aside for orientation on the role-play. The role-play occurs on the fifth day. The sixth day involves a debriefing and the introduction of the essay assignment. On the last day, students work on their essays in class or the computer lab. The biggest keys to success in the Leaders' Forum exercise are the enthusiasm of the teacher, breaking down the assignments into manageable chunks, and carefully guiding students through each stage of the activity.

The Presentations tab on my website, www.sbuenning. com, allows users to download copies of all the documents used in Leaders' Forum. A helpful PowerPoint is also included.

Days One and Two: Choosing a Leader and Starting Research

The Leaders' Forum assignment sheet (see Appendix A on page 130) introduces students to the activity. First, students choose a leader whom they will research and impersonate at Leaders' Forum. The assignment sheet provides extensive lists of possible choices. Students may, with teacher approval, choose an unlisted leader.

These lists emphasize diversity in gender, time period, ethnicity, occupations, and leadership styles. The names of over sixty female and over eighty male leaders are provided, but students may choose leaders of either gender. The listed leaders come from all time periods, including the present. They are grouped according to continent (Africa, Americas, Asia, Europe). Monarchs, generals, democratic leaders, dictators, human rights activists, writers, artists, scientists, philosophers, clerics, and various tyrants are included. They exemplify what psychologist Howard Gardner calls direct leadership (in which leaders "address their public face-to-face") and/or indirect leadership (in which "individuals exert impact through the works that they create").[3]

Prior to the start of the activity, discuss all plans with your school's library media specialist; this professional should be your number one ally! This teacher can help students locate reliable sources, both print and web-based. Avoid Wikipedia, which is not peer-reviewed and, in a general disclaimer, makes no guarantee of its own validity.[4]

On these two days, students use the reference room in the media center to start research. Advise students to focus on the actions of their chosen leader, with emphasis on how the leader influenced others.

Make sure that you impersonate a leader, too. This sets an example for students and allows you to join in the fun! Since our school mascot is the Viking, my own leader is Leif Eriksson—complete with authentic outfit!

Day Three: "What Do I Do Now?"

About ten calendar days before the Leaders' Forum role-play, give the students a letter to show their parents. This letter explains the activity and is accompanied by a parent permission form.

Distribute the "What Do I Do Now?" handout (see Appendix B on page 131). This provides students with more information regarding all requirements of the activity: research (including bibliography), business card, essay, costume, and role-play. Particular attention is paid to instructions on designing the business card.

After answering all questions, initiate a brainstorming discussion about the characteristics of an effective leader. Write responses on the board and encourage students to copy them in their notebooks. Accept all responses except those that will not advance the discussion in a positive manner. The intent is to stimulate serious thought about leadership.

Day Four: Orientation on the Role-Play

By now, students will have quite specific questions concerning the role-play. Many of these questions will center on their costumes. Costumes should demonstrate some effort toward authenticity, but are not expected to involve unreasonable expense. Reassure students that costumes, while required, are only a very minor part of their evaluation. No weapons or look-alike weapons are allowed.

Use this day to answer all questions. Students should understand that, on the day of the role-play, they are expected to bring to class a bibliography (in proper form) and enough business cards so that each student and the teacher will receive one. The students, impersonating their chosen leaders, should be prepared to take part in small-group discussions with other leaders during the role-play. The leaders should be ready to discuss three specific occasions in their life when they demonstrated leadership.

Day Five: Leaders' Forum Role-Play

The process described here has worked smoothly for more than a dozen years. At first glance, it may seem complicated, but teacher and students quickly get used to how it is done!

Prior to the role-play, the teacher needs to do some advance preparation:

- Purchase inexpensive name badges and envelopes (9 x 12 inch).
- Assign each leader a number, and write the leader's number and name on the badge. Do the same with each envelope.
- Prepare two notesheets, one for female leaders and one for male leaders. List each leader's number and name on the appropriate sheet. (Each student receives the notesheets prior to the start of the role-play.)
- On fifteen sheets of paper, write one large letter. Write "A" on the first sheet, "B" on the second sheet, and so on, until the letter "O" is written on the fifteenth sheet. (These will be used by the station chiefs during the role-play.)

In my school, the Leaders' Forum role-play is scheduled as an "in-school field trip" during three consecutive fifty-minute periods, thus allowing for combining students from two or even three world history classes. This format expands the number and diversity of the leaders who will be attending. Naturally, one classroom cannot accommodate that many students, so the role-play occurs in a large room in the school's media center (another example of the importance of collaboration with the librarian!).

Prior to the role-play, custodians have moved tables, desks, and chairs away from the center of the room and toward the walls. Before students arrive, the teacher places the envelopes consecutively around the room (on tables, on top of shelves, on desks or chairs, on the floor). As students arrive, they are told to change into their costumes. Upon returning to the library, each student is given a numbered name badge and asked to submit a bibliography. Then students distribute their business cards, placing one inside each envelope. Give students two notesheets (one for women, one for men). The number and name of each leader are listed consecutively on the two notesheets. Students then line up so they are all moving in the same direction.

Now give students the rotation sequence (see my website). This sequence randomly places students in small groups. The sequence includes lettered columns (A–O) with five numbers in each column. In each rotation, the first number in each column remains the same; students with these numbers are known as station chiefs. Give each station chief one of the lettered sheets of paper (see above) and space the chiefs evenly around the room. The chiefs are the only students who will remain in the same places throughout the role-play.

The role-play begins with the first rotation. Station chiefs hold up their lettered sheets. Tell all the leaders to go to the station corresponding to their number. There, each leader engages in small-group conversation with other leaders; students are encouraged, when possible, to behave as the leaders they are impersonating might have behaved—though you might want to urge Attila or Genghis Khan not to get *too* much into character! The topic of discussion is specific ways in which each leader has influenced the lives of others. Using the two notesheets, leaders take notes on what the other leaders have to say about themselves. (These notes will be important later when students write their essays.)

After a suitable time period, announce the second rotation. Station chiefs hold up their lettered sheets and students move to the next station. The rotation sequence continues accordingly. (Note: The rotation sequence contains numbers one through seventy-five. If more than seventy-five students participate in your role-play, tell the extras to go to any station that needs another person.)

Often Leaders' Forum includes a lunch period, and students need to be fed. We like to order pizza and beverages for delivery; each student pays a nominal charge to cover costs. My suggestion is to schedule food delivery at the end of the role-play. The letter sent to parents on Day Three invites parents to volunteer, particularly with the serving of food. Remind students to ask their parents to do so. Parents enjoy being involved with the event, and their participation will help you focus on the mechanics of leading the role-play. For some students, the chance to dress up in costumes and eat pizza in the library is admittedly the most memorable feature of Leaders' Forum. But if that leaves a good taste in a student's mouth about history, so be it!

Before leaving the role-play, students take their numbered envelopes, with the business cards inserted by all the leaders inside.

Day Six: Debriefing and Introduction of the Essay Assignment

The teacher leads debriefing of the role-play. It is difficult for many self-conscious teens to venture outside their comfort zones by donning a costume and pretending to be a historical figure, so make sure you compliment students on their performances! Ask them to comment on what went well and what needed to be improved or changed. You can get lots of helpful ideas from your students.

In grading Leaders' Forum, 50 percent of the points come from what students do before or during the role-play. The other 50 percent are based on an essay written after the role-play.

The leadership essay assignment sheet (see my website) supplies detailed instructions. Each student writes about two of the leaders at the role-play—the leader that the student impersonated and any other leader of the student's choice. Here is the prompt I use:

Compare and contrast the two leaders. Of the two, who was the more effective leader? Discuss in terms of the following:

a. preparation for leadership
b. influence on others while alive
c. impact on later history

The assignment sheet informs students of the structure and content of the essay. The instructions emphasize using specific evidence to develop and support a thesis that directly answers the prompt. Students should use both their notesheets and the business cards (received in the envelopes) to begin planning their essays. However, they will need to go beyond this information if they want to write a first-rate essay. They need to gather data concerning a leader's preparation for leadership and impact on later history, topics that may not have come up during the role-play. Helpful sources include the classmate who portrayed that leader, the textbook, and other print or online material. As always, students need to pay attention to the validity of their sources and must express ideas in their own words.

Day Seven: Writing the Essay

Students will benefit from a teacher's guidance in writing the essay. You may choose to take them to the computer lab or to bring laptop computers into your classroom. Using class time for this purpose will reduce student anxiety and improve the quality of the essays.

Evaluation

As mentioned above, half the grading points available for the activity are derived from what a student does before or during the role-play. Historical accuracy and proper listing of sources in the bibliography account for twenty points; the ability to portray the leader for the entire exercise (including costume) is worth ten points; the business card can earn ten points. The other forty points come from the essay, which is written after the role-play. A points grid and student score sheet are available on my website, as is a detailed essay rubric. This rubric specifies a variety of criteria for evaluating the essay.

Alternative Suggestions

The Leaders' Forum framework, of course, can be adapted according to the wishes of the teacher. One idea to change the essay prompt. For instance, a prompt could center on Howard Gardner's conceptualization of direct and indirect leadership (see Day One). The prompt could ask students to choose one direct and one indirect leader for comparison and contrast. Students could then discuss which was the more effective leader in terms of the three criteria already provided—or in terms of other criteria of the teacher's preference.

A second idea is to use Leaders' Forum in U.S. history classes. Or students could be asked to write poetry, instead of an essay, as their final product. Both these adaptations were used by Marge Strand, teacher of gifted students at Lake Zurich (IL) Middle School South. After their role-play, Ms. Strand's students wrote two types of poems. The "biopoem" is a biographical poem written by individual students about the leader they impersonated. The "poem for two voices" pairs two students whose collaborative efforts result in a poem that compares and contrasts their leaders' attributes and contributions. These ideas are drawn from the work of consultant Marjorie A. Montgomery.[5]

Another approach is to assign some students the roles of journalists with the task of producing a newspaper covering the events of Leaders' Forum. This approach provides yet another means of developing student skills in writing and graphics.

Conclusion

In teaching world history, we weave through thousands of years as we help our students to appreciate the contributions of our ancestors. But in the blink of a chronological eye, the students in our classrooms will be choosing—

and, perhaps, becoming—the leaders of tomorrow. Each of these future adult citizens will be able to exercise the same rights and responsibilities possessed by each teacher in today's classrooms. Helping our students to think more critically about the nature of leadership is a necessity, and Leaders' Forum is an activity that can help achieve that outcome.

About the Author

Steven L. Buenning, a National Board Certified Teacher, teaches at William Fremd High School, Palatine, Illinois. He received his BA in history from Princeton and his MAT in history and social sciences from University of Chicago. He is author of *The Russian Revolution*, a teaching unit published by the Choices for the 21st Century Education Program at Brown University.

Notes

1. John W. Gardner, *On Leadership* (New York: Free Press, 1990), xix.
2. Peter N. Stearns, "Why Study History?," American Historical Association, 1998, 4, www.historians.org/pubs/free/WhyStudyHistory.htm.
3. Howard Gardner, *Leading Minds: An Anatomy of Leadership* (New York: Basic Books, 1995), ix.
4. General disclaimer, http://en.wikipedia.org/wiki/Wikipedia.
5. Marjorie A. Montgomery, *Accelerating Student Learning in Social Studies: Hands-On Activities, Engaging Projects, and High-Interest Strategies* (Bellevue, WA: Bureau of Education and Research, 2007).

Appendix A: Leader's Forum

Hey, history wannabes! Now you can enjoy the once-in-a-lifetime chance to travel back in your very own personal time machine! Yes, you will be able to go where no person has gone before! You will:

1. choose a man or woman from World History;
2. research the story of that person's life;
3. costume yourself to appear as that person actually appeared;
4. design an informative, attractive business card;
5. attend a gathering of some of the most intriguing people ever to have graced our planet—at the world-renowned Leaders' Forum; and
6. write a well-organized, thoughtful essay on leaders in history.

Sound too good to be true? Well, hold onto your hats, because here's how you can make your historical dreams become reality!

STEP I: Choose a man or woman from World History! Lists are on the reverse side of this sheet! Then see the teacher to get approval of your choice!

STEP II: Research that person! Start your research with your trusty textbook! You may use the good old William Fremd High School library during a study hall or lunch hour! What a school this is! Plus, at no extra charge, there are terrific public libraries just minutes away here in the exciting northwest suburbs! But wait—there's more! You can also utilize the wonders of the World Wide Web (a.k.a. the Internet)!

STEP III: Appear in authentic historical costume! Create your very own fashion statement to show how your character looked while alive! Use your imaginations, but don't include actual weapons or look-alike weapons. See your friendly librarian for books on historical costuming!

STEP IV: Design an informative, attractive business card! The teacher will have some ideas for you on this step!

STEP V: Attend a party given in honor of all invited guests at the world-renowned Leaders' Forum!! Don't forget your business cards; in fact, don't leave home without them!

STEP VI: Write a five-paragraph essay discussing leaders in history.

This sure sounds great! But how do you get started? Well, choose a person from the list and you're on your way!

WOMEN

Africa	Americas	Asia
Hatshepsut	Rigoberta Menchu	Ci Xi
Cleopatra	Eleanor Roosevelt	Mirabai
Amina	Hillary Clinton	Esther
Mbande Nzinga	Jane Addams	Golda Meir
Yaa Asantewaa	Eva Peron	Sondok
Mary Leakey	Frida Kahlo	Indira Gandhi
Shajarat al-Durr	Elizabeth Cady Stanton	Wu Zhao
Queen of Sheba	Sor Juana Ines de la Cruz	Murasaki
Wangari Maathai		Shikibu
Nefertiti		Nur Jahan
		Liliuokalani
		Corazon
		Aquino
		Benazir Bhutto
		Razia
		Aung San
		Suu Kyi
		Mother Teresa
		of Calcutta
		Lakshmi Bai
		Fu Hao

Europe

Christine de Pizan	Teresa of Avila
Emmeline Pankhurst	Anna Comnena
Eleanor of Aquitaine	Boudica
Sofonisba Anguissola	Grace O'Malley
Laura Cereta	Theodora
Victoria	Hildegard of Bingen
Elizabeth Blackwell	Jane Austen
Isabella d'Este	Christina

Artemisia Gentileschi	Princess Diana
Marie Curie	Florence Nightingale
Mary Tudor	Bess of Hardwick
Elizabeth I	
Mary, Queen of Scots	
Maria Theresa	
Margaret Thatcher	
Catherine the Great	
Joan of Arc	
Isabella of Castile	
Catherine de'Medici	
Marie Antoinette	

MEN

Africa	Americas	Asia
Ramses II	Montezuma II	Ibn Sina (Avicenna)
Tutankhamun	Fidel Castro	Solomon
Ibn Battuta	Benito Juarez	Shi Huangdi
Menelik II	Emiliano Zapata	Saladin
Mansa Musa	Simon Bolivar	Suleiman
Sundiata Keita	Thomas Edison	Wudi
Nelson Mandela	Henry Ford	Confucius
Jomo Kenyatta	M.L. King, Jr.	Yasir Arafat
Kwame Nkrumah	Diego Rivera	Asoka
Desmond Tutu	Pancho Villa	Shah Jehan
Shaka	Toussaint L'Ouverture	Mao Zedong
Ezana	Santa Anna	Timur
		Tokugawa Ieyasu
		Mohandas Gandhi

Europe

Michael Collins	Henry VIII	Moses
Alexander the Great	Erwin Rommel	Akbar
Justinian	Marc Antony	Abdul-Azlz ibn Saud
Charlemagne	V.I. Lenin	Dalai Lama
Vladimir of Kiev	Horatio Nelson	Kemal Ataturk
Francis of Assisi	Isaac Newton	Sejong
Charles Darwin	Karl Marx	Kim Dae Jung
Julius Caesar	Martin Luther	Yi Sun-shin
Galileo	Mikhail Gorbachev	Yoritomo Minamoto
Plato	William Shakespeare	David Ben-Gurion
Pericles	Christopher Columbus	Genghis Khan
Augustus	Lech Walesa	Kublai Khan
Michelangelo	Winston Churchill	Nebuchadnezzar
Leonardo da Vinci	Albert Einstein	David
Attila	Albert Schweitzer	Muhammad Yunus
Innocent III	Ibn Rushd	Xerxes
Ivan the Terrible	Moses Ben Maimon	
Marco Polo		
William the Conqueror		
Socrates		
Constantine		
Richard I		
William Wallace		
Napoleon		
Joseph Stalin		
Aristotle		

Appendix B: Leaders' Forum

What Do I Do Now?

Well, let's see . . . two days to go . . .

Research: Hit the libraries, Internet, etc.! Consult at least three sources. No Wikipedia! As part of your grade, you'll be asked to submit a bibliography in proper form. Your textbook may be cited as a fourth source.

What Information Am I Looking For? Find out about the actions of your individual as a leader. Find specific examples as evidence that your individual, as a leader, influenced the behavior of others.

Business Card: Design an informative, attractive business card that you can exchange with the other guests! See reverse for more info.

Essay: During your own research and during Leaders' Forum, you will learn the information you will need to write your essay! More on this later.

Costume: Make plans for your outfit! See your friendly librarian for books on historical costuming. Remember, no actual weapons or look-alike weapons. You'll receive time to change into your costumes prior to the start of Leaders' Forum.

What Will I Do During Leaders' Forum?

You will play the role of the leader you have chosen. From your research, you will learn about what your leader was like as a person. Try to behave as your leader would have behaved when alive!

You will participate in small-group discussions with other leaders. Introduce yourself to the others in your group and strike up a conversation. Talk about specific ways in which you, as a leader, have influenced the lives of others.

During Leaders' Forum, you will take notes on what the other leaders have to say about themselves. These notes will be important to you later on when you write your essay.

How Do I Make Business Cards? What Needs To Be on Each Card?

1. You can purchase business card stock wherever office supplies are sold. Then you can format and print the cards on your computer printer.
2. If you have a PC, you can use the Microsoft Publisher or Microsoft Office programs. Go first to "Tools," then "Templates." Choose "Business Cards." If you have a Mac, use Appleworks. Choose "Show Starting Points" from the File Menu; click on "Assistants," then on "Business Cards."

3. Print cards.
4. Here's what needs to be on each card:

Front of card

- must have name of your person
- include nickname (if one exists)
- include occupation
- specific place(s) where person was important
- dates of the person's birth and death
- a graphic that represents the person's historical role

Back of card

- Indicate **three specific examples** from this person's life that illustrate his/her actions as a leader.

Example

Front of card:

Leif Eriksson
"Leif the Lucky"
Viking Explorer of the
  North Atlantic
c. 970–1020 CE

Back of card:

Actions
Led voyages to Norway,
  Iceland, Greenland, North America
Set up first European
  settlement in North America
Brought Christianity to Greenland

CHAPTER 27

The Procession Portrayed
Using Art History in the Global Curriculum

MARY ROSSABI

Similar themes and subjects appear in the art of most civilizations. Representations of the family, the mother and child, animals, and music-making are found on objects around the world and have been the subjects of scholarly interest. The recurrent theme of the procession, however, has received little attention from historians and art historians, even though, over time, it can be found in the arts of Africa, Asia, Europe, and the Americas. The procession portrays rituals and ceremonies, celebrates civil and religious authority, and illustrates social activities. It therefore reflects a civilization's social structure and its political and religious power in depictions of marriages, funerals, births, coronations, religious activities, pageants, military parades and maneuvers, tribute-bearing, and triumphal entries:

> From the Panathenes or funeral marches of antiquity to the demonstrations of the labor unions, political parties, and "groupuscles" of May 1968 in Paris, from the Corpus Christi procession of the High Renaissance to the Red Square parades during the anniversary celebration of the October Revolution, we can see that order is an essential means for getting across the "message" be that message religious, civic, political, philosophical, or social. Often the intended message becomes complex due to the participants' reciprocal relationships and relative positions within the parade.[1]

The procession throughout art history can become a focal point in any history curriculum; in a global history course, this major theme can unite many diverse cultures. A procession of religious or civil figures, gods, acolytes, worshippers, and warriors can also be read as a sign signifying attitudes toward power, spiritual belief, women, children, and outsiders of any sort. In studying the position of the participants in the procession, their posture, their dress, the contiguity of the figures, and their gaze or eye contact, the viewer learns about social relationships between those signified and their signifiers, between artists, patrons, and those portrayed, and between the viewer and the processional work itself: "generally, parade, cortege, and procession create through their narrative aspect a system of values from which any parade, cortege, procession, or demonstration derives its legitimacy. The process of legitimization or actualization may, in turn, serve to formalize relationships between participants, such as the political relationship between a sovereign and a city."[2]

Since most of the works of art were or are exhibited either on temples or in churches, in town squares, in the residences of patrons, and finally in museums, they have been seen by different audiences, and their reception must, if possible, be considered if their impact is to be analyzed.

The setting of the procession also offers valuable glimpses of the period's architecture and urban and rural landscapes, while the medium and placement or location of the actual procession lead the observer to further conclusions about the place of ritual and authority in a particular society. The art historical genre of history painting, therefore, includes many processions.

A study of the procession rewards the viewer with insights into the prosperity and politics of a particular society, allowing specific questions about the political, social, and economic functions of that society to be addressed. Is the procession generally optimistic in depicting a positive event? Other than funerals (and, as we shall see, not even all funerals), do processions ever reflect the misery and sadness connected to the disasters of war, famine, disease, and political and economic unrest? Is the pictorial procession, as commissioned by a person in authority, a type of visual control in which those portrayed are horizontally organized to complement (or counteract?) the vertical or hierarchical control the rulers or institutions impose on their societies? If so, when does the visual control weaken? Are there fewer depictions of processions in more democratic or unstructured societies? Does the human eye respond to a line of figures positively? Does the procession need beginning and ending points so that this line is aesthetically resolved? These questions help focus analyses and discussions of the artworks and at the same time serve to connect the art to the social and political history surrounding it. The works included in this chapter are accessible and well known, found in basic art history texts, history books, major museums, and on CD-ROMs. A study of why they have become art historical icons or classics serves to uncover some of the stereotypes and values different societies uphold.

An introductory art history course usually begins with a study of the Lascaux frescoes and concludes with the art of the late twentieth century. Most courses concentrate on Western art as it develops out of the art of the Middle East (Mesopotamia and Egypt) and ancient Greece, although units are often devoted to the art of Africa and the Far East. In the texts generally followed in an introductory course, whether Anthony F. Janson's *History of Art*, Helen Gardner's *Art Through the Ages*, Frederick Hartt's *Art: A History*, or Marilyn Stokstad's *Art History* reproductions of processions occur throughout, the earliest being the parade of animals in the galleries and halls at Lascaux. This glorious array of beasts leaves no doubt in the viewer's mind of the priorities of this ancient cave civilization, although it is difficult to categorize this procession. One of the earliest processions after these frescoes is the Sumerian Standard of Ur, a triumphal entry, eliciting praise for the victorious king who subdued the enemy captives he parades behind his chariot. The best-known processions from antiquity, however, are the Parthenon Friezes, the Ara Pacis, and the circular reliefs on Trajan's Column. The first work depicts a religious ceremony in which tribute bearers offer gifts to Athena. The other two reliefs record military victories. The Ara Pacis celebrates the Roman emperor Augustus's victory over Spain, and the reliefs on Trajan's Column describe the subjugation of the Dacians. This procession through Western art history moves into the early Christian era with the Ravenna Mosaics of Theodora and Justinian and their retinues and the Bayeux Tapestry with its depiction of the Norman invasion of England.

During the study of both the classical and the early Christian periods, the instructor can introduce the student to the contemporaneous stone relief processions in the arts of China, India, and Indonesia. Depictions of military and royal processions in the Chou and Han dynasties can be compared to Trajan's spiraling soldiers; Gandharan stair risers, with their classical figures in procession, can be studied against the Ara Pacis; and an Ajanta procession of dwarfs and Borobodur reliefs of Prince Sudhara and his women can be contrasted with the Ravenna Mosaics. There are time discrepancies in some of these comparisons, but by studying the same theme and artistic form in very different cultures, students can ask the questions and follow

the approaches suggested earlier in this chapter as a starting point for further exploration. (Just as the Western art is depicted in the reproductions in the standard texts already mentioned, most of the Asian examples can be found in Sherman Lee's *History of Far Eastern Art*, Jonathan D. Spence's *Search for Modern China*, and John Fairbank, Edwin Reischaur, and Albert Craig's *East Asia: Tradition and Transformation*.)

In Western art, the medieval religious figures have a rigid military air about them, in great part because of their frontal style, lack of perspective, and contrapposto, but also, perhaps, because the early Catholic Church relied on militancy for its survival. In the high Middle Ages, many twelfth-century reliefs, like those on churches along the French pilgrimage route to Santiago de Compostella in Spain, lose some of the stiffness of earlier hierarchical processions. The rows of figures in the reliefs at Autun, Vezelay, and Conques are sent to heaven or thrust into the jaws of hell. At Angkor Wat in Cambodia, a twelfth-century relief of heaven and hell includes "an ecstatic procession of the saved" that offers a rich comparison with the French works.[3] Thirteenth-century animal processions from Mysore in India can also be contrasted.

From the thirteenth and fourteenth centuries, Duccio's *Christ Entering Jerusalem*, Martini's *The Road to Calvary*, and Giotto's *Pieta*, all egg tempera on wood, depict groups of figures in a procession where Christ is the focal point. Duccio's Christ enters Jerusalem triumphantly on a donkey, leading his disciples; Martini's Savior bears his cross to Golgotha surrounded by his devoted followers; and mourners approach Giotto's dead Christ. Lorenzetti's fresco *Good and Bad Government in the Country* uses civil processions of courtiers and urban officials from early Renaissance Siena to expose the uses and abuses of political power.

The Aztec relief on a pyramid outside Mexico City offers a chronological point of comparison with these late medieval–early Renaissance paintings, but because of the very different media, these flat stone sculptures can also be contrasted with the medieval French reliefs:

> The processional type reappears in Aztec sculpture of the fifteenth century, on friezes and slabs in the National Museum, notably the Tizoc stone. The procession of individuals converging from left to right upon an image of the god, or upon a symbol of blood sacrifice, is a recurrent theme. The costumes, attributes, and physical types differ enough in these processions to justify their identification as historical figures, perhaps a convocation of tribal leaders allied under the unifying cult of the Morning Star deity.[4]

The processional theme is found less frequently in the iconic works of Renaissance Italy than in the frescoes and manuscripts used to adorn the palaces of the Italian princes. Perhaps art historians and other connoisseurs preferred to focus on and thus popularize works that illustrated the assumption of individual power and the ascendancy of the princely city-states after the Middle Ages. Perhaps more portraits or intimate religious scenes were selected by Renaissance patrons to reflect or magnify their own importance, making the procession as a theme in Renaissance art less familiar than in the periods already described.

In the Vatican apartments, Raphael's popular fresco *The School of Athens* does, however, offer an intriguing hint of a procession, with Plato and Aristotle the only participants. The use of perspective frontality, physical bulk, and dimensional space separates this work from its medieval predecessors. However, northern European painters of the same period use the processional form in many of their works. The Van Eyck brothers' *Adoration of the Lamb* from the Ghent Altarpiece depicts four processions of religious figures converging on the lamb of God; Bosch's *Garden of Delights* presents a bizarre circular procession of nude men and women mounted on wild beasts; and Peter Brueghel the Elder's *The Blind Leading the Blind* captures a procession of sixteenth-century beggars while illustrating verse 15:14 from the Book of Matthew.

From the fifteenth through the eighteenth centuries, the West African kingdom of Benin produced splendid bronze plaques to decorate the royal palaces of the *oba*, or king. Most of these sculptures exalted the monarch and his rule by depicting him and/or his officials in authoritative stances. "These plaques also served as historical documents, recording people and events."[5] In some of these bronze reliefs, halted processions of warriors, dressed for battle with their swords and shields, face forward. Surrounding them are animals representing the oba. Other plaques show lines of musicians who also serve the ruler of Benin. These West African processions raise the question whether other African societies with a less formal royal structure and court life also employed the processional form in their art.

These processional plaques were fashioned to hang on the walls of the monarch's dwelling in the same way that processional frescoes and other pictures were created for the palaces of the elite of Renaissance Italy. As in the contrast between the stone reliefs of fifteenth-century Mexico and late medieval Italian paintings, the diversity of media, although a hindrance to a precise comparison, suggests where these very different works were placed. Students can then make hypotheses about the architecture, the climate, the economy, patronage, and living styles in these disparate societies.

Like the Benin bronzes, seventeenth-century European processions glorify royal power. Rubens's series celebrating the queen of France, Maria de Medici, includes a painting of her debarkation procession in the Marseilles harbor as she alights from a mighty galleon above cavorting sea nymphs. Rubens's painterly style is in sharp contrast to the stark linear bronzes of the Benin royalty.

Seventeenth- and eighteenth-century European proces-sions also portray the middle class, which, prospering from trade with Africa, Asia, and Latin America, commissioned its own memorials. In Holland, the Dutch burgher class made its triumphal entry in Rembrandt's *Night Watch*. The Chinese reaction to Europe's scramble for trade is recorded in a late eighteenth-century Chinese tapestry in which a procession of Chinese porters, in the employ of British lord Macartney's embassy, carry scientific and technological instruments in the hope of "gaining diplomatic and commercial concessions from the Qing. . . . But Qianlong's responses in an edict to King George III was 'we never valued ingenious articles, nor do we have the slightest need of your country's manufactures.'"[6]

The rise of the merchant class in early Romanov Russia and its reaction to the reforms of Peter the Great are reflected in several satirical woodcuts by anonymous Old Believer artists, whose sect resisted the changes that Peter introduced. In one print, Peter is caricatured as a dead cat, sometimes with his mustachios clipped in the modern fashion so antipathetic to the Old Believers, pulled to his funeral by a procession of mice, each one representing a different trade or geographical area of Russia. This *lubok*, or woodblock print, has become a classic to Russian and foreign viewers who know of it in a variety of reproductions.

By the nineteenth century, processions were a striking feature of several French masterpieces that recorded social and political protest and change. Delacroix's *Liberty Leading the People* of 1830 celebrated the victory of Lady Liberty, leading a rather disorderly band of followers through the burning boulevards of Paris, over the slain bodies of their countrymen. The loosely organized procession reflects this diffuse group of rebels, which moves toward the viewer but makes no eye contact, limiting thereby the emotional impact and casting this work as a history painting rather than a call to arms. A contrasting Japanese print, also from the 1830s, shows two parallel processions of territorial lords (or daimyos) as their "entourages pass the gates of a daimyo mansion on the way to the Shogun's castle on New Year's day."[7] The style is more conventional, with the figures moving from right to left in an orderly file, not toward the picture surface as in Delacroix's work. A comparison of these two processions would encourage students to do research into early nineteenth-century Japanese and French social and political history, as well as studying the conventional characteristics and signifiers of the procession.

Courbet's enormous canvas of 1840–1850, *The Burial at Ornans*, portrays a procession of French peasant mourners gathered at a graveside. The painting was considered outrageous because Courbet did not portray the grand personages usually found in history paintings, but depicted instead the country folk found in popular prints like *Les Images D'Epinal*. Some fifty years after *Liberty Leading the People*, Seurat painted a stratum of French society different from that depicted by either Delacroix or Courbet. In Seurat's *Sunday Afternoon on the Island of La Grande Jatte*, the middle class, in all its finery, enjoys its leisure while strolling in a disjointed, discontinuous parade. Robert Hughes, in *The Shock of the New,* states:

> Seurat wanted to paint the processional aspect of modern life—something formal, rigorous, and impressive. . . . "I want to show moderns moving about on friezes, stripped of their essentials, to place them in paintings arranged in harmonies of colours, in harmonies of line, line and color fitted to each other. . . ." And so, in "La Grande Jatte," the vision of pleasure takes on the gravity of history painting.[8]

There is no formal procession in this painting, only fragments, but the image of a procession of elegant Parisians ambling along the Seine could be imprinted in the viewer's mind's eye. However, the viewer might also "read" the painting as a record of disconnectedness and alienation, as Linda Nochlin suggests in her essay "Seurat's La Grande Jatte: An Anti-Utopian Allegory."[9] The unity of purpose expressed in Delacroix's dramatic processional confrontation, Courbet's funeral cortege, and the grand parades of the daimyos, is gone. Each person remains isolated; even the mother and child do not touch or hold hands. The disintegration of the processional form coincides with the growing significance and power of the individual and the weakening of that individual's affiliation with a larger institution or group, be it religion and the church, a civic organization, or a political hierarchy. The processions discussed earlier in this chapter are all the reflection of some larger entity, while Seurat's fragmented procession mirrors the separation from the group and the isolation of the individual.

Reflections of social change in early twentieth-century West Africa are also found in the processions of the Yoruba, neighbors of the Benin people. Entry doors for the palace at Ikere, completed by the court artists in 1916, depict "a full court ceremonial of 1897 . . . [in which] the Oba received the British Captain Ambrose, travelling Commissioner for the province. Seated in his litter, the European is depicted as smaller than the Yoruba king. Each has his own retinue. . . . The Oba's entourage included a cluster of wives with children on their backs."[10] The members of the captain's procession move toward the king as if about to pay tribute. While the figures in the Western procession appear glum, the followers of the oba smile, displaying their superiority before these Europeans who invaded their territory and made it part of the British colony of Lagos in 1861.

Even before the Ikere palace doors were fashioned, African imagery had exerted a strong influence on European art, as can be seen in Picasso's *Les Demoiselles d'Avignon* of 1907. African masks and their planar construction were instrumental in the development of cubism and the shattering of Renaissance perspective, which had defined European painting for nearly 500 years. This weakening and, for many twentieth-century artists, demise of one-point perspective coincided with the disintegration of the procession as it was seen in many classics of art history.

In some European paintings the procession began to move toward abstraction. Marcel Duchamp's *Nude Descending a Staircase* of 1912 can be read as a time-motion study of one figure or, in spite of the title, as a procession of abstract figures exploding on the canvas. Form is all, and there is no recognizable narrative. What seems merely a representation of shapes in a line, however, can, by its very nonobjectivity, permit the viewer to react to this painting unhindered by more traditional subject matter and convention.

Through this emancipation, an artist like El Lissitsky in revolutionary Russia could use processions of squares, triangles, and circles in his *Beat the Whites with the Red Wedge* to signify a new socialist order. At the same time as the Russian avant-garde artists were using neutral, value-free geometric forms to celebrate the triumphal entry of socialism into Russia, the socialist realists were proclaiming the proletarian state in their victorious processions of flag-bearers, workers, and soldiers. Denikin's portrayal of a procession of troops in *Defense of Petrograd* (1927) is certainly more accessible and moving than the paintings of El Lissitsky. Throughout the Communist world, processions of peasants, workers, and soldiers celebrate the victory of their personal fulfillment through the triumph of the collective state. This theme is illustrated in an anonymous Chinese painting titled *Follow Closely Chairman Mao's Great Strategic Plan, 1968*, in which Mao, in the bottom left corner of the painting, holds up his left hand in front of a winding procession of distant figures.[11] In Mexico City, Diego Rivera's murals in the National Palace, 1929–1935, depict the "past, present and future of mankind . . . as a dialectical march from the glories of the primitive past . . . into the sunlit upland of Marxian communism."[12] The murals are filled with processions of Aztecs, conquistadors, and workers, and the whole series can be seen as the procession of Mexican history, culminating in the triumph of communism. Narrative prevails; there is no abstraction here.

By the mid-twentieth century, however, the procession had ceased to provide the inspiration for most artists who created the icons of art history. Picasso's *Guernica* of 1937, considered by Robert Hughes the last great history painting, is, with its parade of agonized victims, also the last great procession. After *Guernica*, Hughes states, artists no longer believed they could influence their viewers: "The idea that an artist, by making painting or sculpture, could insert images into the stream of public speech and thus change political discourse has gone, probably for good. . . . Mass media took away the political speech of art."[13]

The processional form in relief and in painting thus became irrelevant, replaced by the never-ending procession of television images. In the global curriculum, however, the processional form throughout history and across cultures remains useful in studying the art and civilizations of Africa, Asia, Europe, and the Americas.

About the Author

Mary Rossabi taught history and art history at a variety of schools and colleges for forty years. Since she retired, she has continued to focus on translating from the Mongolian into English biographies, herding manuals, and other works so that they are available to a wider audience. Mary Rossabi's translation of Tserendash Namhaimyambuu's autobiography *Bounty from the Sheep* was published in 2000 with an introduction by Morris Rossabi, the author of *Khubilai Khan: His Life and Times.*

Notes

1. L. Marin, "Notes on a Semiotic Approach to Parade, Cortege, and Procession," in *Time Out of Time: Essays on the Festival*, ed. Alessandro Falassi, 226 (Albuquerque: University of New Mexico, 1987).

2. Ibid., 225.

3. Sherman Lee, *A History of Far Eastern Art* (New York: Abrams, n.d.), 168–170.

4. George Kubler, *The Art and Architecture of Ancient America* (New York: Penguin, 1984), 87–88.

5. Werner Forman, Bedrich Forman, and Philip Dark, *Benin Art* (London: P. Hamlyn, 1960), 11.

6. Jonathan D. Spence, *The Search for Modern China* (New York: W.W. Norton, 1990), following 132.

7. John Fairbank, Edwin Reischauer, and Albert Craig, *East Asia: Tradition and Transformation* (Boston: Houghton Mifflin, 1973), 404.

8. Robert Hughes, *The Shock of the New* (New York: Knopf, 1991), 116.

9. Linda Nochlin, *The Politics of Vision* (New York: Harper and Row, 1991).

10. Larry Silver, *Art in History* (New York: Abbeville Press, 1993).

11. E.J. Laing, *The Winking Owl* (Berkeley: University of California Press, 1988), plate (anonymous, "Mao Zedong's Thought Illumines the Theatre," poster, 1968).

12. B.D. Wolfe, *The Fabulous Life of Diego Rivera* (New York: Stein and Day, 1963), 266.

13. Robert Hughes, *Shock of the New*, 11.

PART VI

LEARNING AND UNDERSTANDING

CHAPTER 28

Fishbones and Forests
Teaching About Argumentation Using a Graphic Organizer

MARYANN BROWN AND MARITA NICHOLAS

One of the joys of teaching is that there is little chance of the day unfolding in the same way as any other. Whenever you are thrown into a new teaching situation, you experience emotional highs and lows. There are lessons that you plan carefully and are rewarded for in abundance. Other lessons are executed with precision yet go horribly wrong. Some fill you with remorse for the lack of forward planning, and the self-evaluation process overflows with ideas for improvement. What is certain is that to continue to try new strategies and to put yourself in challenging situations is beneficial for both teachers and students.

We are both high school teachers in Australia. We have backgrounds in English and humanities teaching and special education. A love of teaching and a desire to learn more and challenge ourselves led us to join Teachers Across Borders Inc. as volunteers running workshops for teachers in Cambodia. This chapter explores our learning from using a fishbone graphic organizer in two different teaching experiences in Cambodia.

Scaffolding learning is a powerful tool to support students who struggle to generate ideas or organize their work into a logical sequence. Challenging students to move outside their comfort zones is valuable for deep learning. All the students you teach come with their own strengths, skills, knowledge, anxieties, challenges, and doubts. If you think any two students are the same, you have not got to know them well enough.

Graphic Organizers

Graphic organizers are visual diagrams that are used to generate and organize ideas and extended pieces of writing. These "visual representations help students to understand some of the information in texts, to order and bundle related information as well as being useful reference guides

. . . [They] are useful pedagogical tools for ESL learners."[1] Graphic organizers encourage a deep understanding of learning and assist long-term retention of concepts.[2]

The fishbone graphic organizer was initially developed by Dr. Kaoru Ishikawa, a Japanese quality control statistician (Figure 28.1). It was developed as a way of analyzing the causes of problems and issues and the resulting effects.[3] This model has been used in many schools as a cause-and-effect organizer.

We had both used the fishbone in a different form as an organizer for argumentative writing. It is ideal for generating and organizing ideas for argumentative and persuasive writing. The idea is to generate a list of arguments for each side of the debate and to align all arguments for and against on the bones on each side of the fish. The model we took was from edHelper.com:

Figure 28.1

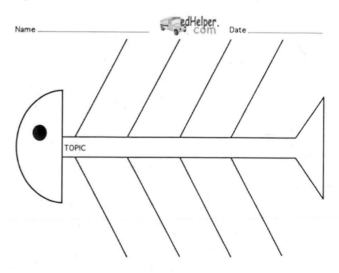

This version of the fishbone seems particularly useful when working with students who are not confident in the language of instruction. The model encourages collaborative learning with all students invited to participate in filling in the different points or fishbones. Another strength is the modeling of joint construction of a text. The teacher can question students: Does this make sense? How will we write this? Can we use a different word here? Is this how you spell the word and so on.

The fact that there are various iterations of the fishbone graphic organizer is interesting. Since many teachers are naturally creative and adaptive, in some ways it makes sense for them to develop models in their own way. However, they should be aware of the risk of adapting models or approaches in education in ways that are so far from the original that the essence or purpose is lost. For example, after Benjamin Bloom's taxonomy of learning had been adopted and adapted with great enthusiasm, Bloom noted that his work was developed in ways he had not imagined.[4] It is important for teachers to consider how far they are adapting models and to ask themselves if the adaptation is suiting the original purpose or their own pedagogical needs. There are good cases to be made for both.

Battambang, January 2007

When we applied to take part in the Teachers Across Borders program, we knew that we would be teaching in a large rural town, Battambang. We were expecting twenty practicing teachers in our workshop as well as a Khmer translator. We had been told that teachers were poorly paid but highly respected, that teacher training was minimal and facilities very basic. We could expect a room with a blackboard and wooden desks. School class sizes were large; sixty students was not unusual. We should not expect electricity in classrooms. We were not certain if there would be a photocopier so we guessed what we would need and copied as much material as we could before going to Cambodia. We had a plan and a number of backup ideas because we really did not know what to expect.

Our workshop, "Teaching and Learning Strategies for the Khmer and English Classroom," aimed to give participants a bag of tricks or strategies that they could use with any age group and across a range of topics and subject areas. One of the strategies was the graphic organizer called the fishbone. We had had success with this organizer on many occasions in our classes in Australia because it assists in organizing ideas effectively and encourages the writer to think about both sides of an issue.

Books are scarce and highly treasured in Cambodia. The Regional Teacher Training Centre in Battambang had a library. Many of the books were donated, some were out of date, and some were so special that they were kept in a glass cabinet. A series of books that we were proudly shown was from an organization called Room to Read. They were beautiful picture storybooks written by local people, each story written in Khmer and English. We asked to borrow one of the books, *My Forest Friend*, which deals with the issues of forest management, malaria, and the value of education. We were very taken by the story and instantly saw its application in our workshop and in classrooms.

In the story, Uncle Sok cuts down trees for a living. When he becomes ill, the family believes he is possessed by evil spirits because he has cut down trees. A younger member of the family, returning from university, realizes that Uncle Sok has malaria and takes him to the hospital for treatment. Uncle Sok recovers and decides to become a nurseryman growing trees, rather than cutting them down.

We used this story and the fishbone graphic organizer to plan an argumentative piece of writing (Table 28.1). The topic, "We should cut down trees," was written across the spine of the fish. The fact that it is written in the spine is symbolically important because it serves as a reminder to students that the statement is central to the piece of writing and that all ideas should stem from it. Each rib is used to formulate an idea. Those above the spine agree with the topic and those below disagree. Ideas can be generated individually or as a group.

In Battambang, the use of a high-quality, local text and the fishbone as a framework led to a level of discussion that seemed to transcend the significant language barrier. In the review of the first trial of the fishbone lesson we noted:

> Reading for a Purpose
>
> A story about the forest, written in Khmer and English, was used to demonstrate this activity. A participant volunteered to read to the class. Using previous modeling, the "teacher" asked participants to identify the story's intended audience and genre and predict what the story would be about. The story was read to the group in Khmer and English. Based on the content of the story, the issue was "We should cut down trees." Participants were asked to record their responses for and against on a fishbone graphic organizer. As the

Table 28.1

We Should Cut Down Trees

Agree	Disagree
The wood is needed to build houses and furniture.	Forests are home to many animals.
The wood is needed as fuel for cooking and heating.	Forests are important to maintain the quality of the air.
Trees can be replaced.	Forests are places of natural beauty and attract tourists to the country.
We need the land to grow food.	Cutting down trees leads to soil erosion and environmental problems.

story was read a second time, participants were asked to call out "Stop" when they heard a relevant argument: "For" arguments were put above the spine of the fish and "Against" arguments below. At the end of the story, participants used the fishbone arguments in a whole-group discussion of the benefits and problems of forestry, brainstorming a range of solutions. This activity could naturally lead to persuasive and argumentative writing or debate.

Phnom Penh, July 2008

When a teaching and learning strategy works you want to use it again. . . . right? Eighteen months after our Battambang teaching we found ourselves running another workshop in Phnom Penh. We used the same graphic organizer and the same text, but the setting and context were very different. This time the fishbone got us into quite a bit of strife!

We arrived to discover that our class had seventy-five students instead of the suggested forty. This number was less than ideal but we decided to be flexible and work with the big group. We had traveled a long way, so we thought we might as well work with whoever was interested. Many of the participants were very experienced senior-level teachers; about half the group were final-year teacher education students who were extremely enthusiastic and very conscious of the privilege of being included in the program. We discovered later that some of the senior teachers resented the big class and the number of education students. We had two teachers, two young translators, and a teaching assistant plus a spare room next door, which could be used for group work.

The next difficulty was that we had signed up to run a workshop on developing literacy skills (to complement recent curriculum developments in the education department), but somehow this had been translated into "Khmer literature." We were unnerved by the mistranslation of the workshop title but, having taught English literature, we decided to see if we could include Khmer literature within our workshops; we managed to find one book of poems in Khmer and English in the International Bookshop.

Our plan for the fourth day of the Phnom Penh workshops was to focus on writing. The class started with a warm-up activity, writing a fifty-word story that conformed to basic conventions (title, beginning, middle, ending). This worked well and a number of stories were shared. This was followed by discussion about developing writing.

Participants were given the book *My Forest Friend* to read in groups. The key question was "How could you use this book in your teaching?"—the idea being that teachers can use a range of resources to develop content in writing.

A fishbone diagram was drawn up. We decided to model this with a general topic and then ask participants to develop their own fishbone using the "We should cut down trees" topic. This procedure seemed logical to us. We knew the forest topic was strong.

Marita's Perspective

I believe that supported and repeated practice is essential for a strategy to become part of a teacher's repertoire. For this reason, I thought that we should leave the easier option for the participants—that was the original statement, "We should cut down trees." Off the top of my head, I came up with another statement—"Education saves lives." I like thinking on my feet and was quite happy with this idea because it linked to the story and it was something we all had background knowledge about. The participants were quick to think of reasons to agree with the statement. Since I was trying to encourage them to think of arguments for both sides, I encouraged discussion of other things, such as medical treatment and clean water, which also saved lives. At the point when the class had suggested two arguments indicating that education may not be significant in changing lives, the atmosphere in the room changed dramatically.

The debate got quite heated. I remember reassuring the young translator that whatever was being said to her in an assertive or angry tone was actually directed at me. She was not the least bit intimidated, but was so caught up in the discussion that she took to arguing rather than translating. Many members of the class were arguing and I had no idea what they were talking about. Finally I rubbed the offending half of the fishbone off the board and allowed a brainstorm of the many ways that education does save lives. As crude as that solution was, the atmosphere relaxed considerably.

On reflection, if the central statement had been "Education is one important thing that saves lives," the discussion would have been more palatable for the participants. Some people interpreted the initial topic to mean that other factors could not be influential in saving lives. Maybe the topic was poorly expressed or the fishbone was not the best graphic organizer for this topic.

Maryann's Perspective

The session started well; the participants were interested in the diagram on the whiteboard. As Marita explained the process, her words were translated. The idea of the model was that students suggest points for and against the topic, giving supporting evidence for each argument. Marita started the discussion asking for points against the topic and immediately a heated discussion developed. Some people, particularly the older, experienced teachers, started arguing with each other while the student teachers watched open-mouthed. One man leaped up and started speaking very passionately. The translator did her best but started actually arguing the points with the man, rather than translating for us. Marita pressed on and wrote some points on the board. She had decided to ask for a point against the topic first. I was standing at the side of the room, watching as the lesson unfolded, and I could see and hear the mood of the room changing from interest to genuine anger. I asked the other translator to translate for me and he tried hard to capture the arguments. Later he explained carefully that it was not possible for teachers to argue against the topic because in Cambodia education is so highly regarded. There was an awkward moment as I tried to indicate to Marita that the lesson was unraveling. Eventually I moved to the front of the room and suggested that we might need to modify the lesson. Marita shifted the discussion to a brainstorm on the value of education.

The Aftermath

Maryann

Back at the hotel we discussed the issue. The power of the response had really distressed me. On reflection I realized that my lack of ability to understand the points that the participants were making left me totally at a loss. I need to understand what people are saying so I can respond and moderate the learning experience as required. I mentioned that we would need to do something to "salvage the lesson." From Marita's perspective the lesson was not a disaster. I remember lying awake that night thinking hard, trying to work out how we could turn the experience into something positive.

The next morning I started the lesson with a new activity: I read some statements and participants had to stand up if they agreed and say "I agree" or stay seated if they disagreed. Here are some of the statements:

- Only women should look after children.
- Cambodia is the best country in Asia.
- All children should attend school.
- Young people are less well behaved than in the past.
- Dancing is good for you.
- Studying history is more important than science.
- Television is educational.

My intention was to shift the focus to the fact that holding different points of view and developing arguments is quite acceptable. The warm-up activity worked; there was much hilarity with some of the questions—the whole class agreed that "men and women should help raise children." I was reminded how much there is to learn about the deep beliefs of different cultures. We eventually returned to our original plan and Marita led a successful session using the fishbone organizer to identify contrasting points of view.

Marita

Maryann felt the initial lesson was a disaster. I felt that was a fairly harsh assessment. What Maryann took to be anger from participants, I considered to be passionate interest. I did not want something I had controlled to be a disaster.

In retrospect I appreciate that Maryann encouraged me to revisit the lesson the next morning. It makes me realize how important a critical friend and team teacher is to professional growth. The fishbone discussion on "We should cut down trees" was broad, deep, and well worth having.

Reflection on Our Learning

- Our class in Battambang was much smaller than the class in Phnom Penh—fifteen students as opposed to seventy-five. This was a major issue. In the small class we had the chance to do much closer language and pronunciation study. We knew all participants by name and we could focus on individual needs. We also knew that a very positive learning environment had been established and that participants had a good rapport with each other.

    In the larger class a few people had the opportunity to contribute, but many were just active or passive observers. We had not been able to learn many names in such a big class and, although the participants were generally positive, some were less than enthusiastic and the group rapport had not been established.
- Our planning was better in Battambang. We thought we had planned carefully for Phnom Penh, but perhaps we had been slightly complacent because we remembered that various activities had been successful and enjoyable. The key issue of repetition without deep planning arises here. So many great ideas are lost in classrooms when teachers (naturally) redo a favorite task and the deeper learning or original purpose is diluted.
- Our purpose was slightly different. The original session was on "Reading for a purpose." Somehow it had become a session on "Models and strategies for supporting students with their writing."
- The "Education saves lives" topic was controversial in a way that we did not appreciate. Education is highly sought in Cambodia. It is understood to be the way to development; we had heard that at the opening ceremony for the workshops.
- Gender and age are significant factors in Cambodian society. The workshop leaders and one translator were female and the majority of experienced teachers were male. As outsiders, we appreciated the Cambodians' respect for age and position, but we had not fully understood how the groups in the class reacted to each other's presence.

- Argument means different things in different cultures and age groups. We had no real idea of the place of argument or holding different points of view in the intellectual culture of Cambodia. This is never a static or simple issue—age, life experience, and personality all play a part. In hindsight, we made a cultural assumption that could have been quite wrong. How could we really understand the cost of holding an opposing position in a country that had experienced the horrors of Pol Pot's regime?
- Planning never ceases to be important for teachers committed to genuine learning for their students.
- The risk of being patronizing due to ignorance is ever present. Teachers must always work to learn about the people in the class, their experiences and their needs.

Questions to Consider

- How do teachers develop cultural knowledge and sensitivity? We had some experience of ESL teaching and there was a briefing prior to our first trip. We had read quite extensively about Cambodian history and culture between trips, but we were still conscious of our lack of knowledge of social structures. We discovered that experience is invaluable and that it is important to get a range of perspectives in interpreting cultural differences.
- As teachers we believe in the value of pushing people out of their comfort zones to encourage deeper learning. Is creating controversy or tension such as we experienced in Phnom Penh still a valuable learning experience?
- How do we find out about our learners and their learning if language is a barrier? How can we ensure that our translators understand the purpose and content of our class? Each day a plan was put on the board in English and Khmer, but in fact we needed extra time to prepare translators for conceptual understanding—and to learn more about potential cultural sensitivities. We will never know how our words were actually translated.
- Events are always interpreted subject to personal experiences. How can we have even an inkling of how people who have lived so differently from us interpret our lessons?
- How can team teaching help us develop insights into our own teaching? We found team teaching, along with shared planning, one of the most interesting, enriching parts of our experience in Cambodia.
- What influences curriculum decision-making on the run? How do we face up to what we have started and ensure that some valuable learning occurs?
- Complacency is a hidden and serious danger in teaching. In our busy lives it is easy to assume that something we have done in the past will still work well.

Are we planning a learning experience with which we have become too comfortable?
- Do graphic organizers and other visual learning tools translate across languages and cultures and have we chosen the right organizer for the task?
- Is the capacity to safely argue and present a point of view the ultimate expression of democracy?
- How do teachers work with students in whose experience expressing an opinion can have high costs and argument can be a cultural challenge?

Conclusion

The strengths of using the fishbone graphic organizer in developing different points of view around a topic are very clear to us. The simplicity of the visual representation is particularly useful when English is not the students' first language. Students can clearly see opposing perspectives on an issue.

The learning we gained from teaching using the same text and graphic organizer in two different settings was very powerful. Lessons are never perfect; teachers must take the time to reflect on their difficulties and insights, thus gaining a deeper understanding of teaching and learning. We learned a great deal about ourselves, each other, our workshop participants, and Cambodian culture and we still have much to learn.

About the Authors

Maryann Brown (BA, Dip Ed, Grad Dip Spec Ed, MEd, EdD) is a secondary teacher and middle school curriculum coordinator at an independent school in Australia. She is a former teacher educator and is currently a senior research fellow of the University of Ballarat.

Marita Nicholas (BA, Dip Ed, Grad Dip Spec Ed) is a secondary teacher and middle years area leader in charge of curriculum development and pastoral care at a high school in Australia.

Notes

1. Sue Bremner, "Talking and Listening Activities for ESL Students," *Primary English Notes* 43 (July 2004): p. 6.
2. Sandra McEwan and John Myers, "Graphic Organizers: Visual Tools for Learning," *Orbit: OISE/UTs Magazine for Schools* (2002): p. 30.
3. NCDENR Office of Organizational Excellence, *Fishbone Diagram: A Problem Analysis Tool*, March 31, 2002, http://quality.enr.state.nc.us/tools/fishbone.htm.
4. L. Anderson and L. Sosniak, eds., *Bloom's Taxonomy: A Forty-Year Retrospective. Ninety-third Yearbook of the National Society for the Study of Education, Part 2* (Chicago: University of Chicago Press, 1994).

CHAPTER 29

Listening to Students Talk About Gender in the World History Classroom

SHARON COHEN

As Sam Wineburg aptly says:

> Professors may assume that their students are stupid or suffer from a learning disability. Often the truth is much simpler: No one has ever bothered to teach them some basic but powerful skills of interpretation. As teachers, we need to remember what the world looked like before we learned our discipline's ways of seeing it. We need to show our students the patient and painstaking processes by which we achieved expertise. Only by making our footsteps visible can we expect students to follow in them.[1]

What can we as teachers learn by listening to how our students talk about the past? How can we analyze what they say in order to hear our students' historical thinking? What is the value of listening to what students say about gender in the world history classroom? The answers to all these questions is that listening to students talk about gender in their analyses of patterns of continuity and change can serve as a useful diagnostic tool to assess their historical thinking skills. In this chapter I will focus on the historical thinking skills of analyzing the patterns of continuity and change in the context of global processes. I also will suggest some ways to help students construct arguments based on those analyses.

Why Teach Students to Use Gender as a Category of Analysis in a World History Survey Course?

Few world history teachers have had formal training in gender studies, and probably even fewer include gender as a regular feature of analysis in the world history course. I hope this chapter will highlight the value of teaching students to use gender as an analytical category in world history.

In the past, many world history teachers approached analysis of gender structures by focusing mainly on "what did the women do?"' Or, perhaps, the teacher occasionally pointed out how interactions among cultures changed what Peter Stearns has identified as the "established ideas about men and women, and their roles."[2] The approach suggested here is to help students see the connections between gender roles, social structures, and political structures across a yearlong world history course. Ultimately, students then can recognize and analyze continuities and changes in the roles for men and women over multiple time periods.

The easiest place for world history teachers to start using gender as an analytical tool is through the development and transformation of social structures, usually in a comparative framework. Students in a world history course also might be encouraged to analyze the processes by which gender, race, and class affected the creation, maintenance, and changes in social hierarchies. By focusing on patterns of continuities and changes over time, the world history teacher can help students recognize the dynamics of continuities and changes over periods of time of varying lengths and relate these dynamics to other global processes such as political, economic, cultural, and ecological developments. In world history classrooms, students can practice the historical thinking skills of recognizing historical patterns and then formulating historical arguments based on their analyses of these patterns by including their perceptions of gender in various times and places in the past.

Over the past ten years, I often found that my world history students felt bewildered by all the different types of political, social, and economic systems in the past. Mostly, my students found the past a "foreign country." In his article "Constructing World History in the Classroom," Ross Dunn encourages world history teachers to help students overcome the tendency "to perceive historical phenomena as exotic and remote." He suggests that we characterize "historical actors in a situation as human beings, not characters playing appointed roles in a culture drama."[3] By using gender as a regular category of analysis, I predicted that my students could relate to the essential human condition of male and female, as well as recognize the ways that different societies defined masculinity and femininity. From the work of John French and Daniel James on Latin American women in the early twentieth century, I learned that gender can be "understood as a relationship rather than a thing, it is viewed as a verb rather than a noun."[4] I realized that I should allow students to discover on their own how past societies defined masculinity and femininity by seeing the relative value given to males and females. From the literature, I concluded that I needed to integrate gender as another category like the traditional ones of "political, social, economic" in teaching world history.

Since I teach mostly juniors in a large, public, suburban high school, I also considered how to develop a technique that would prompt the students' interest in learning about people in the past. (The world history courses I have taught are the advanced placement course, which is equivalent to a yearlong college survey, and a modern world history class that starts about 1400 and proceeds to the present.) It seems trite to say that teenagers spend much of their waking time interpreting the world through the lens of "how does it benefit or hurt me, and what kind of choices do I have?" However, I have found that some of my most successful lessons encouraged students to have some of the human agency or choice that people in the past had.

Furthermore, I had noticed many students' difficulties in seeing the connection between local and global patterns. Integrating gender as a regular category of analysis seemed a possible solution. Students could develop the habit of considering how all societies had definitions of gender roles, while at the same time, students could learn about specific, local patterns. For example, students could learn to recognize global patterns of patriarchy while analyzing the shifts in power of both men and women at different levels of a particular society over specific periods of time. Students could then shift more easily from global to local and from local to global patterns, using gender for analyzing change and continuity in societies over time.

Listening to Students Talk About Gender

The first step in teaching students to use gender as an analytical tool in world history is to define the term. It may be helpful to use the definitions Sonya Michel and Robin Muncy give for "gender" as a term to represent the "meanings attached to sexual differences between men and women."[5] World history teachers can show students that gender structures are related to the definitions of masculinity and femininity within societies. I recommend that when teachers explain the political systems of empires,

kingdoms, colonies, or revolutionary governments, many different personalities and types of people be included in the explanation so that the gender roles of real people can be seen. For example, the Incan Empire's political structure included the male lords of conquered territories serving as local officials and the daughters of the conquered rulers serving in the Inca's royal household or religious centers. The Inca's *mit'a* labor system drew upon most levels of the nonroyal population but divided the tasks by gender. By highlighting what men and women were expected to do within a specific political system in a particular time period, students can then discuss the definitions for masculinity and femininity within and across societies.

A specific approach I developed to using gender as a category of analysis was to require students to imagine themselves as either the son or daughter of a representative type or important person from a specific time period and region. I decided to use the twenty-first–century teenage consumerist approach to life and ask my students to imagine that they had the choice to be someone in the past. I also wanted to reinforce the connection between gender systems and the social systems that I introduced as part of our classroom analysis of any empire, society, or group. The first step was to show students controversial or dramatic primary source examples of both men and women in each political system we studied and then ask students to analyze these print and visual sources within the framework of a timed and scored discussion that included specific questions they had to address. In some cases, the sources revealed uneven amounts of information on male and female roles in those societies.

My ultimate goal was to evaluate students' understanding of the role of gender in each political system we studied. I wanted opportunities to listen to my students talk about gender roles and expectations of gendered behavior in order to assess my students' historical thinking skills, specifically their abilities to recognize historical patterns and formulate arguments using historical evidence. Therefore, I required students to participate in a series of discussions during which I could hear every student express understandings about the global and local patterns of political, social, and gender structures we had discussed in class. I also wanted to encourage students to hear each other's ideas. (Many students told me how much they appreciated the chance to hear analyses from students who did not usually participate in lecture-discussions.) At my school we typically have twenty-eight to thirty-four students in each world history class, so scored class discussions require dividing the students into an inner circle and an outer circle. The inner circle discusses the sources and questions for about fifteen minutes and then switches places with the outer circle. I pair the students so that the ones in the outer circle record the comments, questions, and discussion behaviors of their partners in the inner circle. I also record the students' comments and questions on a grid I create for each class period. The grid lists the students' names and two columns labeled "comments" and "questions." I try to leave enough space to write down what each student says. Mostly, I am listening for recognition of the restrictions or freedom that gender gave people in the past. After the discussion I analyze the students' contributions by highlighting on the grid words such as "has the ability to" or "cannot do without permission" to aid my diagnosis of the level of their historical thinking skills about gender. The written records of the students in the outer circle reinforce what I was able to record and also reveal their own ability to recognize the effects of gender on political, social, and economic structures and institutions when they assess their partner's contribution to the discussion.

A typical discussion in my world history classroom involves students encountering lists of social and political hierarchies in paired political systems along with questions prompting the students to decide who they might prefer to be: the males or the females in any particular society or region. We do at least one discussion for each time period of the advanced placement or modern world history course. By repeating the same procedures of the discussion, the students learn how to ask questions of the sources and challenge each other's choices of gender and class status. They also begin to make connections back to previous seminars as ways to comment on the choices of their peers. For example, we had a discussion on pre-Columbian empires in the Americas as a bridge lesson between postclassical and early modern periods. First, the students had to pretend to be the sons of members of various social and political groups in the Aztec Empire. (The girls were incensed that they could not be females.) During the second half of the forty-seven-minute class period, the students had to pretend to be the daughters of members of various social and political groups in the Incan Empire. (The boys tried to show equal displeasure at being restricted to female roles in Incan society, though they did not seem as bothered as the girls had been.)

In the discussions, students instinctively saw that not all individuals were treated solely on the basis of their gender; people in the past were also affected by their standing in the social hierarchy. Some students also quickly concluded that, despite the pervasiveness of patriarchy in many parts of the world, it was not preferable to be male in all societies. Some male elites were susceptible to being assassinated or serving as military commanders, and some "restricted" elite females had privileges that other women in the society did not. Students also noticed from the sixteenth-century *Codex Mendoza* that the community standards for punishing male and female children were different. I found it interesting that in every one of my five classes, a male student, usually one of East Asian, Latin American, or West African heritage, said, "Well, the punishment for boys was harsher in order

to train them to endure pain when they become soldiers." The formal discussion gave students an open forum to imagine themselves in the past. They also reported that they learned more about the Aztec and the Incan societies from the primary sources by asking questions through the lens of gender roles.

Handout 29.1 **Discussion: Aztec and Incan Empires in the Postclassical Period (600–1450 CE)**

Directions for the Student:

Discuss which type of person you would want to be from the list below. State who you would prefer to be and explain why to demonstrate your analysis of the gender structures in the Aztec and Incan Empires. Be sure to reference the sources and make explicit comparisons with societies and institutions in Afro Eurasia in the postclassical period. Remember to question the validity and reliability of the sources listed below, as well as other primary sources that might help you draw your conclusions about how gender affected the political, economic, and social structures and institutions in the Americas.

Who would you have preferred to be in the Aztec and Incan Empires? Why?

- son of Aztec emperor
- son of Aztec priest
- son of Aztec warrior
- nephew of an Aztec scribe
- son of Aztec feather-shield maker
- daughter of Aztec chinampas maker
- daughter of a stingray fisherman
- son of Aztec merchant
- son of captured enemy of the Aztec
- daughter of the Inca
- daughter of Incan quipu maker
- daughter of Incan tax collector
- daughter of lord who became subordinate to the Inca
- daughter of a potato farmer

Remember you earn points for explaining your choice and for challenging others' choices. You also are expected to reference the primary sources and other texts.

Sources

Berdan, Frances F., and Patricia Rieff Anawalt. *The Essential Codex Mendoza*. Berkeley: University of California Press, 1977. Excerpts from the full folio created circa 1543 for the Spanish.

Poma de Ayala, Felipe Huamán (translated and edited by Christopher Dilke). *Letter to a King: A Peruvian Chief's*

Account of Life Under the Incas and Under Spanish Rule.
New York: E.P. Dutton, 1978, 84–86. In 1615 the author,
descended from Incan and other indigenous royalty, sent
a letter to King Philip III of Spain containing 1,179 pages
and 397 drawings. This excerpt is about the acllas, young
women chosen from among the daughters of local rulers
of defeated territories.

Evidence of Students' Historical Thinking Skills From One Classroom

My goal below is to provide a thick description of student
evidence from one formal discussion of Aztec and Inca
society (fifteen minutes each), my responses to the students,
and my reflection afterward on what the evidence revealed
about their historical thinking and what I should do with this
diagnostic data. The following is a transcript of comments
made by one class of twenty-eight students in one of four
different sections of Advanced Placement World History
that I taught in the fall of 2008.

Aztec Discussion

- Male student #1: "I would like to be the son of the Aztec ruler, because then I would have the best of everything."[6]
- Male student # 2: "But wouldn't you have to be a warrior and undergo the punishments that are worse for boys of the Aztec elite?[7] Look at how they stick the young boys with stingray thorns to punish them when they're bad." (laughter among many students in the class)
- Male student #1: "I would be used to that kind of life; everyone I knew would be doing it, so I wouldn't ask about it, you know?"
- Male student #2: "Yeah, I guess so, but I don't know if I'd like it.[8] Maybe if we had some stuff from men who weren't warriors, because it says in the introduction that the guys who worked with the Spanish to make the *Codex Mendoza* were born into the Nahua elite, you know the Aztec nobles kind of people."
- Male student #3: "You wouldn't know anything else, except maybe that it would be harder work to be a *chinampas* (a garden plot, artificially built above ponds swamp lands) maker, you know, out in the sun and on the water, trying to grow tomatoes and stuff. That'd be too much work for me." (laughter)
- Male student #4: "Well, we know you're lazy. (laughter) But I'd prefer to be a merchant, because I could choose to travel where I want."[9]
- Female student #1: "I don't think the Aztec merchants traveled all that much. The tribute lists on page 89 show mostly local goods, right? And the *Codex Men-*

doza only shows training for kids to be priests and warriors."
- Male student #5: "Well, the *Codex Mendoza* was produced after the Spanish conquest, so maybe the Aztecs didn't want to show the Spanish where their trade routes were. Do you think the Aztecs wanted to hide where they got their gold and silver[10] like the nomad guides along the Silk Roads so they could charge higher prices?"
- Female student #2: "Yeah, maybe it was like *The Emperor's New Groove.*"[11]
- Male student #6: "That was in South America, not Mesoamerica."
- Female student #2: "It's more like *Apocalypto.*"
- Male student #7: "Hey, I saw that—yeah, it was pretty bloody."
- Teacher: "Well, what do the movies or the primary sources show us about expectations of gender behavior or roles in Mesoamerica before the Spanish conquest? Remember to think about how you are constructing your arguments. Remember you can challenge each other on the way you argue your points."[12]
- Female student #3: "Based on the *Codex Mendoza*, I think I'd rather be the son of the merchant, since they didn't seem as important and might escape the tough training to be a warrior and yet not have to work as hard as the peasants."[13]
- Male student #8: "If I were the son of someone in the Aztec elite, I would have to marry someone picked for me. What if I didn't like her?"
- Female student #3: "It's like what he (male student #3) said before—you wouldn't know any better. And that was normal everywhere, like in the Muslim and Chinese empires: they, you know, had to marry someone with connections or power. Remember Jasmine in *Aladdin*—she wasn't supposed to marry a beggar like Ali."[14]
- Male student #9: "I definitely wouldn't want to be the son of a defeated Aztec enemy, because I would likely become a target for human sacrifice. Ouch."
- Female student #4: "It would be worse to be the sons of priests having to do all of that human sacrifice. It must have smelled really bad. I can't believe they thought it was an honor to be covered in human blood."
- Male student #10: "It might be better to be a peasant, so you just have to grow food and not worry about being killed or pulling people's hearts out of them. And it's not like in Europe where they died young, at least not until the Europeans brought over those diseases."
- Teacher: "That's a great start on exploring gender in the Aztec empire. Now, you're going to switch the inner and outer circle seats with your partners and the new inner circle will focus on how gender might have affected people's experiences in the Incan empire."

Incan Discussion

- Female student #4: "Yipee, now we can choose to be a daughter—that's so much better than being warrior boys who only learn how to fight."
- Female student #5: "What about the daughters of defeated lords? Those girls have to become *acllas* or concubines of the Inca. I wouldn't want to be an aclla and not have the chance to make a family; their lives seem pretty limited too."
- Female student #6: "But if your father is made a lord to the Inca, it would be considered an honor. It'd be better to be an aclla than a concubine, because you'd be honored to be an aclla."
- Male student #11: "But old acllas were considered ugly. Most older people are ugly, so I guess that'd be better than being killed or something. Is this a better way to treat the elderly?"
- Male student #12: "They're not going to kill the virgins set aside for their religious temples. It's sort of like the Greek vestal virgins, I guess."
- Female student #7: "I bet the daughter of the Incan ruler got a lot of gold jewelry."
- Female student #8: "No one would see it. They weren't supposed to look at their royalty. It would probably be pretty isolating to live in the royal palace. It'd be like the princess in *Aladdin*."[15]
- Male student #13: "The daughter of a tax collector would have no friends, because everyone hated the tax collector. Maybe the quipu maker was low enough so that the daughter could go outside but high enough to have food and stuff."[16]
- Female student #9: "How would they know who was who? Did they dress for their jobs like uniforms? The excerpt from the source on the acllas didn't really tell us enough about how the Inca lived. But maybe in the other thousand pages there's more information on what they did and how they looked. I can't really say based on just this one page of the source."
- Female student #10: "I agree that the tax collector's family would have it bad; no one would hang out with them. That'd be bad. I'd hate it."
- Male student #14: "Hey, who bought the quipus anyway?"
- Female student #10: "It must have been for the Incan emperor, right? It's the tax records and census, right? In China those kinds of records were really important for keeping control of people, so maybe the quipu maker was considered educated, you know?"[17]
- Male student #14: "I didn't think of them that way, but maybe you're right."
- Female student #11: "Well, maybe it'd be best to be the daughter of a potato farmer; you'd have plenty of food and get exercise, so you'd be in good shape. And like he (#12) said yesterday, they probably didn't have problems with diseases."
- Male student #15: "I'd do that if I could chew coca leaves." (laughter)
- Female student #12: "That's all you think about."
- Female student #10: "I don't think they used recreational drugs; they didn't have time to be hanging out with each other. It was more like going to Starbucks before school, you know?"[18]
- Female student #13: "I'm going to say something about the stingray fisherman. Wouldn't that be for the pricking of royal skin onto the special paper that the priest then burned for the gods?"
- Male student #2: "I think that was the Mayan kings and queens who pricked themselves with the thorns. But I wouldn't want that kind of life picking up stingrays; I got stung once visiting my family in the islands."
- Female student #13: "Anyway, I was thinking about beach life, you know—hanging out on the coast might be nice."
- Male student #2: "Yeah, but your status would be pretty low, so all you'd do would be picking up stingrays all the time. Boring."[19]
- Female student #13: "I don't think people in the past got bored. They were just trying to stay alive most of the time."
- Teacher: "What evidence do you have for the social status of the stingray fisherman? Would the fisherman and his son have a different experience than the wife or daughter? Compare the stingray fisherman to the feather-shield maker's life—would the urban versus rural life affect your analysis of their situations?"
- Female student #13: "Well, it's hard to compare because the *Codex Mendoza* doesn't show us what the adults really did, except for the old people who got to be drunk in public. I guess the husband or wife's experiences would depend on who got to make decisions about what happened every day."
- Male student #14: "I hadn't thought about that. How do we know about their daily life? I guess archaeologists maybe could give us more information."
- Teacher: "We're about to the end of the class period. Tomorrow, I'll give you a set of questions related to the analyses you made in your discussion today. Make sure you think about how gender affected political, economic, and social institutions and processes as you read more tonight about the Aztec and Inca empires in your textbook."

Questions

Here is the list of questions I gave the students to answer at the beginning of the next class period before we went on to analyze and discuss some parts of the journals and letters of Columbus.

1. Compare two occupations that males in the Aztec Empire held in terms of the status of the jobs and the risks involved.
2. Compare two roles females held in the Incan Empire in terms of the status of the roles and the risks involved.
3. Compare the reliability of the two primary sources you read: the *Essential Codex Mendoza* and the excerpt from the letter Felipe Huamán Poma de Ayala wrote to the Spanish king.
4. Identify two other possible types of sources on the Aztecs and the Inca that could help you analyze the effects gender had on their political, economic, and social systems.

Conclusion

The thick description I included above of one discussion about gender in the Aztec and Incan empires exemplifies how I analyze evidence from students' talk to determine the development of their historical thinking skills. From that discussion in early November, I was able to see the progress students made in their ability to break down the effects of gender in these two empires and explain how they came to their conclusions. I saw that they recognized complications in how we can interpret the past because world history often contains competing or incomplete narratives. My students also were beginning to question how the purpose and effects of the Aztec and Incan political, economic, and social structures might compare and contrast to those of other societies in other regions.

I continue to include gender as a regular category of analysis in my world history course. The high school juniors in my classes find analysis of changes in gender roles across cultures and time easier than comparing political or economic systems. Students readily make connections to economic class and the effect of belief systems on the definitions of masculinity and femininity. I conclude that gender is an easier analytical tool because there is no traditional narrative they feel constrained to remember. Instead, when students talk about gender in world history, they have space to comment, to question, and to share their own conclusions. They also seem to understand that expectations for male and female behavior were constrained not just by the overall society's rules, but also by class and status and probably changed over time. Students show interest when using gender as an analytical category, but just as in any other classroom activity they easily get distracted into discussing the details of their own lives. The teacher's role is to keep focusing on the historical thinking skills and especially students' metacognition of their increasing abilities to think and

act like historians. Ultimately, the goal is to guide students to see their thinking made explicit in the classroom so that historical thinking will not seem an unnatural act.

About the Author

Sharon Cohen (AB, history; MA, East Asian studies; MA, international education) is a high school teacher at a public school in suburban Maryland. She contributes to curriculum projects for the College Board, World History For Us All, World History Matters, and Women in World History. In addition, she frequently conducts workshops and institutes about teaching AP World History and creating vertical teams of social studies teachers in one or multiple schools.

Notes

1. Sam Wineburg, "Teaching the Mind Good Habits." *Chronicle of Higher Education*, April 11, 2003, B20.
2. Peter N. Stearns, *Gender in World History*: *Themes in World History* (New York: Routledge, 2000), p. 1.
3. Ross E. Dunn, "Constructing World History in the Classroom," in *Knowing, Teaching and Learning History: National and International Perspectives*, ed. Peter N. Stearns, Peter Seixas, and Sam Wineburg (New York: New York University Press, 2000), p. 133.
4. John D. French and Daniel James, "Women's Factory Labor," in *Gendered Worlds of Latin American Women: From the Household and Factory to the Union Hall and Ballot Box* (Durham, NC: Duke University Press, 1997), p. 4.
5. Sonya Michel and Robin Muncy, *Engendering America: A Documentary History, 1865 to the Present* (Boston: McGraw Hill, 1998), p. 1.
6. I see this student's recognition of the elite control of agricultural surplus through taxation. I also see links being made to the pattern of premodern trade happening mostly in luxury goods. However, there seems to be a nongendered view of how elites benefited from being at the top of the social hierarchy.
7. I see this student's recognition of the gendered expectations of masculinity in the acceptance of harsher physical punishments for boys to train them to bear the pain associated with military conflict.
8. These two students' comments reveal a view of an unchanging past, but also a historian's questioning of what else we might learn from additional sources.
9. Students often use presentist thinking to color their interpretations of the past. Here, the student's comment reveals his assumption that merchants gained freedom by being able to travel, not considering the restrictions that the Aztec government might put on the merchants.
10. This statement demonstrates the student's recognition of the limitation of sources and evidence of seeing patterns in the role of experts' knowledge of trade, such as the settled Afro-Eurasians' interaction with nomads.
11. When students are allowed to determine the content of the discussions, they often refer to popular culture, especially Disney and Hollywood films, which provide the clearest historical images for many young people.

12. I interrupted at this point to direct students back to the main focus of the discussion and to further my goal of hearing them analyze Aztec and Incan social structures using gender as the entry point.

13. The failure of other students to challenge her conclusion based on the absence of merchants from the *Codex* showed me that I needed to show students how to question what is not in a primary source as much as what is in it. I noted that I should model for them how to query the lack of information in a primary source with our next lesson on Columbus.

14. Again, students accept the comments of male student #9 about the Aztecs having arranged marriages even though there is nothing in the text to support his claim. However, I noted female student #3's comparison of the purposes of arranged marriages, especially for the elites, from what she remembered about them in Afro-Eurasia. After absorbing Wineburg's research on how Americans remember history through films, I have come to accept the references to Disney movies and even show clips from YouTube.com when I want students to recall and then amend what they "know" about the past through movies.

15. This whole sequence of the discussion about the acllas shows the students making comparisons with other postclassical societies and analyzing the pros and cons of elite female seclusion. They do not question the reliability of the source, a male after the Spanish conquest who may not have had direct knowledge of the aclla system.

16. It is interesting that no one challenges this comment about tax collectors being hated everywhere.

17. This discussion about the quipu record-keeping system confirmed that the students see the role of civil servants or bureaucrats across cultures; they did not question the gender, though the reference to the Chinese system makes me think they assumed the quipu makers were male.

18. I left in two of these teasing types of comments; there were more but I edited them out for the sake of space. In general, I find that allowing students to speak freely keeps the discussions going. My efforts to restrict what they can say produces silences and isolated comments and questions rather than exchanges of ideas.

19. Again, students neglected to address gender, so my comment attempted to redirect them. Since there were only about three minutes left of the class period, there was not enough time to pursue this issue. The students also veered away from discussing female roles in the Incan empire, but that was because I did not tag the stingray fisherman as living in Mesoamerica.

CHAPTER 30

A Week's Worth of World History Skills
A Reflection

DALE GRIEPENSTROH

When reflecting, choose.
Change all, change little, change nothing.
You'll learn which and when.

The haiku I wrote for you is a simple reminder that the best practice any teacher can pass on is reflection. There is no other way to be an effective teacher. The reader of this essay will witness and evaluate what needs to change or what should remain the same in my instruction based on what works and what does not, aided by student reflections. All best practices are relative to a student population and are subject to change eventually as many variables in education change.

Best practices are a chance for teachers to pass on their knowledge of what has worked—that is, what has worked for a precise student population at a given moment in the immediate past in a very specific educational environment. Being a reflective teacher, I attempt to clarify my instructional insights for you. With humility, I submit my practices for your scrutiny as works in progress. The reflections of my students on these practices and my reasoning for choosing the practices are presented as a dialogue. We together supply you with a typical week in our Advanced Placement (AP) World History classroom. These methods, which could be used in a history classroom at any level, present a routine that often helps struggling students. With open enrollment at my school, my classroom often resembles a typical world history classroom dealing with college-level themes and skills.

Elemental to this student-teacher discussion is its pertinence to my classroom. Assessing your own classroom is a big step in creating any instructional routine.

In order to keep an emphasis on the educational momentum in my classroom, I do not detail the content covered during the week examined. I do not divulge the text I use or specific exam or essay questions so I can focus on the instruction and participation of the students gaining knowledge and skills.

You need to know who my students are to fully understand my choices as a professional. They are a 75 percent second-language student population; more than 50 percent receive free and reduced lunches. The students have few college graduates in their families, and many are first-generation immigrants. There are four levels of world history at my school: bilingual/sheltered, regular, accelerated, and AP. The open-enrollment AP program here usually allows for four or five sections of AP World History. I am the only teacher of this AP subject at my school. The vertically teamed curriculum is still being constructed from the eighth-grade up, so little writing and college-level reading have been attempted and none mastered at the start of the course. Each class meets five times a week for fifty-one minutes.

Monday

To start our reflection on Monday makes the most sense. A typical Monday involves reviewing the test that students took the previous Friday. I use a method introduced to me by Bill Ziegler at San Marcos High School, which makes students responsible for reading a chapter ahead in the text, while in class we cover what they may have had trouble with in the last chapter. For example, students read Chapter 22 over the weekend or during the week and take the test for Chapter 22 on Friday; meanwhile, I cover Chapter 21 in class, tying all content together as students learn scaffolded patterns and skills. I pay close attention to areas of weakness noted on the test for Chapter 21, taken the previous week.

I use scantron multiple-choice tests that provide me with quick printouts of what questions were missed most. Questions are textbook-driven. Most are written by the text's various professors and assistants and are chosen from textbook generators with my revisions. A few questions are additions from other AP sources such as released tests. Every Monday, we review the ten most missed questions (more than ten when time allows) to look for patterns in the students' mistakes. Sometimes a question proves too picky based on guidelines in the College Board AP World History booklet so we discuss the question and evaluate its detractors. What did the writer want to accomplish when writing the question? Is there a reason some recall points are more important than others? I allow these picky questions on the test, but usually do not count their points when tallying final scores. Scoring 50 percent correct on these tests is not uncommon. Students who score 50 percent on tests and do reasonably well on homework and essays receive a C in the class. In our district that is a 3.0 on a 4.0 scale because students receive an inflated point average for advanced placement.

Students have the chance to correct five questions and remediate the class by presenting the information in a mini-lesson that upcoming Thursday. The intent is to have the students teach themselves and to expose the class to content before moving on to the next topic in the text. This method works best when a few students act as role models early in the year. Fifteen-year-olds have great difficulty admitting they made a mistake and do not like admitting it to the class, but when students are prodded to work in groups they are more likely to admit mistakes. I encourage them to be creative and comedic.

The discussion of the test takes thirty to forty minutes. The remaining time is spent preparing for the in-class timed essay the following day. I tell the students which type of essay they will write: an essay on change and continuity over time (CCOT), a compare-and-contrast essay (C&C), or a document-based question (DBQ). I usually hint at the topic and the class reviews the rubric. If the essay is to be a DBQ, the students see the documents for the first time and early in the school year they may take the packet of documents home for further review and prewriting. After they have written a few DBQ's, they are only allowed to see the documents the day before they write the essay and cannot take the document home.

The week I am examining in this chapter is a spring semester week, so the documents were reviewed and returned in class. On this particular occasion one copy of the prompt and documents were missing after lunch, so the prompt had to be changed for the following day.

Student Reflections

Mike (second-generation Chinese male, fluent in Cantonese and English)

Monday: Today we are reviewing the test. This is really helpful because we can point out what we got wrong but more importantly, WHY we got them wrong. I thought I actually did well but I barely mustered a 53 percent.

Justin (African-American and Hispanic male, fluent in English and Spanish)

Monday: Today we went over test 34. With others having different letter forms of tests, it becomes unwise to copy someone's paper, because you never know when Mr. G might switch questions and answers around. (I mean it's not like I copy people's papers, I don't need to do that to pass the class with a good grade. I learned from past experiences that copying someone might give you a lower score than what you would have had by doing it yourself.) I think Mr. G's grading rubric on tests is fair. I mean if you're still below 50 percent you obviously didn't read. I didn't read once and I still got a 50 percent. After a while you know what's going to be on a test. He looks at questions most people got wrong and goes through the steps of why "that answer" is incorrect. Even though he thinks sophomores are stupid, not me of course, he understands why we could have picked that answer. The only thing I don't like about tests are those ones we have to take because we don't know the answers to a question we probably have read about. I mean yes, we do forget things, and others might get mad, Mr. G tells us not just about history, but about life as well. That if we don't try when we have help right now, it's going to be harder when we get to the real world, where we are pretty much by ourselves. People get mad when Mr. G yells at the class, we might make mistakes but it's nothing compared to the screaming of my D.I.'s drill instructors at boot camp.

Denise (white and Hispanic female, bilingual)

Monday: Today we went over the test and reviewed the correct answers. I like doing this because we can really see what we didn't get and ask questions as to why each answer was correct. It's more than seeing what the right answer is, it's understanding why it is right. We also went over and started discussing the DBQ prompt for the next day, I like when we have time to go over it in class because we have time to ask questions and get further understanding of the prompt and documents. This time, it didn't really help me and it was a waste of time because the prompt was changed the next day anyways.

Susan (white and Hispanic female, bilingual)

Monday: After every test, we review the test and the most missed questions. I take notes and write down the correct answer of each question I got wrong to help me improve my knowledge on the chapter.

Nancy (Hispanic female, bilingual)

Monday: I like the fact that we take Mondays to go over our tests. It helps us see how we got the wrong answers or why we choose what we choose. It allows us to see what methods of studying we should use or what we need to do. It also allows us to gain more information for AP exams and what not.

Juan Carlos (Hispanic male, bilingual)

Monday:
    Class Assignments: Grade Test, Prepare for in-class DBQ.
    Evaluation: I feel all questions of the test should be covered in case of a grading error which do occur often. I feel giving the topic for an in-class DBQ is appropriate and pertains to the AP standards

My Reflection

I do agree with Juan Carlos that all questions should be reviewed and in the beginning of the year we do this. He is very competitive and often argues a question's validity. Notice that Susan did expect to remediate herself and perhaps take advantage of the extra points awarded to students who remediate the class. Where there is room for improvement, I allow students to come in at lunch to further examine their tests, but give no extrinsic incentive to do so. Perhaps it is worth a point or two just to have them further their remediation on their own time.

Tuesday

Tuesday's class time could be used for a lesson addressing areas of concern diagnosed from the test data gathered from the previous week, a preview of information on that current week's test, a series of film clips to complement either week's topic, or a timed writing. Most weeks we have a timed writing tying together the information from the previous week's chapters with the current topic of the students' reading. As I stated before, my challenge is to strengthen the students' previous week's content knowledge and connect it to their current reading. They are responsible for keeping up with the reading and not falling behind in their notes.

I chose a DBQ this week. Unfortunately we had a compromised prompt. The DBQ was shared with the class on Monday, but was supposed to remain in the classroom, so students could not do an in-depth prewrite. This simulates a more realistic AP testing experience and makes every classroom minute count on Tuesday. To cut down on printing costs for the school, each DBQ is numbered and aligned with a corresponding desk (i.e., the fourth desk in the front row is DBQ packet #4). This is done to discourage a student from taking a packet home and getting more than the allotted time to examine the documents and start their prewriting. Many students take advantage of open lunch hours to further their study of the documents, but I don't always check to see who has which packet. This particular lunch one of the document packets was missing and it was not until the last class that Monday that I became aware of it. Because of the open use of packets at lunch it was impossible to place blame. To compensate for the missing DBQ, I introduced a new DBQ at the beginning of the class on Tuesday. The new DBQ content aligned with the upcoming test so students who were caught up with their work saw this as an opportunity to further their knowledge. Students in the last class period had the advantage of knowing that I would change the prompt first and that the new DBQ would address a topic from their current reading but they did not know what the prompt would be. Using e-mail and word of mouth, I notified as many students as I could about the new topic at the end of the school day; however, not all got the message. When students saw the new packet on Tuesday, I made sure they had the entire period to write on the new topic. Again, this is more in keeping with an AP testing experience.

It is important to note that all timed essays are taught by scaffolding skills all year long. Tuesday and Wednesday are usually used for this purpose. Students are not exposed to timed essays without first practicing thesis writing, prewriting techniques, point-of-view analysis, and organization. They are also allowed to write rough drafts of essays and ask for advice from classmates and me before they write the timed version in class. In the early months of the year, they have the College Board rubric with them when writing. In ninth grade students wrote five-paragraph essays that helped them in organizing thoughts and writing quickly, but I point out that this format is not always appropriate.

By second semester, the essays are either thirty-minute timed writings for CCOT and C&C essays or fifty-minute timed writings for DBQs. If they are thirty-minute writings, we have time for a quick peer review. The students place only their identification numbers on their essays, but in peer review during the same class, anonymity is impossible. Still students read quickly to see if there was a thesis in place or some other targeted point. We usually only have time to discuss addressing the prompt, and on days with a DBQ timed writing, they write the whole period.

Student Reflections

Mike

Tuesday: Today we wrote a DBQ on Pan-Slavism. I like writing DBQs because the documents provided allow for us to have basis for writing even if we do not have complete knowledge on the information provided. It was originally on indentured servants, but Mr. G changed it and notified us via e-mail, which is a plus because it would have been bad if he hadn't and just surprised us with the new topic.

Justin

Tuesday: We did our DBQs, but had to switch our topic because someone took the documents home to study for. It was about Pan-Slavism in the nineteenth century and we have to assess and group documents and have a POV, point of view. We use evidence, or documents to make plausible arguments.

Denise

Tuesday: Today we took the entire period to write the DBQ. It was difficult for me to finish because it was a lot of documents and I took too much time reading them, but this is what it will be like in the AP test, so it's really good practice. I enjoy doing essays in class. I just wish we could talk about it a little bit more.

After school we had the extra credit film. This week we watched *Paths of Glory*. I really like the after-school movies because they fit in with what we're learning and give us an alternative way to remember things. For me, it's more likely that I'll remember something I learned in a movie than in the textbook. I just wish Mr. G would talk through all the movies and not just some. I understand it and learn much more when he explains many things.

Susan

Tuesday: Today in class, we wrote a timed essay. There are three main types of these essays: a DBQ a C&C, and a CCOT. We are usually given thirty to fifty minutes to complete the essay and they are usually given every other week. In addition we usually are told the topic of the essay and the type of essay the day before so that we can prepare and read up on the topic. I personally feel that these essays have helped me to organize my thoughts and to overcome my need to write a perfect draft.

Nancy

Tuesday: I like DBQs. It gives a better insight to information on subjects that we may have on AP® exams. DBQs are quite fun, if it weren't for someone getting away with the prompt, we all might have gotten better grades, but all in all I like the DBQs because it gives us insight for the AP® exams.

Juan Carlos

Tuesday:
   Class Assignments: DBQ Pan-Slavism
   Evaluation: I felt it is a pretty easy DBQ related to one of the few issues in Chapter 35. I felt it was a much more realistic experience as the essay topic changed last minute and for myself similar to the AP exam and good preparation for it.

My Reflection

Of all the timed writings we do, the students get the most out of DBQs. They synthesize much information and learn history along the way. This week was unusual when someone took an essay from the room at lunch and I could not verify who it was. My threat was to change the subject if one prompt was missing. Effective teachers learn very early that following through on threats is important to maintaining classroom control. I also taught the class the value of electronic media when I e-mailed students. I had only three or four students who did not have e-mail at the beginning of the year and if they took issue with my not notifying them, I would have granted exceptions for them. Most students found out by word of mouth. Flexibility in the classroom on the part of the teacher and students is the key in a surprise change like this.

Denise mentioned that I show extra-credit films after school chosen for their relevance to what the students are reading and testing on that week. I show a film every week and two on the first Saturday of the month. The students write a four-paragraph SAID report: *s*ummary, *a*ccuracy, *i*naccuracy, and *d*irector's point of view. The first three are obvious topics; the fourth is a discussion of the use of film techniques and social atmosphere at the time of the film's creation. Three of these reports can add 5 percent to any student's grade.

Wednesday

Wednesday we did double-blind peer grading of the tests by using student identification numbers for the authors and the evaluators. I switch the papers by class so students are assessing a different group's writing. Still controversial, I know. On the surface, peer grading saves me time by having the students pick out the glaring errors. The idea, of course, is to have students learn from each other's mistakes through peer evaluation and recognize that good writing is what others can understand, not what the author tries to express.

Peer grading is not the answer to evaluating 150 essays at once. It must be used judiciously and with increasing student confidence. I start peer grading in the fall after the students have written two or three essays that I have corrected. They use their essay rubrics when they write the essays during the first semester so they have an idea of what will be scored. They are familiar enough with the rubrics to ascertain if the student they are grading has attempted the points. They are, of course, leery as to whether the attempt warrants a point on the rubric, but Wednesdays are dedicated to going through the rubric point by point and example by example.

Often I will use previously written essays on an overhead projector and correct them on several levels: rubric, grammar, historical accuracy, style, and so on. I encourage the students to write all sorts of notes on their peer's essay so the author will have much feedback on many levels, but in the end it is the rubric score that will be used to evaluate the student's performance. Admittedly, the main drawback with peer grading is the accuracy of the comments and scoring.

When I use peer grading, I always check the highest and lowest rubric scores for accuracy. Later in the week I approach the student readers who awarded scores inappropriately. I make a few low-key, passing comments, but I focus on those students and watch their scoring to see that they are gaining accuracy.

I cannot use this method without allowing for student rebuttals. This is by far the most rewarding part of the process. I gladly give up my lunch hours for office hours dedicated to students who want to learn or demonstrate writing proficiency. Early in the year, we will take a few days to have teacher/student writing conferences during class time, but it is a more valuable learning experience when students must sacrifice some of their lunch to talk to me about their writing. During the first semester I allow students to correct their essay for a grade increase, but they must show me their work personally during their lunch hour.

As mentioned, early in the year we focus on basic necessary skills like writing a clear thesis and then add various other skills. By second semester, students are bringing their peer-scored essay to me with highlighted examples of their attempts to meet rubric criteria. I get a chance to talk to each student about their score and reasoning. In the end, this method may take more time than writing all the comments on the paper, but there is no substitute for individual instruction and student justification.

We ended the class with a brief, ten-minute video. I do not like to show long videos because students tune in and out. This particular video was on the topic of that week's reading, but sometimes they are review videos. When we watch videos, I make students chart "five things I knew already and five things I learned from the film" in order to show the student and me that the video had relevance. These in-class movie notes could be difficult for students with Attention Deficit Disorder, who have a hard time going from notes to film. I allow all students to turn the notes in late or give them five minutes at the end of the period to discuss the notes with a friend to get full credit.

Student Reflections

Mike

Wednesday: Today we peer graded the essays. I understand why Mr. G does this because it is easier for him and for us to learn what to do and what not to do but I feel like the students who grade mine, do not grade them with 100 percent effort or even thoroughly read them.

Justin

Wednesday: Today we checked someone's DBQ, which the main goal of is to develop understandings of diverse ideas, and values in historical context. Sometimes it can be quite confusing, due to the fact that I don't ask questions when I don't understand it. I should at least come in at lunch for help, and ask how to do these essays, (highest grade I got was a 9 out of 10 but we had the weekend to do it. My average score is a 1 or 3. Hopefully, I can go back to the basics, especially on writing a thesis, or buy an AP book for twenty dollars). But besides that it helps us comprehend what different documents are saying and find out what it is that they are trying to tell us. Good for English class.

Denise

Wednesday: Today we peer graded the DBQs in class. I really benefit from this because I get a chance to see what other people wrote to see what I did better, and what I could have done better (so I can compare). It's sometimes unhelpful when you get a really bad or incomplete essay because you don't really learn anything from those, but it happens. After that, we started watching a film about World War I. Like the after school movies, I like these because it paints a picture in my head of what happened and lets me understand the material better.

Susan

Wednesday: Usually, the day after we write an essay, we peer grade another period's essays. I feel that when we discuss the essay, I improve on my writing skills. The fact that we have to grade someone else's essay really helps me to understand how people write and how I can make my writing better. At the end of the period, we watched a video on World War I. We frequently watch short videos and take notes, which really helps me prepare for the test.

Nancy

Wednesday: I think that peer grading is okay. Not really my favorite task. It does allow us, however, to see our mistakes as we correct someone else's. It also gives us an opportunity to see how our own papers are graded. Movies are one of my favorites since we take notes on what we do know, and do not know, it helps a lot. It also helps if what we watch is on the chapter we are going to have a test on next. In all, they are both good though I enjoy watching the movies and taking notes.

Juan Carlos

Wednesday:

Class Assignments: Peer Grade DBQ Pan-Slavism; Movie

Evaluation: I felt the movie was a good one related to the chapter.

Weak points: I feel peer-grading DBQs is generally a bad idea. Oftentimes peers do not do a good job of grading essays giving either grades too high or too low. Hardly ever do they do a good job.

My Reflection

Juan Carlos does not like to give up his lunch to come talk to me about the poor grades he has received from his peers. He feels it is a waste of time, but in general when he does come in we discuss how he could have expressed himself better so another student could have recognized his thought. As I stated before, he is competitive and when a peer does not understand him, he wants to blame it on the other student. Still he has a valid point that other students are not as vested in the process and I do not catch all these students' half-hearted attempts at scoring.

Denise and Susan are frequent lunchtime attendees and see the value of the system. Justin knows he should come, but unfortunately does not. To encourage students in the beginning, I often reward them for coming in at lunch with a courage point. And, as previously stated, during the first semester they can rewrite portions of their essay to get additional points.

If I were to change this system, I would try to find some way of having more writing workshops on Saturdays. I do not want to reduce class time for those who understand the process.

Thursday

Students ask me questions, clarifying the chapter they are currently reading for the first five to fifteen minutes. Then we move on to SPIRITED (*s*ocial, *p*olitical, *i*ntellectual, *r*eligion, *i*nteraction, *t*echnology, *e*conomics, and *d*ependence on the environment) lessons.

I have been using SPIRITED lessons for six years and I give them high marks for helping students review large amounts of information and aiding writing. Thursday's lesson fuses thematic learning and scaffolding with reciprocal

teaching/learning. The former helps students make connections throughout the year and the latter allows for student discussion of read material. Research shows that both are beneficial for low grade levels, but I feel they really improve the higher-level thinking skills needed for AP courses.

It is very important to keep reminding students of historic themes that make analyzing easier and writing in paragraphs second nature. The activity on Thursday is meant to be a review for the Friday test, but it is also setting up students to do well on their Tuesday essays as they learn to analyze material and break chapters down into thematic chunks of information.

In an effort to make the SPIRITED themes ever present in the students' reading, writing, and discussion, there are eight theme bulletin boards that dominate one wall of the classroom. All of these are mentioned in the Acorn book in some fashion or another.

At the beginning of the year we discuss what topics are covered by what themes: *social* includes social classes and the roles of women, men, children; *political* includes rulers and laws and bureaucracies; *intellectual* includes art, architecture, literature, philosophy, and education; *religion* includes gods, worship, afterlife beliefs, and scriptures; *interaction* involves examples of intercultural actions like wars, trade, or migrations; *technology* includes any tools or techniques a society improves upon; *economics* is trade, labor systems, resource development, and monetary systems and problems; *dependence on the environment* includes the influences of a civilization's geography or climate, such as rivers and mountains; available resources, such as animals, minerals, and plants; diseases that arise from that environment; and pollution affecting the environment.

These themes are not absolute and display much overlap; for example, slavery issues can easily be placed in social, economics, and interaction themes. Students learn that a discussion of this overlap allows for justification of placement and leads to better understanding and hopefully better writing skills.

Following a model of cooperative learning researched by Ann Brown and Annemarie Palincsar, students divide into groups of four; since they are seated in rows of four, this is easy and automatic. Each group is assigned a different theme and they rotate through all the themes during the year. Each student in the group takes on the responsibility of one of four different jobs:

The lecturer is responsible for summarizing the information in the chapter for their given theme that week.

The illustrator draws an original picture to encapsulate the theme.

The language expert determines key vocabulary that students should know.

The assessor creates multiple-choice questions that could appear on a test.

Each group then presents their four assigned roles (summary, illustration, vocabulary, and question) to the class, teaching their classmates about their theme and how the chapters involved can be analyzed using that theme. I display the group work on the wall in thematic categories. I wait to display them until after their test to discourage cheating. I replace their work each week after each test to reinforce the themes.

Occasionally a class has more or fewer than thirty-two students. I only give the themes most pertinent for the chapters involved if there are fewer than eight groups, or I allow repetition of certain key themes if there are more than eight groups.

The first time we do this it takes two days, one for the work and one for the presentations. However, in the interest of time and my ultimate goal of making the themes second nature to the students, all groups must arrange their information quickly, presenting it in a fifty-one-minute period. I do not grade these projects as individual students or groups. It is a class effort and they must have all components and finish on time for the class to get a homework credit for that day. Teamwork takes on a whole new meaning for them, as do completion and efficiency. Timed writing becomes easier as well when they are used to working under pressure.

While students are working, I check their notebooks. Students are allowed to take notes using three methods: Cornell, THIEVES, or the SPIRITED thematic method. Each has its advantages, and the students must try the Cornell and THIEVES method at the beginning of the year. We discuss the pros and cons, but students ultimately choose which they prefer. I do not require the thematic notes to be practiced, but some students want options.

Cornell notes are pretty common and can be researched online. Cornell notes require the student to interact with their notes by dividing their note page into three parts. First they split the page vertically into two columns. On the right side they can take outline notes and on the left side they develop sample content questions corresponding with the information on the right side that they can use to study later for their test. A third section is left at the bottom of the page for additional questions they may have about the reading: questions that they may want to ask me, the class or further research on their own. THIEVES may require more explanation than Cornell notes. THIEVES was introduced by Jeff Zwiers in his book *Developing Academic Thinking Skills in Grades 6–12*. I was introduced to the method a few years ago at a Secondary Academic Language Tools training session in California. The students can use THIEVES as a prereading activity or as a skimming technique. Here is a breakdown of how I use the technique. Students organize notes based on the following:

Title: Students write about why the author chose these words for the title of the chapter.

Heading: Students look at the headings (most texts use headings and subheadings in the chapter) and predict or report (depending on how you are using the activity) the main points of the section.

Introduction: After reading the introduction, they summarize in one paragraph in their own words what the author intends to be the focus of the chapter.

Everything I know: Students write what they know about the subject already.

Visuals: Students assess the meaning and importance of all pictures, maps, and graphs.

End of chapter: Students read the summary or end questions and determine what they were supposed to take away from the chapter.

So what?: Most importantly, students determine why the chapter's information is important to their understanding of the particular region and its position in world history.

Students are reluctant to use this method at first, but many see the wisdom of using it.

When I check their notes, I evaluate the students' various methods of note taking and assess understanding quickly by asking key questions. I want the students to have their binder back immediately to study that night for the test the following day. Notebooks and organization are very important in AP or any class where discussion is involved. I encourage them to use their notebooks when we go over tests, prepare for essays (or write essays early in the year), reciprocally teach each other and the class by presenting the roles mentioned in the thematic review lesson, and so on.

Student Reflections

Mike

Thursday: Today we did SPIRITED. I personally don't like this activity. I feel like everyone rushes through it or if not, they concentrate on something minimal. I would rather have Mr. G lecture on the questions we ask during class. Today he also collected notes. I feel that the Cornell notes describing the main headings regarding the chapter are helpful because they require you to read the whole chapter unlike THIEVES.

Justin

Thursday: Today we did SPIRITED notes. SPIRITED focuses on specific themes and thinking skills which involve the impact of interactions among major societies, structure and types of political government, intellectual developments, how religion and philosophies shaped social structures, technological advancements, ideas that molded economic prosperity, and how they used their environment.

The way these themes are structured, they allow you to have an overall view and help us to analyze how societies contributed their efforts to help strengthen and rebuild their system of how everything should happen, which will allow the society to either become more financially, economically, politically, and culturally wealthier and powerful or else lead to the decline and fall of these societies. Usually there are eight groups that will each discuss one of these themes, according to whichever last one they had, they would move on to the next of these themes. In a group there is usually four people, of these four each one will do a certain subject that will help to clarify that particular SPIRITED theme. Even though it may help us understand the lives of those people and how they lived in that time period, I think it helps a little due to the fact that we sometimes only have ten minutes to find information about our theme. Most people just write down what they see in the book, without actually comprehending what's it about (this is not me of course!). Also when people present what they have looked for I bet some don't listen and just want to leave the class with only a few minutes remaining. The people I think that understand are those who have read a part on the weekends. What I would do is make it a game to see who can find such and such information about that theme, and those that get the test question right as a group get a prize. So instead of it just being another class lecture or something that is hard to comprehend, a game will make it fun and will involve more class participation, as groups compete for the "prize." And maybe they might actually learn and remember that information.

Denise

Thursday: Today we reviewed for the test using SPIRITED. Our group had the theme of Society, and we looked in the book and talked to each other about what we already knew concerning this theme.

This method really helps me, because it covers all the major parts of the chapter and you get different perspectives of it. It's also very beneficial because many times, things discussed during the SPIRTED presentations are right in the test the next day. It's also nice to hear information from your classmates than from your teacher or textbook. Especially if you don't understand something.

Susan

Thursday: SPIRITED is a form of reciprocal learning that we use weekly before each test. This method focuses on eight main themes present in our text: Social, Political, Intellect, Religion, Interaction, Technology, Economics and Depends on Environment. I believe that if you work together on a group and really find the most important information for each theme then this form of learning can really help you on the test. On this day, our weekly notes are checked. There are three types of note-taking you can use: THIEVES, SPIRITED, or Cornell. It helped me in the beginning of the year to use THIEVES because that form of notes really helps you to know how the chapters are set up. SPIRITED is helpful if you are having trouble understanding the eight themes, but I feel that Cornell notes are the most useful at understanding the most amount of information possible in the chapter.

Nancy

Thursday: SPIRITED I think helps a lot since it can point out important facts, terms and people. Though we do need to learn how to pinpoint information that should hold priority, but still it improves what we thought was important. There's not much to improve upon and if one or more of the themes are not there we just have to find information that we think the class should know. But overall, SPIRITED does help a lot when we actually get the most important info on the topic of the chapter.

Juan Carlos

Thursday: Class Assignments: SPIRITED and Presentation; movie

SPIRITED is a short in-class project where a group of four or more individuals are assigned a theme of Social, Political, Intellectual, Religious, Interaction, Technological, Economical, and issues on Dependence on Environment.

Evaluation: I feel SPIRITED is a great in-class assignment because it covers and reviews the eight themes of world history in a short presentation. It forces AP students to think about and view world history as a "Big Picture" and get to the main points of the chapter.

Weak points: When students do not properly prepare and do their job, not only do they not benefit from SPIRITED, but also the whole class does not benefit. Often time in groups, some students cannot think for themselves and rely heavily or even copy from the stronger individuals of the group.

Movie: We watched a short video on indentured servants and European oppression of Africans.

Evaluation: It was a good movie related to the chapter.

My Reflection

The students' main concerns involve student participation and buy-in to the process. Some would rather have me lecture, but I want the class to be learner-centered. I agree with Justin that I could make this more of a game or interactive. I may require students to take the test questions they create more seriously by using a few of them on the test or more likely as a pretest quiz so they can see how their questions measure up to the actual test questions.

The types of notes that students use varies as students see

the value of the different types. Susan switched types as she gained understanding. I am generally very flexible here.

Friday

Friday is pretty straightforward. The students have the entire class time to finish a thirty- to forty-question multiple-choice test. As previously stated, I use the test banks of several texts and modify the questions a little. I will use AP released questions to supplement some tests. At the beginning of the year, students do not know enough to answer many released AP test questions, because the questions are comparative across cultures and time periods.

Student Reflections

Mike

Friday: Today we took the test. I feel that it is better on Fridays because it is more convenient compared to Thursdays.

Justin

Friday: Today we took a test on Chapter 34 and showed Mr. G our SPIRITED or THIEVES notes. I think it seems to help to do this so you understand the overview of the chapter. But doing these notes and just copying down stuff in the book won't help you as much as if you read some of it. I also noticed students print out overviews of the chapters from Mr. G's website. It might help a little, but Mr. G puts things on the test, it may be a little thing, that tells if you read. P.S. with more practice and more tests you can sometimes infer what is going to be on the test.

Denise

Friday: Today we took the Chapter 34 test. The tests are always very fair and come from the book. I just don't like how many times there are very picky questions on there.

Susan

Friday: Today we took our weekly test on the chapter or chapters we were studying this week. We are supposed to do the reading and most of the notes over the weekend and then study the information over the week. Which I admit, doesn't always happen, but I try my best to always complete the work. Our test is usually twenty-five to fifty questions depending on the importance and length of the chapters.

Nancy

Friday: If we're smart, we ask questions throughout the week about the chapter to better understand the material. I

like the fact that Mr. G says to think that the first five minutes of class is ours to ask questions, this is a method that I love most because of its openness. We take notes over the weekend and read the chapters for next week. This is also a good method to use since it clears up the next week to summarize and review and learn more about what we read.

Juan Carlos

Friday:
   Class Assignments: Test Chapter 34
   Evaluation: Good test that covered the eight main themes.
   Weak points: Some questions I felt were irrelevant.

My Reflection

A few students who did not show me their notes on Thursday showed me on Friday. The major issue here is the pickiness of the questions. I put these questions on the test to allow for some discussion of the issues and how they pertain to the eight themes. If the question is too picky I may throw it out, but my tests are curved based on the highest score. So whoever has the highest score receives 100 percent by adding enough percentage points to his or her score to equal 100. All other students receive the same amount of percentage points added to their scores. Students who score below 50 percent before any points are added must have their parents sign the test.

I need to start meeting with parents who sign more than three tests. I arrange only one big meeting a semester at this point, but I think I will schedule more meetings next year.

Concluding Thoughts

It is a great honor to share with others the procedures I use in my classroom. They are effective for most students in my class, but there is always room for improvement. Having instructional routines is very important for student empowerment and learning of very complex material, but I would say that the most important routine for the teacher is to be reflective and remain flexible. Change is inevitable in all aspects of education.

About the Author

Dale Griepenstroh (BA, MS, National Board Certified Teacher–Social Science) is a secondary teacher in the border region of southern California, south of San Diego. He has served on curriculum assessment and design committees in two San Diego county districts, taught a social science methods class at San Diego State University, and currently serves as a San Diego county coordinator of the Secondary Academic Literacy Tools cohort for the California Reading and Literacy Project.

PART VII

HISTORIOGRAPHY

CHAPTER 31

Why Historiography Belongs in the Classroom

CRISTÓBAL T. SALDAÑA

It does not matter if one is a novice teacher or a veteran teacher. For the world history teacher, historiography drives the course. Every decision teachers make in what they choose to incorporate or disregard in their curriculum is based on historiography. Whether the teacher is cognizant of this reason does not matter: it is a simple fact. Many states have standards for world history courses, and these, too, are driven by a much larger historiographical debate.

If historiography plays such a big role in driving our curriculum, does it belong in the classroom? In other words, how can we teach students the historiography of world history, when we have so much to cover and so little time to cover it? What is historiography? Loosely defined, historiography is the history of history. The modern world history course took root only in the latter half of the twentieth century, and its historiography has been the topic of debate. For an in-depth look at the historiography of the modern world history course, Ross Dunn's *The New World History*[1] should prove a useful tool for any world history teacher or professor.

Aside from the usual trek to grade Advanced Placement (AP) World History essays last summer, I had the opportunity to participate in an AP Summer Institute that coincided with the World History Association's annual conference in Milwaukee, Wisconsin. During that week and a half, historiography was a continual topic of discussion. As the conference and institute came to a close, it became apparent that teaching students historiography was a fundamental skill that needed to be included in every world history classroom.

As I came to that conclusion, I realized that teaching historiography to my students would be no easy task. I had been teaching world history for five years, and not once had I thought to discuss historiography. I had been teaching this skill, but I had never discussed it explicitly. In fact, it was not until my third year of teaching, when I decided to pursue a master's degree in history, that I began to understand what historiography is, and now I had come to the conclusion that I needed to teach my students this skill explicitly. If I found this task difficult, imagine how enormous this would appear to a first-year world history teacher.

However, before continuing, there is a glaring question I must address. What makes historiography a fundamental skill to teach within the realm of the high school world history class? The simple answer to this question is that students need to be able to "interpret diverse points of view." This phrase comes from the AP World History Course Description Guide. In a best-of-all-worlds scenario, I believe that the AP World History Course Description Guide provides an invaluable tool for those who are beginning to teach world history. This guide can aid teachers in designing their curriculum for any level of world history—not just the advanced placement level. It helps novice teachers focus their time on developing their curriculum to reflect the skills that will be required of students when they enter college. It develops the idea that world history is about point of view, and this is what lies at the very heart of the historiography of world history.

Historians debate teaching students the skills required to interpret documents from a historiographical standpoint. This must be the basis for any world history course, as it is this one skill that all students should demonstrate proficiently. If society is not to be doomed to repeat the mistakes of the past, as Santayana noted, then citizens must be able to understand not only what happened as in the "how's" and the "why's" but also the thinking that occurs when secondary sources seek to explain those same "how's" and "why's."

History is written through the lens of the present. Some say history is a conversation with the past. The writing of history thus varies from generation to generation. At that AP Summer Institute in Milwaukee, Dr. Tim Keirn noted that historical representation changes for various reasons. New evidence might give historians a deeper understanding of historical or even current events. Also, a change in current values would impact the writing of history. In addition, new technology might uncover new evidence. Lastly, new theory might lead to a change in historical representation. Keirn argued that history is a matter of interpreting historical data. He also argued that historians borrow theory from other fields to draw conclusions about that historical data. For example, historians analyze historical economic data according to accepted economic theory.

So what does "understanding the diversity of interpretation" actually mean? This is a call for incorporating some basic level of historiography in the classroom. There are many ways to do this. Using various media can be helpful, at least on the introductory level. One of the movies I love to show in my classes is *Rocky IV*. It is a movie with which all of my students are familiar, but before beginning the film, I tell them to watch it from the point of view of a Soviet student. I provide some basic information on life in the Soviet Union. At the end of the movie, I quiz the students on their observations: "Do you think the Russians would really be cheering Rocky at the end of a real fight?" and "What does it mean to have Rocky draped in an American flag in Moscow at the end of the movie?" At this point they begin to understand the underlying political overtones in a movie made during the cold war. Since most non-AP students are visual learners with short attention spans, I find that doing this activity works best with them.

For my AP students, we begin analyzing documents almost immediately. I think it is important to delve into terms like bias and point of view. This is probably the most difficult part in teaching students to understand the interpretation of documents. Students struggle with the idea that nothing can be written in a truly objective fashion. Every life experience is different, and therefore the written account will reflect as much. I emphasize this idea so that when my students enter college or the workforce, they learn to question everything. If they read a historical source about Africa from the 1960s, they will realize that it is going to have a very different connotation than a source written in 1995.

When an AP student can understand that, and when a non-AP student can understand that things are not always what they seem, then I know I have accomplished my job in teaching the diversity of interpretation. Helping students understand the diversity of interpretation is just the beginning of helping students understand historiography. Understanding historiography is not just about point of view, but also about understanding the big picture in which history is written. Because there is so much material to cover and so little time to cover that material, this is probably as deep as teachers can delve, at least in a high school classroom. But at least, in doing so, teachers will have introduced the concept of historiography to students, should they go on to study it in a university setting.

However, for the world history teacher, the necessity for understanding historiography goes deeper than documents and movies. Almost all teachers have to deal with state standards and a state standardized test. Novice and veteran teachers should be aware of the era in which most of these standards were written. From the mid-1960s to the early 1980s, the world history movement was undergoing a phase often called "the West and the rest." This comparative approach to world history sought to explain why the West's view predominated while the "rest" struggled to survive. It often highlighted the highs of the West and the lows of the rest. It was in this era in world history that most state standards were written. For example, this is why, in Texas, the dates of importance in world history according to the Texas Essential Knowledge and Skills (TEKS) standards are 1066, 1215, 1492, 1521, 1789, 1914–1918, and 1939–1945. With two exceptions, each one of these dates refers to an event in Europe. The two events that occur outside Europe, in 1492 and 1521, give agency (those doing the action) to Europeans. How can this be a true "world history" class if the important dates are all European? Where is the global perspective? Europe is not the entire world.

I should acknowledge that TEKS does try to atone by setting historical teaching standards for other areas around the world. Unfortunately, these tend to be very broad in nature, such as, "The student will understand the political, social, and economic development of sub-Saharan Africa." Entire books and graduate classes have been devoted to each part of this standard (political, social, and economic), and those books and classes only scratch the surface. How can high school students "understand" this topic in a few short weeks? This is why it is important to know the background under which most state standards were written. It is also important to know that until recently, most world history teachers had no formal training in world history, only in more specific specialized areas. This leads to further confusion, especially when the novice world history teacher looks to the standards to decide what to incorporate and what to disregard. Again, in the best of all worlds, the AP World History Course Description Guide is a very useful guide for any world history class. The secret is to tweak it to fit your students, whether you teach AP or non-AP students.

World history continues to evolve. As humans seek a deeper understanding of past events, new meaning is found in the actions of those in the past. It is left to the teachers of world history to help students, the future leaders, to understand the context in which those events and those actions occur. This can be accomplished by incorporating historiography on the basic levels. When students see the bigger picture, teachers can be confident that they are teaching the most fundamental skill all students should take from any world history class.

About the Author

Cristóbal T. Saldaña (BA, government and international studies; MA, history and politics) is a world history teacher at Harlingen High School in Harlingen, Texas. He has been an AP reader for world history since 2004. He has been intrigued by the impact of social studies since his time at Notre Dame. The focus of his master's thesis is teaching writing in the AP World History classroom.

Note

1. Ross E. Dunn, ed. *The New World History: A Teacher's Companion.* New York: Bedford/St. Martin's, 2000.

CHAPTER 32

A Basic, Briefly Annotated Bibliography
for Teachers of World History

JERRY H. BENTLEY

Since about 1975 the subfield of world history has expanded dramatically. Many schools, colleges, and universities have replaced courses in Western civilization with introductions to world history or have at least added world history as an alternative to established courses. Recognizing that history is not the exclusive property of national communities or ethnic groups, professional historians have increasingly taken comparative, cross-cultural, systematic, and global approaches to the past. From its foundation in 1982, the World History Association (WHA) has promoted teaching and research in world history, and the WHA newsletter, the *World History Bulletin*, has published reflective essays and articles on teaching world history. The *Journal of World History*, founded in 1990, provides a forum for research and scholarship in world history. In 2006 the *Journal of Global History* made its appearance as an additional platform for articles and essays in world history. At least two online journals—*World History Connected* (founded in 2003) and *New Global Studies* (founded in 2007)—also serve the needs of world historians. Other journals that frequently feature articles on transnational and global themes are *American Historical Review*, *Comparative Studies in Society and History*, *Itinerario*, *Journal of Asian Studies*, *Journal of Early Modern History*, and *Journal of Modern History*, to mention only the most prominent.

Rapid expansion has caused some growing pains for the subfield of world history. Instructors at all educational levels have found themselves teaching about historical issues and world regions that they did not study during their own school years. On the scholarly front, world history has faced challenges from two directions in particular: most professional historians have continued to work in traditionally recognized fields of local and national history, while many postmodern and postcolonial critics have rejected any project to analyze large-scale processes in favor of local

studies addressing the interests of identity politics. Nor have world historians agreed among themselves on a paradigm of world history. At the beginning of the twenty-first century, there is no commonly accepted vision of world history, but rather a series of alternatives that rarely engaged the issues raised by competing schools of analysis.

In spite of these problems, it seems certain that world history will occupy a prominent place in the educational landscape for the foreseeable future. Although the number of courses in world history has grown in recent years, more and better instruction at all levels is needed. Schoolteachers need courses on global themes that will prepare them to offer survey courses in the K–12 curriculum. They need not only high-quality introductory courses in colleges and universities, but also advanced undergraduate courses that explore global themes in detail. As world history gains recognition in the larger discipline of history, there is a need for graduate seminars that introduce advanced students to the scholarly literature and encourage them to undertake research on themes in world history. Finally, there is also a need for courses on world history and global themes for the general public. In an era of increasing global interdependence, it is crucial for educated citizens to understand that human societies have engaged in processes of cross-cultural interaction from earliest times, that the world has been the site of globalization for a very long time indeed.

The purpose of this bibliography is to serve the needs of instructors teaching world history at various levels. The bibliography is eclectic: it does not favor or slight any particular school of analysis—at least, not intentionally. Instead it seeks to include the most important and influential publications that take comparative, cross-cultural, systematic, or global approaches to the past. It does not list primary sources, textbooks, or readers. Nor does it mention theoretical works that reflect the experiences of any single society, but it does include theoretical works that cross the boundary lines of societies and seek to understand historical dynamics from larger perspectives. It does not mention works on individual lands or world regions—even though many such works are important for the organization of courses in world history—except to the extent that they place individual lands or regions in a larger context. It is by no means a complete bibliography of all the relevant scholarship, but it will serve at least as a starting point for instructors designing courses in world history.

Many thanks to the following scholars who contributed to the construction of this bibliography: Edmund Burke III, Ross E. Dunn, Craig Lockard, Robert B. Marks, Kevin Reilly, and Merry E. Wiesner-Hanks.

Historiography, Periodization, Conceptualization, and Teaching Aids

Alongside the classic literature of world history—some of which takes the form of philosophy of history rather than historical analysis as generally understood—this section mentions historiographical studies, works dealing with periodization, scholarship developing alternatives to national states and discrete societies as categories of historical analysis, contributions on conceptual issues, and teaching aids.

The Classic Literature of World History

McNeill, William H. *The Rise of the West: A History of the Human Community*. Chicago: University of Chicago Press, 1963. The starting point for contemporary historical approaches to the global past.
———. *"The Rise of the West* after Twenty-Five Years." *Journal of World History* 1 (1990): 1–21. The author's critical reflections on his own work.
Nehru, Jawaharlal. *Glimpses of World History*. New York: John Day, 1942. Letters to his daughter, Indira Gandhi, offering a South Asian perspective on the global past.
Spengler, Oswald. *The Decline of the West*. 2 vols. Trans. by C.F. Atkinson. New York: Knopf, 1934. Cultural determinism writ large.
Toynbee, Arnold. *A Study of History*. 12 vols. Oxford: Oxford University Press, 1934–1961. An erudite effort to distill lessons from historical experience.
Wells, H.G. *The Outline of History*. New York: Macmillan, 1920. A popular work with a global perspective.

Historiographical Studies

Adas, Michael, ed. *Islamic and European Expansion: The Forging of a Global Order*. Philadelphia: Temple University Press, 1993. Ten essays, originally published as pamphlets, dealing with issues in global history.
Allardyce, Gilbert. "Toward World History: American Historians and the Coming of the World History Course." *Journal of World History* 1 (1990): 23–76. Thoughtful, witty analysis of mid-century efforts in global history.

Arnold, David. *The Problem of Nature: Environment, Culture and European Expansion*. Oxford, UK: Blackwell, 1996. Critical reflections on environmental history.
Bentley, Jerry H. "The New World History." In *A Companion to Western Historical Thought*, ed. Lloyd Kramer and Sarah Maza, 393–416. Oxford, UK: Blackwell, 2002. Focuses on scholarly approaches and themes of recent scholarship in world history.
———. *Shapes of World History in Twentieth-Century Scholarship*. Washington, DC: American Historical Association, 1996. A pamphlet that seeks to sort through recent scholarship in world history.
Costello, Paul. *World Historians and Their Goals: Twentieth-Century Answers to Modernism*. DeKalb: Northern Illinois University Press, 1993. Argues that twentieth-century world history has been largely a response to modernism.
Croizier, Ralph. "World History in the People's Republic of China." *Journal of World History* 1 (1990): 151–169. Chinese conceptions of the world's past.
Gargan, Edward T., ed. *The Intent of Toynbee's History: A Cooperative Appraisal*. Chicago: Loyola University Press, 1961. Scholarly essays evaluating Toynbee's work.
Geyer, Michael, and Charles Bright. "World History in a Global Age." *American Historical Review* 100 (1995): 1034–1062. Views recent scholarship as a reflection of contemporary globalization.
Hughes, H. Stuart. *Oswald Spengler: A Critical Estimate*. New York: Scribner's, 1952. An insightful critique of Spengler.
Kopf, David. "A Look at Nehru's *World History* from the Dark Side of Modernity." *Journal of World History* 2 (1991): 47–63. Analysis of Nehru's vision of world history.
Lockard, Craig A. "The Contributions of Philip Curtin and the 'Wisconsin School' to the Study and Promotion of Comparative World History." *Journal of Third World Studies* 11 (1994): 180–223. Deals with Curtin's work and influence.
Manning, Patrick. *Navigating World History: Historians Create a Global Past*. New York: Palgrave Macmillan, 2003. Historiographical, methodological, and organizational discussions.
McNeill, William H. *Arnold J. Toynbee: A Life*. Oxford, UK: Oxford University Press, 1989. The best biography and evaluation.
Sorokin, Pitirim A. *Modern Historical and Social Philosophies*. New York: Dover, 1963. A sociologist's review of the philosophy of history.

Periodization

Barraclough, Geoffrey. *An Introduction to Contemporary History*. Harmondsworth, UK: Penguin, 1967. Sketches some main themes of contemporary history from a global point of view.
Bentley, Jerry H. "Cross-Cultural Interaction and Periodization in World History." *American Historical Review* 101 (1996): 749–70. Argues that cross-cultural interaction can serve as a basis for global historical periodization.
———. "Early Modern Europe and the Early Modern World." In *Between the Middle Ages and Modernity: Individual and Community in the Early Modern World*, ed. Charles H. Parker and Jerry H. Bentley, 13–31. Lanham, MD: Rowman and Littlefield, 2007. Argues for a coherent early modern era of world history.
———. "Hemispheric Integration, 500–1500 C.E." *Journal of World History* 9 (1998): 237–254. Emphasizes commercial, biological, and cultural exchanges in the postclassical era.
Dunn, Ross E. "Periodization and Chronological Coverage in a

World History Survey." In *What Americans Should Know: Western Civilization or World History?* ed. Josef W. Konvitz, 129–140. East Lansing: Michigan State University, 1985. Emphasizes large-scale processes like the construction of the Mongol empires and epidemic plague.

Fletcher, Joseph F. "Integrative History: Parallels and Interconnections in the Early Modern Period, 1500–1800." *Journal of Turkish Studies* 9 (1985): 37–57; reprinted in Joseph F. Fletcher, *Studies on Chinese and Islamic Inner Asia*. Brookfield, VT: Variorum, 1995, article X. Argues for an interconnected early modern world.

Goldstone, Jack A. "The Problem of the 'Early Modern' World." *Journal of the Economic and Social History of the Orient* 41 (1998): 249–284. Questions the coherence of the concept of an early modern era in world history.

Green, William A. *History, Historians, and the Dynamics of Change*. Westport, CT: Praeger, 1993. General discussion of periodization issues.

———. "Periodization in European and World History." *Journal of World History* 3 (1992): 13–53. Concentrates on modern times.

Manning, Patrick. "The Problem of Interactions in World History." *American Historical Review* 101 (1996): 771–782. Questions meaning of interactions for periodization.

Richards, John F. "Early Modern India and World History." *Journal of World History* 8 (1997): 197–209. Briefly characterizes the early modern world and locates India in early modern times.

Stearns, Peter. "Periodization in World History Teaching: Identifying the Big Changes." *History Teacher* 20 (1987): 561–580. A practical and useful approach.

Beyond National States and Discrete Societies: Alternative Categories of Historical Analysis

Bender, Thomas. *A Nation Among Nations: America's Place in World History*. New York: Hill and Wang, 2006. Examines U.S. history in global context.

———, ed. *Rethinking American History in a Global Age*. Berkeley: University of California Press, 2002. Essays placing U.S. history in global context.

Bentley, Jerry H. "Sea and Ocean Basins as Frameworks of Historical Analysis." *Geographical Review* 89 (1999): 215–224. On maritime regions as historical categories.

Bentley, Jerry H., Renate Bridenthal, and Kären Wigen, eds. *Seascapes: Maritime Histories, Littoral Cultures, and Transoceanic Exchanges*. Honolulu: University of Hawai'i Press, 2007. Scholarly essays exploring historical issues in the contexts of maritime regions.

Bentley, Jerry H., Renate Bridenthal, and Anand A. Yang, eds. *Interactions: Transregional Perspectives on World History*. Honolulu: University of Hawai'i Press, 2005. Scholarly essays exploring historical issues in transregional context.

Bose, Sugata. *A Hundred Horizons: The Indian Ocean in the Age of Global Empire*. Cambridge, MA: Harvard University Press, 2006. Traces cross-cultural interactions over the Indian Ocean.

Buschmann, Rainer. *Oceans in World History*. New York: McGraw Hill, 2006. Brief analysis.

Chaudhuri, K.N. *Trade and Civilisation in the Indian Ocean: An Economic History from the Rise of Islam to 1750*. Cambridge, UK: Cambridge University Press, 1985. Applies a Braudelian approach to the Indian Ocean.

Cunliffe, Barry. *Facing the Ocean: The Atlantic and Its Peoples.* Oxford, UK: Oxford University Press, 2001. An archaeologist considers the Atlantic region from prehistoric times to the modern age.

Egerton, Douglas, et al. *The Atlantic World: A History, 1400–1888*. Wheeling, WV: Harlan Davidson, 2007. Detailed discussion of interactions and exchanges.

Guarneri, Carl. *America in the World: United States History in Global Context*. New York: McGraw-Hill, 2007. Brief analysis of the United States in context of world history.

Lewis, Martin W., and Kären E. Wigen. *The Myth of Continents: A Critique of Metageography*. Berkeley: University of California Press, 1997. A critical review of conventional geographical constructs.

Pearson, Michael. *The Indian Ocean*. New York: Routledge, 2003. Historical analysis of a maritime region.

Shaffer, Lynda. "Southernization." *Journal of World History* 5 (1994): 1–21. Explores influences of tropical regions on temperate lands.

White, Richard. *The Middle Ground: Indians, Empires, and Republics in the Great Lakes Region, 1650–1815*. Cambridge, MA: Cambridge University Press, 1991. Fresh approach to the study of borderlands.

Other Conceptual Issues and Approaches

Bentley, Jerry H. "Myths, Wagers, and Some Moral Implications of World History." *Journal of World History* 16 (2005): 51–82. Explores political and moral issues raised by world history.

———. "World History and Grand Narrative." In *Writing World History, 1800–2000*, ed. Benedikt Stuchtey and Eckhardt Fuchs, 47–65. Oxford, UK: Oxford University Press, 2003. Seeks appropriate ways to construct grand narratives in world history.

Burke, Edmund, III. "Marshall G.S. Hodgson and the Hemispheric, Interregional Approach to World History." 6 (1995): 237–250. Outlines Hodgson's approach.

Christian, David. "The Case for 'Big History.'" *Journal of World History* 2 (1991): 223–238. Not just human history—world history from the big bang forward.

———. *Maps of Time: An Introduction to Big History*. Berkeley: University of California Press, 2005. A major statement situating human history in a much larger context.

Diamond, Jared. *Guns, Germs, and Steel: The Fates of Human Societies*. New York: W.W. Norton, 1997. Environmental and geographical interpretation of world history.

Fernández-Armesto, Felipe. *Civilizations: Culture, Ambition, and the Transformation of Nature*. New York: Free Press, 2002. Environmental interpretation of human societies.

Frank, Andre Gunder. "A Plea for World System History." *Journal of World History* 2 (1991): 1–28. Spirited call for global historical analysis.

Hodgson, Marshall G.S. *Rethinking World History: Essays on Europe, Islam, and World History,* ed. by Edmund Burke III. Cambridge, UK: Cambridge University Press, 1993. Posthumous writings on conceptions of world history.

———. *The Venture of Islam: Conscience and History in a World Civilization*. 3 vols. Chicago: University of Chicago Press, 1974. An influential analysis that places Islam in a hemispheric context.

Hughes-Warrington, Marnie, ed. *Palgrave Advances in World Histories*. New York: Palgrave Macmillan, 2005. Ten essays on aspects of world history.

Mazlish, Bruce, and Ralph Buultjens, eds. *Conceptualizing Global History*. Boulder, CO: Westview Press, 1993. Essays seeking to distinguish global history from world history, universal history, and total history.

McNeill, J.R., and William H. McNeill. *The Human Web: A Bird's-Eye View of World History*. New York: W.W. Norton, 2003. Considers the roles of networks in world history.

McNeill, William H. *Mythistory and Other Essays*. Chicago: University of Chicago Press, 1986. Collected essays and presentations, mostly on issues in world history.

———. *Polyethnicity and National Unity in World History*. Toronto: University of Toronto Press, 1986. Argues that the ideal of national ethnic homogeneity was a very recent development in world history.

Pomper, Philip, Richard H. Elphick, and Richard T. Vann, eds. *World History: Ideology, Structures, and Identities*. Oxford, UK: Blackwell, 1998. Scholarly essays on the problems and possibilities of world history.

Stavrianos, L.S. *Lifelines from Our Past: A New World History*. New York: Pantheon, 1989. A large-scale view based on social organization.

Teaching Aids

Adams, Steven, Michael Adas, and Kevin Reilly, eds. *World History: Selected Course Outlines and Reading Lists from American Colleges and Universities*. New ed. Princeton: Markus Wiener, 1998. A collection of syllabi.

Dunn, Ross E., ed. *The New World History: A Teacher's Companion*. Boston: Bedford St. Martins, 2000. Essays and excerpts from previously published writings on conceptions of world history.

Dunn, Ross E., and David Vigilante, eds. *Bring History Alive! A Sourcebook for Teaching World History*. Los Angeles: National Center for History in the Schools, UCLA, 1996. Includes essays and teaching activities geared toward *National Standards for World History*.

National Center for History in the Schools. *National Standards for World History*. Los Angeles: National Center for History in the Schools, UCLA, 1994. Comprehensive and challenging.

Roupp, Heidi, ed. *Teaching World History: A Resource Book*. Armonk, NY: M.E. Sharpe, 1997. Essays, syllabi, and lesson plans.

Development Studies: Modernization, Dependency, World Systems, and Beyond

Some of the most influential recent theories of world history have emerged from analytical schools seeking to understand modern economic development, underdevelopment, and the rise of the West. These schools have all generated an enormous literature. The works cited here represent some of the most useful for purposes of understanding the implications of modernization, dependency, world-system, and more recent approaches for global history. Several critical historiographical works also appear on this list.

Modernization Analysis

Black, Cyril E. *The Dynamics of Modernization: A Study in Comparative History*. New York: Harper and Row, 1966. A primer in modernization thinking.

Jones, E.L. *The European Miracle: Environments, Economies, and Geopolitics in the History of Europe and Asia*. 3rd ed. Cambridge, UK: Cambridge University Press, 2003. An effort to update modernization analysis by shedding its ethnocentrism.

———. *Growth Recurring: Economic Change in World History*. Oxford, UK: Oxford University Press, 1988. Seeks to globalize modernization theory.

Landes, David S. *The Wealth and Poverty of Nations: Why Some Are So Rich and Some So Poor*. New York: W.W. Norton, 1998. Cultural explanation of development.

Lockard, Craig A. "Global History, Modernization, and the World-Systems Approach: A Critique," *History Teacher* 14 (1981): 489–515. Thoughtful comparison and critique.

Rostow, W.W. *How It All Began: Origins of the Modern Economy*. New York: McGraw-Hill, 1975. Interpretion of modern economic history from the modernization viewpoint.

———. *The Stages of Economic Growth: A Non-Communist Manifesto*. 3rd ed. Cambridge, UK: Cambridge University Press, 1991. A classic articulation of modernization economic theory.

Dependency Analysis

Amin, Samir. *Unequal Development*. New York: Monthly Review Press, 1976. A classic statement of dependency theory.

Frank, Andre Gunder. *Dependent Accumulation and Underdevelopment*. New York: Monthly Review Press, 1979. Dependency view of modern history.

———. *World Accumulation, 1492–1789*. New York: Monthly Review Press, 1978. Interprets early modern world history from a dependency viewpoint.

Rodney, Walter. *How Europe Underdeveloped Africa*. Washington, DC: Howard University Press, 1974. Application of dependency analysis to Africa.

White, Richard. *The Roots of Dependency: Subsistence, Environment, and Social Change Among the Choctaws, Pawnees, and Navajos*. Lincoln: University of Nebraska Press, 1983. Application of dependency analysis to the indigenous peoples of North America.

Williams, Eric. *Capitalism and Slavery*. Chapel Hill: University of North Carolina Press, 1944. A classic work anticipating dependency analysis.

World-System Analysis

Abu-Lughod, Janet L. *Before European Hegemony: The World System, A.D. 1250–1350*. Oxford, UK: Oxford University Press, 1989. Influential study that pushes world-system analysis into premodern times.

Bagchi, Amiya Kumar. *Perilous Passage: Mankind and the Global Ascendancy of Capital*. Lanham, MD: Rowman and Littlefield, 2005. Provocative analysis of the rise of capitalist Europe.

Braudel, Fernand. *Civilization and Capitalism, 15th–18th Century*. 3 vols. Trans. by S. Reynolds. New York: Harper and Row, 1981–1984. Reflects the influence of world-system analysis.

Chase-Dunn, Christopher, and Thomas D. Hall. *Rise and Demise: Comparing World Systems*. Boulder, CO: Westview Press, 1997. A synthesis of world-system theory and analysis.

Frank, Andre Gunder. *ReORIENT: Global Economy in the Asian Age*. Berkeley: University of California Press, 1998. Rejects Eurocentric social theory in favor of global economic and historical analysis.

Frank, Andre Gunder, and Barry K. Gills, eds. *The World System: Five Hundred Years or Five Thousand?* New York: Routledge, 1993. Essays exploring world systems before modern times.

Islamoglu-Inan, Huri, ed. *The Ottoman Empire and the World-Economy*. Cambridge, UK: Cambridge University Press, 1987. Scholarly essays.

Lockard, Craig A. "Global History, Modernization, and the World-Systems Approach: A Critique." *History Teacher* 14 (1981): 489–515. Thoughtful comparison and critique.

Ragin, Charles, and Daniel Chirot. "The World System of Immanuel Wallerstein." In *Vision and Method in Historical Sociology*, ed. Theda Skocpol, 276–312. Cambridge, UK: Cambridge University Press, 1984. Insightful essay on Wallerstein.

Schneider, Jane. "Was There a Pre-Capitalist World System?" *Peasant Studies* 6 (1977): 20–29. An important critique of Wallerstein's views on trade.

Shannon, Thomas Richard. *An Introduction to the World-System Perspective*. 2nd ed. Boulder, CO: Westview Press, 1996. A reliable and helpful introduction.

So, Alvin. *Social Change and Development: Modernization, Dependency, and World-System Theories*. Newbury Park, CA: Sage, 1990. Discusses three approaches to modern history.

So, Alvin, and Stephen W.K. Chiu. *East Asia and the World Economy*. Newbury Park, CA: Sage, 1995. Interprets East Asian history from a world-system perspective.

Stavrianos, L.S. *Global Rift: The Third World Comes of Age*. New York: William Morrow, 1981. Spirited analysis of the third world from world-system perspective.

Voll, John Obert. "Islam as a Special World-System," *Journal of World History* 5 (1994): 213–226. Views the Islamic world as a community of discourse.

Wallerstein, Immanuel. *Essential Wallerstein*. New York: New Press, 2000. Collected essays that place the author's views in context.

———. *Historical Capitalism*. London: Verso, 1983. Brief sketch of the author's views.

———. *The Modern World-System*. 3 vols. to date. New York: Academic Press, 1974– . The classic argument for a modern, capitalist, European-dominated world system.

Wolf, Eric. *Europe and the People Without History*. Berkeley: University of California Press, 1982. An anthropologist's adaptation of world-system analysis.

Beyond Modernization, Dependency, and World Systems: Fresh Views on the Rise of the West

Bayly, C.A. *The Birth of the Modern World, 1780–1914: Global Connections and Comparisons*. Oxford, UK: Blackwell, 2003. Dense but brilliant analysis of emerging modernity.

Frank, Andre Gunder. *ReORIENT: Global Economy in the Asian Age*. Berkeley: University of California Press, 1998. Provocative effort to develop an alternative to Eurocentric analyses of modern world history.

Goldstone, Jack A. "Efflorescences and Economic Growth in World History: Rethinking the 'Rise of the West' and the Industrial Revolution." *Journal of World History* 13 (2002): 323–389. Fresh interpretation of the rise of the West in light of recent scholarship.

———. *Why Europe? The Rise of the West in World History, 1500–1850*. New York: McGraw-Hill, 2008. Brief analysis reflecting recent scholarship.

Goody, Jack. *Capitalism and Modernity: The Great Debate*. Oxford, UK: Oxford University Press, 2004. A distinguished anthropologist's review of recent debates on modernity and the rise of the West.

———. *The East in the West*. Cambridge, UK: Cambridge University Press, 1996. Emphasizes Asian rationality and Asian influences on Europe.

———. *The Theft of History*. Cambridge, UK: Cambridge University Press, 2007. Argues for large-scale influence of Asian values and institutions on Europe.

Hobson, John M. *The Eastern Origins of Western Civilisation*. Cambridge, UK: Cambridge University Press, 2004. Spirited but sometimes overstated polemic about Asian influences on Europe.

Hopkins, A.G., ed. *Globalization in World History*. New York: W.W. Norton, 2002. Scholarly essays emphasizing transregional historical processes.

———, ed. *Global History: Interactions Between the Universal and the Local*. New York: Palgrave Macmillan, 2006. Scholarly studies on global processes in local contexts.

Lieberman, Victor, ed. *Beyond Binary Histories: Re-imagining Eurasia to c. 1830*. Ann Arbor: University of Michigan Press, 1999. Essays testing the editor's hypothesis about the value of large-scale comparisons of societies across the Eurasian continent.

Marks, Robert B. *The Origins of the Modern World: Fate and Fortunes in the Rise of the West*. Rev. ed. Lanham, MD: Rowman and Littlefield, 2007. Brisk synthesis of recent scholarship.

Pomeranz, Kenneth. *The Great Divergence: China, Europe, and the Making of the Modern World Economy*. Princeton: Princeton University Press, 2000. Brilliant analysis of the foundations for the rise of the West.

Vries, P.H.H. "Are Coal and Colonies Really Crucial? Kenneth Pomeranz and the Great Divergence." *Journal of World History* 12 (2001): 407–446. Critical but appreciative review of Pomeranz.

Wong, R. Bin. *China Transformed: Historical Change and the Limits of European Experience*. Ithaca, NY: Cornell University Press, 2000. Sophisticated argument calling for reciprocal comparisons.

Migrations and Diasporas

Large-scale migrations of peoples have figured among the most important processes in all of world history. They have profoundly influenced both the experiences of individual societies and the development of the world as a whole. The literature on migrations is vast, but most of it takes a very limited perspective. Works cited here take a broad approach to migrations, seeking to understand their larger historical significance. Another section mentions works that employ the category of diaspora in studying the social and cultural effects of migrations and that sometimes also construe groups in diaspora as alternatives to national communities.

Migrations

Anthony, David W. *The Horse, the Wheel, and Language: How Bronze-Age Riders from the Eurasian Steppes Shaped the Modern World*. Princeton: Princeton University Press, 2007. Important study of the origins and migrations of Indo-European speakers.

Cohen, Robin, ed. *The Cambridge Survey of World Migrations*. Cambridge, UK: Cambridge University Press, 1995. Scholarly syntheses.

Curtin, Philip D. *The Atlantic Slave Trade: A Census*. Madison:

University of Wisconsin Press, 1969. The starting point for contemporary discussions on the number of slaves transported to the Western Hemisphere.

Emmer, Pieter C., ed. *Colonialism and Migration: Indentured Labor before and after Slavery*. Dordrecht, Netherlands: Martinus Nijhoff, 1986. An important collection of scholarly essays on indentured labor migrations.

Gamble, Clive. *Timewalkers: The Prehistory of Global Colonization*. Cambridge, MA: Harvard University Press, 1994. Deals with the earliest human migrants—those who established human species in all parts of the world.

Hoerder, Dirk. *Cultures in Contact: World Migrations in the Second Millennium*. Durham, NC: Duke University Press, 2002. Massive study of migration systems over the past thousand years.

Inikori, Joseph E., and Stanley Engerman, eds. *The Atlantic Slave Trade: Effects on Economies, Societies, and Peoples in Africa, the Americas, and Europe*. Durham, NC: Duke University Press, 1992. Scholarly essays.

Mallory, J.P. *In Search of the Indo-Europeans: Language, Archaeology, and Myth*. London: Thames and Hudson, 1989. Dated but generally reliable discussion of Indo-European origins and early migrations.

Mallory, J.P., and Victor H. Mair. *The Tarim Mummies: Ancient China and the Mystery of the Earliest Peoples from the West*. London: Thames and Hudson, 2000. Focuses on early Indo-European migration to what is now western China.

Manning, Patrick. *Migration in World History*. London: Routledge, 2005. Brief large-scale analysis.

———. *Slavery and African Life: Occidental, Oriental, and African Slave Trades*. Cambridge, UK: Cambridge University Press, 1990. An important survey synthesizing recent scholarship.

McKeown, Adam. "Global Migration, 1846–1940." *Journal of World History* 15 (2004): 155–189. Fresh look at patterns in global migration.

Northrup, David. *Indentured Labor in the Age of Imperialism, 1834–1922*. Cambridge, UK: Cambridge University Press, 1995. Revises the argument of Tinker, cited below.

Rouse, Irving. *Migrations in Prehistory: Inferring Population Movements from Cultural Remains*. New Haven, CT: Yale University Press, 1986. Throws important light on several prehistoric migrations.

Solow, Barbara, ed. *Slavery and the Rise of the Atlantic System*. Cambridge, UK: Cambridge University Press, 1991. Scholarly essays.

Tinker, Hugh. *A New System of Slavery: The Export of Indian Labour Overseas, 1830–1920*. 2nd ed. London: Hansib, 1993. Portrays the trade in indentured labor as a new system of slavery.

Wang Gungwu, ed. *Global History and Migrations*. Boulder, CO: Westview Press, 1997. Scholarly essays on historical migrations.

Diasporas

Cohen, Robin. *Global Diasporas: An Introduction*. Seattle: University of Washington Press, 1997. A useful introduction to the literature.

Clifford, James. *Routes: Travel and Translation in the Late Twentieth Century*. Cambridge, MA: Harvard University Press, 1997. Essays dealing with migration and diaspora themes.

Conniff, Michael, et al. *Africans in the Americas: A History of the Black Diaspora*. New York: St. Martin's, 1994. A comprehensive survey.

Gilroy, Paul. *The Black Atlantic: Modernity and Double Consciousness*. Cambridge, MA: Harvard University Press, 1993. Offers a challenging, distinctive perspective on the African diaspora.

Harris, Joseph E., ed. *Global Dimensions of the African Diaspora*. 2nd ed. Washington, DC: Howard University Press, 1993. Scholarly essays.

Ho, Engseng. *The Graves of Tarim: Genealogy and Mobility Across the Indian Ocean*. Berkeley: University of California Press, 2006. Traces a Yemeni diaspora to destinations throughout the Indian Ocean basin.

Kilson, Martin L., and Robert I. Rotberg, eds. *The African Diaspora: Interpretive Essays*. Cambridge, MA: Harvard University Press, 1976. Scholarly essays.

Sheffer, Gabriel, ed. *Modern Diasporas in International Politics*. London: Croom Helm, 1986. Scholarly essays.

Thornton, John. *Africa and Africans in the Making of the Modern World, 1400–1800*. 2nd ed. Cambridge, UK: Cambridge University Press, 1998. Well-documented study of the early African diaspora.

Empires and Imperialism

Like movements of peoples, the building of imperial states has also profoundly influenced the development of world history. As in the case of migrations, most studies focus tightly on specific experiences. Works cited here, however, take a broader approach, seeking to gauge the role of empires and imperialism in historical development. Apart from works on empires and imperialism proper, there are citations also to geographical travel and exploration, which has often figured as a prelude to imperial and colonial projects, as well as postcolonial scholarship addressing issues of identity and cross-cultural representation.

Geographical Travel and Exploration

Alam, Muzaffar, and Sanjay Subrahmanyam. *Indo-Persian Travels in the Age of Discoveries, 1400–1800*. Cambridge, UK: Cambridge University Press, 2007. Summaries of travel accounts.

Dreyer, Edward L. *Zheng He: China and the Oceans in the Early Ming Dynasty, 1405–1433*. New York: Longman, 2006. Situates Zheng He's career and voyages in context of Ming dynasty.

Fernández-Armesto, Felipe. *Pathfinders: A Global History of Exploration*. New York: W.W. Norton, 2006. Engaging survey of exploration from ancient times to the present.

Frye, Richard N., ed. *Ibn Fadlan's Journey to Russia*. Princeton: Markus Wiener, 2005. Translation of an important travel account.

Hopkins, J.F.P., and Nehemia Levtzion, eds. *Corpus of Early Arabic Sources for West African History*. Cambridge, UK: Cambridge University Press, 1981. Important collection of translated travel accounts.

Levathes, Louise. *When China Ruled the Seas: The Treasure Fleet of the Dragon Throne, 1405–1433*. New York: Oxford University Press, 1997. Good popular account of Zheng He's expeditions.

Parry, J.H. *The Age of Reconnaissance: Discovery, Exploration and Settlement, 1450–1650*. London: Littlehampton Book Services, 1962. Dated survey of early European empires.

Phillips, J.R.S. *The Medieval Expansion of Europe.* Oxford, UK: Oxford University Press, 1988. Synthesizes scholarship on European expansion and imperialism before 1500.

Phillips, William D., Jr., and Carla Rahn Phillips. *The Worlds of Christopher Columbus.* New York: Cambridge University Press, 1992. The best general study, locating Columbus properly in European and global context.

Ringrose, David. *Expansion and Global Interaction, 1200–1700.* New York: Longman, 2000. Explores empire-building as a global historical process in the early modern era.

Subrahmanyam, Sanjay. *The Career and Legend of Vasco da Gama.* Cambridge, UK: Cambridge University Press, 1997. The best study of Vasco da Gama.

Verlinden, Charles. *The Beginnings of Modern Colonization.* Trans. by Y. Freccero. Ithaca, NY: Cornell University Press, 1970. Important essays on early European exploration and colonization of the Atlantic islands.

Premodern and Early Modern Empires

Barfield, Thomas J. *The Perilous Frontier: Nomadic Empires and China, 221 B.C. to A.D. 1757.* Cambridge, MA: Blackwell, 1989. Valuable study of empire-building in China and central Asia.

Cunliffe, Barry. *Greeks, Romans and Barbarians: Spheres of Interaction.* New York: Methuen, 1988. Explores the social and political results of interactions in the classical Mediterranean world.

Di Cosmo, Nicola. *Ancient China and Its Enemies: The Rise of Nomadic Power in East Asian History.* Cambridge, UK: Cambridge University Press, 2004. On relations between Chinese and nomadic peoples.

Doyle, Michael. *Empires.* Ithaca, NY: Cornell University Press, 1986. A sociological analysis.

Gruzinski, Serge. *The Conquest of Mexico: The Incorporation of Indian Societies into the Western World, 16th–18th Centuries.* Trans. by E. Corrigan. Cambridge: Polity Press, 1993. Concentrates on cultural issues.

Herman, John E. *Amid the Clouds and Mist: China's Colonization of Guizhou, 1200–1700.* Cambridge, MA: Harvard University Press, 2007. Explores Chinese absorption of the southwestern region.

Hostetler, Laura. *Qing Colonial Enterprise: Ethnography and Cartography in Early Modern China.* Chicago: University of Chicago Press, 2005. Examines Chinese use of ethnography and cartography as intellectual tools for consolidation of imperial rule.

Kasinec, Wendy, and Michael A. Polushin, eds. *Expanding Empires: Cultural Interaction and Exchange in World Societies from Ancient to Early Modern Times.* Wilmington, DE: Scholarly Resources, 2002. Essays on premodern empires.

Kedar, Benjamin Z. *Crusade and Mission: European Approaches Toward the Muslims.* Princeton: Princeton University Press, 1984. On conquest and conversion as European aims during the Crusades.

Mintz, Sidney, *Sweetness and Power: The Place of Sugar in Modern History.* New York: Viking, 1985. Explores connections between sugar and power, including imperial and colonial power.

Morgan, David. *The Mongols.* Oxford, UK: Blackwell, 1986. Excellent brief introduction to the Mongol empires.

Pagden, Anthony. *Lords of All the World: Ideologies of Empire in Spain, Britain, and France, c. 1500–c. 1800.* New Haven, CT: Yale University Press, 1995. On early European theories of empire.

Perdue, Peter C. *China Marches West: The Qing Conquest of Central Eurasia.* Cambridge, MA: Harvard University Press, 2005. Detailed study of Chinese empire-building in early modern times.

Rossabi, Morris. *Khubilai Khan: His Life and Times.* Berkeley: University of California Press, 1988. Best study of the great khan.

Russell-Wood, A.J.R. *The Portuguese Empire, 1415–1808: A World on the Move.* Baltimore: Johns Hopkins University Press, 1998. Perhaps the best general study of the Portuguese global empire.

Subrahmanyam, Sanjay. *The Portuguese Empire in Asia, 1500–1700: A Political and Economic History.* London: Longman, 1993. A well-researched and judicious study.

Yü, Ying-shih. *Trade and Expansion in Han China: A Study in the Structure of Sino-Barbarian Economic Relations.* Berkeley: University of California Press, 1967. An important study focusing on trade and political relations between Han China and nomadic peoples.

Modern Imperialism

Adas, Michael P. *Machines as the Measure of Men: Science, Technology, and Ideologies of Western Dominance.* Ithaca, NY: Cornell University Press, 1989. Holds that European imperialists judged other peoples by their technological capacities.

———. *Prophets of Rebellion: Millenarian Protest Movements against the European Colonial Order.* Cambridge, UK: Cambridge University Press, 1987. Focuses on religious, cultural, and political responses to imperialism.

Beasley, William G. *Japanese Imperialism, 1894–1945.* Oxford, UK: Oxford University Press, 1987. Solid study of the Japanese empire.

Boahen, A. Adu. *African Perspectives on Colonialism.* Baltimore: Johns Hopkins University Press, 1987. Views of the colonized.

Chaudhuri, Nupur, and Margaret Strobel, eds. *Western Women and Imperialism: Complicity and Resistance.* Bloomington: Indiana University Press, 1992. Scholarly essays on women and imperialism.

Cohn, Bernard S. *Colonialism and Its Forms of Knowledge: The British in India.* Princeton: Princeton University Press, 1996. Explores the cultural dimensions of colonial rule.

Cooper, Frederick, and Ann Laura Stoler, eds. *Tensions of Empire: Colonial Cultures in a Bourgeois World.* Berkeley: University of California Press, 1997. Sophisticated studies of metropolitan-colonial relationships.

Curtin, Philip D. "The Environment Beyond Europe and the European Theory of Empire." *Journal of World History* 1 (1990): 131–150. Studies environmental justifications of European imperialism.

Darwin, John. *After Tamerlane: The Global History of Empire Since 1405.* New York: Bloomsbury Press, 2008. Views early modern and modern imperialism in the context of political economy.

Davis, Mike. *Late Victorian Holocausts: El Niño Famines and the Making of the Third World.* London: Verso, 2001. Provocative analysis linking imperial and environmental histories.

Doyle, Michael. *Empires.* Ithaca, NY: Cornell University Press, 1986. A sociological analysis.

Gallagher, John. *The Decline, Revival and Fall of the British Empire.* Ed. by Anil Seal. Cambridge, UK: Cambridge University Press, 1982. Collection of influential essays on the British empire.

Guha, Ranajit, and Gayatri Chakravorty Spivak, eds. *Selected Subaltern Studies*. New York: Oxford University Press, 1988. A collection of scholarly essays from the subaltern school.

Headrick, Daniel R. *The Invisible Weapon: Telecommunications and International Politics, 1851–1945*. New York: Oxford University Press, 1991. On telegraphy and radio communications.

———. *The Tentacles of Progress: Technology Transfer in the Age of Imperialism, 1850–1940*. New York: Oxford University Press, 1988. Spotlights the cultural and political obstacles to technology transfer.

———. *The Tools of Empire: Technology and European Imperialism in the Nineteenth Century*. Oxford, UK: Oxford University Press, 1981. Focuses on technology.

Kiernan, Victor G. *Lords of Human Kind: European Attitudes Toward the Outside World in the Imperial Age*. Harmondsworth, UK: Penguin, 1972. Focuses on imperialists' perceptions of subject peoples.

McCormick, Thomas J. *America's Half-Century: United States Foreign Policy in the Cold War*. Baltimore: Johns Hopkins University Press, 1989. Interprets U.S. foreign policy from a world-system perspective.

Metcalf, Thomas. *Imperial Connections: India in the Indian Ocean Arena, 1860–1920*. Berkeley: University of California, 2008. India as the nexus of imperial power.

Myers, Ramon H., and Mark R. Peattie, eds. *The Japanese Colonial Empire, 1895–1945*. Princeton: Princeton University Press, 1984. Scholarly essays on the Japanese empire.

Osterhammel, Jürgen. *Colonialism: A Theoretical Overview*. Trans. by S.L. Frisch. Princeton: Markus Wiener, 1997. A succinct statement.

Parsons, Timothy H. *The British Imperial Century, 1815–1914: A World History Perspective*. Lanham, MD: Rowman and Littlefield, 1999. A concise but comprehensive overview.

Strobel, Margaret. *European Women and the Second British Empire*. Bloomington: Indiana University Press, 1991. Introduces the gender perspective into studies of imperialism.

Williams, William Appleman. *The Roots of the American Empire: A Study of the Growth and Shaping of Social Consciousness in a Marketplace Society*. New York: Random House, 1969. Critical study of U.S. imperialism.

Young, Louise. *Japan's Total Empire: Manchuria and the Culture of Wartime Imperialism*. Berkeley: University of California Press, 1999. On the creation of the Japanese empire in northeast Asia.

Postcolonial Perspectives

Ashcroft, Bill, Gareth Griffiths, and Helen Tiffin, eds. *The Empire Writes Back: Theory and Practice in Post-Colonial Literatures*. London: Routledge, 1989. An influential collection of postcolonial writings.

Breckenridge, Carol, ed. *Orientalism and the Postcolonial Predicament: Perspectives on South Asia*. Philadelphia: University of Pennsylvania Press, 1993. Essays on the orientalism debate.

Chakrabarty, Dipesh. *Provincializing Europe: Postcolonial Thought and Historical Difference*. New ed. Princeton: Princeton University Press, 2007. Insightful critique of professional historical scholarship and conceptions of modernity.

Clifford, James. *The Predicament of Culture: Twentieth-Century Ethnography, Literature, and Art*. Cambridge, MA: Harvard University Press, 1988. Essays dealing with postcolonial themes.

Dirlik, Arif. *The Postcolonial Aura: Third World Criticism in the Age of Global Capitalism*. Boulder, CO: Westview Press, 1997. Essays criticizing postcolonial scholarship.

Pratt, Mary Louise. *Imperial Eyes: Travel Writing and Transculturation*. London: Routledge, 1992. A rich study analyzing travel writing in the context of imperialism.

Said, Edward W. *Culture and Imperialism*. New York: Knopf, 1993. Explores the influence of empire in nineteenth-century literature.

———. *Orientalism: Western Representations of the Orient*. New York: Routledge and Kegan Paul, 1978. Most prominent postcolonial critique of historical representations.

Thomas, Nicholas. *Colonialism's Culture: Anthropology, Travel, and Government*. Princeton: Princeton University Press, 1994. Critical reflections on recent studies dealing with cultural issues in imperial context.

Young, Robert J.C. *Colonial Desire: Hybridity in Theory, Culture and Race*. London: Routledge, 1995. Views the construction of racial and ethnic differences in imperial context.

———. *White Mythologies: Writing History and the West*. London: Routledge, 1990. Draws on postcolonial perspectives to question historical knowledge.

Cross-Cultural Trade

Much of the recent scholarship in world history has to do with exchanges—especially commercial, biological, and cultural exchanges—between peoples of different societies. The literature on commercial exchange is especially voluminous. The most important works deal with premodern and early modern times.

Premodern Trade

Abu-Lughod, Janet L. *Before European Hegemony: The World System, A.D. 1250–1350*. Oxford, UK: Oxford University Press, 1989. Influential study that pushes world-system analysis into premodern times.

Begley, Vimala, and Richard Daniel De Puma, eds. *Rome and India: The Ancient Sea Trade*. Madison, WI: University of Wisconsin Press, 1991. Scholarly essays.

Chaudhuri, K.N. *Asia before Europe: Economy and Civilisation of the Indian Ocean from the Rise of Islam to 1750*. Cambridge, UK: Cambridge University Press, 1990. Views all of Asia as an integrated region centered on the Indian Ocean.

———. *Trade and Civilisation in the Indian Ocean: An Economic History from the Rise of Islam to 1750*. Cambridge, UK: Cambridge University Press, 1985. Analyzes the Indian Ocean basin as a large-scale commercial zone.

Curtin, Philip D. *Cross-Cultural Trade in World History*. Cambridge, UK: Cambridge University Press, 1984. Important general study emphasizing the role of trade diasporas.

Fernández-Armesto, Felipe. *Before Columbus: Exploration and Colonization from the Mediterranean to the Atlantic, 1229–1492*. Philadelphia: University of Pennsylvania Press, 1987. The best work on European colonization of the Atlantic islands.

Goitein, S.D. *A Mediterranean Society: The Jewish Communities of the Arab World as Portrayed by the Documents of the Cairo Geniza*. 6 vols. Berkeley: University of California Press, 1967–1993. A masterful work exploiting a rich cache of documents.

Hodges, Richard, and David Whitehouse. *Mohammed, Char-*

lemagne and the Origins of Europe: Archaeology and the Pirenne Thesis. Ithaca, NY: Cornell University Press, 1983. Brings archaeological evidence to bear on the trading world of postclassical times.

Hourani, George F. *Arab Seafaring in the Indian Ocean in Ancient and Early Medieval Times*. 2nd ed. Princeton: Princeton University Press, 1992. A brief study of the Indian Ocean basin.

Liu Xinru. *Ancient India and Ancient China: Trade and Religious Exchanges, A.D. 1–600*. Delhi: Oxford University Press, 1988. Emphasizes the role of trade in the spread of Buddhism.

———. *Silk and Religion: An Exploration of Material Life and the Thought of People, A.D. 600–1200*. New Delhi: Oxford University Press, 1996. Studies the role of silk—including its manufacture, trade, and consumption—in Eurasian religious life.

McCormick, Michael. *Origins of the European Economy: Communications and Commerce, A.D. 300–900*. Cambridge, UK: Cambridge University Press, 2001. Brilliant, detailed study that situates early European trade and economic development in larger Mediterranean context.

Miller, J. Innes. *The Spice Trade of the Roman Empire, 29 B.C. to A.D. 641*. Oxford, UK: Oxford University Press, 1969. Dated but still useful.

Phillips, William D. *Slavery from Roman Times to the Early Transatlantic Slave Trade*. Minneapolis: University of Minnesota Press, 1985. An important survey and synthesis.

Ratnagar, Shereen. *Trading Encounters: From the Euphrates to the Indus in the Bronze Age*. New Delhi: Oxford University Press, 2004. Relies mostly on archaeological evidence in studying trade between the Indus River valley and Mesopotamia.

Sen, Tansen. *Buddhism, Diplomacy, and Trade: The Realignment of Sino-Indian Relations, 600–1400*. Honolulu: University of Hawai'i Press, 2003. Examines linkages between trade, diplomacy, and Buddhism.

Smith, Richard L. *Premodern Trade in World History*. London: Routledge, 2009. A concise survey.

Yü, Ying-shih. *Trade and Expansion in Han China: A Study in the Structure of Sino-Barbarian Economic Relations*. Berkeley: University of California Press, 1967. An important study focusing on trade and political relations between Han China and nomadic peoples.

Early Modern Trade

Blussé, Leonard, and F.S. Gaastra, eds. *Companies and Trade: Essays on Overseas Trading Companies during the Ancien Régime*. Leiden, Netherlands: Leiden University Press, 1981. Scholarly essays.

———, eds. *On the Eighteenth Century as a Category of Asian History: Van Leur in Retrospect*. Brookfield, VT: Ashgate, 1998. Scholarly essays on early modern trade.

Brook, Timothy. *Vermeer's Hat: The Seventeenth Century and the Dawn of the Global World*. London: Bloomsbury Press, 2007. Cross-cultural trade and much more.

Chaudhuri, K.N. *The Trading World of Asia and the English East India Company, 1660–1760*. Cambridge, UK: Cambridge University Press, 1978. Perhaps the best study of any of the early modern trading companies.

Chaudhury, Sushil, and Michael Morineau, eds. *Merchants, Companies, and Trade: Europe and Asia in the Early Modern Era*. New York: Cambridge University Press, 1999. Scholarly essays on European, Asian, and transregional trade.

Curtin, Philip D. *Cross-Cultural Trade in World History*. Cambridge, UK: Cambridge University Press, 1984. Important general study emphasizing the role of trade diasporas.

———. *The Rise and Fall of the Plantation Complex*. 2nd ed. Cambridge, UK: Cambridge University Press, 1998. Pioneering study of plantation societies.

Dale, Stephen F. *Indian Merchants and Eurasian Trade, 1600–1750*. Cambridge, UK: Cambridge University Press, 1994. A rare and important study of Indian merchants engaged in long-distance trade

Das Gupta, Ashin. *The World of the Indian Ocean Merchant, 1500–1800*. New Delhi: Oxford University Press, 2001. Collected essays on early modern trade in the Indian Ocean basin.

Flynn, Dennis O., and Arturo Giráldez. "Arbitrage, China, and World Trade in the Early Modern Period." *Journal of the Economic and Social History of the Orient* (1995). Emphasizes the role of American silver in early modern trade.

———. "Born with a 'Silver Spoon': The Origin of World Trade in 1571." *Journal of World History* 6 (1995): 201–221. Argues that Chinese demand for silver drove global trade in early modern times.

———. "China and the Manila Galleons." In *Japanese Industrialization and the Asian Economy*, ed. A.J.H. Latham and H. Kawakatsu. London: Routledge, 1994. Argues that a great deal of American silver went to China across the Pacific Ocean by way of the Manila galleons.

———. "Cycles of Silver: Global Economic Unity Through the Mid-Eighteenth Century." *Journal of World History* 13 (2002): 391–427. Traces global silver flows in early modern times.

Frank, Andre Gunder. *ReORIENT: Global Economy in the Asian Age*. Berkeley: University of California Press, 1998. Argues for an early modern world system centered on China.

Furber, Holden. *Rival Empires of Trade in the Orient, 1600–1800*. Minneapolis: University of Minnesota Press, 1976. Dated but still useful study of European trading companies in Asia.

Hamashita, Takeshi. *China, East Asia and the Global Economy: Regional and Historical Perspectives*. London: Routledge, 2008. Collected essays by a noted scholar of East Asian trade.

Hugill, Peter. *World Trade since 1431: Geography, Technology, and Capitalism*. Baltimore: Johns Hopkins University Press, 1993. Emphasizes importance of transportation technologies.

Israel, Jonathan. *Dutch Primacy in World Trade, 1585–1740*. Oxford, UK: Oxford University Press, 1989. Focuses usefully on the organization of Dutch trade in political and economic contexts.

Meilink-Roelofsz, M.A.P. *Asian Trade and European Influence in the Indonesian Archipelago between 1500 and about 1630*. The Hague: Nijhoff, 1962. A richly documented study, though now somewhat dated.

Pomeranz, Kenneth, and Steven Topik. *The World That Trade Created: Society, Culture, and the World Economy, 1400 to the Present*. Armonk, NY: M.E. Sharpe, 1999. Fascinating vignettes.

Ptak, Roderich, and Dietmar Rothermund, eds. *Emporia, Commodities and Entrepreneurs in Asian Maritime Trade, c. 1400–1750*. Stuttgart: Steiner Verlag, 1991. Scholarly essays.

Reid, Anthony. *Southeast Asia in the Age of Commerce, 1450–1680*. 2 vols. New Haven, CT: Yale University Press, 1988–1993. A work in the mold of Braudel and Chaudhuri that portrays Southeast Asia as a region deeply influenced by cross-cultural trade.

Richards, John F., ed. *Precious Metals in the Later Medieval and Early Modern World*. Durham, NC: Carolina Academic Press, 1983. Scholarly essays on global bullion flows.

Steensgaard, Niels. *The Asian Trade Revolution of the Seventeenth*

Century: The East India Companies and the Decline of the Caravan Trade. Chicago: University of Chicago Press, 1974. Deals with the eclipse of overland trade by maritime trade.

Subrahmanyam, Sanjay. *The Career and Legend of Vasco da Gama*. Cambridge, UK: Cambridge University Press, 1997. The best study of Vasco da Gama.

————. *The Portuguese Empire in Asia, 1500–1700: A Political and Economic History*. London: Longman, 1993. A well-researched and judicious study.

Tracy, James D., ed. *The Political Economy of Merchant Empires: State Power and World Trade, 1350–1750*. Cambridge, UK: Cambridge University Press, 1991. Companion volume to the one cited below and equally important.

————. *The Rise of Merchant Empires: Long-Distance Trade in the Early Modern World, 1350–1750*. Cambridge, UK: Cambridge University Press, 1990. Important collection of essays on early modern trade.

Wills, John E. "Maritime Asia, 1500–1800: The Interactive Emergence of European Domination." *American Historical Review* 98 (1993): 83–105. Important review of recent literature, much of it on early modern trade.

Biological Exchanges and Environmental Change

Diffusions of biological species—including plants, animals, disease pathogens, and human communities—have profoundly influenced the development of individual societies and the world as a whole. Although they often came about as a result of trade, migration, or imperialism, a distinctive literature has focused usefully on biological exchanges and environmental change. This list mentions works that deal with biological exchanges in particular and those that deal more generally with environmental conditions and environmental change in cross-cultural perspective.

Biological Exchanges

Cook, Noble David. *Born to Die: Disease and New World Conquest*. Cambridge, UK: Cambridge University Press, 1998. A brief survey dealing with all of the Americas.

Crosby, Alfred W. *The Columbian Exchange: Biological and Cultural Consequences of 1492*. Westport, CT: Greenwood Press, 1972. A pioneering work and a classic.

————. *Ecological Imperialism: The Biological Expansion of Europe*. 2nd ed. Cambridge, UK: Cambridge University Press, 2004. Seeks to explain why European species have flourished in the larger world.

Curtin, Philip D. *Death by Migration: Europe's Encounter with the Tropical World in the Nineteenth Century*. Cambridge, UK: Cambridge University Pres, 1989. A precise, quantitative study based on military records.

Dols, Michael W. *The Black Death in the Middle East*. Princeton: Princeton University Press, 1977. The best work on bubonic plague in the Muslim world.

Henige, David. *Numbers from Nowhere: The American Indian Contact Population Debate*. Norman: University of Oklahoma Press, 1998. A critical examination of historical demography especially as applied to the societies of the pre-Columbian Americas.

Mazumdar, Sucheta. *Sugar and Society in China: Peasants, Technology, and the World Market*. Cambridge, MA: Harvard

University Press, 1998. Explores the role of sugar in Chinese society.

McNeill, William H. *Plagues and Peoples*. Garden City, NJ: Anchor Books, 1976. An important work of historical epidemiology.

Watson, Andrew. *Agricultural Innovation in the Early Islamic World: The Diffusion of Crops and Farming Techniques, 700–1100*. Cambridge, UK: Cambridge University Press, 1983. Charts the spread of food crops and industrial crops in postclassical times.

Watts, Sheldon. *Epidemics and History: Disease, Power, and Imperialism*. New Haven, CT: Yale University Press, 1997. Views epidemic disease in social and cultural context.

Environmental Conditions and Environmental Change

Chew, Sing C. *World Ecological Degradation: Accumulation, Urbanization and Deforestation, 3000 B.C.–A.D. 2000*. Walnut Creek, CA: AltaMira Press, 2001. Important long-term, large-scale analysis of environmental change.

Cronon, William. *Changes in the Land: Indians, Colonists, and the Ecology of New England*. New York: Hill and Wang, 1983. An outstanding study of environmental change in colonial New England.

Diamond, Jared. *Collapse: How Societies Choose to Fail or Succeed*. New York: Viking, 2005. Focuses on environmental effects of human policies and decisions.

————. *Guns, Germs, and Steel: The Fates of Human Societies*. New York: W.W. Norton, 1997. Environmental interpretation of world history.

Fagan, Brian M. *The Little Ice Age: How Climate Made History, 1300–1850*. New York: Basic Books, 2001. Popular account of the little ice age.

————. *The Long Summer: How Climate Changed Civilization*. New York: Basic Books, 2004. Popular account focusing on the medieval warm period and its effects.

Grove, Richard. *Green Imperialism: Colonial Expansion, Tropical Island Edens, and the Origins of Environmentalism*. Cambridge, UK: Cambridge University Press, 1995. Places the emergence of environmental consciousness in the context of European imperialism.

Hughes, J. Donald. *An Environmental History of the World: Humankind's Changing Role in the Community of Life*. London: Routledge, 2001. A thoughtful, sensitive synthesis.

McNeill, John R. "Of Rats and Men: A Synoptic Environmental History of the Island Pacific." *Journal of World History* 5 (1994): 299–349. Comprehensive survey of environmental change in Pacific islands.

————. *Something New under the Sun: An Environmental History of the Twentieth-Century World*. New York: W.W. Norton, 2001. Charts dramatic environmental changes in recent times.

Ponting, Clive. *A Green History of the World*. London: Penguin, 1991. A critical environmental history of the world.

Pyne, Stephen J. *Vestal Fire: An Environmental History, Told through Fire, of Europe and Europe's Encounter with the World*. Seattle: University of Washington Press, 1997. Fire in European and world history.

————. *World Fire: The Culture of Fire on Earth*. New York: Henry Holt, 1995. Comparative study of fire and its effects.

Richards, John F. *The Unending Frontier: An Environmental History of the Early Modern World*. Berkeley: University of California Press, 2003. A particularly insightful global analysis.

Silver, Timothy. *A New Face on the Countryside: Indians,*

Colonists, and Slaves in South Atlantic Forests. Cambridge, UK: Cambridge University Press, 1990. Deals with environmental change in the southeastern portion of colonial North America.

Tucker, Richard P. *Insatiable Appetite: The United States and the Ecological Degradation of the Tropical World.* Berkeley: University of California Press, 2000. Effects of concentrated demand on fragile environments.

Worster, Donald, ed. *The Ends of the Earth: Perspectives on Modern Environmental History.* Cambridge, UK: Cambridge University Press, 1988. Scholarly essays on environmental change.

———. *Rivers of Empire: Water, Aridity, and the Growth of the American West.* New York: Oxford University Press, 1985. Studies the hydraulic society of the American West.

Cultural Exchanges

Throughout history, processes of cross-cultural interaction have brought cultural as well as commercial and biological exchanges. Although many studies deal with individual cases, there are few large-scale studies, and there is little consensus among scholars about how best to explore processes of cultural interaction and exchange. This list mentions works dealing with cultural and religious exchanges, cross-cultural interactions, and frontier dynamics.

Cultural and Religious Exchanges

Ahmad, Aziz. *Studies in Islamic Culture in the Indian Environment.* Oxford, UK: Clarendon Press, 1964. A scholarly analysis.

Bentley, Jerry H. *Old World Encounters: Cross-Cultural Contacts and Exchanges in Pre-Modern Times.* New York: Oxford University Press, 1993. Seeks to problematize religious conversion.

Bernal, Martin. *Black Athena: The Afroasiatic Roots of Classical Civilization.* 2 vols. to date. New Brunswick: Rutgers University Press, 1987– . Controversial study arguing for Egyptian and Semitic influences in ancient Greece.

Burkert, Walter. *The Orientalizing Revolution: Near Eastern Influence on Greek Culture in the Early Archaic Age.* Cambridge, MA: Harvard University Press, 1992. Scholarly study of Mesopotamian influences in ancient Greece.

Comaroff, Jean, and John Comaroff. *Of Revelation and Revolution: Christianity, Colonialism, and Consciousness in South Africa.* 2 vols. Chicago, 1991–1997: University of Chicago Press. Views Christian missions in South Africa as a colonial project.

Gernet, Jacques. *Buddhism in Chinese Society: An Economic History from the Fifth to the Tenth Centuries.* Trans. by F. Verellen. New York: Columbia University Press, 1995. An economic and social interpretation of Buddhism in China.

Hefner, Robert W. *Conversion to Christianity: Historical and Anthropological Perspectives on a Great Transformation.* Berkeley: University of California Press, 1993. Scholarly essays.

Ikram, S.M. *Muslim Civilization in India.* New York: Columbia University Press, 1964. A valuable introduction.

Johnson, Donald, and Jean Johnson. *Universal Religions in World History: Buddhism, Christianity, and Islam.* New York: McGraw-Hill, 2007. Focuses on the spread of religious traditions.

Levtzion, Nehemia, ed. *Conversion to Islam.* New York: Holmes and Meier, 1979. Scholarly essays.

Lieu, Samuel N.C. *Manichaeism in the Later Roman Empire and Medieval China.* 2nd ed. Tübingen: J.C.B. Mohr, 1992. Fascinating study of an explosive missionary faith.

MacCormack, Sabine. *Religion in the Andes: Vision and Imagination in Early Colonial Peru.* Princeton: Princeton University Press, 1991. Deals with the efforts to convert indigenous peoples to Christianity in colonial Peru.

MacMullen, Ramsay. *Christianizing the Roman Empire (A.D. 100–400).* New Haven, CT: Yale University Press, 1984. A social history of conversion to Christianity.

Thornton, John. "'I Am the Subject of the King of Congo': African Political Ideology and the Haitian Revolution." *Journal of World History* 4 (1993): 181–214. Argues for the influence of specific African cultural elements during the Haitian revolution.

Vryonis, Speros. *The Decline of Medieval Hellenism in Asia Minor and the Process of Islamization from the Eleventh through the Fifteenth Century.* Berkeley: University of California Press, 1971. Detailed study of Islamization.

Waley-Cohen, Joanna. *The Sextants of Beijing: Global Currents in Chinese History.* New York: W.W. Norton, 1999. Emphasizes interactions and exchanges over the long term of Chinese history.

Cross-Cultural Interactions

Adas, Michael P. *Prophets of Rebellion: Millenarian Protest Movements against the European Colonial Order.* Cambridge, UK: Cambridge University Press, 1987. Focuses on religious, cultural, and political responses to imperialism.

Axtell, James. *The European and the Indian: Essays in the Ethnohistory of Colonial North America.* New York: Oxford University Press, 1981. Insightful scholarly essays.

———. *The Invasion Within: The Contest of Cultures in Colonial North America.* New York: Oxford University Press, 1985. Studies the interaction of English, French, and indigenous peoples.

Dening, Greg. *Beach Crossings: Voyaging across Times, Cultures, and Self.* Philadelphia: University of Pennsylvania Press, 2004. Investigations and reflections on cross-cultural relationships.

———. *Islands and Beaches: Discourse on a Silent Land—Marquesas, 1774–1880.* Honolulu: University of Hawai'i Press, 1980. Rich, reflective analysis of interactions between European and Marquesan peoples.

Elliott, J.H. *The Old World and the New, 1492–1650.* Cambridge, UK: Cambridge University Press, 1970. Elegant essays on European thought about the Americas.

Gruzinski, Serge. *The Conquest of Mexico: The Incorporation of Indian Societies into the Western World, 16th–18th Centuries.* Trans. by E. Corrigan. Cambridge: Polity Press, 1993. Concentrates on cultural issues.

Hall, Edith. *Inventing the Barbarian: Greek Self-Definition through Tragedy.* Oxford, UK: Oxford University Press, 1989. Argues that classical Greeks defined themselves against "barbarians."

Hartog, François. *The Mirror of Herodotus: The Representation of the Other in the Writing of History.* Berkeley: University of California Press, 1988. On cross-cultural representation in historical writing.

Helms, Mary W. *Ulysses' Sail: An Ethnographic Odyssey of Power, Knowledge, and Geographical Distance.* Princeton: Princeton University Press, 1988. Important study exploring the political and cultural implications of long-distance travel and knowledge from afar.

Karttunen, Frances. *Between Worlds: Interpreters, Guides, and Survivors*. New Brunswick: Rutgers University Press, 1994. Focuses on individuals caught in cross-cultural interactions.

Kupperman, Karen Ordahl. *America in European Consciousness, 1493–1750*. Chapel Hill: University of North Carolina Press, 1995. Scholarly essays.

Liu, Xinru, and Lynda Shaffer. *Connections Across Eurasia: Transportation, Communication, and Cultural Exchange on the Silk Roads*. New York: McGraw-Hill, 2007. On trade and cultural exchanges on the silk roads.

Miyoshi, Masao. *As We Saw Them: The First Japanese Embassy to the United States*. Berkeley: University of California Press, 1979. Fascinating account of the first Japanese embassy to the United States.

Pagden, Anthony. *European Encounters with the New World: From Renaissance to Romanticism*. New Haven, CT: Yale University Press, 1993. Studies the interpretation of the Americas by European scholars.

Pearson, Michael N. *Pilgrimage to Mecca: The Indian Experience, 1500–1800*. Princeton: Marcus Weiner, 1996. Pioneering work.

Rafael, Vicente. *Contracting Colonialism: Translation and Christian Conversion in Tagalog Society under Early Spanish Rule*. Ithaca, NY: Cornell University Press, 1988. Deals with early interactions of Spanish and Filipino peoples.

Ranger, Terence. "Europeans in Black Africa." *Journal of World History* 9 (1998): 255–268. Reviews recent literature from a distinctive perspective.

Schwartz, Stuart B. *Implicit Understandings: Observing, Reporting, and Reflecting on the Encounters between European and Other Peoples in the Early Modern Era*. Cambridge, UK: Cambridge University Press, 1994. Important collection of scholarly essays.

Takaki, Ronald T. *A Different Mirror: A History of Multicultural America*. Boston: Little, Brown, 1993. Makes room for the experiences of European, African, Asian, and indigenous American peoples.

Thornton, John. *Africa and Africans in the Making of the Atlantic World, 1400–1800*. 2nd ed. Cambridge, UK: Cambridge University Press, 1998. Offers an Afrocentric perspective on the Atlantic world.

Frontier Dynamics

Barfield, Thomas J. *The Perilous Frontier: Nomadic Empires and China*. Cambridge, MA: Blackwell, 1989. Provocative interpretation of relations between Chinese and nomadic peoples.

Callaway, Colin G. *New Worlds for All: Indians, Europeans, and the Remaking of Early America*. Baltimore: Johns Hopkins University Press, 1997. Studies interactions in colonial North America.

Clendinnen, Inga. *Ambivalent Conquests: Maya and Spaniard in Yucatan, 1517–1570*. Cambridge, UK: Cambridge University Press, 1987. Insightful analysis.

Cunliffe, Barry. *Greeks, Romans and Barbarians: Spheres of Interaction*. New York: Methuen, 1988. Explores the social and political results of interactions.

Eaton, Richard. *The Rise of Islam and the Bengal Frontier, 1204–1760*. Berkeley: University of California Press, 1993. A landmark study.

Farriss, Nancy M. *Maya Society under Colonial Rule: The Collective Enterprise of Survival*. Princeton: Princeton University Press, 1984. A richly documented study.

Giersch, C. Patterson. *Asian Borderlands: The Transformation of Qing China's Yunnan Frontier*. Cambridge, MA: Harvard University Press, 2006. Focuses on Chinese-Tai relations in Yunnan.

Harrell, Stevan, ed. *Cultural Encounters on China's Ethnic Frontiers*. Seattle: University of Washington Press, 1995. Scholarly essays.

Limerick, Patricia Nelson. *The Legacy of Conquest: The Unbroken Past of the American West*. New York: W.W. Norton, 1987. A spirited contribution.

McNeill, William H. *The Great Frontier: Freedom and Hierarchy in Modern Times*. Princeton: Princeton University Press, 1983. Lectures.

Shepherd, John Robert. *Statecraft and Political Economy on the Taiwan Frontier, 1600–1800*. Stanford: Stanford University Press, 1993. Focuses on interactions of indigenous, Chinese, and foreign peoples.

Shin, Leo. *The Making of the Chinese State: Ethnicity and Expansion on the Ming Borderlands*. New York: Cambridge University Press, 2006. Argues that Chinese expansion helped create ethnic identities.

Weber, David J. *The Spanish Frontier in North America*. New Haven, CT: Yale University Press, 1992. A synthesis of recent scholarship.

White, Richard. *The Middle Ground: Indians, Empires, and Republics in the Great Lakes Region, 1650–1815*. Cambridge, UK: Cambridge University Press, 1991. Richly documented study of the interactions between colonists and indigenous peoples in North America.

Science, Technology, and Technological Exchanges

The comparative study of science and technology has brought salient differences between the world's major societies into useful focus, while the analysis of the dissemination, diffusion, and exchange of technologies has contributed to the understanding of the rise of the West as well as conflicts and interactions between societies.

Adas, Michael P. *Machines as the Measure of Men: Science, Technology, and Ideologies of Western Dominance*. Ithaca, NY: Cornell University Press, 1989. Holds that European imperialists judged other peoples by their technological capacities.

Anthony, David W. *The Horse, the Wheel, and Language: How Bronze-Age Riders from the Eurasian Steppes Shaped the Modern World*. Princeton: Princeton University Press, 2007. Important study of the origins and migrations of Indo-European speakers.

Bulliet, Richard W. *The Camel and the Wheel*. Cambridge, MA: Harvard University Press, 1975. Fascinating study of camels and related transportation technologies.

Campbell, I.C. "The Lateen Sail in World History." *Journal of World History* 6 (1995): 1–23. Discusses multiple inventions and diffusions of lateen sails.

Casson, Lionel. *The Ancient Mariners: Seafarers and Sea Fighters of the Mediterranean in Ancient Times*. 2nd ed. Princeton: Princeton University Press, 1991. A popular work on ancient maritime technology.

Chase, Kenneth. *Firearms: A Global History to 1700*. Cambridge, UK: Cambridge University Press, 2003. Brings together a great deal of research and argues a provocative thesis.

Crosby, Alfred W. *Children of the Sun: A History of Humanity's Unappeasable Appetite for Energy*. New York: W.W. Norton, 2006. A brief and provocative survey.

Finlay, Robert. "The Pilgrim Art: The Culture of Porcelain in World History." *Journal of World History* 9, no. 2 (1998): 141–187. Fascinating study of invention, production, distribution, and consumption of porcelain.

Headrick, Daniel R. *The Invisible Weapon: Telecommunications and International Politics, 1851–1945*. New York: Oxford University Press, 1991. On telegraphy and radio communications.

———. *The Tentacles of Progress: Technology Transfer in the Age of Imperialism, 1850–1940*. New York: Oxford University Press, 1988. Spotlights the cultural and political obstacles to technology transfer.

———. *The Tools of Empire: Technology and European Imperialism in the Nineteenth Century*. Oxford, UK: Oxford University Press, 1981. Focuses on technology.

———. *When Information Came of Age: Technologies of Knowledge in the Age of Reason and Revolution, 1700–1850*. Oxford, UK: Oxford University Press, 2000.

Huff, Toby. *The Rise of Early Modern Science: Islam, China, and the West*. Cambridge, UK: Cambridge University Press, 1993. Important comparative study.

McClellan, James E., III, and Harold Dorn. *Science and Technology in World History: An Introduction*. 2nd ed. Baltimore: Johns Hopkins University Press, 2006. Excellent survey.

McNeill, William H. *The Pursuit of Power: Technology, Armed Force, and Society since A.D. 1000*. Chicago: University of Chicago Press, 1982. Emphasizes transfers of military technology.

Mokyr, Joel. *The Lever of Riches: Technological Creativity and Economic Progress*. Oxford, UK: Oxford University Press, 1990. Impressive general argument about the importance of technological development.

Needham, Joseph. *Science and Civilisation in China*. 7 vols. to date. Cambridge, UK: Cambridge University Press, 1954. A massive project of fundamental importance.

———. *Science in Traditional China: A Comparative Perspective*. Hong Kong: Harvard University Press/Chinese University Press, 1981. Briefly reviews some of the major points of Needham's larger work.

Pacey, Arnold. *Technology in World Civilization: A Thousand-Year History*. Oxford, UK: Blackwell, 1990. Argues for technological dialogue or dialectic rather than diffusion.

Ralston, David B. *Importing the European Army: The Introduction of European Military Techniques and Institutions into the Extra-European World, 1600–1914*. Chicago: University of Chicago Press, 1990. Studies transfers of military technologies and their effects.

Smil, Vaclav. *Energy in World History*. Boulder, CO: Westview Press, 1994. Pathbreaking study.

Smith, Merritt Roe, and Leo Marx, eds. *Does Technology Drive History? The Dilemma of Technological Determinism*. Cambridge, MA: MIT Press, 1994. Scholarly essays.

Stearns, Peter N. *The Industrial Revolution in World History*. Boulder, CO: Westview Press, 1993. A global look at industrialization and its effects.

White, Lynn, Jr. *Medieval Technology and Social Change*. Oxford, UK: Oxford University Press, 1962. Dated but still useful.

Social History, Women's History, and Gender History

Within the larger discipline of history, the fields of social history, women's history, and gender history have become staples since the 1960s. Within the subfield of world history, however, they have loomed much less large. World historians have focused their attention instead on large-scale comparisons and processes of cross-cultural interaction and exchange. While they have often noted the social or gender dimensions of their analyses, they have rarely made social or gender relations the principal focus. The works cited here represent efforts to make a more prominent place for social and gender relations in the subfield of world history.

Clay, Catherine, et al. *Envisioning Women in World History: Prehistory to 1500*. New York: McGraw-Hill, 2008. Brief survey of women's history in premodern times.

Lerner, Gerda. *The Creation of Feminist Consciousness: From the Middle Ages to 1870*. New York: Oxford University Press, 1993. Companion volume to *The Creation of Patriarchy*.

———. *The Creation of Patriarchy*. New York: Oxford University Press, 1986. Controversial effort to account for the origins and reproduction of patriarchal social forms.

McVay, Pamela. *Envisioning Women in World History: 1500–Present*. New York: McGraw-Hill, 2008. A companion volume to Clay et al. surveying women's history in modern times.

Pomeranz, Kenneth. "Social History and World History: From Daily Life to Patterns of Change." *Journal of World History* 18 (2007): 69–98. Promotes engagement of social history and world history.

Smith, Bonnie G., ed. *Women's History in Global Perspective*. 3 vols. Urbana: University of Illinois Press, 2004–2005. Includes contributions by foremost leaders in the field.

Stearns, Peter N. *Childhood in World History*. New York: Routledge, 2005. Brief large-scale analysis.

———. "Social History and World History: Prospects for Collaboration." *Journal of World History* 18 (2007): 43–52. Review article on tensions and possibilities.

Strobel, Margaret. *European Women and the Second British Empire*. Bloomington: Indiana University Press, 1991. Introduces the gender perspective into studies of imperialism.

Wiesner-Hanks, Merry E. *Christianity and Sexuality in the Early Modern World: Regulating Desire, Reforming Practice*. London: Routledge and Kegan Paul, 2000. Global influence of Christianity on sexuality and gender relations.

———. *Gender in History*. Oxford, UK: Blackwell, 2001. Globalizes the historical study of gender.

———. "World History and the History of Women, Gender, and Sexuality." *Journal of World History* 18 (2007): 53–67. Valuable review article.

Zinsser, Judith P. *History and Feminism: A Glass Half-Full*. New York: Twayne, 1993. Traces the effects of feminism on history and historiography.

———. "Women's History, World History, and the Construction of New Narratives." *Journal of Women's History* 12 (2000): 196–206. Review article focusing on the four volumes of the important Restoring Women to History series.

Individuals in World History

Most scholarship in world history deals with large-scale processes. Individuals often make appearances in analyses of these processes, but scholarship in world history has not often focused on individuals and their experiences. While historians have considered the significance of individual experiences for local and national history for more than a century, world historians have only begun to exploit archives and other primary sources for purposes of studying the effects of large-scale processes on individuals and local communities. The works listed here represent some especially important and useful contributions.

Colley, Linda. *The Ordeal of Elizabeth Marsh: A Woman in World History.* New York: Pantheon, 2007. Travels of a Jamaican woman illuminate the eighteenth-century world.

Dunn, Ross E. *The Adventures of Ibn Battuta: A Muslim Traveler of the Fourteenth Century.* Rev. ed. Berkeley: University of California Press, 2005. Places Ibn Battuta squarely in hemispheric context.

Kraemer, Joel L. *Maimonides: The Life and World of One of Civilization's Greatest Minds.* New York: Doubleday, 2008. Biography of the great medieval Jewish philosopher.

Phillips, William D., Jr., and Carla Rahn Phillips. *The Worlds of Christopher Columbus.* Cambridge, UK: Cambridge University Press, 1992. The best general study, which locates Columbus properly in European and global context.

Price, Richard. *Alabi's World.* Baltimore: Johns Hopkins University Press, 1990. Concentrates on relationships between Saramaka maroons and their neighbors.

———. *First-Time: The Historical Vision of an Afro-American People.* Baltimore: Johns Hopkins University Press, 1983. Fascinating reconstruction of the historical experience and historical vision of the Saramaka maroon community in modern-day Surinam.

Rachewiltz, Igor de. "Marco Polo Went to China." *Zentralasiatische Studien* 27 (1997): 34–92. Critical review of Frances Wood's book (cited below) arguing persuasively that Marco Polo did indeed go to China.

———. *Papal Envoys to the Great Khans.* Stanford: Stanford University Press, 1971. Reliable survey of Roman Catholic missionaries to China during the Mongol era.

Rossabi, Morris. *Voyager from Xanadu: Rabban Sauma and the Journey from China to the West.* New York: Kodansha International, 1992. Deals with the first known individual born in China to visit Western Europe.

Storey, William K. "Big Cats and Imperialism: Lion and Tiger Hunting in Kenya and Northern India, 1898–1930." *Journal of World History* 2 (1991): 135–173. Imaginative analysis of racial and social relations in the imperial era.

Thomas, Nicholas. Cook: *The Extraordinary Voyages of Captain James Cook.* New York: Walker, 2003. Provocative study of Cook and his voyages.

Thompson, Jason. "Osman Effendi: A Scottish Convert to Islam in Early Nineteenth-Century Egypt." *Journal of World History* 5 (1994): 99–123. Experiences of a cross-cultural convert.

Wheatley, Helen. "From Traveler to Notable: Lady Duff Gordon in Upper Egypt, 1862–1869." *Journal of World History* 3 (1992): 81–104. Experiences of Lady Duff Gordon seen as a prism for refracting cross-cultural relationships.

Whitfield, Susan. *Life along the Silk Roads.* Berkeley: University of California Press, 2000. Focuses on personal experiences of silk roads travelers.

Wood, Frances. *Did Marco Polo Go to China?* Boulder, CO: Westview Press, 1996. Questions whether Marco Polo actually traveled to China.

Wriggins, Sally Hovey. *The Silk Road Journey with Xuanzang.* Boulder, CO: Westview Press, 2003. Synthesizes studies of the most famous Chinese Buddhist pilgrim.

About the Author

Jerry H. Bentley is professor of history at the University of Hawai'i and editor of the *Journal of World History*. He is the author of *Old World Encounter: Cultural Contacts and Exchanges in Pre-Modern Times* (1993); *Shapes of World History in Twentieth-Century Scholarship* (1996); and (with Herbert Ziegler) *Traditions and Encounters: A Global Perspective on the Past* (3rd ed., 2005).

Index

H

I

About the Editor

Heidi Roupp (BA, University of Wyoming, and MA, Columbia University) was a founding member of the World History Association. She hosted three world history conferences at the Aspen Institute, which led to the first World History Institute for professors and teachers developing world history courses. She was the first recipient of the American Historical Association's Beveridge Teaching Prize. During her tenure as president of the World History Association, she organized a nationwide program for the National Endowment for the Humanities consisting of twenty-seven world history institutes for educators preparing to teach advanced placement world history. She served as the CNN education consultant for the Millennium Series and was a chief adviser for the Bridging World History series. Heidi Roupp is presently the executive director of *World History Connected Inc.*, an electronic journal for teachers of world history, and serves as executive director of Teachers Across Borders, an international, non-profit organization. TAB volunteers help colleagues teaching in fragile educational environments with professional development and teaching materials "in the belief that education changes lives."